Communications in Computer and Information Science 2187

Rationale

The CCIS series is devoted to the publication of proceedings of computer science conferences. Its aim is to efficiently disseminate original research results in informatics in printed and electronic form. While the focus is on publication of peer-reviewed full papers presenting mature work, inclusion of reviewed short papers reporting on work in progress is welcome, too. Besides globally relevant meetings with internationally representative program committees guaranteeing a strict peer-reviewing and paper selection process, conferences run by societies or of high regional or national relevance are also considered for publication.

Topics

The topical scope of CCIS spans the entire spectrum of informatics ranging from foundational topics in the theory of computing to information and communications science and technology and a broad variety of interdisciplinary application fields.

Information for Volume Editors and Authors

Publication in CCIS is free of charge. No royalties are paid, however, we offer registered conference participants temporary free access to the online version of the conference proceedings on SpringerLink (http://link.springer.com) by means of an http referrer from the conference website and/or a number of complimentary printed copies, as specified in the official acceptance email of the event.

CCIS proceedings can be published in time for distribution at conferences or as post-proceedings, and delivered in the form of printed books and/or electronically as USBs and/or e-content licenses for accessing proceedings at SpringerLink. Furthermore, CCIS proceedings are included in the CCIS electronic book series hosted in the SpringerLink digital library at http://link.springer.com/bookseries/7899. Conferences publishing in CCIS are allowed to use Online Conference Service (OCS) for managing the whole proceedings lifecycle (from submission and reviewing to preparing for publication) free of charge.

Publication process

The language of publication is exclusively English. Authors publishing in CCIS have to sign the Springer CCIS copyright transfer form, however, they are free to use their material published in CCIS for substantially changed, more elaborate subsequent publications elsewhere. For the preparation of the camera-ready papers/files, authors have to strictly adhere to the Springer CCIS Authors' Instructions and are strongly encouraged to use the CCIS LaTeX style files or templates.

Abstracting/Indexing

CCIS is abstracted/indexed in DBLP, Google Scholar, EI-Compendex, Mathematical Reviews, SCImago, Scopus. CCIS volumes are also submitted for the inclusion in ISI Proceedings.

How to start

To start the evaluation of your proposal for inclusion in the CCIS series, please send an e-mail to ccis@springer.com.

Frans A. Oliehoek · Manon Kok · Sicco Verwer
Editors

Artificial Intelligence and Machine Learning

35th Benelux Conference, BNAIC/Benelearn 2023
Delft, The Netherlands, November 8–10, 2023
Revised Selected Papers

Springer

Editors
Frans A. Oliehoek
Delft University of Technology
Delft, The Netherlands

Manon Kok
Delft University of Technology
Delft, The Netherlands

Sicco Verwer
Delft University of Technology
Delft, The Netherlands

ISSN 1865-0929 ISSN 1865-0937 (electronic)
Communications in Computer and Information Science
ISBN 978-3-031-74649-9 ISBN 978-3-031-74650-5 (eBook)
https://doi.org/10.1007/978-3-031-74650-5

This Springer imprint is published by the registered company Springer Nature Switzerland AG
The registered company address is: Gewerbestrasse 11, 6330 Cham, Switzerland

Preface

In this volume, we are happy present the post-proceedings of BNAIC/BeNeLearn 2023, the joint conference on Artificial Intelligence and Machine Learning in the BeNeLux, which took place at TU Delft. It is the main regional conference on these topics and has a long tradition: in 2018, the 30th Benelux Conference on Artificial Intelligence (BNAIC) and the 27th Belgian Dutch Conference on Machine Learning (Benelearn) were jointly organized in 's Hertogenbosch, and this has been repeated annually since.

The conference took place from Wednesday November 8th to Friday November 10th, filling nearly three full days with invited and contributed talks, poster presentations, demo's and an industry session. The conference was preceded by a co-located ELLIS Benelux PhD event. The scientific track consisted of different types of papers: A) regular papers, B) encore abstracts of recently published work, C) demonstration papers, and D) thesis abstracts. A total of 139 submissions were received (47 type A papers, 49 encore abstracts, 5 demonstration papers, and 38 thesis abstracts), out of which 122 were selected for presentation, following a single-blind peer review process in which the type A, C and D papers received at least two reviews each. Decisions on type B papers, which report on work that has already passed peer review, were made by the program chairs. Following a round of revisions and another round of peer review with a minimum of two reviews per paper, 14 papers were selected for these post-proceedings.

The contributed type A and B papers were given 20 min to present their work, as well as the opportunity to present a poster. The thesis abstracts were presented in the poster session and advertised in lightning poster pitch sessions. Furthermore, the program featured two exciting keynotes by Jan-Willem van der Meent (Universiteit van Amsterdam) and Ann Nowé (Vrije Universiteit Brussel), a panel on "AI in the scientific world and industry: opportunities and challenges", a session led by BNVKI with invited talks from the Polish AI Society, and a FACt session to highlight upcoming faculty in AI. We gave awards for the best paper by Yannick Molinghen, Raphaël Avalos, Mark Van Achter, Ann Nowé and Tom Lenaerts, the best student abstract by Eline Bovy, Marnix Suilen and Nils Jansen, and the best demo by Junhan Wen, Andrei Dascalu, Dragomir Drashkov, Marinski, Bhatti, Herrebout and Michael Weinmann.

Organizing a conference takes an incredible effort, and we would like to thank our co-organizers, student volunteers, and the support staff of TU Delft Mechanical Engineering faculty. The conference sponsors are also warmly thanked. These were at level platinum: BNVKI, SIKS; at level gold: Convergence AI Port Center, Dyflexis, ORTEC, TU Delft AI Initiative; and at level silver: ASML.

July 2024

Frans A. Oliehoek
Manon Kok
Sicco Verwer

Organization

General Chairs

Bilge Atasoy	TU Delft, The Netherlands
Neil Yorke Smith	TU Delft, The Netherlands

Program Committee Chairs

Frans A. Oliehoek	TU Delft, The Netherlands
Manon Kok	TU Delft, The Netherlands
Sicco Verwer	TU Delft, The Netherlands

Local Organization Committee

Pedro Vergara Barrios	TU Delft, The Netherlands
Lolke Boonstra	TU Delft, The Netherlands
Issa Hanou	TU Delft, The Netherlands
Zlatan Ajanović	TU Delft, The Netherlands
Simon Goede	Mondai, The Netherlands
Patty Bokop-van der Stap	TU Delft, The Netherlands
Joost Poort	Mondai, The Netherlands
Kerem Yoner	TU Delft, The Netherlands
Clinton Cao	TU Delft, The Netherlands

Program Committee

Wannes Meert	Katholieke Universiteit Leuven, Belgium
Gerasimos Spanakis	Maastricht University, The Netherlands
Luca Laurenti	TU Delft, The Netherlands
Johan Kwisthout	Radboud University, The Netherlands
Thiago D. Simão	Radboud University, The Netherlands
Laurens Bliek	Eindhoven University of Technology, The Netherlands
Floris Bex	Utrecht University, The Netherlands
Nils Jansen	Radboud University, The Netherlands

Daan Bloembergen	City of Amsterdam, The Netherlands
Chris Develder	Ghent University, Belgium
Paul Van Eecke	Vrije Universiteit Brussel, Belgium
Bert Bredeweg	University of Amsterdam, The Netherlands
Tony Belpaeme	Ghent University, Belgium
Leon van der Torre	University of Luxembourg, Luxembourg
Arjen Hommersom	Open University of the Netherlands, The Netherlands
Amin Sharifi Kolarijani	Delft University of Technology, The Netherlands
Peter van der Putten	Leiden University & Pegasystems, The Netherlands
Jan Lemeire	Vrije Universiteit Brussel, Belgium
Christoph Schommer	University of Luxembourg, Luxembourg
Raj Thilak Rajan	Delft University of Technology, The Netherlands
Mustafa Mert Çelikok	TU Delft, The Netherlands
M. Birna van Riemsdijk	University of Twente, The Netherlands
Tom Lenaerts	Université libre de Bruxelles, Belgium
Raf Van de Plas	Delft University of Technology, The Netherlands
Jan Ramon	Inria, France
Yingqian Zhang	Eindhoven University of Technology, The Netherlands
Marco Loog	Radboud University, The Netherlands
Mohammad Khosravi	Delft University of Technology, The Netherlands
Hendrik Blockeel	Katholieke Universiteit Leuven, Belgium
Emir Demirović	Delft University of Technology, The Netherlands
Egon L. van den Broek	Utrecht University, The Netherlands
Tibor Bosse	Radboud University, The Netherlands
Ad Feelders	Utrecht University, The Netherlands
Vincent Francois	VU Amsterdam, The Netherlands
Sebastijan Dumancic	Katholieke Universiteit Leuven, Belgium
Dirk Thierens	Utrecht University, The Netherlands
Walter Kosters	Leiden University, The Netherlands
Shenghui Wang	University of Twente, The Netherlands
Stephan Sigg	Aalto University, Finland
Remco Veltkamp	Utrecht University, The Netherlands
Mitra Baratchi	University of Twente, The Netherlands
John Lee	Université catholique de Louvain, Belgium
Matthijs T. J. Spaan	Delft University of Technology, The Netherlands
Yuliya Shapovalova	Radboud University, The Netherlands
Yvan Saeys	Ghent University, Belgium
Pierre Geurts	University of Liège, Belgium
Jens Kober	Delft University of Technology, The Netherlands

Mathias Verbeke	KU Leuven, Belgium
Tom Claassen	Radboud University, The Netherlands
Jef Wijsen	University of Mons, Belgium
Isel Grau	Eindhoven University of Technology, The Netherlands
Stephan Bongers	Delft University of Technology, The Netherlands
Zaharah A. Bukhsh	Eindhoven University of Technology, The Netherlands
Floris Geerts	University of Antwerp, Belgium
Peter Lucas	University of Twente, The Netherlands
Jakub Tomczak	Vrije Universiteit Amsterdam, The Netherlands
Suk-Chung Yoon	Widener University, USA
Michel Klein	Vrije Universiteit Amsterdam, The Netherlands
Len Feremans	Universiteit Antwerpen, Belgium
Jilles Dibangoye	University of Groningen, The Netherlands
John-Jules Meyer	Utrecht University, The Netherlands
Tim van Erven	University of Amsterdam, The Netherlands
Zhao Yang	Leiden University, The Netherlands
Mark H.M. Winands	Maastricht University, The Netherlands
Luis A. Leiva	University of Luxembourg, Luxembourg
Nicolas Gillis	Université de Mons, Belgium
Tom Heskes	Radboud University, The Netherlands
Fatiha Saïs	Paris Saclay University, France
Walter Daelemans	University of Antwerp, Belgium
Joost Vennekens	KU Leuven, Belgium
Aske Plaat	Leiden University, The Netherlands
Davide Grossi	University of Groningen, The Netherlands
Hui Wang	Leiden University, The Netherlands
Arnoud Visser	University of Amsterdam, The Netherlands
Yaoxin Wu	Eindhoven University of Technology, The Netherlands
Henry Prakken	University of Utrecht & University of Groningen, The Netherlands
Menno van Zaanen	South African Centre for Digital Language Resources, South Africa
Mark Hoogendoorn	Vrije Universiteit Amsterdam, The Netherlands
Elvin Isufi	Delft University of Technology, The Netherlands
Mehdi Dastani	Utrecht University, The Netherlands
Bart Bogaerts	Vrije Universiteit Brussel, Belgium
Willem Waegeman	Ghent University, Belgium
Marieke van Vugt	University of Groningen, The Netherlands
Cédric Pruski	Luxembourg Institute of Science and Technology, Luxembourg

Benoit Macq	UCL, Belgium
Yolanda Spinola-Elias	University of Seville, Spain
Sven Mayer	LMU Munich, Germany

Contents

No Imputation Without Representation

Oliver Urs Lenz[1,2(✉)], Daniel Peralta[3], and Chris Cornelis[2]

[1] Leiden Institute of Advanced Computer Science, Leiden University, Leiden, The Netherlands
o.u.lenz@liacs.leidenuniv.nl

[2] Research Group for Computational Web Intelligence, Department of Applied Mathematics, Computer Science and Statistics, Ghent University, Ghent, Belgium
chris.cornelis@ugent.be

[3] Department of Information Technology, Ghent University, Ghent, Belgium
daniel.peralta@ugent.be
https://cwi.ugent.be

Abstract. By filling in missing values in datasets, imputation allows these datasets to be used with algorithms that cannot handle missing values by themselves. However, missing values may in principle contribute useful information that is lost through imputation. The missing-indicator approach can be used in combination with imputation to instead represent this information as a part of the dataset. There are several theoretical considerations why missing-indicators may or may not be beneficial, but there has not been any large-scale practical experiment on real-life datasets to test this question for machine learning predictions. We perform this experiment for three imputation strategies and a range of different classification algorithms, on the basis of twenty real-life datasets. In a follow-up experiment, we determine attribute-specific missingness thresholds for each classifier above which missing-indicators are more likely than not to increase classification performance. And in a second follow-up experiment, we evaluate numerical imputation of one-hot encoded categorical attributes. We reach the following conclusions. Firstly, missing-indicators generally increase classification performance. Secondly, with missing-indicators, nearest neighbour and iterative imputation do not lead to better performance than simple mean/mode imputation. Thirdly, for decision trees, pruning is necessary to prevent overfitting. Fourthly, the thresholds above which missing-indicators are more likely than not to improve performance are lower for categorical attributes than for numerical attributes. Lastly, mean imputation of numerical attributes preserves some of the information from missing values. Consequently, when not using missing-indicators it can be advantageous to apply mean imputation to one-hot encoded categorical attributes instead of mode imputation.

Keywords: Missing data · Missing-indicators · Imputation · Classification · Data-centric machine learning

F. A. Oliehoek et al. (Eds.): BNAIC/Benelearn 2023, CCIS 2187, pp. 1–21, 2025.
https://doi.org/10.1007/978-3-031-74650-5_1

1 Introduction

Missing values are a frequent issue in real-life datasets, and the subject of a large body of ongoing research. Some implementations of machine learning algorithms can handle missing values natively, requiring no further action by practitioners. But whenever this is not the case, a common general strategy is to replace the missing value with an estimated value: imputation. An advantage of imputation is that we obtain a complete dataset, to which we can apply any and all algorithms that make no special provision for missing values. However, missing values may be informative, and a disadvantage of imputation is that it removes this information.

The missing-indicator approach [12] is an old proposal to represent and thereby preserve the information encoded by missing values. For every original attribute, it adds a new binary 'indicator' or 'dummy' attribute that takes a value of 1 if the value for the original attribute is missing, and 0 if not (Fig. 1).[1] The missing-indicator approach is often presented as an alternative to imputation, but since it does not resolve the missing values in the original attributes, it can only be used in addition to, not instead of imputation.

a_1	a_2	a_3	i_1	i_2	i_3
0.92	aap	2.50	0	0	0
?	aap	1.00	1	0	0
8.42	?	3.00	0	1	0
2.23	noot	0.05	0	0	0
?	?	?	1	1	1
0.41	mies	?	0	0	1
⋮	⋮	⋮	⋮	⋮	⋮

Fig. 1. Illustrative example of a dataset with three attributes (a_1, a_2, a_3) with missing values ('?'), and corresponding missing-indicators (i_1, i_2, i_3)

It is an open question whether missing-indicators should be used for predictive tasks in machine learning [75]. Both imputation and the missing-indicator approach originate in the statistical literature. While imputation strategies have been the subject of a rich body of research, the missing-indicator approach has not received a large amount of attention, and is often dismissed or disregarded in overviews of approaches towards missing values.

In the context of machine learning, the effect of missing-indicators can be framed as follows. On the one hand, the addition of missing-indicators results in a more complete, higher-dimensional representation of the data. On the other hand, their omission corresponds to a form of dimensionality reduction,

[1] Some authors use the opposite convention, letting the indicator express non-missingness.

which may increase the efficiency and effectiveness of a dataset by eliminating redundancy.

To determine whether this trade-off is useful, a key question is to which extent missing values in a given dataset are informative. If they are not, the phrase "missing at random" (MAR) [66] is used to indicate that the distribution of missing values is dependent on the known values, while the stricter phrase "missing completely at random" (MCAR) denotes values that are distributed truly randomly. In contrast, informative missing values are often denoted as "missing not at random" (MNAR).

In this respect, it is often argued that one should distinguish between missing values that could in principle have been obtained, and missing values that fundamentally do not exist, like attributes related to pregnancy tests for male subjects.[2] In the latter case, the missing values are definitely informative. However, such clear-cut cases may be comparatively rare. Moreover, it does not follow that the missing values in the former case are definitely non-informative. In fact, for real-life datasets, unless we have specific knowledge about the process responsible for the missing values, we have to assume some degree of informativeness in principle.[3]

Nonetheless, it has been argued that in practice, the attributes of a dataset can be sufficiently redundant that one can get away with assuming that its missing values are MAR [69]. This means that most of the information contained by the missing values should in principle be recoverable through imputation. But even if this is so, imputation may not always perform optimally, in which case missing-indicators may still prove useful for machine learning.

A more subtle point is that even when missing values are informative, the information they encode need not be lost completely through imputation. This is particularly evident in the case of numerically encoded binary attributes (e.g. 0 and 1), where imputation can represent missing values as a third, intermediary value (e.g. 0.5). More generally, Le Morvan et al. [49] have recently observed that almost all deterministic imputation functions map records with missing values to distinct manifolds in the attribute space that can in principle be identified by sufficiently powerful algorithms. Nevertheless, missing-indicators can potentially make this learning task easier.

In light of these conflicting theoretical arguments, the usefulness of missing-indicators for real-life machine learning problems is an interesting empirical question. However, previous experiments in this direction have been limited in scope and number. These limitations include the use of only one or a handful of datasets, the use of datasets from which values have been removed artificially,

---

[2] We are grateful to an anonymous reviewer for this example.

[3] This is acknowledged by authors working under the assumption of MAR, e.g. "When data are missing for reasons beyond the investigator's control, one can never be certain whether MAR holds. The MAR hypothesis in such datasets cannot be formally tested unless the missing values, or at least a sample of them, are available from an external source." [69].

and not comparing the same imputation strategies with and without missing-indicators.

The purpose of the present paper is straightforward. On the basis of twenty real-life classification problems with naturally occurring missing values, we measure the performance of a range of popular classification algorithms, using three common types of imputation, with and without missing-indicators. This allows us to evaluate the effect of using missing-indicators, as well as the choice of imputation strategy.

Moreover, we conduct three follow-up experiments to gain a better understanding of when and why missing-indicators can be useful. In the first, we determine whether this is influenced by the type (categorical or numerical) and the amount of missing values of a given attribute. In the second, we test the hypothesis that numerical imputation partially preserves the information from missing values. And in the third follow-up experiment, we compare missing-indicators to two model-specific approaches to missing values for nearest neighbour and decision tree classifiers.

In Sect. 2, we provide a brief overview of the existing literature on missing-indicators, including previous experimental evaluations. In Sect. 3, we describe our experimental setup. We report our results in Sect. 4 and conclude in Sect. 5.

2 Background

We start with a brief discussion of the origins and reception of the missing-indicator approach, as well as previous experimental evaluations of the use of missing-indicators in prediction tasks.

2.1 Origins and Reception

The missing-indicator approach originates in the literature on linear regression. It dates back to at least Cohen [12], who pointed out that values in real-life datasets are typically not missing completely at random, and that the distribution of missing values may in particular depend on the values of the attribute that is to be predicted. He proposed that each attribute could be said to have two 'aspects', its value, and whether that value is present to begin with, which should be encoded with a pair of variables. For missing attribute values, the first of these variables was to be filled in with the mean of the known values, although other applications might call for different values. Cohen's proposal was subsequently expanded in [13], but received only limited recognition in the following years [4,11,42,46,57,76].

Cohen's proposal was subjected to a formal analysis by Jones [44], who showed that, if one assumes that missing values are MAR, and the true linear regression model does not contain any terms related to missingness, it produces biased estimates of the regression coefficients (unless the sample covariance between independent variables is zero). However, these assumptions run directly counter to the position set out in [13] that a priori, the missingness of each attribute is a possible explanatory factor, that it is safer not to assume that missing values are distributed randomly, and that the usefulness of missing-indicators is ultimately an empirical question.

Allison [2], motivated by [44] and working under the general assumption of MAR, dismissed missing-indicators as "clearly unacceptable", before conceding that they in fact produce optimal estimates when the missing value is not just missing, but cannot exist, such as the marital quality of an unmarried couple. However, this semantic distinction may not always be clear-cut in practice, and the more pertinent question may be whether missing values are informative. Allison [3] later acknowledged that missing-indicators may lead to better predictions and their use for that purpose was acceptable. Missing-indicators have also been dismissed in [5,36,61,70], and are frequently omitted in overviews of missing data strategies [16,23,25,32,69].

2.2 Previous Experiments

Only a handful of experimental comparisons of missing data approaches have included the missing-indicator approach, and these have been limited in scope. [81] and [56] only use a single dataset with randomly removed values, and base their evaluation on the performance of a single algorithm (respectively a neural network and linear regression). The authors of [59] use three classification algorithms and 22 datasets, but again with randomly removed values, explicitly assuming an MCAR context. They conclude that imputation outperforms missing-indicators, but the comparison is not like-for-like, since it involves several forms of imputation but only combines indicator attributes with zero imputation. The authors of [41] compare missing-indicators with zero imputation against several other forms of imputation without missing-indicators on one real dataset, for logistic regression. However, they do not evaluate predictive performance.

Ding & Simonoff [18] conduct a more extensive investigation, using insights from a series of Monte Carlo simulations to systematically remove values from 36 datasets to simulate different forms of missingness. They use these datasets to compare zero imputation[4] with indicator attributes against mean/mode imputation without, as well as a number of other missing data approaches, for logistic regression. In addition, the authors evaluate a related representation of missing values[5] on the same set of 36 datasets, and on one real-life dataset with missing values, for decision trees. They find that there is strong evidence that representing missing values is the best approach when they are informative; when this is not the case their results show no strong difference.

[4] Presumably, they use one-hot encoding for categorical attributes, in which case zero imputation is equivalent to treating missing values as a separate category, but they do not state this explicitly.

[5] For categorical values, encoding missing values as a separate category; for numerical values, encoding missing values as an extremely large value that can always be split from the other values.

The comparison by Grzymala-Busse & Hu [38] is based on 10 datasets with naturally occurring missing values. However, the setting is purely categorical—all attributes are transformed into categorical attributes—the only form of imputation is mode imputation, and the missing value approaches are evaluated on the basis of the LERS classifier (Learning from Examples based on Rough Sets [37]).

Marlin [52] compares zero imputation with missing-indicators (*augmentation with response indicators*) against several forms of imputation without, for logistic regression and neural networks, on the basis of an extensive series of simulations, one dataset with artificially removed values, and three real datasets. For the real datasets, there is no strong difference in performance between the different approaches.

Most recently, building on earlier experiments with simulated regression datasets [45,49], Perez-Lebel et al. [60] compare four different imputation techniques with and without missing-indicators (*missingness mask*) on seven prediction tasks derived from four real medical datasets, and conclude that missing-indicators consistently improve performance for gradient boosted trees, ridge regression and logistic regression.

We point out that the Missingness in Attribute (MIA) proposal [80] for decision trees and decision tree ensembles can be understood as an implicit combination of missing-indicators with automatic imputation, and has also been shown to outperform imputation without missing-indicators in small-scale experimental studies [45,60].

Finally, even experimental comparisons of missing data that do not feature the missing-indicator approach generally do not involve more than a handful of real-life datasets with naturally occurring missing values. We have only found the connected works [50,51], which feature 21 datasets from the UCI repository, but 12 of these are problematic.[6]

[6] The target column of the *echocardiogram* dataset ('alive-at-1') is supposed to denote whether a patient survived for at least one year, but it doesn't appear to agree with the columns from which it is derived, that denote how long a patient (has) survived and whether they were alive at the end of that period. The *audiology* dataset has a large number of small classes with complex labels and should perhaps be analysed with multi-label classification. In addition, it has ordinal attributes where the order of the values is not entirely clear, and three different values that potentially denote missingness ('?', 'unmeasured' and 'absent'), and it is not completely clear how they relate to each other. The *house-votes-84* dataset contains '?' values, but its documentation explicitly states that these values are not unknown, but indicate different forms of abstention. The *ozone* dataset is a time-series problem, while the task associated with the *sponge* and *water-treatment* datasets is clustering, with no obvious target for classification among their respective attributes. Finally, the *breast-cancer* (9), *cleveland* (7), *dermatology* (8), *lung-cancer* (5), *post-operative* (3) and *wisconsin* (16) datasets contain only very few missing values, and any performance difference between missing value approaches on these datasets may to a large extent be coincidental.

3 Experimental Setup

To evaluate the effect of the missing-indicator approach on classification performance, we conduct a series of experiments, using the Python machine learning library *scikit-learn* [58].

3.1 Questions

The aim of our experiments is to answer the following questions:

- Do missing-indicators increase performance, and does it matter which imputation strategy they are paired with?
- When do missing-indicators start to become useful in terms of missingness?
- Does using mean imputation instead of mode imputation allow for more information to be learned from missing categorical values?
- How do missing-indicators compare to model-specific approaches to missing values?

3.2 Evaluation

We preprocess datasets by standardising numerical attributes and one-hot encoding categorical attributes (as required by the implementations in scikit-learn).

We measure classification performance by performing stratified five-fold cross-validation, repeating this for five different random states (which determine both the dataset splits and the initialisation of algorithms with a random component), and calculating the mean area under the receiver operator curve (AUROC). For multi-class datasets, we use the extension of AUROC defined in [40].

To compare two alternatives A and B, we consider the p-value of a one-sided Wilcoxon signed-rank test [82] on the mean AUROC scores for our selection of datasets. When we compare A vs B, a score below 0.5 means that A increased performance on our selection of datasets; the lower the scores, the more confident we can be that this generalises to other similar datasets. Conversely, a score higher than 0.5 means that A decreased performance on our selection of datasets.

3.3 Imputation Strategies

We consider the following three imputation strategies:

- *Mean/mode imputation* replaces missing values of numerical and categorical attributes by, respectively, the mean and the mode of the non-missing values.
- *Nearest neighbour imputation* [79] replaces missing values of numerical and categorical attributes by, respectively, the mean and the mode of the 5 nearest non-missing values, with distance determined by the corresponding non-missing values for the other attributes.

– *Iterative imputation*, as implemented in scikit-learn, based on [8], predicts missing values of one attribute on the basis of the other attribute values using a round-robin approach. For numerical attributes, this uses Bayesian ridge regression [77], initialised with mean imputation, while for categorical attributes, we use logistic regression, initialised with mode imputation.

The scikit-learn implementations of nearest neighbour and iterative imputation can currently only impute numerical features, so we had to adapt them for categorical imputation. In all other aspects, we follow the default settings of scikit-learn.[7]

3.4 Classification Algorithms

We consider the classification algorithms listed in Table 1, as implemented in scikit-learn. Hyperparameters take their default values, except for SVM-L, LR and MLP, where we increase the maximum number of iterations to 10 000 to increase the probability of convergence.

For a number of these algorithms, specific ways have been proposed to handle missing values: e.g. NN-2-D [19], SVM-G [72], MLP [43,73,78] and CART [63, 80]. The purpose of the present experiment is to evaluate the general approach of using imputation with missing-indicators when these solutions have not been implemented, as is the case in scikit-learn.

Table 1. Classification algorithms.

Name	Description
NN-1	Nearest neighbours [28] with (Boscovich) 1-distance
NN-2	Nearest neighbours with (Euclidean) 2-distance
NN-1-D	Nearest neighbours with 1-distance, distance-weighted [21]
NN-2-D	Nearest neighbours with 2-distance, distance-weighted
SVM-L	Soft-margin Support Vector Machine [14] with linear kernel
SVM-G	Soft-margin Support Vector Machine with Gaussian kernel
LR	Multinomial logistic regression [15]
MLP	Multilayer perceptron [65] with ReLu activation [31], Glorot initialisation [34] and Adam optimisation [47]
CART	Classification and Regression Tree [7]
RF	Random Forest [6]
ERT	Extremely Randomised Trees [33]
ABT	Ada-boosted trees [29] with SAMME (stagewise additive modeling using a multi-class exponential loss function) [83]
GBM	Gradient Boosting Machine [30]

[7] For the *nomao* dataset, iterative imputation diverged, so we had to restrict imputation to the interval $[-100, 100]$.

3.5 Datasets

We use twenty real-life datasets with naturally occurring missing values from the UCI repository for machine learning [20] (Table 2). These datasets are quite varied—they cover a number of different domains and contain between 155 and 76 000 records, between 4 and 590 attributes, between 2 and 21 decision classes and missing value rates between 0.0032 and 0.43.

We have preprocessed these datasets in the following manner. We have removed attributes that were non-informative according to the accompanying documentation, as well as identifiers and alternative target values. When it was clear from the description that an attribute was categorical, we have treated it as such, even if it was originally represented with numerals. Conversely, where the possible values of an attribute admitted a semantic order, we have encoded them numerically. We have left binary attributes in their original encoding (categorical or numerical). To enable 5-fold cross-validation, we have removed classes with fewer than 5 records.

Table 2. Real-life classification datasets with missing values from the UCI repository for machine learning.

Dataset	Records	Classes	Attributes			Missing value rate			Source
			Num	Cat	Total	Num	Cat	Total	
adult	48842	2	5	8	13	0.0	0.017	0.010	[48]
agaricus-lepiota	8124	2	1	21	22	0.0	0.015	0.014	[71]
aps-failure	76000	2	170	0	170	0.083		0.083	[27]
arrhythmia	443	10	279	0	279	0.0032		0.0032	[39]
bands	540	2	19	15	34	0.054	0.054	0.054	[26]
ckd	400	2	14	10	24	0.14	0.059	0.11	[67]
crx	690	2	6	9	15	0.0060	0.0068	0.0065	[62]
dress-sales	500	2	3	9	12	0.20	0.19	0.19	
exasens	399	4	7	0	7	0.43		0.43	[74]
hcc	165	2	49	0	49	0.10		0.10	[68]
heart-disease	1611	2	13	1	14	0.18	0.0	0.17	[17]
hepatitis	155	2	19	0	19	0.057		0.057	[22]
horse-colic	368	2	19	1	20	0.25	0.39	0.26	[54]
mammographic-masses	961	2	2	2	4	0.042	0.041	0.042	[24]
mi	1700	8	111	0	111	0.085		0.085	[35]
nomao	34465	2	89	29	118	0.38	0.37	0.38	[9]
primary-tumor	330	15	16	1	17	0.029	0.20	0.039	[10]
secom	1567	2	590	0	590	0.045		0.045	[53]
soybean	683	19	22	13	35	0.099	0.096	0.098	[55]
thyroid0387	9172	18	7	16	23	0.22	0.0021	0.069	[64]

Table 3. One-sided p-values, imputation with missing-indicators versus without.

Classifier	Imputation strategy		
	Mean/mode	Neighbours	Iterative
NN-1	0.0088	0.0015	0.0017
NN-2	0.015	0.0024	0.00048
NN-1-D	0.0045	0.0019	0.0011
NN-2-D	0.0019	0.0031	0.00027
SVM-L	0.13	0.27	0.099
SVM-G	0.0032	0.0027	0.0021
LR	0.079	0.063	0.068
MLP	0.0027	0.0063	0.0056
CART	0.44	0.39	0.40
RF	0.038	0.051	0.17
ERT	0.28	0.0099	0.026
ABT	0.089	0.078	0.47
GBM	0.17	0.012	0.36

4 Results and Discussion

Using the experimental setup detailed in the previous section, we now try to answer the questions listed in Subsect. 3.1.

4.1 Do Missing-Indicators Increase Performance, and Does it Matter Which Imputation Strategy They are Paired With?

The p-values obtained by comparing imputation with and without missing-indicators are displayed in Table 3. Missing-indicators generally lead to increased performance—with the notable exception of CART, to which we return below. The more complicated imputation strategies do not result in much better results than mean/mode imputation when we pair imputation with missing-indicators (Table 4). At best, nearest neighbour and iterative imputation only lead to a modest improvement, and for many classifiers, they actually decrease performance. Therefore, we focus on mean/mode imputation for the remainder of this section.

A possible reason for the failure of missing-indicators to increase performance with CART, is that by default, the scikit-learn implementation of this classifier does not perform pruning, making it prone to overfitting. To test this hypothesis, we repeat our experiment for CART and mean imputation, but this time we apply cost complexity pruning ($\alpha = 0.01$). This clearly improves performance

Table 4. One-sided p-values, missing-indicators with iterative and nearest neighbour versus mean/mode imputation.

Classifier	Imputation strategy	
	Neighbours	Iterative
NN-1	0.94	0.15
NN-2	0.78	0.19
NN-1-D	0.97	0.55
NN-2-D	0.84	0.23
SVM-L	0.53	0.61
SVM-G	0.47	0.94
LR	0.40	0.83
MLP	0.30	0.55
CART	0.69	0.79
RF	0.61	0.86
ERT	0.61	0.64
ABT	0.33	0.78
GBM	0.93	0.85

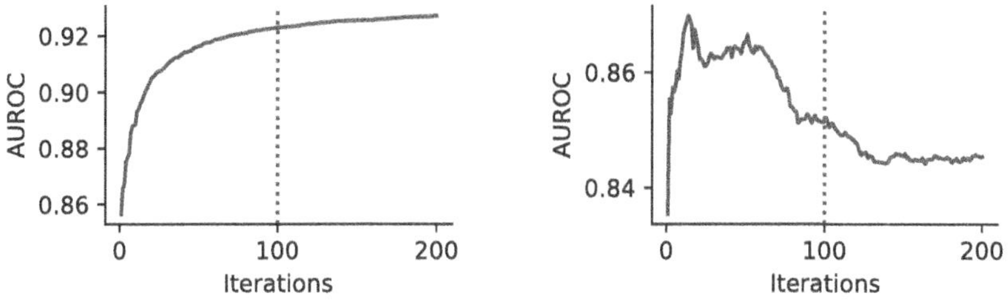

(a) adult (b) mammographic-masses

Fig. 2. GBM test AUROC for two illustrative datasets, using mean/mode imputation without missing-indicators, for one random state and one cross-validation fold. The default hyperparameter value of 100 iterations leads to under- (a) and overfitting (b).

($p = 0.0069$ without missing-indicators, $p = 0.015$ with missing-indicators), and now missing-indicators have a slight advantage ($p = 0.23$).

We have also taken a closer look at ERT and GBM, for which the performance increase from missing-indicators is not very significant. For ERT, this may be due to underfitting. If we increase the number of trees from the default 100 to 1000, this improves performance ($p = 0.0011$ without missing-indicators, $p = 0.0032$ with missing-indicators), and makes the advantage of missing-indicators somewhat clearer ($p = 0.092$).

For GBM, the default choice of 100 iterations of gradient descent can lead to both under- or overfitting, depending on the dataset (Fig. 2). We believe that it is generally preferable to continue training until an early-stopping criterion is met. However, applying the same criterion as with MLP[8] does not improve performance over the default of 100 ($p = 0.81$ without missing-indicators, $p = 0.85$ with missing-indicators) and does not change the relative advantage due to missing-indicators ($p = 0.20$).

4.2 When Do Missing-Indicators Start to Become Useful in Terms of Missingness?

The theoretical motivation for representing missing values through missing-indicators is that this allows classifiers to learn the information encoded in their distribution. In principle, this should be easier when there are more examples to learn from. We can use this principle to obtain a better understanding of when missing-indicators might be useful on a per-attribute level.

The challenge that we have to overcome is that we would like to study individual attributes, but classification performance is measured on the dataset level. We tackle this by studying datasets with only one attribute with missing values, allowing us to investigate the relation between the properties of the attribute and classification performance on the dataset.

We conduct the following experiment. For each attribute with missing values in each dataset, we reduce the original dataset by removing all other attributes with missing values. We thus obtain 1148 reduced datasets with only one attribute with missing values, onto which we apply each of our classifiers (with pruning for CART, 1000 trees for ERT and early-stopping for GBM) and consider whether missing-indicators increase or decrease AUROC (we dismiss ties). Finally, for each classifier we fit a logistic regression model with cluster robust covariance (clustered by the originating dataset), with the following potential parameters: categoricalness (whether the attribute is categorical) and either the number of missing values (log-transformed) or the missing rate. We use the Akaike information criterion [1] to decide whether to select these parameters.

We find that for most classifiers, either the absolute or the relative number of missing values is an informative parameter with positive coefficient. For MLP, neither parameter is informative, while for RF, the number of missing values is an informative parameter with negative coefficient, for which we have no explanation at present. For every classifier, categoricalness is an informative parameter with positive coefficient, meaning that missing-indicators are more beneficial for categorical than for numerical attributes.

The fitted logistic regression models allow us to calculate attribute-specific thresholds above which missing-indicators are more likely than not to increase AUROC, for all classifiers except MLP and RF (Table 5). In many cases, these thresholds are 1 or 0.0, indicating that missing-indicators are always likely to increase AUROC.

[8] Setting aside 10% of the data for validation, stopping when validation loss has not decreased by at least 0.0001 for ten iterations, with a maximum of 10 000 iterations.

Table 5. Thresholds above which missing-indicators are more likely than not to increase AUROC, in terms of the absolute number of missing values or the missing rate.

Classifier	Missing values		Missing rate	
	Cat	Num	Cat	Num
NN-1	1	302		
NN-2	2	130		
NN-1-D	1	291		
NN-2-D	1	73		
SVM-L			0.0	0.0
SVM-G			0.0	0.40
LR			0.0	0.0
CART			0.0	0.12
ERT			0.0	1.0
ABT	1	23200		
GBM			0.0	0.0

4.3 Does Using Mean Imputation Instead of Mode Imputation Allow for More Information to Be Learned from Missing Categorical Values?

As indicated above, missing-indicators are generally more likely to increase performance for categorical than for numerical attributes. A potential explanation for this is the fact that the mode of a categorical attribute is one of the non-missing values, whereas the mean of a numerical attribute is generally not equal to one of the non-missing values. Therefore, categorical imputation renders missing values truly indistinguishable from non-missing values, whereas numerical imputation does not—the information expressed by missing values may be partially recoverable, as argued by Le Morvan et al. [49] and discussed in the Introduction.

We can achieve a similar partial representation of missing categorical values by changing the order in which we perform imputation and one-hot encoding, i.e. by performing numerical imputation on one-hot encoded categorical attributes with missing values. For imputation without missing-indicators, this indeed leads to better performance for some classifiers, while in combination with missing-indicators, it does not make much of a difference (Table 6)[9].

4.4 How Do Missing-Indicators Compare to Model-Specific Approaches to Missing Values?

While not the primary focus of this paper, we may also wonder how the missing-indicator approach compares to model-specific approaches to missing values.

[9] LR is an exception here, we have no explanation for this.

Table 6. One-sided p-values, mean imputation after one-hot encoding versus mode imputation of missing categorical values.

Classifier	Without —	With missing-indicators
NN-1	0.020	0.077
NN-2	0.14	0.031
NN-1-D	0.016	0.12
NN-2-D	0.16	0.031
SVM-L	0.43	0.57
SVM-G	0.17	0.56
LR	0.81	0.057
MLP	0.16	0.60
CART	0.44	0.30
RF	0.046	0.57
ERT	0.030	0.95
ABT	0.48	0.62
GBM	0.077	0.54

For CART and RF, we consider the proposal by [80], that a decision tree should evaluate two variants of each split, with missing values sent to either side. This has been implemented in the latest version of scikit-learn (1.4.0), which was released after the previous experiments in this section were conducted. In addition, we have modified the implementation of the nearest neighbour classifier in scikit-learn to obtain the approach labelled as 'normal' in [19]. This calculates the distance between two records by linearly extrapolating the distance calculated only on the basis of all non-missing feature values. We note that every model-specific approach is different—we expect that their effect on classification performance will differ from case to case—so our evaluation of these two approaches only serves an illustrative purpose.

We find (Table 7, Test 1) that the model-specific approach for the nearest neighbour classifiers performs significantly worse than mean/mean imputation with missing-indicators. In contrast, there is no difference for CART, and the model-specific approach appears to perform better for RF. We can also ask whether these model-specific approaches benefit from adding missing-indicators—here this only appears to be the case for the nearest neighbour classifiers (Table 7, Test 2), i.e. when the model-specific approach performs badly. However, even with missing-indicators the model-specific approach for the nearest neighbour classifiers does not perform better than mean/mean imputation with missing indicators (Table 7, Test 3).

Table 7. One-sided p-values, model-specific missing value approaches. Test 1: Mean/mean imputation with missing-indicators vs model-specific approach without; Test 2: Model-specific approach with missing-indicators vs model-specific approach without; Test 3: Model-specific approach vs mean/mean imputation, both with missing-indicators.

Classifier	Test 1	Test 2	Test 3
NN-1	0.00036	0.00017	0.56
NN-2	0.00074	0.00015	0.94
NN-1-D	0.00020	0.00015	0.89
NN-2-D	0.00023	0.00011	0.93
CART	0.50	0.86	0.66
RF	0.92	0.60	0.092

5 Conclusion

We have presented the first large-scale experimental evaluation of the effect of the missing-indicator approach on classification performance, conducted on real datasets with naturally occurring missing values, paired with three different imputation techniques. The central question was whether, on balance, more benefit can be derived from the additional information encoded in a representation of missing values, or from the lower-dimensional projection of the data obtained by omitting missing-indicators.

On the whole, missing-indicators increase performance for the classification algorithms that we considered. An exception was CART, which suffers from overfitting in its default scikit-learn configuration. When pruning is applied, missing-indicators do increase performance. For ERT, the advantage of missing-indicators becomes more significant when underfitting is controlled.

We also found that, in the presence of missing-indicators, nearest neighbour and iterative imputation do not significantly increase performance over simple mean/mode imputation. This is a useful finding, because implementations of more sophisticated imputation strategies may not always be available to practitioners working in different frameworks, or easy to apply.

In a follow-up experiment, we determined attribute-specific missingness thresholds, above which missing-indicators are more likely than not to increase performance. For categorical attributes, this threshold is generally very low, while for numerical attributes, there is more variation among classifiers, in particular as to whether this threshold is absolute or relative to the total number of records.

The greater usefulness of missing-indicators for categorical than for numerical attributes can be explained by the fact that the mean of a numerical attribute is not generally identical to any of the non-missing values, and that mean imputation therefore preserves some of the information of missing values. This is supported by the results of a further experiment, which showed that, in the absence of missing-indicators, applying mean imputation to one-hot encoded categorical attributes results in somewhat better performance than mode imputation.

While we have mainly considered the use of missing-indicators with imputation, there also exist model-specific solutions for missing values, that can in turn be combined with missing-indicators. Whether missing-indicators outperform these model-specific approaches has to be determined on a case-by-case basis. This was illustrated by our third follow-up experiment for nearest neighbour and decision tree classifiers.

We conclude that the combination of mean/mode imputation with missing-indicators is a safe default approach towards missing values in classification tasks. While over- or underfitting is a concern for certain classifiers, it is a concern for these classifiers with or without missing-indicators. However, practitioners may want to omit missing-indicators when the classification algorithm to be used has a special provision for missing values, when the missingness thresholds that we determined are not met, or on the basis of specific information about the distribution of missing values in the dataset. The use of missing-indicators can also be combined with dimensionality reduction algorithms to increase the information density of the resulting dataset.

The problem of missing data has been the subject of a rich body of theoretical literature. We hope to have contributed with this paper to the practical evaluation of some of that theory. In particular, we are happy to have identified twenty real-life datasets with missing values, and hope that in the future, more such datasets will be collected.

Acknowledgement. The research reported in this paper was conducted with the financial support of the Odysseus programme of the Research Foundation – Flanders (FWO). This publication is part of the project Digital Twin with project number P18-03 of the research programme TTW Perspective, which is (partly) financed by the Dutch Research Council (NWO). We would like to express our thanks to Geert van der Heijden for answering a question about [41].

Data and Code. Datasets and the code to reproduce our experiments are available at https://cwi.ugent.be/~oulenz/code/lenz-2024-no.tar.gz.

Disclosure of Interests. The authors have no competing interests to declare that are relevant to the content of this article.

References

1. Akaike, H.: Information theory and an extension of the maximum likelihood principle. In: Proceedings of the 2nd International Symposium on Information Theory, pp. 267–281. Akadémiai Kiadó (1971)
2. Allison, P.D.: Missing Data. Sage Publications, Thousand Oaks (2001)
3. Allison, P.D.: Missing data. In: Marsden, P.V., Wright, J.D. (eds.) Handbook of Survey Research, 2nd edn., chap. 20, pp. 631–657. Emerald Group Publishing, Bingley (2010)

4. Anderson, A.B., Basilevsky, A., Hum, D.P.J.: Missing data: a review of the literature. In: Rossi, P.H., Wright, J.D., Anderson, A.B. (eds.) Handbook of Survey Research. Quantitive Studies in Social Relations, chap. 12, pp. 415–494. Academic Press, New York (1983)
5. Aste, M., Boninsegna, M., Freno, A., Trentin, E.: Techniques for dealing with incomplete data: a tutorial and survey. Pattern Anal. Appl. **18**(1), 1–29 (2015)
6. Breiman, L.: Random forests. Mach. Learn. **45**(1), 5–32 (2001)
7. Breiman, L., Friedman, J.H., Olshen, R.A., Stone, C.J.: Classification and Regression Trees. The Wadsworth Statistics/probability Series. Wadsworth, Monterey, California (1984)
8. van Buuren, S., Groothuis-Oudshoorn, K.: MICE: multivariate imputation by chained equations in R. J. Stat. Softw. **45**(3), 1–67 (2011)
9. Candillier, L., Lemaire, V.: Design and analysis of the Nomao challenge: active learning in the real-world. In: ECML-PKDD 2012: Active Learning in Real-world Applications Workshop (2012)
10. Cestnik, B., Kononenko, I., Bratko, I.: ASSISTANT 86: a knowledge-elicitation tool for sophisticated users. In: EWSL 87: Proceedings of the 2nd European Working Session on Learning, pp. 31–45. Sigma Press (1987)
11. Chow, W.K.: A look at various estimators in logistic models in the presence of missing values. Technical report, N-1324-HEW. Rand Corporation, Santa Monica (1979)
12. Cohen, J.: Multiple regression as a general data-analytic system. Psychol. Bull. **70**(6), 426–443 (1968)
13. Cohen, J., Cohen, P.: Missing data. In: Applied Multiple Regression/Correlation Analysis for the Behavioral Sciences, pp. 265–290. Lawrence Erlbaum Associates, Hillsdale (1975)
14. Cortes, C., Vapnik, V.: Support-vector networks. Mach. Learn. **20**(3), 273–297 (1995)
15. Cox, D.R.: Some procedures connected with the logistic qualitative response curve. In: David, F.N. (ed.) Research Papers in Statistics: Festschrift for J. Neyman, pp. 55–71. Wiley, London (1966)
16. Das, S., Datta, S., Chaudhuri, B.B.: Handling data irregularities in classification: foundations, trends, and future challenges. Pattern Recogn. **81**, 674–693 (2018)
17. Detrano, R., et al.: International application of a new probability algorithm for the diagnosis of coronary artery disease. Am. J. Cardiol. **64**(5), 304–310 (1989)
18. Ding, Y., Simonoff, J.S.: An investigation of missing data methods for classification trees applied to binary response data. J. Mach. Learn. Res. **11**(1), 131–170 (2010)
19. Dixon, J.K.: Pattern recognition with partly missing data. IEEE Trans. Syst. Man Cybern. **9**(10), 617–621 (1979)
20. Dua, D., Graff, C.: UCI machine learning repository (2019). http://archive.ics.uci.edu/ml
21. Dudani, S.A.: The distance-weighted k-nearest-neighbor rule. IEEE Trans. Syst. Man Cybern. **6**(4), 325–327 (1976)
22. Efron, B., Gong, G.: Statistical theory and the computer. In: Eddy, W.F. (ed.) Computer Science and Statistics: Proceedings of the 13th Symposium on the Interface, pp. 3–7. Springer, New York (1981). https://doi.org/10.1007/978-1-4613-9464-8_1
23. Eirola, E.: Machine learning methods for incomplete data and variable selection. Ph.D. thesis, Aalto University, Espoo (2014)

24. Elter, M., Schulz-Wendtland, R., Wittenberg, T.: The prediction of breast cancer biopsy outcomes using two CAD approaches that both emphasize an intelligible decision process. Med. Phys. **34**(11), 4164–4172 (2007)
25. Enders, C.K.: Applied Missing Data Analysis. Methodology in the Social Sciences. The Guilford Press, New York (2010)
26. Evans, B., Fisher, D.: Overcoming process delays with decision tree induction. IEEE Expert **9**(1), 60–66 (1994)
27. Costa, C.F., Nascimento, M.A.: IDA 2016 industrial challenge: using machine learning for predicting failures. In: Boström, H., Knobbe, A., Soares, C., Papapetrou, P. (eds.) IDA 2016. LNCS, vol. 9897, pp. 381–386. Springer, Cham (2016). https://doi.org/10.1007/978-3-319-46349-0_33
28. Fix, E., Hodges Jr., J.: Discriminatory analysis—nonparametric discrimination: consistency properties. Technical report, 21-49-004, USAF School of Aviation Medicine, Randolph Field, Texas (1951)
29. Freund, Y., Schapire, R.E.: A desicion-theoretic generalization of on-line learning and an application to boosting. In: Vitányi, P. (ed.) EuroCOLT 1995. LNCS, vol. 904, pp. 23–37. Springer, Heidelberg (1995). https://doi.org/10.1007/3-540-59119-2_166
30. Friedman, J.H.: Greedy function approximation: a gradient boosting machine. Ann. Stat. **29**(5), 1189–1232 (2001)
31. Fukushima, K.: Visual feature extraction by a multilayered network of analog threshold elements. IEEE Trans. Syst. Sci. Cybern. **5**(4), 322–333 (1969)
32. García, S., Luengo, J., Herrera, F.: Data Preprocessing in Data Mining, Intelligent Systems Reference Library. Dealing with Missing Values vol. 72, chap. 4. Springer, Cham (2015). https://doi.org/10.1007/978-3-319-10247-4
33. Geurts, P., Ernst, D., Wehenkel, L.: Extremely randomized trees. Mach. Learn. **63**(1), 3–42 (2006)
34. Glorot, X., Bengio, Y.: Understanding the difficulty of training deep feedforward neural networks. In: AISTATS 2010: Proceedings of the Thirteenth International Conference on Artificial Intelligence and Statistics. Proceedings of Machine Learning Research, vol. 9, pp. 249–256. JMLR Workshop and Conference Proceedings (2010)
35. Golovenkin, S.E., et al.: Trajectories, bifurcations, and pseudo-time in large clinical datasets: applications to myocardial infarction and diabetes data. GigaScience **9**(11), giaa128 (2020)
36. Graham, J.W.: Missing data analysis: making it work in the real world. Annu. Rev. Psychol. **60**, 549–576 (2009)
37. Grzymala-Busse, J.W.: Knowledge acquisition under uncertainty-a rough set approach. J. Intell. Rob. Syst. **1**(1), 3–16 (1988)
38. Grzymala-Busse, J.W., Hu, M.: A comparison of several approaches to missing attribute values in data mining. In: Ziarko, W., Yao, Y. (eds.) RSCTC 2000. LNCS, vol. 2005, pp. 378–385. Springer, Heidelberg (2000). https://doi.org/10.1007/3-540-45554-X_46
39. Güvenir, H.A., Acar, B., Demiröz, G., Çekin, A.: A supervised machine learning algorithm for arrhythmia analysis. In: Proceedings of the 24th Annual Meeting of Computers in Cardiology. Computers in Cardiology, vol. 24, pp. 433–436. IEEE (1997)
40. Hand, D.J., Till, R.J.: A simple generalisation of the area under the ROC curve for multiple class classification problems. Mach. Learn. **45**(2), 171–186 (2001)

41. van der Heijden, G.J.M.G., Donders, A.R.T., Stijnen, T., Moons, K.G.M.: Imputation of missing values is superior to complete case analysis and the missing-indicator method in multivariable diagnostic research: A clinical example. J. Clin. Epidemiol. **59**(10), 1102–1109 (2006)
42. Hutcheson, J.D., Jr., Prather, J.E.: Interpreting the effects of missing data in survey research. Southeastern Polit. Rev. **9**(2), 129–143 (1981)
43. Ipsen, N., Mattei, P.A., Frellsen, J.: How to deal with missing data in supervised deep learning? In: Artemiss 2020: First ICML Workshop on the Art of Learning with Missing Values (2020)
44. Jones, M.P.: Indicator and stratification methods for missing explanatory variables in multiple linear regression. J. Am. Stat. Assoc. **91**(433), 222–230 (1996)
45. Josse, J., Chen, J.M., Prost, N., Varoquaux, G., Scornet, E.: On the consistency of supervised learning with missing values. Stat. Papers **65**(9) (2024). https://doi.org/10.1007/s00362-024-01550-4
46. Kim, J.O., Curry, J.: The treatment of missing data in multivariate analysis. Sociol. Methods Res. **6**(2), 215–240 (1977)
47. Kingma, D.P., Ba, J.L.: Adam: a method for stochastic optimization. In: ICLR 2015: 3rd International Conference on Learning Representations (2015)
48. Kohavi, R.: Scaling up the accuracy of naive-bayes classifiers: a decision-tree hybrid. In: KDD-96: Proceedings of the Second International Conference on Knowledge Discovery and Data Mining, pp. 202–207. AAAI Press (1996)
49. Le Morvan, M., Josse, J., Scornet, E., Varoquaux, G.: What's a good imputation to predict with missing values? In: NeurIPS 2021: Proceedings of the Thirty-fifth Conference on Neural Information Processing Systems. Advances in neural information processing systems, vol. 34, pp. 11530–11540. NIPS Foundation (2021)
50. Luengo, J., García, S., Herrera, F.: On the choice of the best imputation methods for missing values considering three groups of classification methods. Knowl. Inf. Syst. **32**(1), 77–108 (2012)
51. Luengo, J., Sáez, J.A., Herrera, F.: Missing data imputation for fuzzy rule-based classification systems. Soft. Comput. **16**(5), 863–881 (2012)
52. Marlin, B.M.: Missing data problems in machine learning. Ph.D. thesis, University of Toronto (2008)
53. McCann, M., Li, Y., Maguire, L., Johnston, A.: Causality challenge: benchmarking relevant signal components for effective monitoring and process control. In: NIPS 2008: Proceedings of Workshop on Causality. Proceedings of Machine Learning Research, vol. 6, pp. 277–288. JMLR Workshop and Conference Proceedings (2008)
54. McLeish, M., Cecile, M.: Enhancing medical expert systems with knowledge obtained from statistical data. Ann. Math. Artif. Intell. **2**(1–4), 261–276 (1990)
55. Michalski, R.S., Chilausky, R.L.: Learning by being told and learning from examples: an experimental comparison of the two methods of knowledge acquisition in the context of developing an expert system for soybean disease diagnosis. Int. J. Policy Anal. Inf. Syst. **4**(2), 125–161 (1980)
56. Ng, C.G., Yusoff, M.S.B.: Missing values in data analysis: ignore or impute? Educ. Med. J. **3**(1) (2011)
57. Orme, J.G., Reis, J.: Multiple regression with missing data. J. Soc. Serv. Res. **15**(1–2), 61–91 (1991)
58. Pedregosa, F., et al.: Scikit-learn: machine learning in Python. J. Mach. Learn. Res. **12**(85), 2825–2830 (2011)
59. Pereira Barata, A., Takes, F.W., van den Herik, H.J., Veenman, C.J.: Imputation methods outperform missing-indicator for data missing completely at random. In: ICDM 2019: Proceedings of the Workshops, pp. 407–414. IEEE (2019)

60. Perez-Lebel, A., Varoquaux, G., Le Morvan, M., Josse, J., Poline, J.B.: Benchmarking missing-values approaches for predictive models on health databases. GigaScience **11**(1), giac013 (2022)
61. Pigott, T.D.: A review of methods for missing data. Educ. Res. Eval. **7**(4), 353–383 (2001)
62. Quinlan, J.R.: Simplifying decision trees. Int. J. Man Mach. Stud. **27**(3), 221–234 (1987)
63. Quinlan, J.R.: Unknown attribute values in induction. In: Proceedings of the Sixth International Workshop on Machine Learning, pp. 164–168. Morgan Kaufmann (1989)
64. Quinlan, J.R., Compton, P.J., Horn, K.A., Lazarus, L.: Inductive knowledge acquisition: a case study. In: Proceedings of the Second Australian Conference on Applications of Expert Systems, pp. 157–173. Turing Institute Press (1986)
65. Rosenblatt, F.: Principles of neurodynamics—perceptrons and the theory of brain mechanisms. Technical report VG-1196-G-8, Cornell Aeronautical Laboratory, Buffalo, New York (1961)
66. Rubin, D.B.: Inference and missing data. Biometrika **63**(3), 581–592 (1976)
67. Rubini, L.J., Eswaran, P.: Generating comparative analysis of early stage prediction of chronic kidney disease. Int. J. Mod. Eng. Res. **5**(7), 49–55 (2015)
68. Santos, M.S., Abreu, P.H., García-Laencina, P.J., Simão, A., Carvalho, A.: A new cluster-based oversampling method for improving survival prediction of hepatocellular carcinoma patients. J. Biomed. Inform. **58**, 49–59 (2015)
69. Schafer, J.L.: Analysis of Incomplete Multivariate Data, Monographs on Statistics and Applied Probability, vol. 72. Chapman & Hall, London (1997)
70. Schafer, J.L., Graham, J.W.: Missing data: our view of the state of the art. Psychol. Methods **7**(2), 147–177 (2002)
71. Schlimmer, J.C.: Concept acquisition through representational adjustment. Ph.D. thesis, University of California, Irvine (1987)
72. Śmieja, M., Struski, Ł, Tabor, J., Marzec, M.: Generalized RBF kernel for incomplete data. Knowl.-Based Syst. **173**, 150–162 (2019)
73. Śmieja, M., Struski, Ł., Tabor, J., Zieliński, B., Spurek, P.: Processing of missing data by neural networks. In: NeurIPS 2018: Proceedings of the Thirty-second Annual Conference on Neural Information Processing Systems. Advances in Neural Information Processing Systems, vol. 31, pp. 689–696. NIPS Foundation (2018)
74. Soltani Zarrin, P., Röckendorf, N., Wenger, C.: In-vitro classification of saliva samples of COPD patients and healthy controls using machine learning tools. IEEE Access **8**, 168053–168060 (2020)
75. Sperrin, M., Martin, G.P., Sisk, R., Peek, N.: Missing data should be handled differently for prediction than for description or causal explanation. J. Clin. Epidemiol. **125**, 183–187 (2020)
76. Stumpf, S.A.: A note on handling missing data. J. Manag. **4**(1), 65–73 (1978)
77. Tipping, M.E.: Sparse Bayesian learning and the relevance vector machine. J. Mach. Learn. Res. **1**, 211–244 (2001)
78. Tresp, V., Neuneier, R., Ahmad, S.: Efficient methods for dealing with missing data in supervised learning. In: NIPS-94: Proceedings of the Eighth Annual Conference on Neural Information Processing Systems. Advances in neural information processing systems, vol. 7, pp. 689–696. MIT Press (1994)
79. Troyanskaya, O., et al.: Missing value estimation methods for DNA microarrays. Bioinformatics **17**(6), 520–525 (2001)
80. Twala, B.E., Jones, M., Hand, D.J.: Good methods for coping with missing data in decision trees. Pattern Recogn. Lett. **29**(7), 950–956 (2008)

81. Vamplew, P., Adams, A.: Missing values in a backpropagation neural net. In: ACNN 1992: Proceedings of the Third Australian Conference on Neural Networks, pp. 64–66. Sydney University Electrical Engineering (1992)
82. Wilcoxon, F.: Individual comparisons by ranking methods. Biomet. Bull. **1**(6), 80–83 (1945)
83. Zhu, J., Zou, H., Rosset, S., Hastie, T.: Multi-class AdaBoost. Stat. Interface **2**(3), 349–360 (2009)

Relevance Feedback Strategies for Reducing Review Effort in Recall-Oriented Neural Information Retrieval

Timo Kats[1], Peter van der Putten[1(✉)], and Jan Scholtes[2]

[1] LIACS, Leiden University, P.O. Box 9512, 2300 RA Leiden, The Netherlands
{t.p.a.kats,p.w.h.van.der.putten}@liacs.leidenuniv.nl
[2] Maastricht University, Minderbroedersberg 4-6, 6211 LK Maastricht, The Netherlands
scholtes@msc.nl

Abstract. In a number of information retrieval applications, such as patent search, literature review, and due diligence, preventing false negatives is more important than preventing false positives. However, approaches designed to reduce review effort, such as 'technology assisted review', can create false negatives, since these are often based on active learning systems that exclude documents automatically based on user feedback. To address this issue, we propose a recall-oriented approach to reducing review effort, through iteratively re-ranking the relevance rankings based on user feedback. We propose and experiment with various relevance feedback strategies. Best results are obtained by using a BERT-based dense-vector search for relevance rankings, and basing relevance feedback on cumulatively summing the queried and selected embeddings. Our results show that this method can reduce review effort between 17.85% and 59.04%, compared to a baseline approach of no feedback, given a fixed recall target.

Keywords: high recall information retrieval · dense-vector search · relevance feedback · neural information retrieval

1 Introduction

In a diverse range of information retrieval applications, reaching certain minimal recall goals is key, when identifying which documents in a large corpus are relevant to an information need. This is particularly important in contexts such as intelligence and law enforcement, searching for adverse effects of medicines, patent due diligence, or legal search applications. In these scenarios, preventing false negatives often takes precedence over preventing false positives [23].

Manually reviewing all documents is cost intensive and error-prone [17]. Therefore, technology is often used to reduce review effort. However, technolo-

F. A. Oliehoek et al. (Eds.): BNAIC/Benelearn 2023, CCIS 2187, pp. 22–39, 2025.
https://doi.org/10.1007/978-3-031-74650-5_2

gies aimed at reducing review effort, such as 'technology assisted review' can create false negatives, since they often rely on active learning systems that exclude documents automatically based on user feedback [10].

Therefore, in this research we propose a more recall-oriented approach to reducing review effort while cumulatively identifying relevant documents. For this, we combine two major components: textual similarity and relevance feedback. Textual similarity is used to produce relevance rankings, while relevance feedback iteratively refines these relevance rankings based on user feedback. Hence, our first research question are: 'what text similarity methods are most suitable for relevance feedback?', and building upon this: 'to what extent can relevance feedback contribute to reducing review effort?'

For textual similarity, we evaluate TF-IDF and BERT-based dense-vector representations. For relevance feedback, we compare text-based and vector-based feedback strategies. Additionally, we experiment with varying levels of textual granularity in both components. In the text similarity component this is done through paragraph-based document rankings and in the relevance feedback component this is done through feedback amplification.

This combination of representation methods, feedback strategies and levels of granularity has elements that contribute to scientific novelty, and leads to substantial improvements in results. In fact, given a recall target of 80%, our proposed method reduces review effort between 17.85% and 59.04% compared to our baseline approach of no relevance feedback.

The remainder of this paper is structured as follows. Section 2 discusses the background. Next, we describe our methodology (Sect. 3) and experimental setup (Sect. 4). In Sect. 5 we share the results of our experiments, and the paper ends with a discussion section (Sect. 6) and conclusion (Sect. 7).

2 Background

In this section we discuss work related to the two main components of our method: text similarity methods and relevance feedback strategies. For the text similarity methods we discuss term-based and context-based approaches. Next, for the relevance feedback strategies, we review text-based and vector-based strategies.

2.1 Term-Based Similarity Methods

Term-based similarity methods compute text similarity through taking the common features between two pieces of text into account [6]. As a result, these methods do not incorporate contextual language properties like homonymy or synonymy in their similarity computations.

A simple and commonly used [12] implementation of term-based similarity is Jaccard similarity [11], which computes text similarity based on how many features two texts have in common divided by the total number of features across both texts. The formula for this is given below. Here, A and B refer to the set of unique words for both documents.

$$Jaccard(A,B) = \frac{|A \cap B|}{|A \cup B|} = \frac{|A \cap B|}{|A| + |B|} \tag{1}$$

However, a shortcoming of Jaccard similarity is that frequent terms (that are more likely to match) within a document are unlikely to be distinctive or important [5]. To deal with this shortcoming, there are two approaches. The first approach is based on manually filtering out frequent words based on a predefined list of words that are known to be common in a given language. These words are often referred to as 'stop words'. Removing stop words when searching for textually similar documents generally has a beneficial effect [5], though this is task dependent [25]. Hence, we filter out stop words in our experiment.

The second approach is based on reducing the influence of words that are common in a corpus [5]. An advantage of this method compared to filtering stop words is that it is more dynamic. Certain words that are common within a specific context (e.g., the word 'patient' in medical data) might not be included in predefined lists of stop words. This approach is implemented in our TF-IDF-based similarity method through *inverse document frequency*. Terms are given a measure of uniqueness by dividing the number of documents in total by the number of documents that have a specific term. The formula for this metric is given below. Here, D refers to the number of documents in the dataset whereas d refers to the number of documents that contain term t. As a result, terms that appear in many documents (and are therefore less unique) are given a diminished value [22].

$$idf(t,D) = log\frac{|D|}{1 + |\{d \in D : t \in d\}|} \tag{2}$$

2.2 Context-Based Similarity Methods

In this research we also use context-based similarity methods. In contrast to the term-based similarity methods mentioned previously, these methods do incorporate a form of semantics. This is based on the 'distributional hypothesis' [9], which is built on the idea that 'words that occur in the same contexts tend to have similar meanings' [6]. Given this hypothesis, this research uses pre-trained word embeddings that provide vector-based representations of texts. This enables us to compute the textual similarity based on the similarity between the vectors (e.g., with cosine similarity) [6].

In this category of pre-trained word embeddings, we specifically focus on BERT [8, 26]. The transformer-based architecture of BERT allows it to capture context-sensitive word properties (like homonymy and synonymy) in its embeddings. There are versions of BERT made for specific tasks. For example, Sentence-BERT (SBERT) is a BERT model specifically made for measuring text similarity using cosine distance [19]. The key advantage of SBERT over other BERT models for text similarity tasks is its reduction in computational overhead. The researchers found that for finding the most similar pairs in a collection of 10.000 sentences, BERT would take ≈65 h whereas SBERT would take 5 s. Moreover, it enables a similarity search between larger bodies of text (like sentences and paragraphs) through mean-pooling the word embeddings.

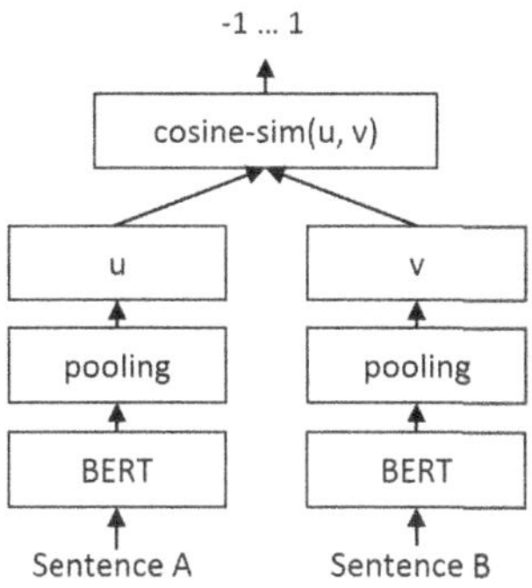

Fig. 1. Simplified architecture of SBERT [19].

A simplified overview of this architecture can be found in Fig. 1. Here, the (word-level) BERT embeddings are first mean-pooled to create paragraph or sentence level embeddings. Thereafter, these embeddings are compared through their cosine similarity. Note, for the mean-pooling process, text that exceeds 384 words in length is truncated [19]. As a result, this approach cannot be implemented on a level of text granularity that exceeds this amount.

2.3 Text-Based Feedback Strategies

Relevance feedback refers to changing the relevance ranking through user feedback, generally in multiple iterations [16]. A commonly used text-based relevance feedback strategy is 'keyword expansion'. Here, keywords from the selected search results are appended to the query. A frequently used implementation of this approach is based on the *inverse document frequency* mentioned earlier in this section. Here, the underlying assumption is that more unique words are more valuable to the search. In this research we will use this strategy for selecting keywords to expand our queries with.

2.4 Vector-Based Feedback Strategies

Assuming vector representations of the query and search results are available, user feedback can also be applied to the queried vector directly. This is referred to as vector-based pseudo-relevance feedback. There are two commonly used methods for this [13]. First, the queried vector can be averaged with the positive search results. Second, the queried vector can be summed with the selected search results. Both strategies are implemented in our research.

A commonly used variation of averaging query vectors is based on Rocchio's method for relevance feedback [13]. The high-level idea of this method is to move the query vector towards the selected vectors through assigning different weights to selected and queried vectors [20]. The version of Rocchio's method implemented by most researchers today [3,4] differs slightly from the original method, since it omits the negative feedback (i.e. non-selected documents) from the formula. As a result, this version of Rocchio can be seen as a weighted average between the (original) queried embedding and the (averaged) selected embeddings.

The weight of the queried embedding (α) and the weight of the averaged selected embeddings (β) can be set by a user. Still, the default/consensus values most research adheres to is $\alpha = 0.5$ and $\beta = 0.5$ [3]. Hence, we use Rocchio with those parameter values as a baseline method in our experiment.

3 Methodology

In this research we evaluate different relevance feedback strategies and text similarity methods with the objective of reducing review effort. As shown in Fig. 2, the method for accomplishing this is based on iteratively presenting the user with a set of (10) results to accept or decline. Thereafter, the accepted documents are used to improve the query (and consequently results) for the next iteration.

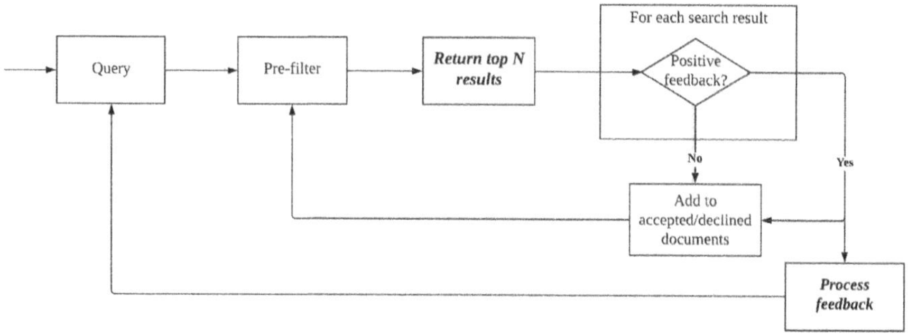

Fig. 2. Flowchart of the method.

For returning the results (i.e. relevance ranking) we experiment with different text similarity methods, levels of textual granularity, and ranking methods. These methods are explained in the first and second subsections. Next, for processing the feedback given after each iteration, we experiment with different feedback strategies. These are explained in the third and fourth subsections.

3.1 TF-IDF-Based Text Similarity

Our baseline method is based on TF-IDF, which vectorizes text based on multiplying the frequency of a word in a document with the *inverse* frequency of that word in the entire data set. Hence, TF-IDF looks at the 'uniqueness' of a word instead of just the frequency. The result of TF-IDF is a sparse vector where all the words that exist in a document are given their TF-IDF value (words that do not appear in a specific document have zero values).

In our research we use TF-IDF to find similar documents using 'More-LikeThis' (MLT). In summary, MLT queries the terms from a document (that have the highest TF-IDF values) individually using the document index. The documents returned by these queries are ranked based on combining their MLT scores, which is defined as the sum of the TF-IDF values of the matching terms between the queried document and the returned document.

Note, we are aware that a commonly used implementation of TF-IDF to identify textually similar texts is based on computing the cosine distance between the TF-IDF vectors. However, computing the cosine distance between n vectors results in quadratic time and space complexity ($O(n^2)$). Hence, we use MLT instead.

3.2 BERT-Based Text Similarity

Our semantic similarity method is based on Sentence-BERT (SBERT) embeddings. These embeddings can be used to find similar texts using 'dense-vector search' (DVS). The distance metric used for this is cosine similarity, which computes the similarity between two vectors (i.e. embeddings) based on the cosine value of the angle between the two vectors [18]. This angle is computed through dividing the dot-product (which is the sum of products from both vectors) by the length of the vectors. This means that the potential values of this similarity measure range from -1 (completely opposite) to 1 (completely similar). The formula for this is given below:

$$cosine\ similarity = \cos(\theta) = \frac{\mathbf{A}\mathbf{B}}{\|\mathbf{A}\|\|\mathbf{B}\|} = \frac{\sum_{i=1}^{n} \mathbf{A}_i \mathbf{B}_i}{\sqrt{\sum_{i=1}^{n} (\mathbf{A}_i)^2} \sqrt{\sum_{i=1}^{n} (\mathbf{B}_i)^2}} \quad (3)$$

In order to find embeddings with a high cosine similarity in a large dataset efficiently we use Hierarchical Navigable Small Worlds (HNSW) based vector search [15]. HNSW is an algorithm that finds the k most similar documents to a query with logarithmic time and space complexity (O(log(N))).

3.3 Paragraph-Based Document Rankings

Because relevant information can be exclusive to a specific part of a document [1], we conduct experiments on two levels of text granularity: the document and paragraph levels. Here, the paragraph level means that we query and retrieve paragraphs instead of documents. However, for the relevance ranking we only consider documents. As a result, the experiments on the paragraph level require a document ranking to be derived from the returned paragraphs. For this, we define two different paragraph-based document rankings.

The first ranking method is based on taking the highest ranked paragraph of a document in the ranking as the overall document ranking. For example, say we return 6 paragraphs from 3 unique documents in the following order: $\{d_1, d_2, d_2, d_3, d_3, d_3\}$ where d_i refers to a paragraph from document i. Then, our document ranking will be as follows: $\{1, 2, 3\}$. Note how the ranking from the first paragraph of a document determines its position in the document ranking.

The second ranking method is based on counting the number of paragraphs per document in the ranking, and using that to rank the documents. For example, say we return the same 6 paragraphs in the following order: $\{d_1, d_2, d_2, d_3, d_3, d_3\}$ where d_i refers to a paragraph from document i. Then, our document ranking will be as follows: $\{3, 2, 1\}$. Note how in contrast to the previous ranking method, the number of paragraphs per document determines the ranking.

3.4 Baseline Feedback Strategies

We use three methods for the relevance feedback experiments. The first baseline method is to re-use the original queried embedding. If a user accepts/declines documents, the ranking of documents remains constant. This is referred to as 'no feedback'. The second baseline method is based on keyword expansion. In keyword expansion, each iteration a number of keywords from the documents with *positive* pseudo-relevance feedback is selected and appended to the original query using an OR operator. As a result, the selected keywords serve as a pre-filter for the original query where the documents should contain at least 1 of the collected keywords to be considered. In our research, this selection is done based on the (highest) *inverse document frequency* value.

3.5 Vector-Based Feedback Strategies

Since the queried and collected texts are represented by vectors (BERT or TF-IDF), the relevance feedback methods are based on vector operations. These vector operations are based on summing and averaging the vectors. For this, we experiment with both cumulative (i.e. include the queried vector in the average/sum) and non-cumulative feedback (i.e. exclude the queried vector in the average/sum).

Also, for text similarity methods implemented on the paragraph level, relevance feedback can be amplified to the document level. If a given paragraph receives positive relevance feedback, then that feedback can be extended to other paragraphs that have the same parent document. In our research this will be referred to as 'amplified feedback' (or 'amp' in tabular formats). Note, feedback amplification is not applicable to any of our baseline methods.

4 Experimental Setup

This section provides an overview of the experiments and our data (and preprocessing). The first experiment focuses on comparing the performances of different text similarity methods. The second experiment focuses on implementing the best performing similarity method using different relevance feedback strategies.

4.1 Data and Preprocessing

Our research uses the RCV-1 v2 dataset in all experiments [2]. This dataset was made public in 2005 by Reuters News and consists of 806784 news articles. Due to hardware constraints, we did not use the complete dataset in our experiment. Instead, we randomly sampled 300 articles per topic. For this, we sampled 15 (unrelated) topics that are equally split in train, validation, and test. We call this data set the 'default set'. Moreover, besides these topics we also sampled 4 topics that share the same parent topics. This set will be referred to as the 'ambiguous' set.

As for preprocessing, in TF-IDF we filter out stop words, numbers, and convert the text to lowercase. The stop word list used for this is publicly available on GitHub[1]. For the SBERT-based experiments, we only remove numbers and special characters.

Finally, for the experiments on the paragraph level, we first split the text into sentences using the `<p>...</p>` tags in the XML files from RCV-1 v2 dataset [2]. Next, a paragraph is created through concatenating every 3 adjacent sentences of a document (and the remainder). For SBERT the number of words in a paragraph cannot exceed 384. Hence, we verified that the paragraphs in the topic sets do not exceed that limit.

4.2 Text Similarity Methods

For the text similarity methods, we compare two approaches: MLT (which is based on TF-IDF) and DVS (which is based on SBERT). For both methods, we iterate through our set using 'query by document' (QBD). Each time we query a document/paragraph to return other documents/paragraphs that belong to the same topic.

For MLT, we set two parameters. First, the minimum document frequency for words to be considered (minDf). Second, the maximum document frequency for words to be considered (maxDf). Due to limited computing resources, we didn't conduct a full grid search to find the optimal values for these parameters. Instead, we conducted a manual search on the train and validation sets and used the average of the most performant parameter values on our default (and ambiguous) test set. Note, we conduct these experiments on the paragraph *and* document level.

For DVS, we do not have parameters to set. Hence these experiments are conducted directly on our default and ambiguous set. However, we do experiment with three different pre-trained SBERT models. These are selected based on being the general-purpose models in the SBERT documentation [19]. An overview of these models can be found in Table 1. Note, due to SBERT's maximum context length, we conduct these experiments on the paragraph level only.

Finally, we evaluate the similarity methods based on (the macro averaged) recall, precision and F1 scores. For these metrics, the definition of a 'true positive'

[1] https://github.com/stopwords-iso/stopwords-en.

Table 1. Selected BERT models' characteristics according to [19].

Model name	Size	#Dimensions	Speed (sentences/sec)
all-mpnet-base-v2	420 MB	768	2800
all-MiniLM-L12-v2	120 MB	384	7500
all-MiniLM-L6-v2	80 MB	384	14200

Algorithm 1: Pseudo relevance feedback experiment

```
input : paragraph, maxRecall
output: Iterations needed to achieve recall
iterations = 0
while recall(acceptedDocuments) ≤ maxRecall do
    filter = acceptedDocuments + declinedDocuments
    results = query(paragraph, filter)            // Returns top 10 results.
    for result in results do
        if feedback for result is positive then
            paragraph = processFeedback(result)
            acceptedDocuments += result
        else
            declinedDocuments += result
    iterations + = 1
return iterations
```

is a returned document that is of the same set as the queried document. This positive set is based on the annotations of the dataset. For example, if we query a document annotated as 'sports', then the document returned (as similar) should also be annotated as 'sports' to be considered a true positive.

4.3 Relevance Feedback

For our relevance feedback experiments we implement a form of pseudo-relevance feedback. The pseudo-code of this experiment can be found in Algorithm 1. In summary, the algorithm iteratively collects relevant documents until a predefined recall threshold is reached. For each iteration, the 10 most relevant documents are collected based on our selected text similarity method. Next, the relevant documents in this set are used to improve the query for the next iteration using relevance feedback.

Note, documents are considered relevant based on the same definition of a true positive as mentioned earlier. As a result, this experiment is based on pseudo-relevance feedback. Finally, for performance evaluation, we record the average number of iterations needed to achieve exactly 80% recall (which is a commonly used threshold in information retrieval [21]).

4.4 Configuration

The experiments are conducted on a local device. The CPU of this device is an Intel(R) Core(TM) i7-10610U CPU @ 1.80 GHz and it has 16 GB of RAM memory. As for software, the TF-IDF and DVS based text similarity experiments including MLT were conducted using Solr[2], which is built on top of Lucene[3]. Finally, the source code used in this experiment is publicly available on GitHub[4].

5 Results

This section provides an overview of the results from our experiments. In the first subsection, we discuss the results of the individual text similarity methods. In the second subsection, we present the results of the different relevance feedback strategies.

5.1 Text Similarity Methods

For our TF-IDF-based approach, the manual search on the train and validation sets resulted in the parameter values of maxDf = 0.8 and minDf = 0 on both the paragraph and document level. Hence, the TF-IDF related results are based on these parameter values. Next, for the DVS experiments, *all-mpnet-base v2* was the best performing pre-trained SBERT model. Hence, the results of this model are shown in this section.

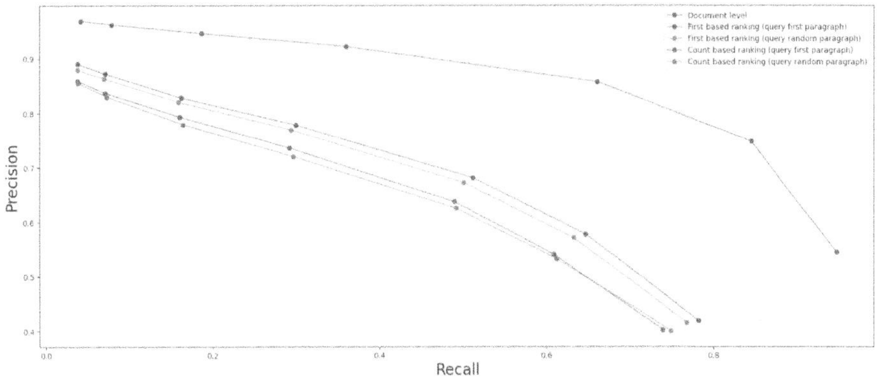

Fig. 3. Different configurations for the TF-IDF-based approach on the default set.

2 https://solr.apache.org/.
3 http://lucene.apache.org/java/340/scoring.html.
4 https://github.com/TimoKats/MasterThesis.

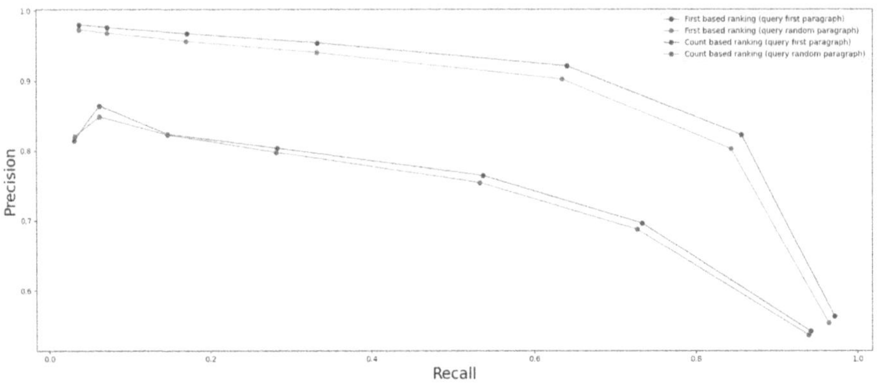

Fig. 4. Different configurations for DVS on the default set.

For our default test set, the recall-precision graphs are shown in Fig. 3 and Fig. 4. In both figures, it is apparent that deriving a document ranking from its *highest* ranked paragraph outperforms ranking documents based on *counting* the paragraphs. Moreover, for both methods querying the first paragraph of a document slightly outperforms querying random paragraphs. Next, for the TF-IDF-based method specifically, the experiments on the document level outperform the experiments on the paragraph level.

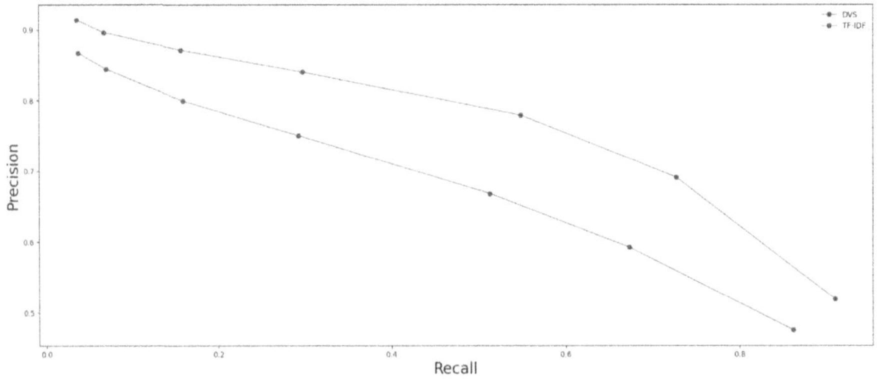

Fig. 5. Identified configurations of DVS and TF-IDF-based approach on the ambiguous set.

Finally, when comparing the performance of the optimal configuration of both approaches, DVS (with a first-based ranking) outperforms all TF-IDF-based approaches. Next, when comparing the optimal configurations of the approaches on the *ambiguous* set, we again see that DVS outperforms the TF-IDF-based approach (see Fig. 5).

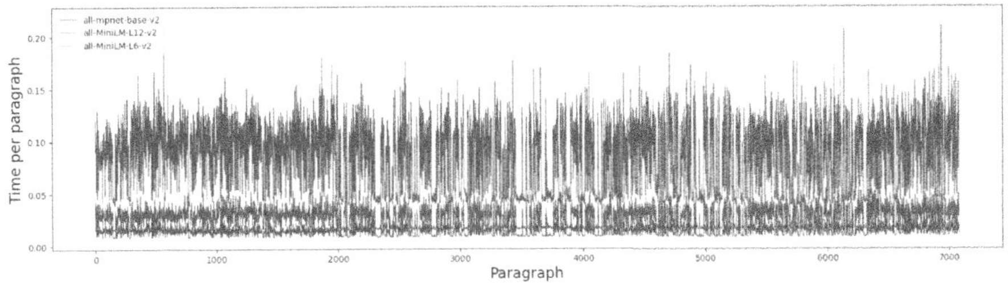

Fig. 6. Time consumed to create SBERT embeddings per paragraph.

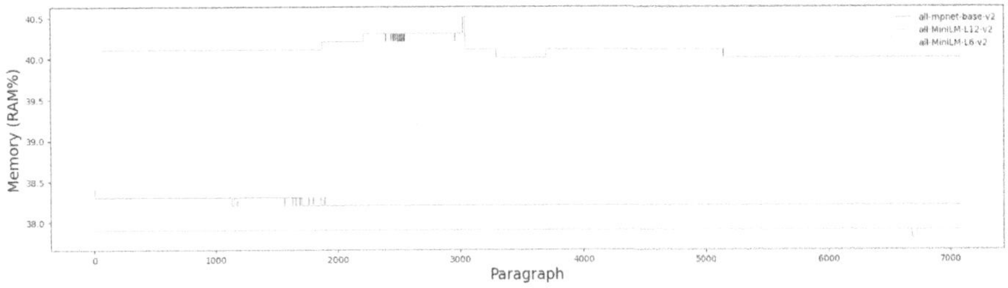

Fig. 7. RAM% consumed to create SBERT embeddings per paragraph.

For all pre-trained SBERT models used in our experiments, RAM usage and computation time per embedding are shown in Fig. 6 and 7. In these figures, the x-axis refers to the individual paragraphs (i.e. each x-tick is a paragraph) and the y-axis refers to the time taken/memory consumed to create an embedding for that paragraph. Here, despite the large variance of results shown in Fig. 6, both these figures confirm the pattern described in the documentation from SBERT (shown in Table 1), which is that the larger models are more time and memory consumptive. Hence, the results of *all-mpnet-base v2* shown in this section do have extra computational costs.

5.2 Relevance Feedback

For the second set of experiments, we experimented with different feedback strategies using the identified text similarity method (DVS). For these experiments, the average number of iterations (and standard deviation) needed to achieve 80% recall for all methods and datasets is shown in Table 2. Note, every iteration translates to a review effort of 10 paragraphs. Similar to the previous experiments, the results are available on the default and ambiguous set.

First, the results on the default test set. Here, it is apparent that the feedback methods based on vector operations require fewer iterations and have a lower standard deviation than the baseline methods. The best performing feedback method is summing the vectors. Next, the results on the ambiguous set. Here, all similarity methods require more iterations to reach 80% recall and have a

Table 2. Iterations needed to achieve 80% recall (baselines are in the top cells, cumulative approaches are in the middle cells, non-cumulative approaches are in the bottom cells).

Feedback strategy	Mean (Default)	Std Dev (Default)	Mean (Ambiguous)	Std Dev (Ambiguous)
No feedback	33.36	8.84	46.77	10.04
Keyword expansion	32.24	8.03	44.23	9.94
Rocchio ($\alpha = 0.5$, $\beta = 0.5$)	29.50	3.79	37.98	5.11
Average	29.43	1.51	32.65	2.97
Average (amp)	30.17	1.03	32.99	1.80
Sum	***28.29***	0.75	***29.41***	2.13
Sum (amp)	28.46	***0.50***	30.54	***1.31***
Average	31.54	1.14	38.68	4.41
Average (amp)	32.81	1.08	38.41	2.64
Sum	32.80	1.12	38.80	5.28
Sum (amp)	32.20	0.87	38.20	3.77

higher standard deviation than they have on the default set. Still, feedback methods based on summing the vectors (cumulatively) gives the best results.

It is apparent that cumulative feedback methods outperform non-cumulative feedback methods for all vector-based relevance strategies. Moreover, the difference between averaging and summing vectors is smaller when using non-cumulative strategies.

A noteworthy finding when comparing the results from the default and ambiguous set is the gap between the minimal baseline method (of no feedback) and the optimal feedback method (of cumulatively summing the vectors). On the default set, the reduction of review effort (measured in the number of iterations to achieve 80% recall) is 17.85%. On the ambiguous set however, this reduction of review effort equals 59.04%. Another noteworthy finding is that amplifying the feedback to sibling paragraphs reduces the standard deviation, but not the number of iterations needed to achieve 80% recall.

Finally, for all methods we measured average time taken per iteration. The results for this are shown in Table 3. These results show that relevance feedback strategies based on vector operations (average and sum) add little latency to the experiment compared to no feedback. Still, amplifying feedback to sibling paragraphs does add some latency to the experiment for both averaging and summing vectors. However, keyword expansion adds the most latency to the experiments.

6 Discussion

This section is a discussion of the results. First, we interpret the results for our two main experiments. Second, we discuss the limitations of our research and the resulting suggestions for future work.

Table 3. Average execution times for different relevant feedback strategies.

Strategy	Average time per iteration (in seconds)
No feedback	0.02298
Average	0.02386
Sum	0.02417
Rocchio	0.02901
Sum (amp)	0.04982
Average (amp)	0.05097
Keyword expansion	0.12093

6.1 Text Similarity Methods

For all of text similarity methods, some common denominators emerge from the results. First, querying the first paragraph gives better results than querying a random paragraph. This coincides with findings from related work, since prior research found that the effectiveness of 'query by document' approaches depends on the prevalence of relevant terms in the queried text [27]. Combining this finding with our results, it is probable that the first paragraphs in the RCV-1 v2 dataset outperform random paragraphs because they have a higher prevalence of relevant terms. This property could be exclusive to the news articles used in our research, and therefore might not apply to the data used in other domains.

Another commonality between the methods is related to the paragraph-based document rankings. Here, we see that for all methods ranking documents based on the first paragraph in the ranking gives better results than querying documents based on counting their paragraphs in the ranking. Potentially, this could be related to differences in the number of paragraphs per document. If a document only has one paragraph, then it is always bound to be at the bottom of a count-based ranking, regardless of how related/similar that document is.

As for comparing the different text similarity methods, both sets of experiments show that DVS outperforms the TF-IDF-based approach. Considering our DVS approach is based on BERT instead of TF-IDF, this finding makes sense. Because, BERT's bidirectional self-attention mechanism [8] enables it to understand more ambiguous and context-sensitive language properties. For example, the usage of synonymy, homonymy and referrals.

However, it must also be noted that our findings are based on a pre-trained SBERT model (*all-mpnet-base v2*) that had higher computational costs with regards to RAM usage (see Fig. 7) and computation time (see Fig. 6) than the other pre-trained models in our experiment.

6.2 Relevance Feedback

For the second experiment, the best performing text similarity method (DVS, with a first-based document ranking) was implemented for relevance feedback.

For both the default and the ambiguous set, the experiments show that relevance feedback methods based on cumulatively summing the vectors reduce review effort the most. Interestingly, this improvement does not seem to come at a computational cost. Since Table 3 shows that the execution time of these methods (without feedback amplification to sibling paragraphs) is fairly similar to our minimal baseline method (of no feedback). Note, when optimizing for a low standard deviation, amplifying feedback to sibling paragraphs is beneficial, which does add latency to the experiment.

6.3 Reflection on Implementation and Contributions

With regards to implementation, our results show that review effort can be decreased using text similarity-based relevance feedback methods. An important side note in this finding is that relevance feedback accomplishes this through only re-ranking documents. As a result, this strategy does not produce false negatives automatically without the awareness of the user (in contrast to an active learning based approach). This is particularly important in use-cases that require a high recall.

In terms of scientific novelty and contributions, we should state that the concept of relevance feedback has been studied before [28]. However, certain parts within our implementation are (to our knowledge) novel and therefore contribute to science. First, the evaluation of different paragraph-based document rankings contribute to the domain of paragraph-based document-to-document retrieval. Given the rise of large language models (that are generally limited to the paragraph level [14]) and the fact that relevant information can be exclusive to a specific part of a document [1], these findings are applicable beyond the technologies/embeddings used in this research. Second, our results show that the usage of sibling paragraphs in relevance feedback can reduce the standard deviation of review effort. To our knowledge, this technique and finding is novel. Moreover, a more 'stable' reduction of review effort could be favorable in real-world scenarios.

Hence, our findings are not just novel, but also applicable and practically implementable.

6.4 Limitations

First, data in real-world information retrieval scenarios tends to be heterogeneous (e.g. emails, documents, direct messages, etc.) [24]. But, the data used in this research is fairly homogeneous, since it only consists of news articles. Hence, there's a slight mismatch between the type of data used in this experiment and the real-world data this technique could be applied to. Thus, the lack of data heterogeneity in this experiment is a limitation of this research.

Second, the size of the dataset (only 300 articles per topic) is smaller than most real-world information retrieval scenarios. Moreover, our data only consists of news articles. Therefore, certain findings in our research (e.g., the fact that querying the first paragraph slightly outperforms querying random paragraphs) might not apply on other datasets. Still, given the fact that the RCV-1 v2 dataset is commonly used as a benchmark dataset in information retrieval [7], the results are still an adequate indication of our method's performance.

6.5 Future Work

Our first suggestion for future work is related to the size of our dataset. As mentioned, due to computational constraints we only sampled 300 articles per topic. However, datasets in real-world information retrieval applications can be much larger than that. As a result, future work could run these methods on larger datasets to research their scalability.

Our second suggestion for future work is related to the level of data heterogeneity in the experiments. As mentioned in the previous subsection, data used in real-world information retrieval scenarios tend to be heterogeneous whereas the data used in this experiment is fairly homogeneous. As a result, future work could research to what extent heterogeneous data impacts the ability of different text similarity methods to return similar documents.

Next, this research uses Solr's 'MoreLikeThis' functionality to increase the speed of our TF-IDF-based similarity experiments. Meaning, we didn't use any vector space scoring to compute the similarities between the TF-IDF vectors. The reasoning behind this is that computing the (cosine) similarities between n TF-IDF vectors results in quadratic ($\mathrm{O}(\mathrm{n}^2)$) time and space complexity, which is simply not viable in a real-world application. However, recent innovations have made it possible to compute the pairwise similarities between (sparse) vectors much faster. An example of this is the ChunkDot Python library[5], which splits the TF-IDF matrix into chunks and computes the similarities in parallel. Future work could use this innovation to experiment with TF-IDF-based cosine similarity as an additional text similarity method.

Finally, it will be interesting to further experiment with our relevance feedback strategies in combination with using large language models for the embeddings, or potentially also for pseudo or proxy feedback, both in the context of discovery and information retrieval tasks, as well as other tasks such as retrieval augmented generation.

7 Conclusion

This research evaluates the impact of changing the (text similarity-based) relevance rankings based on relevance feedback. For this, the first research question was formulated as follows: what text similarity methods are most suitable for relevance feedback? Our results show that the most suitable text similarity method for this is DVS (using BERT-based dense-vector representations) where the highest ranked paragraph determines the document ranking.

Next, the second research question was formulated as follows: to what extent can relevance feedback help to reduce review effort? We have outlined a variety

[5] https://pypi.org/project/chunkdot/.

of relevance feedback strategies. Our results show that (compared to processing no relevance feedback) our best-scoring the relevance feedback strategy reduces review effort between 17.85% and 59.04%, given a target recall level of 80%.

Given the recall-oriented nature of many information retrieval applications [23], the results for the relevance feedback experiments are encouraging. Since, in contrast to an active learning based strategy (which typically used for this purpose), this approach reduces review effort through only re-ranking documents. As a result, there are no false negatives created without the awareness of the user.

References

1. Adebayo, K.J.: Multimodal legal information retrieval. Ph.D. thesis, University of Luxembourg, Luxembourg (2018)
2. Amini, M.-R., Goutte, C.: Reuters RCV1 RCV2 multilingual, multiview text categorization test collection. UCI Machine Learning Repository (2013)
3. Arampatzis, A., Peikos, G., Symeonidis, S.: Pseudo relevance feedback optimization. Inf. Retrieval J. 269–297 (2021)
4. Cai, T., et al.: Scalable relevance ranking algorithm via semantic similarity assessment improves efficiency of medical chart review. J. Biomed. Inform. 104109 (2022)
5. Chai, C.P.: Comparison of text preprocessing methods. Nat. Lang. Eng. 509–553 (2023)
6. Chandrasekaran, D., Mago, V.: Evolution of semantic similarity—a survey. ACM Comput. Surv. 1–37 (2022)
7. Deolalikar, V.: How valuable is your data? A quantitative approach using data mining. In: 2015 IEEE International Conference on Big Data (Big Data), pp. 1248–1253. IEEE (2015)
8. Devlin, J., Chang, M.W., Lee, K., Toutanova, K.: BERT: pre-training of deep bidirectional transformers for language understanding. In: Burstein, J., Doran, C., Solorio, T. (eds.) Proceedings of the 2019 Conference of the North American Chapter of the Association for Computational Linguistics: Human Language Technologies, vol. 1, pp. 4171–4186. Association for Computational Linguistics, Minneapolis (2019)
9. Gorman, J., Curran, J.R.: Scaling distributional similarity to large corpora. In: Proceedings of the 21st International Conference on Computational Linguistics and 44th Annual Meeting of the Association for Computational Linguistics, pp. 361–368 (2006)
10. Grossman, M.R., Cormack, G.: Continuous active learning for TAR. Journal 1–7 (2016)
11. Jaccard, P.: Nouvelles recherches sur la distribution florale. Bull. Soc. Vaud. Sci. Nat. 223–270 (1908)
12. Joshi, S., Contractor, D., Ng, K., Deshpande, P.M., Hampp, T.: Auto-grouping emails for faster e-discovery. Proc. VLDB Endow. 1284–1294 (2020)
13. Li, H., Mourad, A., Zhuang, S., Koopman, B., Zuccon, G.: Pseudo relevance feedback with deep language models and dense retrievers: successes and pitfalls. ACM Trans. Inf. Syst. 1–40 (2023)
14. Liu, Y., et al.: Summary of ChatGPT-related research and perspective towards the future of large language models. Meta-Radiol. **1**(2), 100017 (2023)

15. Malkov, Y.A., Yashunin, D.A.: Efficient and robust approximate nearest neighbor search using hierarchical navigable small world graphs, pp. 824–836. IEEE Computer Society (2020)
16. Manning, C.D.: Introduction to Information Retrieval. Syngress Publishing (2008)
17. Piramuthu, O.B.: Multiple choice online algorithms for technology-assisted reviews. In: Proceedings of the 38th ACM/SIGAPP Symposium on Applied Computing, pp. 639–645 (2023)
18. Rahutomo, F., Kitasuka, T., Aritsugi, M.: Semantic cosine similarity. In: The 7th International Student Conference on Advanced Science and Technology ICAST, p. 1 (2012)
19. Reimers, N., Gurevych, I.: Sentence-BERT: sentence embeddings using Siamese BERT-networks. In: Inui, K., Jiang, J., Ng, V., Wan, X. (eds.) Proceedings of the 2019 Conference on Empirical Methods in Natural Language Processing and the 9th International Joint Conference on Natural Language Processing (EMNLP-IJCNLP), pp. 3982–3992. Association for Computational Linguistics, Hong Kong (2019)
20. Rocchio, J.J.: Document retrieval system-optimization and evaluation. In: DIR 2009 Dutch-Belgian Information Retrieval Workshop, p. 99 (2009)
21. Roitblat, H.L.: Probably reasonable search in ediscovery (2022). arXiv:2201.12376
22. Sánchez, D., Batet, M.: A semantic similarity method based on information content exploiting multiple ontologies. Expert Syst. Appl. 1393–1399 (2013)
23. Song, J.J., Lee, W., Afshar, J.: An effective high recall retrieval method. Data Knowl. Eng. **123**, 101603 (2019)
24. Sperling, M., Jin, R., Rayvych, I., Li, J., Yi, J.: Similar document detection and electronic discovery: so many documents, so little time. In: ICAIL 2013 Workshop on Standards for Using Predictive Coding, Machine Learning, and Other Advanced Search and Review Methods in E-Discovery (DESI V Workshop), Rome, Italy (2013)
25. Teernstra, L., van der Putten, P., Noordegraaf-Eelens, L., Verbeek, F.: The morality machine: tracking moral values in tweets. In: Boström, H., Knobbe, A., Soares, C., Papapetrou, P. (eds.) IDA 2016. LNCS, vol. 9897, pp. 26–37. Springer, Cham (2016). https://doi.org/10.1007/978-3-319-46349-0_3
26. Vaswani, A., et al.: Attention is all you need. In: Advances in Neural Information Processing Systems (2017)
27. Yang, E., Lewis, D.D., Frieder, O., Grossman, D.A., Yurchak, R.: Retrieval and richness when querying by document. In: Biennial Conference on Design of Experimental Search & Information Retrieval Systems, pp. 68–75 (2018)
28. Zhang, H., Cormack, G.V., Grossman, M.R., Smucker, M.D.: Evaluating sentence-level relevance feedback for high-recall information retrieval. Inf. Retrieval J. 1–26 (2020)

Defining and Evaluating the Degrees of Abstraction in Explanations with Kolmogorov Complexity

Jan Lemeire[1,2] and Stefan Buijsman[3(✉)]

[1] Department of Industrial Sciences (INDI), Vrije Universiteit Brussel (VUB), Pleinlaan 2, 1050 Brussels, Belgium
jan.lemeire@vub.be
[2] Department of Electronics and Informatics (ETRO), Vrije Universiteit Brussel (VUB), Pleinlaan 2, 1050 Brussels, Belgium
[3] Section of Ethics and Philosophy of Technology, TU Delft, Jaffalaan 5, 2628 BX Delft, The Netherlands
s.n.r.buijsman@tudelft.nl

Abstract. What variables should be used to get explanations (of AI systems) that are easily interpretable? The challenge to find the right degree of abstraction in explanations, also called the 'variables problem', has been actively discussed in the philosophy of science. The challenge is striking the right balance between specificity and generality. Concepts such as proportionality and exhaustivity are investigated and discussed. We propose a new and formal definition based on Kolmogorov complexity and argue that this corresponds to our intuitions about the right level of abstraction. First, we require that variables are uniform, so that they cannot be decomposed into less abstract variables without increasing the Kolmogorov complexity. Next, uniform variables are optimal for an explanation if they can compose the explanation without increasing its Kolmogorov complexity. For this, the concepts K-decomposability and K-composability of sets are defined. Explanations of a certain instance should encompass a maximal set of instances without being K-decomposable. Although Kolmogorov complexity is uncomputable and depends on the choice of programming language, we show that it can be used effectively to evaluate and reason about explanations, such as in the evaluation of XAI methods.

Keywords: Explainability · Explainable AI · Kolmogorov complexity · Abstraction

1 Introduction

How do we best explain a particular outcome of a binary function in terms of the properties of the input? One of the challenges in answering this question is finding the right variables to use in these explanations. Intuitively, we prefer an

F. A. Oliehoek et al. (Eds.): BNAIC/Benelearn 2023, CCIS 2187, pp. 40–53, 2025.
https://doi.org/10.1007/978-3-031-74650-5_3

Fig. 1. Images of coffee that are correctly identified by a trained Convolutional Neural Network.

explanation that is *not too specific, nor too abstract.* Consider a Convolutional Neural Network (CNN) that is trained to recognize coffee in images and assume the network successfully recognizes coffee in all the images shown in Fig. 1. An explanation for the identification of coffee in image (a) is the dark brown color and the foam. But if image (b) also leads to a positive identification, the property 'dark brown' is too specific; 'brown' is sufficient and seems to better capture the behaviour of the network. Similarly, image (c) is linked to coffee by the shape of the cup and the steam, but a very specific description of the cup may lead us to believe that the system generalizes less than it does if the more abstract cup in image (d) is also classified as a coffee cup. This can be observed again in image (e) where the 'flower pattern' in the foam may not be necessary for identification if image (f) is also classified correctly. Vice versa, 'rounded shapes' may be too general a variable for the explanation, even if it matches these examples. The final image (g) illustrates this again, where one may use 'food' or 'medium-sized objects' to describe what is on the image, but these are likely too abstract compared to options such as 'croissant' and 'coffee cup'.

However, it is a challenge to specify formally what an optimal degree of abstraction is and on which concepts, called *variables* in the philosophical literature, an explanation should be based. This is a general problem for theories of explanation [5,8], but one that reasserts itself in the field of XAI [6]. Especially in the philosophy of science there has been earlier work on precisely this question, which we survey in Sect. 2. In Sect. 3 we show that current definitions for the upper bound of the level of abstraction are falling short. Our aim in this paper is to build upon this work by giving a formal definition of this degree of abstraction using descriptive complexity. We therefore first introduce Kolmogorov complexity theory in Sect. 4. In Sect. 5 we provide an alternative formal specification for optimal degrees of abstraction of variables in an explanation. We then show in Sect. 6 how this definition applies and resolves the current problems. In the final section we illustrate how this theoretical discussion applies to XAI methods for explanations.

2 Related Work

There is a wide-ranging literature on explanations of AI systems [1]. Methods showing how important different features were for the output [17,19] are one option, as are methods extracting rules (e.g. decision trees) to describe the (local) behaviour of the AI system and counterfactuals showing what should be changed to the input to achieve the desired output [14]. And while there is still disagreement about how we should define explanations, both in the computer science literature [11] and in the philosophical literature on explanation [3], the overall goal on all of these definitions is to let recipients of explanations better understand the AI system.

In all of these cases, too, explanations require the use of variables: either the input variables of the system, or a set of (often more abstract) variables that are closer to the variables humans are used to working with. Examples of XAI methods doing the latter are so-called concept-based explainability methods, such as Concept Activation Vectors [10,24] which attempt to extract (some of) the patterns that a convolutional neural network uses to arrive at the output classification. Alternative methods use crowd workers to attribute concepts to highlighted regions in images [2,4], thus abstracting from highlighted individual pixels to more abstract concepts. This makes explanations not only more interpretable, as humans are more used to reasoning with concepts such as chairs and tables than we are with sets of pixel values. It also makes explanations more general, as more abstract variables typically cover a wider set of cases.

This is important, as a common standard for the quality of an explanation is how general the explanation is [6]. In other words, "powerful explanations should, just like any predictor, generalize as much as possible" [14, p.36]. However, finding the point where an explanation has generalized *as much as possible* is difficult. The 'variables problem' [8,21] in the philosophy of explanation shows the challenge of identifying optimal degrees of abstraction for explanations. To illustrate with an example commonly used in philosophical literature, there is an intuitive sense that of the following three factually correct explanations the second is the best, being neither too specific nor too general:

(1) The pigeon pecked because it was presented with a scarlet stimulus
(2) The pigeon pecked because it was presented with a red stimulus
(3) The pigeon pecked because it was presented with something stimulating

Specifying why this is so is non-trivial, but by now two approaches can be found. Blanchard [5] suggests that we opt for the most abstract variables that are still specific when compared to even less abstract variables, where abstraction and specificity are defined as follows:

> An explanation with explanans variable(s) e_1 is more abstract than an explanation with explanans variable(s) e_2 when the actual value of e_1 is implied by the actual value of e_2, but not vice versa

An explanation with explanans variable(s) e_1 is more specific than an explanation with explanans variable(s) e_2 when e_2 is a function f of e_1 and other variables $e_3, \dots e_n$ such that ...neither e_1 nor $G(e_2) = G(f(e_1, e_3 \dots e_n))$ change value if the variables $e_3, \dots e_n$ are varied. G refers to the explanation provided by the variables.

The proposed definitions apply as follows: using *red* leads to a better explanation than using *scarlet* because it is more abstract (if $scarlet = 1$ then $red = 1$, but not vice versa) without being more specific. On the other hand, using *red* leads to a better explanation than using *something stimulating* because it is more specific (*something stimulating* can be seen as a function $f(red, food, tickle) = red \vee food \vee tickle$ where the value of f remains the same as long as $red = 1$).

Woodward [23] takes a slightly different approach to the same problem, stating that a requirement of proportionality instead motivates the choice of variable. This principle of *proportionality* states that "other things being equal, we should prefer those causal claims/explanations that more fully represent or exhibit those patterns of dependence that hold" [23, p. 247]. It then functions as follows: using *scarlet* suggests the following relation: if *scarlet* is set to 1 then $peck = 1$, if *scarlet* is set to 0 then $peck = 0$ (all other things being equal, so without the presentation of other kinds of stimuli that will make the bird peck) The latter part is false, because we can change the colour of the stimulus to other shades of red (meeting the requirements of setting *scarlet* to 0) while the bird will still peck. Hence, the explanation that if *red* is set to 1 then $peck = 1$, if *red* is set to 0 then $peck = 0$ (all other things being equal) is better because it better represents how the pecking depends on the colour; changing the colour to anything other than red will, all else being equal, entail that the bird stops pecking at it.

Our approach instead links the choice of degree of abstraction to descriptive complexity, based on the intuitive idea that we should choose variables in our explanations that minimize the complexity of these explanations (given equal accuracy). This may be linked to philosophical discussions on effective conversational communication in common social situations. Grice's four maxims of conversation [12][1] describe the rationality behind what people expect from effective communication, and stress conveying as much as possible while as relevant and brief as possible. One way to comply with these norms of communication is to minimize descriptive complexity through variable choice.

To make this idea of using the descriptive complexity of an explanation more precise we need an objective complexity measure. Although it has its limitations (discussed in Sect. 4.2) we will use Kolmogorov complexity in this paper. Alternatives are of course available, such as Minimum Description Length (MDL) [13], but Kolmogorov complexity is well-suited due to its generality as MDL is mainly used for finding the optimal model within an a priori chosen model class. That being said, our approach will also work with other approaches to

[1] https://www.sas.upenn.edu/~haroldfs/dravling/grice.html for a summary of the 4 principles.

descriptive complexity, as one can simply replace the Kolmogorov measure in our definitions with another way to formalize descriptive complexity. In order to utilize the formal precision that Kolmogorov complexity brings we now need to further formalize the problem of variable choice.

3 Formalization of the Challenge

With the context of XAI as part of the motivation for formalizing the discussion on abstraction, we will consider a binary classifier b which outputs 0 or 1 for each input $x \in X$. x is a multi-dimensional feature vector. The set of all inputs for which b outputs 1 is called the *positive subset*, which we denote with S_b. b is also called the *indicator function* for set S_b. An explanation of an instance $b(x)$ for a particular x is then based on the properties of the input that ensured the outcome. For this paper, we assume that an explanation defines a *sufficient condition* for b, in line with definitions of explanations from [22] and [6] that see them as generalizations describing a set of outputs. Zooming in on a particular instance, this points us to the idea that an explanation G for $x \in S_b$ corresponds to a description of a subset S_G of the positive subset S_b; it defines a set with elements that are all identified by the classifier. The question we address in this paper is then (1) the optimal choice of subset S_G, how large the subset S_G should be, and (2) which features to use to define the subset.

To illustrate these two points, consider a scenario where a pigeon pecks at both red and yellow stimuli inspired by the work in the philosophical literature. Here, the choice will be formalized based on what we consider to be the relevant S_G to describe this behaviour. We can opt for one explanation per colour, separating the behaviour into two possible scenario's and arriving at the explanation:

(4) The pigeon pecked because it was presented with a red stimulus OR The pigeon pecked because it was presented with a yellow stimulus

Or we could use a broader subset S_G along with a single composed variable $redow = red \vee yellow$ to generate the following explanation:

(5) The pigeon pecked because it was presented with a redow stimulus

If we compare these two explanations there seems to be a clear preference for (4), where no new abstract variable is introduced to cover the two cases in one go. However, judging by the criteria of [5] we should in fact prefer (5). The variable is more abstract ($yellow = 1$ implies $redow = 1$ and $red = 1$ implies $redow = 1$) but not more specific (*red* changes values if the value of *yellow* is changed and vice versa). We will propose a definition that makes a clear distinction between (4) and (5), and gives a preference for (4).

This definition is based on the idea that the crucial difference between (4) and (5) is the uniformity of the explanatory domain S_G, as *red* is a uniform set (informally, one can test membership directly, for the formal definition see Definition 5) whereas *redow* is not (one needs to look whether the stimulus is either red, or yellow to determine its value). To further illustrate this idea consider a second variation on the same example. Here, there is a range of different colours that a pigeon responds to. What they all have in common is that they are bright colours, such as red, orange and yellow. So, we again have two options for an explanation (assuming here that in this case we decide to opt for a domain S_G that covers all these colour shades in a single explanation). Either we use a disjunction of less abstract variables or we use the more abstract variable *bright colour*:

(6) The pigeon pecked because it was presented with a bright red or a bright orange or a bright yellow stimulus
(7) The pigeon pecked because it was presented with a bright coloured stimulus

Here, it seems that the abstract variable in (7) is preferable whereas the abstract variable *redow* in (5) is not. As both are specifiable as disjunctions of incompatible colour concepts this raises the question: what is the difference? In our view, it is that there is a separate, undecomposable way to define *bright colour*. Specifically, colours can be defined using the HSV colour space (https://en.wikipedia.org/wiki/HSL_and_HSV), where the V-component defines the brightness using a single numerical value. There is no such unifying measure for *redow*, which could be why we find this a less illuminating concept to use. This brings us back to the descriptive complexity of the explanation.

The underlying idea behind the formal definitions that we introduce below is that variables should be both general and, at the same time, undecomposable. In other words, the variable should track a single property that can be tested for in a *canonical* manner. Explanation should moreover only contain the relevant information that makes the instance positive, prompting our choice for S_G. An explanation that is too specific contains information about the properties that are not essential for the classifier. On the other hand, an explanation that is too general contains information that is not essential for the classification of the given instance. Descriptive complexity, formalized here using Kolmogorov complexity, can help to make these ideas more precise.

4 The Kolmogorov Complexity of Functions and Sets

To introduce Kolmogorov complexity, we consider first how we can describe an indicator function of a set. Most arbitrary sets (e.g. by randomly picking elements) can only be described by an enumeration of its elements because the elements have no properties in common. In most cases, however, we are interested in sets that mean something, of which the elements have properties in common on which the indicator function can be built. Then, the implementation of the indicator function will become shorter than a literal enumeration. This can be formalized by algorithmic information or 'Kolmogorov complexity', a concept put forward as an objective measure of complexity.

4.1 Definition of Kolmogorov Complexity

First we define the Kolmogorov complexity (KC) of a single object:

Definition 1. *For a binary sequence $x \in \{0,1\}^*$, the algorithmic information $K(x)$ (or 'Kolmogorov complexity') is defined as the length of the shortest program on a universal Turing machine that generates x and then stops:*

$$K(x) = \min_{p:\mathcal{U}(p)=x} l(p) \tag{1}$$

with $\mathcal{U}$ a universal computer, and $l(\cdot)$ the length in bits of a binary sequence.

The shortest program is denoted with p^*_x.

To illustrate this definition, consider the following two sequences of 1000 bits:

- 01111000011001100111 ...00001111100100011101
- 00010001000100010001 ...00010001000100010001

The first string is arbitrary without any patterns, while the second repeats "0001". $K(x)$ is maximal for the random string, namely around 1000 bits. The shortest program literally encodes the string. The second string can be described by program `REPEAT 250 TIMES"0001"+` and needs far fewer bits. The program exploits the 'regularities' (patterns) of the string to *compress* its description. It is these regularities that make up the meaningful information we are interested in. This same idea can then be applied to indicator functions:

Definition 2. *The* ***Kolmogorov complexity of a binary function*** *b that takes as argument $x \in X$ and returns 0 or 1, is defined as the length of the shortest program p^* that when executed by a universal Turing machine together with any argument $x \in X$ returns the same output as $b(x)$: $\mathcal{U}(p^*, x) = b(x)$. The shortest program is denoted as p^*_b,*

Definition 3. *The* ***Kolmogorov complexity of a set*** *$S \subseteq X$ is defined as the Kolmogorov complexity of the indicator function of S.*

4.2 Limitations and Practical Use of Kolmogorov Complexity

There are two problems to apply Kolmogorov complexity to practical problems [13]. First, Kolmogorov complexity is not computable. It is proven that there is no algorithm that given a bitstring will output the length of the shortest program and halts [7]. For a lot of cases, however, the shortest program is indisputable, as will be shown in the discussed examples. Still, for more intricate programs it is not trivial, as for example in the case of neural networks trained to detect objects – which quickly use millions of parameters. Instead of trying to identify the absolute shortest implementation (and with that the absolute best concept to use in the explanation), we will therefore use the definitions to *compare and validate implementations* in the same way as explanations are compared in philosophical literature.

Second, Kolmogorov complexity depends on the choice of programming language (or Turing machine) up to a constant. Since one programming language can be translated into another one with a program of length C, the difference of describing x in both languages, can be maximally be C, a constant which does not dependent on x. Therefore, theorems often have to incorporate this constant [15]. This can be seen in the additivity rule (which we need later) for the joint Kolmogorov complexity, which has the following formulation:

$$K(x, y) \stackrel{+}{=} K(x) + K(y|p_x^*), \tag{2}$$

where $K(y|p_x^*)$ denotes the conditional Kolmogorov complexity of y, given the shortest program p_x^* of x. As usual in algorithmic information theory, $\stackrel{+}{=}$ denotes equality up to a constant that is independent of the string x, but does depend on the chosen Turing machine. Since information is symmetric [9], see also [16, Eq. 2.1]:

$$K(x) + K(y|p_x^*) \stackrel{+}{=} K(y) + K(x|p_y^*), \tag{3}$$

we can write that:

$$K(x, y) \stackrel{+}{=} K(y, x) \stackrel{+}{=} K(y) + K(x|p_y^*). \tag{4}$$

5 Abstraction and Undecomposable Concepts

We will now formalize our proposed definitions.

5.1 Formal Definition of Uniformity

Formalizing this idea of having a unifying measure and undecomposable definition available for a concept we can appeal to Kolmogorov complexity to define when a concept meets this requirement. To make this translation we have to interpret concepts as sets, where the set has as members every element to which the concept applies. The question of whether the corresponding concept is appropriately uniform can then be approached in terms of the Kolmogorov complexity of the description of the set:

Definition 4. *A set S is K-decomposable if there exist different and non-empty subsets S_1 and S_2 such that:*

- $S = S_1 \cup S_2$, *and*
- $K(S) \stackrel{+}{=} K(S_1) + K(S_2|p_{S_1}^*)$.

The conditional in the second term of the last equation indicates that the identification of the S_1 by $p_{S_1}^*$ can be reused for describing S_2. If the description of both sets is nevertheless of equal complexity as S, it signifies that S_1 and S_2 contain no additional information that is not already required to describe S. *K-decomposability* thus refers to the possibility of decomposing a set into multiple sets keeping the descriptive complexity invariant. The description of the total set can be decomposed into a separate description of subsets. Note that this definition has the same form as the additivity rule (Eq. (2) in Sect. 4.2), which always holds for Kolmogorov complexities. In the case of K-decomposability, however, we only get additivity if the set decomposition does not bring in new information on the right side of the equation that is not present on the left side: information that is required to identify S_1 and S_2 but which is not required for identifying S. Moreover, by Eq. (3), the definition is symmetric, the roles of S_1 and S_2 can be swapped.

Applied to the example of *something stimulating* we can see that it is in fact *K-decomposable.* The three variables *red, food,* and *tickle* are identified with three separate functions and so $K(S) \stackrel{+}{=} K(red) + K(food|p^*_{red}) + K(tickle|p^*_{red}, p^*_{food})$. The Kolmogorov complexity of the set S is the sum of the KCs of the three subsets. On the other hand, a concept that is appropriately uniform cannot be decomposed. Consider the set of all squares. To decompose this set, we would have to segregate the squares according to a certain criterion. For example, we could apply a threshold on their size to distinguish small from large squares. But then we have to include this criterion in the indicator functions of both subsets, which makes the total description larger than the original one and invalidates the decomposition. Thus, we can plausibly say that 'square' is not *K-decomposable.*

Using the notion of *K-decomposable* sets we can then define when a variable V is uniform, in accordance with the informal characterization above:

Definition 5. *V is a **uniform** variable if the set S_V that corresponds to V is not K-decomposable*

In other words, the variables that we are looking for are those that attach to a unified characteristic, such as *red* or *brightness*, guaranteed by the fact that the concepts used are not *K-decomposable.* Importantly, for any explanation and element x there is a wide range of uniform variables that can be used. A specific x could be both red (one uniform variable), and a rectangle (a second uniform variable) and a large object (a third uniform variable) at the same time. Furthermore, variables at various levels of abstraction can be uniform: *scarlet* is uniform, as is *red* and *colour*. Which uniform variables one chooses then depends on the specific explanation (and to be more precise the domain of that explanation), to which we turn next.

Here, we will say that an explanation $G(x)$ of $b(x)$ regarding element x aims to cover as large a set as possible while still using only patterns (of dependence) relevant to x.

Definition 6. *An explanation $G(x)$ is called optimal if it has domain $S_G \subseteq S_b$, where S_G is a maximal non-K-decomposable set which contains x*

For optimal explanations of x there is then a guarantee that S_G contains as many inputs as possible, while it does not include irrelevant information for x (as in this case it would be possible to K-decompose S_G). Note that there is always a non-K-decomposable set that contains x, namely the trivial set, which only contains x.

5.2 Formal Definition of Optimal Variable in an Explanation

To arrive at our final definition of optimal variables for an explanation we then also need the notion of *K-composability*. The idea here is that in explanations we often use more than one variable to capture the set of inputs X for whose outputs Y the explanation is supposed to provide additional insight. The interaction of these different variables needs to be accounted for, as they should be complementary. To capture this aspect we therefore define *K-composability* as follows:

Definition 7. *A set S is K-composable if there exist different and non-empty subsets S_1 and S_2 such that:*

- $S_1 \setminus S_2 \neq \emptyset$,
- $S_2 \setminus S_1 \neq \emptyset$,
- $S = S_1 \cap S_2$, *and*
- $K(S) \stackrel{+}{=} K(S_1) + K(S_2|p^*_{S_1})$.

Using both K-decomposability (based on the union of sets) and K-composability (based on the intersection of sets) we can then define when variables are of an optimal degree of abstraction for an explanation of an input x. Our definition states that these optimal variables together identify this subset S_G of inputs in a complementary fashion, building on the definition of a uniform variable.

Definition 8. *Uniform variables $V_1, \ldots V_n$, associated with set $S_{V_1}, \ldots S_{V_n}$, are* ***optimal variables in explanation*** *$G(x)$ of input x for $b(x)$ if the set S_G associated with the explanation is such that the sets $S_{V_1}, \ldots S_{V_n}$ corresponding to uniform $V_1, \ldots V_n$ K-compose S_G.*

Figure 2 helps to visualize what this definition states. Our choice of S_G as the maximal subset of S_b that is non-K-decomposable and contains x is illustrated on the left. On the right we see how an explanation of x is then built up using optimal variables. The composability requirement states that if we use different variables in an explanation then they have to overlap, to together characterize S_G. However, they have to do so in complementary fashion (and with a minimal number of variables). So, these sets will be similar to those seen on the right-hand side in the image. For example, if S_G is the set of all big, red rectangles then it is K-composed of the sets S_{V_1}: 'rectangles', S_{V_2}: 'big objects' and S_{V_3}: 'red objects'. The requirement that the difference sets are non-empty helps to exclude the possibility to further compose the set of rectangles based on the set of 'quadrilaterals' or 'polygons'. This is not a valid composition of 'rectangles' by our definition since 'rectangles' minus 'quadrilaterals' is the empty set. This, together with the requirement that the Kolmogorov complexity does not increase through K-composition, helps prevent the move to more abstract concepts.

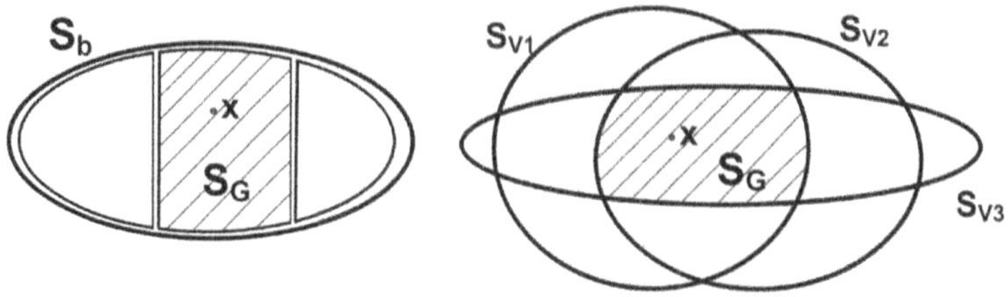

Fig. 2. An explanation G for X explains inputs in subset S_G of the positive subset S_b (left), and does so using the intersection of global variables S_{V1}, S_{V2} and S_{V3} (right).

6 Application of the Definition to the Pigeon Case

If we apply this proposed definition to the examples depicted in Sect. 3, we see that it tracks exactly the judgements we are inclined to make. According to our definition, we should prefer *red* over *scarlet* because the resulting explanation covers a larger subset (namely all red stimuli rather than only the scarlet stimuli), while *red* can be defined in simpler (i.e. shorter) terms than as a disjunction of the different shades of red. The subset S_G is in this case the set of all red stimuli, assuming that x is a specific red stimulus. While we could describe this with variables of different shades of red (which are uniform variables), this increases the Kolmogorov complexity of the set as red is not *K-decomposable*. Hence, we should prefer *red* over a disjunction of shades of red. We should also prefer it over *scarlet*, as *scarlet* does not K-compose S_G on its own. Finally, more abstract variables such as *colour* are ruled out as composition of more abstract variables is more complex than simply using *red* (violating the last condition of K-composition). However, had the bird pecked only at scarlet stimuli, our definition would state that *scarlet* is an optimal variable to use. In that case, S_b would not have contained other shades of red and so likewise $S_G \subseteq S_b$ would have been restricted to the specific set of scarlet stimuli, which are then captured by the uniform variable *scarlet*.

Furthermore, we should prefer *red* over *something stimulating* in the situation where the bird pecks at a wider range of stimuli. Despite the broader reach of *something stimulating* it is *K-decomposable* in terms of *red*, *food* and *tickle*. As a result, we first fix S_G as one of the maximal non-K-decomposable subsets, in the case of a red stimulus this will be *red*. This means that *something stimulating*, the variable that covers all S_b, is ruled as being too abstract. Instead, we should look at the minimal number of non-K-decomposable sets that together K-compose the smaller set S_G, which is simply *red* again. Should we want a more general explanation of the behaviour of the pigeon then we can simply go for the disjunction of the explanations corresponding to our K-decomposed subsets: *red* $\vee$ *food* $\vee$ *tickle*. For the follow-up examples we get again the desired results: *red* is preferable to *redow* because *redow* is *K-decomposable* in terms of *red* and *yellow* (which affects the choice of S_G), whereas *bright coloured* is preferable because it is not *K-decomposable*, again assuming that the set of positive instances that we aim to explain is in the first case that of red and yellow stimuli and in the second case that of bright coloured stimuli.

To consider this in the pigeon example just discussed, we can imagine a setting in which the brain of the pigeon is studied and neural signals are measured. Based on these measurements it is observed that when a particular part of the brain gets stimulated it cause the pecking. In such a context, with the knowledge of what's going on in the brain, 'something stimulating' can provide a good (uniform) explanation for the pecking. For each of the different stimuli (a bright color, food or tickle), a similar process in the brain can be observed. This shows that an explanation might depend on the features available to the binary classifier b.

7 Explanations in AI

A popular option in XAI for explaining black-box algorithms is to fit decision trees to them, which aim to approximate the input-output relation of b [14,20]. They offer a human-understandable description, thanks to the explicit variables and clear decision paths (for trees that are not too large). Can they represent/describe the level of abstraction we defined in this paper? Decision trees are based on clauses that form conditions on the input variables by conjunctions, negations, and disjunctions. Also rule-based systems are based on such clauses.

Figure 3 shows the decision tree for the Pigeon example (4) in which the color might be red or yellow. The decision tree provides an explanation for all positive instances, where each node is an optimal variable for an explanation and each leaf represents the right level of abstraction for an explanation of an individual outcome (an S_G-set).

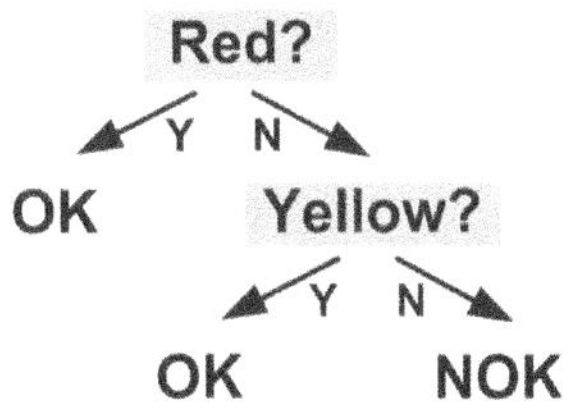

Fig. 3. Decision tree for the Pigeon2 example (Red or Yellow). (Color figure online)

In this example, the decision tree is the shortest description of the partitioning. But this is not always true: for more regular structures, a shorter description is possible. Consider the partitioning of a chessboard into 64 squares. Describing all black squares separately results in a large tree. An algorithm can do this in a more succinct way by exploiting the regularities of a chessboard. The KC of the black squares is smaller than a literal enumeration of all squares.

Likewise, the set of images containing a pattern, such as a rectangle which is recognized by a NN, cannot be explained succinctly by a decision tree. The NN employs multiple layers of various operations applied to the image pixels to achieve the recognition. This cannot be described by simple clauses. Patterns are the regularities that reduce the KC, while constraints on parameters do not reduce the KC. Consider the set S_b of the rectangles of a certain size and color. An explanation for S_b is K-composed of 3 optimal variables: the rectangular shape, the size and the color. The variables can be extracted without increasing the KC. The first one describes the pattern. The second and third are constraints. Such constraints can be formed by conditions on the input variables, but also conditions on the parameters of the patterns. Conditions can be described succinctly by a decision tree or rules. Patterns, however, cannot. To overcome this challenge, [18] propose to use decision trees containing *prototypes* that are representative for a set of similar instances. By checking against the prototype in the node it is possible to classify a case using more abstract concepts.

8 Conclusion

How abstract should variables in explanations be? We have proposed an account based on Kolmogorov complexity which, although not computable, gives us a formal definition of optimal degrees of abstraction. As shown in Sect. 5, our formal definition handles the examples in the philosophical literature well. We have done so by first defining the notion of a uniform, i.e. undecomposable, variable. Which of these uniform variables is optimal for a given explanation is then based on what variables can be combined to characterize the patterns of dependence captured by the explanation with minimal Kolmogorov complexity. Ultimately, therefore, we approach the problem of abstraction by arguing that optimal degrees of abstraction are those which lead to the least complex description of the patterns and constraints in the explanation. As abstraction is precisely meant to simplify description, we consider it a natural link to say that optimal degrees of abstraction are those which optimally reduce the complexity of descriptions.

References

1. Arrieta, A.B., et al.: Explainable artificial intelligence (XAI): concepts, taxonomies, opportunities and challenges toward responsible AI. Inf. Fusion **58**, 82–115 (2020)
2. Balayn, A., Soilis, P., Lofi, C., Yang, J., Bozzon, A.: What do you mean? Interpreting image classification with crowdsourced concept extraction and analysis. In: Proceedings of the Web Conference 2021, pp. 1937–1948 (2021)
3. Beisbart, C., Räz, T.: Philosophy of science at sea: clarifying the interpretability of machine learning. Philos. Compass **17**(6) (2022)
4. Biswas, S., Corti, L., Buijsman, S., Yang, J.: CHIME: causal human-in-the-loop model explanations. In: Proceedings of the AAAI Conference on Human Computation and Crowdsourcing, vol. 10, pp. 27–39 (2022)

5. Blanchard, T.: Explanatory abstraction and the goldilocks problem: interventionism gets things just right. Br. J. Philos. Sci. (2020)
6. Buijsman, S.: Defining explanation and explanatory depth in XAI. Mind. Mach. **32**(3), 563–584 (2022)
7. Chaitin, G.J., Arslanov2, A., Calude3, C.: Program-size complexity computes the halting problem. Bull. EATCS **57** (1995)
8. Franklin-Hall, L.R.: High-level explanation and the interventionist's 'variables problem'. Br. J. Philos. Sci. (2016)
9. Gács, P.: On the symmetry of algorithmic information. In: Soviet Mathematics - Doklady, vol. 15, pp. 1477–1480 (1974)
10. Ghorbani, A., Wexler, J., Zou, J.Y., Kim, B.: Towards automatic concept-based explanations. Adv. Neural Inf. Process. Syst. **32** (2019)
11. Gilpin, L.H., Paley, A.R., Alam, M.A., Spurlock, S., Hammond, K.J.: "Explanation" is not a technical term: the problem of ambiguity in XAI. arXiv preprint arXiv:2207.00007 (2022)
12. Grice, H.P.: Logic and conversation. In: Cole, P., Morgan, J.L. (eds.) Syntax and Semantics: Vol. 3: Speech Acts, pp. 41–58. Academic Press (1975)
13. Grünwald, P.: The Minimum Description Length Principle. MIT Press, Cambridge (2007)
14. Guidotti, R., Monreale, A., Ruggieri, S., Turini, F., Giannotti, F., Pedreschi, D.: A survey of methods for explaining black box models. ACM Comput. Surv. **51**(5) (2018)
15. Li, M., Vitányi, P.: An Introduction to Kolmogorov Complexity and its Applications. Springer, Heidelberg (1997)
16. Li, M., Chen, X., Li, X., Ma, B., Vitányi, P.M.: The similarity metric. IEEE Trans. Inf. Theory **50**(12), 3250–3264 (2004)
17. Lundberg, S.M., Lee, S.I.: A unified approach to interpreting model predictions. Advances Neural Inf. Process. Syst. **30** (2017)
18. Nauta, M., Van Bree, R., Seifert, C.: Neural prototype trees for interpretable fine-grained image recognition. In: Proceedings of the IEEE/CVF Conference on Computer Vision and Pattern Recognition, pp. 14933–14943 (2021)
19. Ribeiro, M.T., Singh, S., Guestrin, C.: "Why should I trust you?" Explaining the predictions of any classifier. In: Proceedings of the 22nd ACM SIGKDD International Conference on Knowledge Discovery and Data Mining, pp. 1135–1144 (2016)
20. Sagi, O., Rokach, L.: Explainable decision forest: transforming a decision forest into an interpretable tree. Inf. Fusion **61**, 124–138 (2020)
21. Weatherson, B.: Explanation, idealisation and the goldilocks problem. Res. **84**(2), 461–473 (2012)
22. Woodward, J.: Making Things Happen: A Theory of Causal Explanation. Oxford University Press, Oxford (2005)
23. Woodward, J.: Explanatory autonomy: the role of proportionality, stability, and conditional irrelevance. Synthese **198**, 237–265 (2021)
24. Yeh, C.K., Kim, B., Arik, S., Li, C.L., Pfister, T., Ravikumar, P.: On completeness-aware concept-based explanations in deep neural networks. Adv. Neural. Inf. Process. Syst. **33**, 20554–20565 (2020)

Assessing Aggressive Driving Behaviour Using Attention Based Models

Jonathan Aechtner(✉), Anna Wilbik, and Mirela Popa

Department of Advanced Computing Sciences, Maastricht University, Maastricht, The Netherlands
jonathan.aechtner@student.maastrichtuniversity.nl, {a.wilbik,mirela.popa}@maastrichtuniversity.nl
https://www.maastrichtuniversity.nl/research/department-advanced-computing-sciences

Abstract. As aggressive driving behavior threatens road safety, we investigate it using attention-based models and feature extraction techniques, applied on the METEOR driving dataset. After refining the dataset for our specific research needs, we implemented and evaluated the attention-based models OadTR and Colar, each showing distinct strengths and limitations. Notably, there's a consistent correlation between the frequency of an action in the training data and a model's classification accuracy. Our research offers two primary contributions. Firstly, we combined the OadTR and Colar models into a novel hybrid architecture that leverages categorical exemplars while predicting future frames. Secondly, we extract salient cues for model interpretability by tracing agent paths across spatial and temporal dimensions. These insights are especially valuable for autonomous vehicle applications where real-time interpretability and efficient computation are vital. The code is made available at https://github.com/unofficial-Jona/assessing_ADB/tree/main.

Keywords: Online action detection · Explainable Artificial Intelligence · Temporal Modeling · Driving Behaviour

1 Introduction

Aggressive driving behavior (ADB) poses a significant threat to road safety. Its roots are tracing back to the early days of modern road infrastructure. J.J. Leeming highlighted the competitive and aggressive attitudes of drivers as early as 1969 [22]. Since then, research in this area has evolved, leading to a distinction between road rage and ADB. While road rage involves the intent to harm, ADB is characterized by a disregard for the safety and well-being of other road users, often motivated by impatience, annoyance, or time-saving [32].

With the advent of autonomous vehicles, understanding and predicting ADB becomes even more critical. Autonomous vehicles interact with human

F. A. Oliehoek et al. (Eds.): BNAIC/Benelearn 2023, CCIS 2187, pp. 54–81, 2025.
https://doi.org/10.1007/978-3-031-74650-5_4

drivers, who may exhibit unpredictable and aggressive behavior. The ability of autonomous vehicles to recognize and respond to such behavior is essential for ensuring road safety.

This research pursues two primary objectives: firstly, to determine the most suitable attention-based model architecture for identifying Aggressive Driving Behavior (ADB), and secondly, to enhance the model's explainability by identifying salient cues essential for driving behavior assessment.

Historically, online action detection primarily relied on Recurrent Neural Networks (RNNs) and Long Short Term Memory networks (LSTMs). However, these models grappled with challenges, most notably their limited computational parallelizability and challenges in effectively retrieving significant information over extended sequences [15]. To circumvent these limitations, more recent research has embraced the attention mechanism. Notably, the **O**nline **a**ction **d**etection **TR**ansformer (OadTR) [38] leverages the power of the transformer architecture, particularly using its decoder layers to anticipate future frames. While this methodology has shown promising results, it demands substantial computational resources for both training and inference. In contrast, Colar [41] innovatively bypasses the need to anticipate future frames. Instead, it identifies characteristic exemplars for each action category and expeditiously compares current frames to these pre-established exemplars, a strategy somewhat analogous to contemporary advances in information retrieval for language models. The fusion of these divergent strategies into a singular model architecture represents one of the salient contributions presented in this paper.

The second contribution made by this research regards the identification of salient cues. Prior works are often times tailored towards image data [11,26,29,30], designed for specific model architectures [11] and/or require extensive optimization [16,23]. To address these shortcomings, we present an occlusion based, optimization free and model agnostic approach, to generate local explanations, by harvesting prior information about agents.

This research enhances road safety by developing models that predict aggressive driving, crucial for autonomous vehicles. Using attention-based models, it introduces a real-time, optimization-free method to assess each agent's relevance, informing policies for autonomous vehicle regulation.

2 Related Work

The task of detecting aggressive driving behavior in video data intersects several distinct research areas. The discussion begins with an examination of feature extraction methods, followed by a comprehensive overview of various model designs and approaches. Additionally, the psychological and behavioral aspects of aggressive driving behavior are explored, providing a broader context for understanding the problem at hand. A subsection dedicated to explainable artificial intelligence (XAI) methods for online action detection models is also included, highlighting their significance in ensuring the interpretability and accountability of the developed models.

2.1 Online Action Detection

The task of online action detection can be regarded as a specialized variant of action detection, where the model is restricted to using only past and present frames to make predictions.

This constraint limits the model's ability to leverage the full temporal context of the action, which often contains crucial information about the action's progression and outcome [13]. This makes the task of online action detection more demanding, as the model must be able to accurately predict actions based on potentially incomplete information [17].

For the detection of ADB, this constitutes a major challenge, because the appearance of aggression may be at the very end of the action. An exemplary situation would be an overtaking maneuver that seems non-aggressive until the final lane change. At that point, if the overtaking driver cuts in too closely, it might force the overtaken vehicle to brake abruptly. However, to provide valuable predictions it would be desirable to label instances as aggressive, before the real aggression takes place. On the other hand, aggressive drivers demonstrate clues constantly, implying that even a detection after an initial offence may be valuable.

In the early stages of online action detection, the focus was on extracting handcrafted features, such as dense trajectories [34] and improved dense trajectories [35], to represent and analyze video data. With the emergence of deep learning, researchers explored more advanced models, including 3D CNNs [33] and two-stream CNNs [28], which effectively leveraged spatial and temporal information from video sequences. The adoption of recurrent neural networks (RNNs), particularly long short-term memory (LSTM) networks [15], further facilitated the modeling of temporal dependencies in video data. However, LSTMs faced limitations such as difficulty in capturing long-range dependencies and lack of parallelizability.

A method to address the limitation of inaccessible future frames is to *anticipate future frame representations*, employing these predictions to enhance the classification accuracy at the current frame f_t. This idea is inspired by the fact that humans consistently think about present actions by anticipating the future [12]. Typically, this approach employs an encoder-decoder architecture [17,38]. In this architecture, the encoder is set up to learn frame representations that are most informative to the task. The decoder, on the other hand, is learned to provide predictions about future frame representations. Earlier works rely on LSTM and/or Temporal Recurrent Networks (TRN) cells [17,39] to model temporal dependencies. The introduction of the online action detection transformer (OadTR) constitutes a shift towards the transformer architecture, where encoder and decoder both employ the multi-headed self-attention mechanism (MSA) [38]. While this yields good results, computing MSA across all input frames presents a computational challenge, that can be alleviated by using a different strategy called *consulting exemplars*. The idea of this approach is to utilise the fact, that examples of a category share characteristics and can therefore be described by representatives. This presents the problem of finding these representatives, which the authors of the Colar paper (derived from consulting exemplars) solve by clustering all examples of a single category and subsequently defining the example(s) closest to the cluster center as exemplars. This yields representative exemplars per category [41]. The differences between the implementations however, exceed aforementioned conceptual differences and will be discussed in Sect. 3.

2.2 Explainability and Interpretability in Video Data

Deep learning models have gained widespread adoption in the field of computer vision due to their remarkable performance and ability to automatically learn complex features from large-scale data. However, these models are often referred to as "black-box" models, as their internal workings and decision-making processes can be challenging to interpret and understand [8]. This lack of explainability and interpretability poses significant concerns for stakeholders, particularly in high-stakes applications where transparency, trust, and accountability are crucial [18]. Moreover, the opaqueness of deep learning models can hinder the identification and resolution of biases or errors in predictions, which may have far-reaching consequences [20]. Consequently, there is a growing interest in developing Explainable Artificial Intelligence (XAI) techniques that can enhance the interpretability of deep learning models in computer vision and facilitate human understanding of their underlying mechanisms [4]. In order to optimize the efficacy of the generated explanations, it is imperative to consider not only the specific problem at hand but also the characteristics and needs of the intended user [2].

Two distinct approaches define the XAI landscape in computer vision today. While attribution methods and gradient based approaches focus on the model itself, perturbation approaches try to modify the input data to generate explanations. Attribution methods and gradient based approaches have shown remarkable results. Their explanations are usually visualised as heatmaps, where the most influential regions of the image are highlighted [11]. Gradient-based methods leverage the backpropagation process, essential for training neural networks, to obtain gradients concerning each layer's input [27,29,30]. In contrast, attribution methods generate explanations by recursively decomposing a network's decisions into the contributions from preceding layers, with the theoretical foundation laid by Deep Taylor Decomposition (DTD) [24]. Notable contributions include Layer-wise Relevance Propagation (LRP) [5], Contrastive-LRP [19], Softmax-Gradient-LRP [21], and TIBAV [11].

Perturbation approaches [16], introduce minor alterations to the data, while monitoring the model's varying behavior. However, if cast as an optimisation problem, these methods are computationally demanding due to the requirement for separate model inference with each data perturbation. Shapley value methods [23] encounter similar issues.

The majority of explainable AI (XAI) approaches in computer vision are tailored to image input [11,16,23,26,29,30]. Adapting these methods to video data is not a trivial task. Partially, because computational overhead challenges are exacerbated when incorporating a temporal dimension.

2.3 Aggressive Driving Behavior

Driving behavior is influenced by a multitude of factors such as personality traits, age, experience, gender, distraction, weather conditions, and the influence of alcohol and drugs. Studies have shown that personality traits such as aggression, sensation-seeking, and anxiety can affect driving behavior [36]. Various methodologies have been proposed to assess the aggressiveness of driving behavior, many of which have emerged from the fields of sociology and traffic modeling [3,37].

The vast majority of these metrics such as the Driving Anger Scale and the Total Aggressive Expression Index rely on survey data to measure the extent of anger experienced by the driver in a given situation [9,14].

A similar, driver centered research direction was adopted by [40] and [31], where machine learning based approaches are used to identify the aggressiveness of a driver. While these approaches offer valuable insights into the sociological and psychological underpinnings of aggressive driving, their applicability to autonomous driving is limited, as they primarily focus on the individual driver. In the case of autonomous vehicles, the challenge becomes identifying aggressive driving through the vehicle's driving style, rather than attempting to understand, avoid or mitigate driver aggressiveness.

3 Methodology

3.1 Research Design

The primary goal of this research is to determine if and how aggressive driving can be assessed using attention-based deep learning models. The findings of this study will serve as a stepping stone for the automotive industry, particularly for autonomous vehicle development, as such vehicles could use information about aggressive driving agents to alter their future interactions with these agents.

The dataset used in this research is approximately 100GB of video data from the METEOR Dataset. Apart from the RGB-videos provided in the METEOR Dataset, no additional features or data sources were incorporated into the research. Deep learning models were chosen for this research due to their widespread adoption in contemporary related work and their ability to handle large datasets, and learn complex patterns.

The first research objective is investigated by testing two attention based model architectures (OadTR and Colar)and evaluating their performance. Additionally, these two distinct architectures were aggregated, resulting in a third model (OadTR_v4) that was also evaluated on the online action detection task.

To address the second research objective, an occlusion based approach was employed. This approach excludes one agent at a time from the video and compares the resulting classification output to the classification of the original video.

This strategy results in local explanations, providing an understanding of the influence of individual agents on the overall classification.

To alleviate the computational burden of the training process, this research uses a *ResNet-50 i3D* to extract spatio-temporal features. This model was pre-trained on the Kinetics dataset [7]. Even though this fine-tuning is not driving-specific, it was chosen for its wide adoption in literature, including the original implementation of the **Colar** online action detection model [41]. The model configuration used for feature extraction returns one feature vector for every 8 frames, implying that the extracted feature f is defined as $\mathbb{R}^{t \times h \times w \times c} \rightarrow \mathbb{R}^{\lfloor \frac{t}{8} \rfloor \times 2048}$.

3.2 Dataset and Label Refinement

The METEOR driving dataset offers annotations for a large selection of rare and unusual behaviors, that are rarely featured in other driving datasets. Figure 4 in Appendix A provides a comprehensive overview on which behaviors are present in the data. While some of these behaviors can hardly be considered aggressive, others are explicitly described as aggressive in the accompanying publication [10].

Deriving Labels Encoding ADB from METEOR Dataset. To train models capable of detecting aggressive driving behaviors, we mapped the behaviors established as aggressive (based on the definitions from related work) to the labels native to the METEOR dataset [10].

To best utilize the given dataset, it was decided that labels explicitly affirming the existence of aggression should be considered alongside labels matching the definition from [32]. Additionally, the METEOR label *cutting* was approved for the final list of labels. The METEOR paper states that cutting represents an agent of interest interrupting the road crossing of a slower entity (e.g., bicycle, pedestrian, etc.). Since the only difference between the labels for *LaneChanging (m)* (= lane change with lane markings) and *LaneChanging* (= lane change **without** lane markings) is exclusively related to the nature of the road, thus these labels were combined into one. Lastly, a *background* label was added as is standard practice in the reviewed literature [6], being defined as the absence of all considered actions. This gives the final list of considered labels: *OverTaking, LaneChanging, WrongLane, Cutting, Background.*

To convert agent-level labels to frame-level, each frame is assigned a binary label based on the actions of all agents within it. It is noted that these actions are independent of one another, implying that an agent can show multiple aggressive actions at the same time. This constitutes a multilabel case, where different labels can co-exist at the same time. This is noted, as it has far reaching consequences for model implementation and training.

Label Refinement. Initial experiments were conducted with all available agents and actions in the dataset. However, due to poor results, the scope of the experiments was iteratively narrowed. At first the number of actions was reduced based on their occurrence in the dataset. As can be seen in Table 2, the number of frames featuring interesting behaviors as well as agents varies greatly. Following the intuition that aggressive actions are typically performed in relation to another agent (Overspeeding being the exception to the rule), the initial configuration had an upper bound of $N^2 * A$ combinations of aggressive behavior where N is the number of agents and A is the number of aggressive actions. Following the findings from Table 2 only the agents *Car, MotorBike* and *Scooter* were included into the final configuration based on their frequent involvement in ADB. The ADB labels in the final configuration are: *OverTaking, LaneChanging, WrongLane*, *Cutting* and *Background.*

3.3 Models for Online Action Detection

OadTR. As outlined in Sect. 2, the Online Action Detection Transformer (OadTR) represents a significant advancement over previous designs, incorporating the transformer architecture into the online action detection task [38]. OadTR consists of two main components, the encoder and the decoder, both of which are inspired by the standard encoder-decoder architecture of current transformer models. As such they employ multi-headed self attention.

The encoder incorporates a class token to learn global features pertinent to the online action detection task. This is done to ensure that the final feature representation is not disproportionately influenced by the initial value of a specific feature.

Conversely, the class token, via its adaptive interplay with other tokens within the encoder, can yield a semantic embedding more fitting for feature representation and for capturing the global context of the video sequence. Empirical support for these theoretical postulates is provided by experiments showing that the feature similarity for $t = 0$ dramatically diminishes before and after a pass through the network when a class token is employed.

While the encoder's responsibility lies in accurately capturing temporal dependencies and relations, the decoder's function can be understood, as predicting the future of $t = 0$, achieved via learnable predictive queries. To optimally leverage semantic information from the encoder, the decoder incorporates the encoder-decoder cross-attention mechanism.

An important difference to the original Vision Transformer is that the OadTR implementation permits the parallelization of the prediction queries' decoding at each decoding layer [38].

The initial implementation of OadTR is tailored to a multiclass problem. To adapt it to multilabel problems, a few modifications were required. The most significant adjustment involved updating the loss function. Following initial trials, the PyTorch implementation of BCEWithLogitsLoss was employed [25]. As can be seen in Eq. 1, this loss function amalgamates binary cross-entropy loss with a sigmoid layer, offering an additional advantage of eliminating the necessity of the softmax operation implemented by OadTR for the final classification outputs and the supervised training of the decoder.

$$\ell(x, y) = \frac{1}{N} \sum_{n=1}^{N} -w_n \left[y_n \cdot \log \sigma(x_n) + (1 - y_n) \cdot \log(1 - \sigma(x_n)) \right] \tag{1}$$

We used Adam as implemented by PyTorch, to optimize the model. A notable divergence from the OadTR implementation was the use of a CosineAnnealingLR scheduler, which allows for dynamic updates of the learning rate during training. This modification was considered necessary as the original OadTR implementation employed a StepLR scheduler, which is significantly influenced by the step-size. This is a hyper-parameter that would have necessitated substantial effort to optimize. The revised approach thus aimed to make the training process more efficient, without compromising on model performance.

In terms of regularization, two distinct strategies were employed. The first involved the use of the *weight_decay* parameter within the Adam optimizer, and the second incorporated dropout layers dispersed throughout the network. Furthermore, the size of the model itself served as an additional regularization factor. This multi-faceted approach to regularization aimed to prevent overfitting and enhance the generalization capabilities of the model.

Colar. The second model employed for online action detection is the Colar Model [41]. This model was chosen for its novelty, its lower computational footprint compared to the OadTR model and its innovative approach to action detection by consulting representative examples of each action category.

The Colar Model operates by comparing each frame in a video sequence with both previous frames and category exemplars. This dual comparison is facilitated in distinct branches, named dynamic branch and static branch.

The dynamic branch models the temporal process of actions. It does this by comparing each frame with its predecessors. During this process, local features are aggregated to obtain a combined feature representation of the entire input sequence.

The static branch, on the other hand, is designed to capture the unique characteristics of each action category. It does this by comparing each frame with a set of representative exemplars for each category. These exemplars are selected based on a simple clustering approach where instances closest to the cluster centers are used as exemplars.

The original Colar implementation fuses predictions from dynamic and static branches according to the following formula: $s = \beta\hat{s}^s + (1 - \beta)\hat{s}^d$, where $\hat{s}^s$ are the predictions from the static branch and $\hat{s}^d$ are the predictions from the dynamic branch. Ablation studies found the configuration $\beta = 0.3$ to be optimal. However, in order to make the fusion of the final predictions learnable as well, our modification concatenates predictions from static and dynamic branches along the first dimension. The subsequent prediction vector is then fed into a MLP to aggregate a final prediction score per class.

Since the Colar model was implemented for a multiclass problem and does not natively support the multilabel case, some modifications were necessary. Similarly to the OadTR model, the most significant change was the implementation of the BCEWithLogitsLoss [25]. Other modifications regarded the replacement of Softmax Layers with Sigmoid layers, for both the final classification and the measure of similarity within the static branch.

We used Adam as implemented by PyTorch, to optimize the model. Regularization was facilitated, by utilizing Adam's *weight_decay* parameter. Following the same intuition as with OadTR, a CosineAnnealingLR scheduler was used to reduce the learning rate over the course of the experiments.

Combining OadTR and Colar. The exploration of a comprehensive approach to online action detection in this study involves the integration of the static branch of the Colar model with the OadTR model resulting in a new model named *OadTR_v4*. The static branch of the Colar model provides a robust mechanism for capturing category-specific features, thereby enhancing the model's ability to distinguish between different action categories. The OadTR model contributes its efficient and effective handling of temporal dependencies, enhancing the model's ability to track the evolution of actions over time.

The integration of these models is designed to harness the unique strengths of each. It is expected to yield a model with only slightly increased computational demands (compared to OadTR baseline), yet significantly improved classification performance.

OadTR already aggregates features right before computing the final classification scores. Extending this aggregation to also include the output of the static branch of the Colar model emerges as a straightforward implementation.

Following the notations from the Colar and OadTR papers, Eq. 2 is derived, explaining how the final prediction p_0 is made. A visual representation of the proposed architecture can be found in Fig. 1.

$$p_0 = \mathrm{sigmoid}(\mathrm{Concat}[m_N^{\mathrm{token}}, \tilde{Q}, \hat{s}^s]W_c) \tag{2}$$

In Eq. 2, the parameter m_N^{token} represents the task-related features in the OadTR encoder, $\tilde{Q}$ depicts the pooled-predicted features from the OadTR decoder and $\hat{s}^s$ is the output of the static branch of the Colar model. W_c are the parameters of a fully connected layer that is used to combine features.

3.4 Identifying Salient Cues

This study employs a masking technique to identify salient cues in video data, a perturbation-based approach that significantly reduces computational overhead by avoiding optimizations. By leveraging prior information on agents' bounding boxes, the method involves running $n + 1$ inferences, where n is the number of agents in the latest video frame. A baseline is established through an initial inference on the unaltered video, followed by n inferences each masking a different agent. The effect of each agent on the prediction is measured against the baseline, as defined in Eq. 3:

$$\mathrm{Influence}_{\mathrm{agent}_i} = \mathrm{classification}(\mathrm{baseline}) - \mathrm{classification}(\mathrm{video\ excluding\ agent}_i) \tag{3}$$

An example is shown in Fig. 2, where occluding the red agent changes the LaneChange prediction from 0.996 to 0.012, indicating a high influence of 0.984 by the red agent.

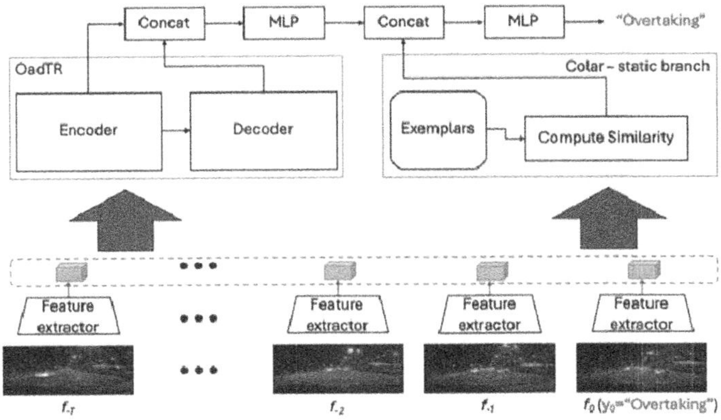

Fig. 1. Proposed new model architecture (OadTR_v4) obtained by combining OadTR and Colar models (adapted from the original figures in [38] and [41]).

While novel in the context of online action detection and aggressive driving behavior assessment, this technique draws parallels with other computer vision strategies, like key-frame analysis in action recognition. It offers localized explanations for model performance enhancement and could be pivotal in autonomous vehicle technologies for identifying critical agents in a scene. However, it's essential to acknowledge its inability to account for background elements and their potential impact on classification. It is noted that this approach may face limitations with occluding agents.

4 Experiments and Results

4.1 Model Training and Evaluation

To improve training speed, the training process was split into two stages, where stage one was dedicated to extracting features from the video data and stage two revolved around model training.

The dataset was split randomly according to video names using 80% for training and 20% for testing. This approach averted scenarios where the model would use time steps for evaluation that were also used for training, thus preventing data leakage. Despite the split being done without regards for the number of frames per category in each video, Fig. 5 in Appendix A shows that the result approximates the intended 80/20 ratio.

The hyperparameters and regularization techniques varied for different models and were discussed in the introduction of the model architectures. To address the issue of class imbalance among the different labels, a weighted loss function was used, where the weights are calculated based on the Eq. 4.

$$\text{Weight}_{\text{Category } i} = \frac{\text{TotalFrames} - \text{Frames}_{\text{Category } i}}{\text{Frames}_{\text{Category } i}} \tag{4}$$

Fig. 2. Salient Cues Identification example - at the top of the legend the classification scores without occlusion are depicted; underneath there is one row for each agent (color-coded) that gives information on the true label (*true label*), the new classification scores with occlusion (*predictions*) and the difference (*diff to org.*).

Model performance was evaluated using the ROC-AUC score to assess how much better the model performed compared to a random classifier. Additionally, the metrics F1 score, precision and recall are used to compare the performance of different model configurations. These metrics are used as implemented by sklearn [1]. To reduce the impact of the class imbalance on the metric results, the parameter *average* was set to *weighted*. Based on this, the support of each class is used as a weight, so that the average is calculated according to the class distribution. Additionally, the widely used metric Mean Average Precision (mAP) is also computed by taking the mean of average precision per class.

Furthermore, multilabel confusion matrices were generated and used to visualize the model performance as well.

This research was made possible, in part, using the Data Science Research Infrastructure (DSRI) hosted at Maastricht University, by training and evaluating our models on a single NVIDIA Tesla V100 - 32 GB GPU.

4.2 Experimental Setup

To maintain uniform experimental conditions, consistent hyperparameters were used. An exhaustive list of model hyperparameters can be found in the accompanying repository.

OadTR. To ensure fair comparison with the Colar model, the number of timesteps given to the model was increased from 63 to 64. Based on each feature incorporating information of 8 frames, this implies that the model can utilise information from $8 * 64 = 512$ frames.

Colar. As outlined in Sect. 3.3, some small changes were made to the original implementation of the Colar model. Most notably a change was done in the fusing procedure between the static and dynamic branches. Additionally, some changes were necessary to accommodate the multilabel nature of the problem.

4.3 Testing Different Model Architectures

In the pursuit to answer the first research objective, three different architectures were explored. As introduced in Sect. 3, these models are the OadTR model, the Colar model and an integrated model using the OadTR skeleton, but enhancing it by the static branch of the Colar model. Subsequently this integrated model will be dubbed OadTR_v4, complying with naming conventions introduced by OadTR [38].

For fair comparison, all three models were trained for 50 epochs, regardless of wall-clock time. It is noted, that training the Colar model is significantly faster than OadTR. Besides the aggregated experiment depicted in Table 1, we also present results for each architecture and action label in Appendix B, Table 3.

Table 1. Performance metrics represent the weighted class average of the impact of different model architectures.

Experiment	ROC_AUC	F1	Precision	Recall
OadTR	**0.668**	0.671	0.686	0.659
OadTR_v4	0.661	0.658	0.685	0.633
Colar	0.613	**0.682**	**0.688**	**0.688**

The OadTR model showcased outstanding results, with an ROC_AUC of 0.668 and a precision of 0.686 according to Table 1. While it excelled in the 'Background' category with an F1 score of 0.799, there is potential for enhancement in other categories. In comparison, the OadTR_v4 model had notable precision (0.685) but showed room for growth in the 'WrongLane' and 'Cutting' categories. Noteworthy is its superior performance in the 'LaneChange' category, achieving an F1 score of 0.138.

Differing from the others, the Colar model was balanced in its metrics, boasting the highest F1 and recall scores at 0.682. Specifically in the 'Background' category, it achieved an impressive precision of 0.832. Additionally, its strength in detecting 'OverTaking' instances was evident with a recall of 0.682, and it outperformed in the 'WrongLane' and 'Cutting' categories compared to its counterparts.

Among all models, the Background category had the strongest performance. F1 scores ranged from 0.777 (OadTR_v4) to 0.799 (OadTR). Colar demonstrated superior precision, marking its effectiveness in recognizing true positives. In the *OverTaking* category, performance was slightly lower across all models. However, Colar stood out with a recall of 0.682, indicating its capability in detecting 'OverTaking' instances and reducing false negatives. All models showed sub-par performance in the *LaneChange* category, highlighting the difficulty in predicting this action. OadTR_v4 had a slightly better F1 score of 0.138, showcasing balanced precision and recall. Correctly predicting the *WrongLane* category proved difficult for all models as well. However, the Colar model did indicate a marginally better F1 score, suggesting potential for improvement with further adjustments. For the *Cutting* category all models faced challenges due to limited representation in the training data. Still, Colar managed to achieve the highest F1 score of 0.041, hinting at its resilience for this category.

In summary, all models demonstrated varying performance across different categories, each excelling in certain areas while requiring improvements in others. The Colar model showed balanced performance, OadTR outperformed in precision and ROC_AUC, and OadTR_v4 exhibited strength in the 'LaneChange' category. Despite the strong performance in the 'Background' category, all models demonstrated a need for further optimization for the less represented categories such as 'Cutting'. A more visual representation of the model performance can be found in Fig. 6 in Appendix B.

4.4 Generating Salient Cues as Explanations

The methodology employed to identify salient cues for the elucidation of the model's predictions is detailed in Sect. 3.4. In these experiments, a masking technique was employed which involved setting parts of the input video to zero, thus effectively 'removing' certain agents from the frame.

This masking approach creates a suite of $n+1$ videos, where n represents the total number of agents in the frame. The prediction results from these masked videos are then compared against a baseline prediction from the unmasked video. The comparison provides a measure of influence of each agent on the classification outcome.

In addition to the primary method, an alternative technique utilizing negative masks was also investigated. This technique deviates from the positive masking approach, in that it preserves only the actor of interest within each frame, with all other regions being set to zero. However, the use of negative masks led to undesirable outcomes, in that the classification results appeared to be random and yielded no noticeable improvements. In fact, the lack of contextual data within the frames due to negative masking, led to significant declines in classification accuracy.

Hence, following initial exploratory trials, the strategy of using negative masks was abandoned due to its detrimental effects on classification performance. However, it is noteworthy that the current codebase is designed to allow for swift adaptation and potential future exploration of negative masks.

The reported values are generated by applying a sigmoid function to the last layer of the neural network. Given the nature of the multilabel classification problem at hand, the outputs of this operation can be interpreted as probabilities. Each output corresponds to the probability of the associated class label being present, as estimated by the model. This is because each output logit represents a separate binary classification problem, independent of the others. It's worth noting that these 'probabilities' do not sum to 1 across classes, reflecting the fact that multiple class labels can be simultaneously present in this multilabel context.

Generally speaking it would be difficult to incorporate video explanations into this paper. In order to provide some visualization and allow for a mapping of probability differences and agents, it was decided to use the last frame as a reference. Therefore each explanation consists of a visual representation of the last image next to a legend, which maps the colored bounding boxes to probability estimates and the difference between these new differences and the original ones. An example for this approach can be found in Fig. 2. Additionally, Fig. 3 as well as Figs. 7, 8 and 9 (in Appendix C) demonstrate how this technique can be used to generate examples for different models and action categories.

5 Discussion

The discussion section seeks to elaborate on the findings presented earlier, provide possible explanations, and propose future research avenues. To aid further discussion, the first part focuses on the generation of salient cues, which is important as these are used in subsequent parts of this discussion. The second part focuses on the performance of three evaluated architecturally different online action detection models.

5.1 Discussion of the Results Achieved by Different Model Architectures

The results from the experiment examining various model architectures reveal distinct strengths and weaknesses for each model, highlighting potential areas for improvement.

OadTR. The OadTR model demonstrated notable performance in terms of ROC_AUC and precision, leading the three models with respective values of 0.668 and 0.686. This model exhibited a particular strength in discerning the 'Background' category, attaining the highest F1 score of 0.799. However, its somewhat subdued performance in other categories suggests opportunities for further refinement. The model's suboptimal results in the *LaneChange*, *WrongLane*, and *Cutting* categories underline the need to enhance its proficiency for less represented categories in the dataset.

Colar. The Colar model demonstrated robust overall performance, registering the highest F1 and recall scores of all models at 0.682. Its strong proficiency in handling the 'Background' category, denoted by the highest precision score of 0.832, indicates a particular strength in identifying true positives. Additionally, the model showed superior sensitivity in the *OverTaking* category with a recall score of 0.682, surpassing the other two models' performance. The Colar model notably outperformed other models in the *WrongLane* and *Cutting* categories. However, its relatively lower ROC_AUC and precision compared to the OadTR model suggest potential areas for further refinement. Its comparatively superior performance on underrepresented categories suggests that categories with fewer training/testing examples especially benefit from comparison with representative exemplars.

OadTR_v4. The OadTR_v4 model, a synthesis of OadTR and Colar concepts, exhibits remarkable precision, scoring 0.802 for the 'Background' category. The model however underperforms in overall ROC_AUC and recall. Interestingly, OadTR_v4 outshines all other models in the less frequently encountered 'WrongLane' category, with an F1 score of 0.076 - almost twice the score of its predecessor, OadTR. This suggests that the integration of Colar and OadTR methodologies is particularly effective for rare labels. On the other side, the model failed to classify any instances of 'Cutting', as indicated by zeroes across all metrics for this category. This underscores the need for further refinements in the merging of OadTR and Colar concepts. Despite these shortcomings, the unique strengths displayed by OadTR_v4 imply a potential for the integrated model, particularly when adjustments are made for better assimilation of the constituent models' features.

The comparable performance across the models, particularly in less represented categories, may be more reflective of the characteristics of the dataset rather than the inherent capabilities of the models. This observation suggests that enhancements in the dataset, such as increasing the representation of underrepresented categories, could potentially augment the performance of these models.

5.2 Discussion on Salient Cue Generation

While no quantitative observations have been made, several factors appear to qualitatively influence the efficacy of the generated explanations.

Actor Size. By definition, larger, more prominent agents have a greater impact on the extracted image features and thus are more likely to cause substantial variation in classification results. This effect is exemplified in Fig. 3c, where the explanations for *Cutting* are dominated by the orange agent, which is more prominently positioned than the red or blue agent. Additional examples in Fig. 9 in Appendix C confirm this effect for the other implemented models.

Number of Agents. The effectiveness of the explanations seems to be inversely correlated with the number of agents. As the scene becomes more crowded, the explanation is less likely to identify the correct agent with a high level of certainty.

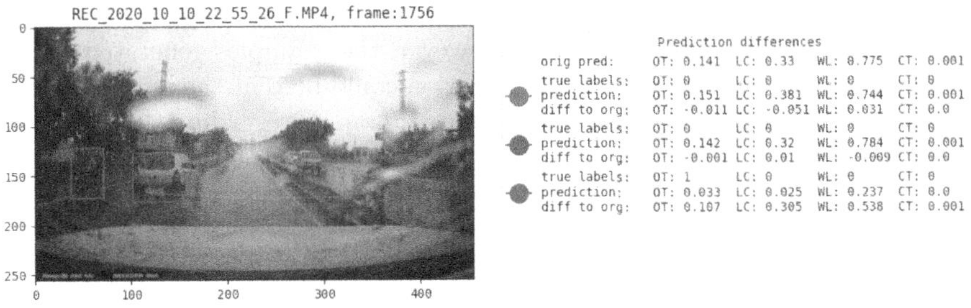

(a) OverTaking

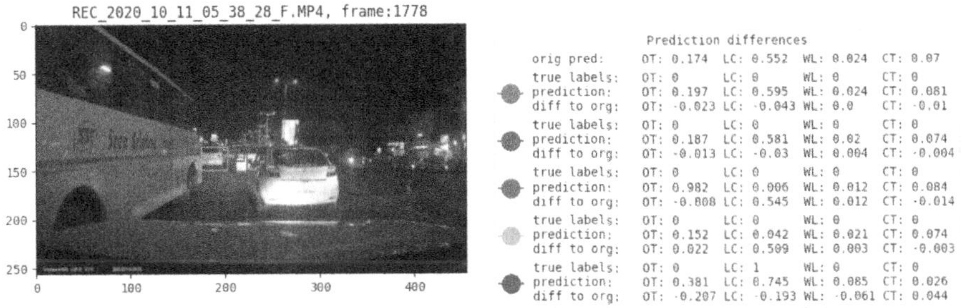

(b) LaneChanging

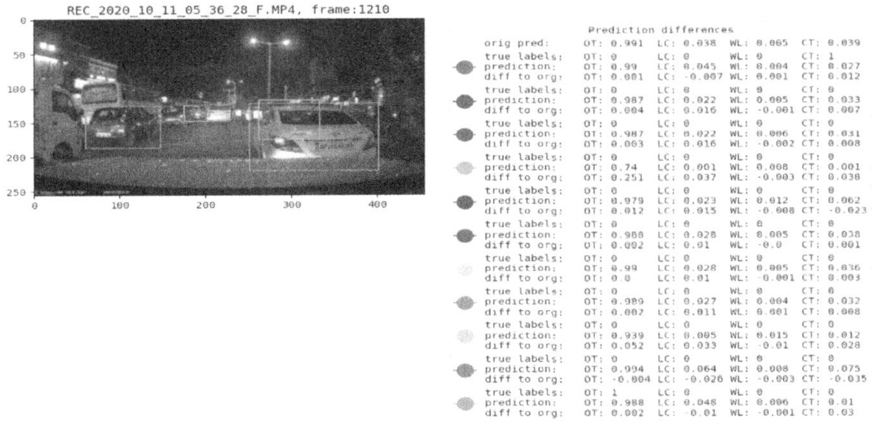

(c) Cutting

Fig. 3. Explanations generated using OadTR_v4

Contrasting Aggressors and Victims. A key challenge of this approach is the lack of a reliable way to differentiate between an aggressor and a victim of aggression. In terms of the generated explanations, there is minimal conceptual difference if the aggressor or the victim of aggression is omitted from the scene. Specifically, an overtaking maneuver can only be labeled as aggressive if there is an agent being overtaken aggressively. Removing one of the two from the frame should yield similar results.

Background Light. It was initially hypothesized that masking agents in black would be less effective in night scenes. However, the examples generated contradict this assumption. One possible explanation could be that the model predominantly focuses on the lower half of the frames, often disregarding the upper half which tends to be less critical for its objective. Moreover, even during nighttime, the frames rarely, if ever, contain entirely black pixels, especially within the road sections.

Utilizing Visual Explanations. We examine examples from the *OadTR_v4* model (see Fig. 3) to understand its performance in interpreting actions like *OverTaking*, *LaneChanging*, and *Cutting*. In the first example (Fig. 3a), the model confuses *OverTaking* with *WrongLane* or *LaneChange*, likely due to the overlapping elements of these actions. It identifies the green agent as the aggressor despite prediction inaccuracies. The second example (Fig. 3b) introduces challenges with scene crowding and partial occlusion, affecting the model's ability to accurately attribute aggressive actions, particularly underlining the limitations of the masking method used for explanation. The third example (Fig. 3c) increases complexity with 11 agents and mixed actions, revealing the model's struggles with accurately identifying actions like *Cutting* and attributing them correctly, especially in scenes with multiple agents and occlusions.

Comparative analysis with other models (referenced in Appendix C) indicates similar challenges across models.

6 Concluding Remarks

In the quest for road safety, understanding aggressive driving behavior is essential. This research offers a comprehensive exploration into such behaviors by leveraging attention-based models and feature extraction techniques applied on the METEOR driving dataset. Two significant innovations were introduced: the integration of the OadTR and Colar models and the generation of salient cues. Despite the hybrid model not outperforming individual models in global metrics, there is a marked improvement for lesser-represented labels, underscoring the potential of the combined approach. Model interpretability is emphasized, by producing transparent and efficient explanations, particularly crucial for real-time applications like autonomous vehicles.

6.1 Ethical Considerations

As models become more advanced and capable, ethical and privacy considerations become increasingly important. Future research should consider the ethical implications of assessing driving behavior, particularly in terms of data privacy, consent, and the potential for bias in model assessments. Additionally, the classification of drivers in *aggressive* and *non-aggressive* sparks the question where and how this information will be used. The goal of this research is to understand human driving patterns for supporting autonomous driving, not for misusing this information for increasing revenues (e.g. car insurance providers or rental car companies could raise premiums for potentially aggressive drivers).

A Additional Dataset Statistics

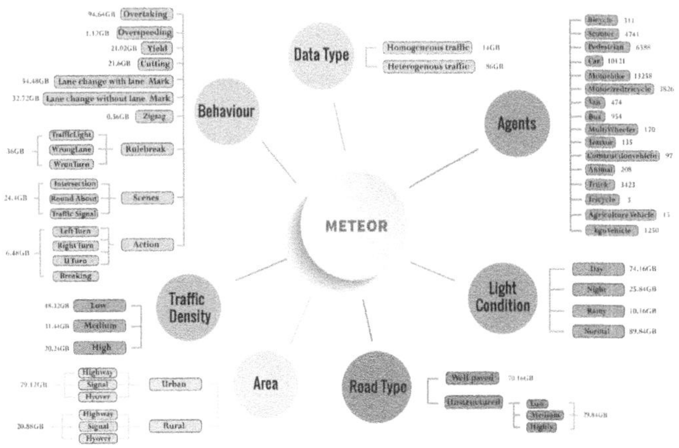

Fig. 4. Labels overview in the METEOR Dataset [10].

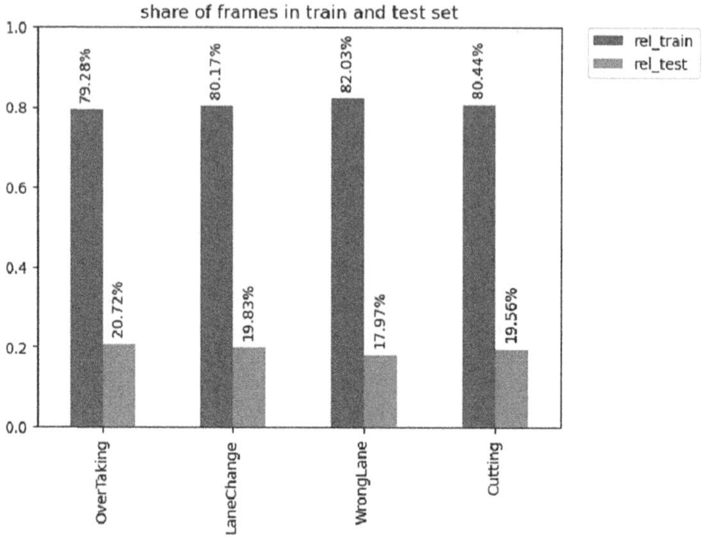

Fig. 5. Share of frames used for training and testing.

Table 2. Number of Frames where a certain actor is annotated as showing a specific aggressive behaviour. Categories and Actors that are part of the final configuration are marked with a * LaneChanging (m) refers to lane changes with visible lane markings. LaneChanging to lane changes without visible lane markings.

	OverTaking*	OverSpeeding	LaneChanging(m)*	LaneChanging*	TrafficLight	WrongLane*	WrongTurn	Cutting*
EgoVehicle	227225	9	165866	37371	32	23733	187	4595
MotorizedTricycle	66556	209	9974	3800	7	4985	2	1233
Car*	304322	87	88686	28558	208	8515	24	5534
Van	6501	0	929	820	0	268	0	0
MotorBike*	319702	285	14271	6917	727	40863	115	4994
Pedestrian	45	0	0	0	0	377	4	5180
Bicycle	852	0	18	0	0	2762	1	142
MultiWheeler	0	0	0	0	0	332	0	0
Truck	63728	89	18889	4376	0	4532	0	3868
Scooter*	130465	7	7237	2897	220	15440	281	2289
Tractor	57	0	0	0	0	2598	0	0
Bus	33756	10	9263	3296	0	4852	0	817
ConstructionVehicle	802	0	245	0	0	0	0	21
Animal	0	0	0	0	0	0	0	390
AgricultureVehicle	0	0	0	0	0	0	0	0
Pedestrain	0	0	0	0	0	0	0	0
Tricycle	0	0	0	0	0	0	0	0

B Additional Experiment Results

(See Tables 4, 5, 6 and 7).

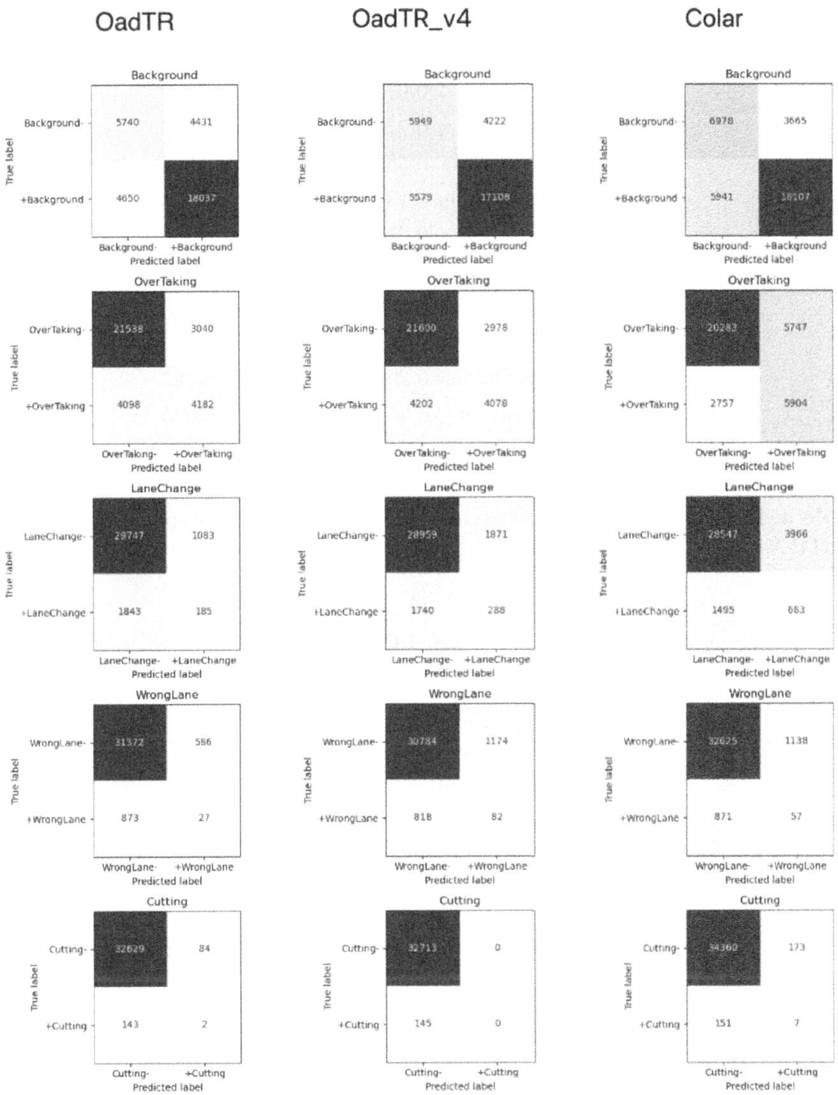

Fig. 6. Confusion Matrices for different Model Architectures.

Table 3. Performance metrics for different model architectures, for each driving action.

	category	F1	recall	precision	mAP
OadTR	Background	0.799	0.795	0.803	0.858
	OverTaking	0.540	0.505	0.579	0.542
	LaneChange	0.112	0.091	0.146	0.107
	WrongLane	0.036	0.030	0.044	0.046
	Cutting	0.017	0.014	0.023	0.012
OadTR_v4	Background	0.777	0.754	0.802	0.849
	OverTaking	0.532	0.493	0.578	0.546
	LaneChange	0.138	0.142	0.133	0.1
	WrongLane	0.076	0.091	0.065	0.041
	Cutting	0.000	0.000	0.000	0.077
Colar	Background	0.790	0.753	0.832	0.875
	OverTaking	0.581	0.682	0.507	0.574
	LaneChange	0.200	0.314	0.147	0.125
	WrongLane	0.054	0.061	0.048	0.045
	Cutting	0.041	0.044	0.039	0.029

Table 4. Impact of the number of decoder layers on classification performance for the OadTR_v4 model.

Metric	3	4	5	6
ROC_AUC	0.690	**0.697**	0.686	0.691
F1	0.676	**0.679**	0.644	0.666
Precision	0.676	**0.678**	0.673	0.675
Recall	0.699	**0.707**	0.664	0.691
mAP	0.303	**0.307**	0.296	0.301

Table 5. Impact of the number of encoder layers on classification performance for the OadTR_v4 model.

Metric	2	3	4	5
ROC_AUC	0.695	0.693	0.698	**0.700**
F1	**0.679**	0.671	0.675	0.651
Precision	0.676	0.678	0.679	**0.685**
Recall	**0.709**	0.693	0.700	0.671
mAP	**0.316**	0.305	0.305	0.302

Table 6. Impact of dropout probability on classification performance for the OadTR_v4 model.

Metric	0.1	0.2	0.3	0.4	0.5
ROC_AUC	**0.702**	0.698	0.694	0.690	0.701
F1	0.662	0.666	0.667	0.676	**0.682**
Precision	**0.684**	0.681	0.676	0.676	0.681
Recall	0.681	0.687	0.689	0.699	**0.711**
mAP	**0.312**	0.309	0.311	0.303	0.309

Table 7. Impact of hidden dimension size on classification performance for the OadTR_v4 model.

Metric	128	256	512	1024
ROC_AUC	0.680	0.682	0.690	**0.691**
F1	0.657	0.658	**0.676**	0.674
Precision	0.668	0.670	**0.676**	0.674
Recall	0.679	0.677	**0.699**	**0.699**
mAP	**0.306**	0.305	0.303	0.305

C Visual Explanations

(a) Colar

(b) OadTR

Fig. 7. Explanations using the salient cues identification technique for the action category *OverTaking.*

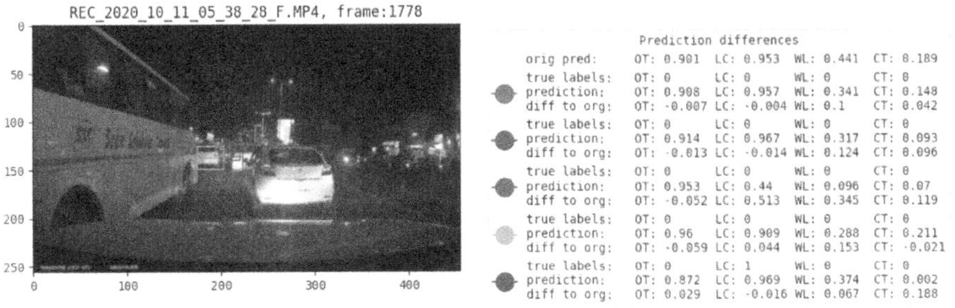

(a) Colar

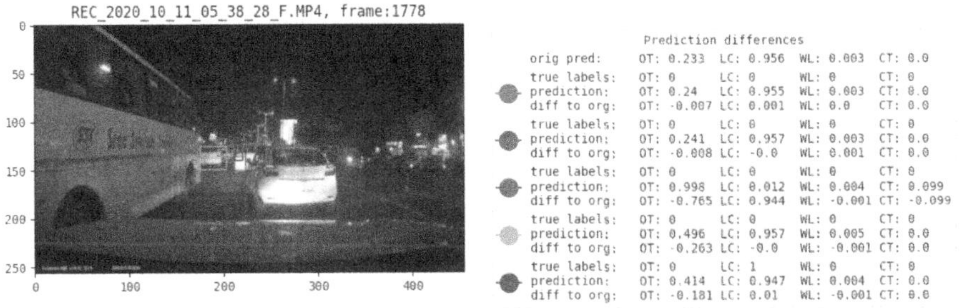

(b) OadTR

Fig. 8. Explanations using the salient cues identification technique for the action category *LaneChanging*.

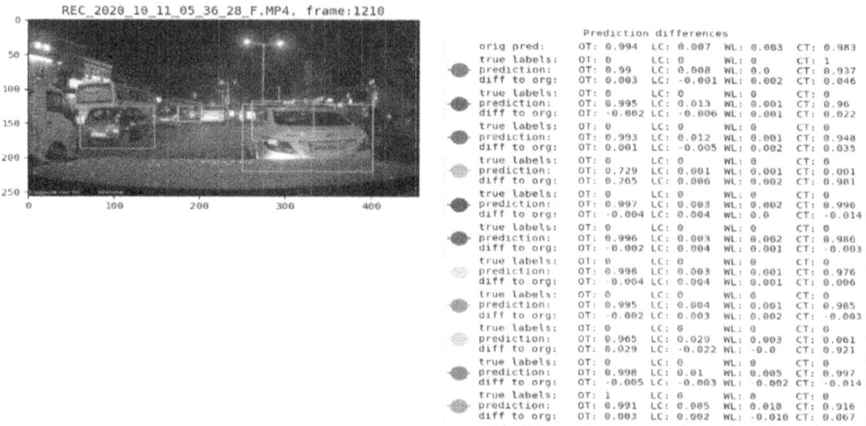

(a) Colar

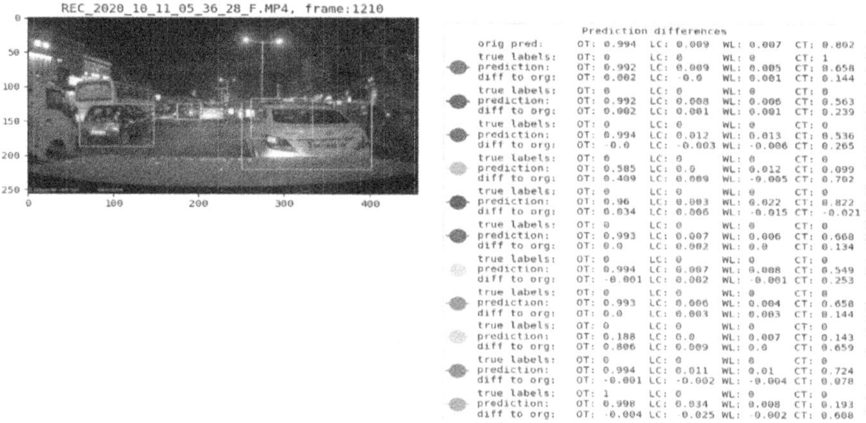

(b) OadTR

Fig. 9. Explanations using the salient cues identification technique for the action category *Cutting*.

References

1. Scikit-learn: Machine learning in Python. https://scikit-learn.org/stable/modules/classes.html#module-sklearn.metrics. Accessed 11 June 2023
2. Aechtner, J., Cabrera, L., Katwal, D., Onghena, P., Valenzuela, D.P., Wilbik, A.: Comparing user perception of explanations developed with XAI methods. In: International Conference on Fuzzy Systems (FUZZ-IEEE), pp. 1–7. IEEE (2022). https://doi.org/10.1109/FUZZ-IEEE55066.2022.9882743
3. Aljaafreh, A., Alshabatat, N., Al-Din, M.S.N.: Driving style recognition using fuzzy logic. In: International Conference on Vehicular Electronics and Safety (ICVES 2012), pp. 460–463. IEEE (2012). https://doi.org/10.1109/ICVES.2012.6294318

4. Arrieta, A.B., et al.: Explainable artificial intelligence (XAI): concepts, taxonomies, opportunities and challenges toward responsible AI. Inf. Fusion **58**, 82–115 (2020). https://doi.org/10.1016/j.inffus.2019.12.012
5. Bach, S., Binder, A., Montavon, G., Klauschen, F., Müller, K.R., Samek, W.: On pixel-wise explanations for non-linear classifier decisions by layer-wise relevance propagation. PLoS ONE **10**(7), e0130140 (2015). https://doi.org/10.1371/journal.pone.0130140
6. Baptista-Ríos, M., López-Sastre, R.J., Caba Heilbron, F., Van Gemert, J.C., Acevedo-Rodríguez, F.J., Maldonado-Bascón, S.: Rethinking online action detection in untrimmed videos: a novel online evaluation protocol. IEEE Access **8**, 5139–5146 (2020). https://doi.org/10.1109/ACCESS.2019.2961789
7. Carreira, J., Noland, E., Hillier, C., Zisserman, A.: A short note on the kinetics-700 human action dataset. CoRR abs/1907.06987 (2019). http://arxiv.org/abs/1907.06987
8. Castelvecchi, D.: Can we open the black box of AI? Nat. News **538**(7623), 20 (2016). https://doi.org/10.1038/538020a
9. Chandra, R., Bhattacharya, U., Mittal, T., Bera, A., Manocha, D.: CMetric: a driving behavior measure using centrality functions. In: International Conference on Intelligent Robots and Systems (IROS), pp. 2035–2042. IEEE (2020). https://doi.org/10.1109/IROS45743.2020.9341720
10. Chandra, R., et al.: Meteor: a massive dense & heterogeneous behavior dataset for autonomous driving. arXiv preprint arXiv:2109.07648 (2021)
11. Chefer, H., Gur, S., Wolf, L.: Transformer interpretability beyond attention visualization. In: Proceedings of the IEEE/CVF Conference on Computer Vision and Pattern Recognition, pp. 782–791 (2021). https://doi.org/10.1109/CVPR46437.2021.00084
12. Clark, A.: Whatever next? Predictive brains, situated agents, and the future of cognitive science. Behav. Brain Sci. **36**(3), 181–204 (2013). https://doi.org/10.1017/S0140525X12000477
13. De Geest, R., Gavves, E., Ghodrati, A., Li, Z., Snoek, C., Tuytelaars, T.: Online action detection. In: Leibe, B., Matas, J., Sebe, N., Welling, M. (eds.) ECCV 2016. LNCS, vol. 9909, pp. 269–284. Springer, Cham (2016). https://doi.org/10.1007/978-3-319-46454-1_17
14. Deffenbacher, J.L., Oetting, E.R., Lynch, R.S.: Development of a driving anger scale. Psychol. Rep. **74**(1), 83–91 (1994). https://doi.org/10.2466/pr0.1994.74.1.83
15. Donahue, J., et al.: Long-term recurrent convolutional networks for visual recognition and description. In: Proceedings of the IEEE CVPR Conference (2015). https://doi.org/10.21236/ADA623249
16. Fong, R., Patrick, M., Vedaldi, A.: Understanding deep networks via extremal perturbations and smooth masks. In: Proceedings of the CVPR Conference, pp. 2950–2958 (2019). https://doi.org/10.1109/ICCV.2019.00304
17. Gao, J., Yang, Z., Nevatia, R.: Red: reinforced encoder-decoder networks for action anticipation. arXiv preprint arXiv:1707.04818 (2017). https://doi.org/10.5244/C.31.92
18. Goebel, R., et al.: Explainable AI: the new 42? In: Holzinger, A., Kieseberg, P., Tjoa, A.M., Weippl, E. (eds.) CD-MAKE 2018. LNCS, vol. 11015, pp. 295–303. Springer, Cham (2018). https://doi.org/10.1007/978-3-319-99740-7_21
19. Gu, J., Yang, Y., Tresp, V.: Understanding individual decisions of CNNs via contrastive backpropagation. In: Jawahar, C.V., Li, H., Mori, G., Schindler, K. (eds.)

ACCV 2018. LNCS, vol. 11363, pp. 119–134. Springer, Cham (2019). https://doi.org/10.1007/978-3-030-20893-6_8
20. Guidotti, R., Monreale, A., Ruggieri, S., Turini, F., Giannotti, F., Pedreschi, D.: A survey of methods for explaining black box models. ACM Comput. Surv. (CSUR) **51**(5), 1–42 (2018). https://doi.org/10.1145/3236009
21. Iwana, B.K., Kuroki, R., Uchida, S.: Explaining convolutional neural networks using softmax gradient layer-wise relevance propagation. In: 2019 IEEE/CVF International Conference on Computer Vision Workshop (ICCVW), pp. 4176–4185. IEEE (2019). https://doi.org/10.1109/ICCVW.2019.00513
22. Leeming, J., Mackay, G., Pole, K., Fitzgerald, P.: Road accidents: prevent of punish? (1969)
23. Lundberg, S.M., Lee, S.I.: A unified approach to interpreting model predictions. In: Advances in Neural Information Processing Systems, vol. 30 (2017). https://proceedings.neurips.cc/paper_files/paper/2017/file/8a20a8621978632d76c43dfd28b67767-Paper.pdf
24. Montavon, G., Lapuschkin, S., Binder, A., Samek, W., Müller, K.R.: Explaining nonlinear classification decisions with deep Taylor decomposition. Pattern Recogn. **65**, 211–222 (2017). https://doi.org/10.1016/j.patcog.2016.11.008
25. PyTorch: Pytorch vision models (2022). https://pytorch.org/docs/stable/generated/torch.nn.BCEWithLogitsLoss.html
26. Selvaraju, R.R., Cogswell, M., Das, A., Vedantam, R., Parikh, D., Batra, D.: Grad-CAM: visual explanations from deep networks via gradient-based localization. In: Proceedings of the IEEE International Conference on Computer Vision, pp. 618–626 (2017). https://doi.org/10.1109/ICCV.2017.74
27. Shrikumar, A., Greenside, P., Shcherbina, A., Kundaje, A.: Not just a black box: learning important features through propagating activation differences. arXiv preprint arXiv:1605.01713 (2016)
28. Simonyan, K., Zisserman, A.: Two-stream convolutional networks for action recognition in videos. In: Advances in Neural Information Processing Systems, vol. 27 (2014). https://doi.org/10.48550/arXiv.1406.2199
29. Smilkov, D., Thorat, N., Kim, B., Viégas, F., Wattenberg, M.: Smoothgrad: removing noise by adding noise. arXiv preprint arXiv:1706.03825 (2017)
30. Sundararajan, M., Taly, A., Yan, Q.: Axiomatic attribution for deep networks. In: International Conference on Machine Learning, pp. 3319–3328. PMLR (2017). https://doi.org/10.48550/arXiv.1703.01365
31. Talebloo, F., Mohammed, E.A., Far, B.: Deep learning approach for aggressive driving behaviour detection (2021). https://doi.org/10.48550/arXiv.2111.04794
32. Tasca, L.: A review of the literature on aggressive driving research (2000). https://www.stopandgo.org/research/aggressive/tasca.pdf
33. Tran, D., Bourdev, L., Fergus, R., Torresani, L., Paluri, M.: Learning spatiotemporal features with 3D convolutional networks. In: Proceedings of the IEEE International Conference on Computer Vision (ICCV) (2015). https://doi.org/10.1109/ICCV.2015.510
34. Wang, H., Kläser, A., Schmid, C., Liu, C.L.: Dense trajectories and motion boundary descriptors for action recognition. Int. J. Comput. Vis. **103**, 60–79 (2013). https://doi.org/10.1007/s11263-012-0594-8
35. Wang, H., Schmid, C.: Action recognition with improved trajectories. In: Proceedings of the IEEE International Conference on Computer Vision, pp. 3551–3558 (2013). https://doi.org/10.1109/ICCV.2013.441
36. Wang, L., Li, Z., Li, M.: Impact of personality traits on driving behavior: a systematic review. Transport. Res. F: Traffic Psychol. Behav. **55**, 342–358 (2018)

37. Wang, W., Xi, J., Chong, A., Li, L.: Driving style classification using a semisupervised support vector machine. IEEE Trans. Hum.-Mach. Syst. **47**(5), 650–660 (2017). https://doi.org/10.1109/THMS.2017.2736948
38. Wang, X., et al.: OadTR: online action detection with transformers (2021). https://doi.org/10.48550/ARXIV.2106.11149
39. Xu, M., Gao, M., Chen, Y.T., Davis, L.S., Crandall, D.J.: Temporal recurrent networks for online action detection. In: Proceedings of the International Conference on Computer Vision (ICCV) (2019). https://doi.org/10.1109/ICCV.2019.00563
40. Xu, W., Wang, J., Fu, T., Gong, H., Sobhani, A.: Aggressive driving behavior prediction considering driver's intention based on multivariate-temporal feature data. Accid. Anal. Prevention **164**, 106477 (2022). https://doi.org/10.1016/j.aap.2021.106477
41. Yang, L., Han, J., Zhang, D.: Colar: effective and efficient online action detection by consulting exemplars. In: Proceedings of the IEEE/CVF Conference on Computer Vision and Pattern Recognition, pp. 3160–3169 (2022). https://doi.org/10.1109/CVPR52688.2022.00316

Multi-Agent Counterfactual Communication Using Difference Rewards Policy Gradients

Simon Vanneste[1(✉)], Astrid Vanneste[1], Tom De Schepper[2], Siegfried Mercelis[1], Peter Hellinckx[3], and Kevin Mets[1]

[1] IDLab - Faculty of Applied Engineering, University of Antwerp - imec, Sint-Pietersvliet 7, 2000 Antwerp, Belgium
{simon.vanneste,astrid.vanneste,siegfried.mercelis, kevin.mets}@uantwerpen.be

[2] IDLab - Department of Computer Science, University of Antwerp - imec, Sint-Pietersvliet 7, 2000 Antwerp, Belgium
tom.deschepper@uantwerpen.be

[3] Faculty of Applied Engineering, University of Antwerp, Antwerp, Belgium
peter.hellinckx@uantwerpen.be

Abstract. Communication learning while learning a behaviour policy is a challenging problem within the multi-agent reinforcement learning domain. In this work, we combine the MACC (Multi-Agent Counterfactual Communication) method with the DR.PG (Difference Reward Policy Gradient) method and propose the novel DR.MACC (Difference Reward Multi-Agent Counterfactual Communication) method. The DR.MACC method enables us to create an agent-specific difference return for the action and communication policy of the agents. This policy-specific difference return minimizes the credit-assignment problem compared to using the team reward directly. The DR.MACC method does not require us to learn a joint Q-function, like the MACC method, but instead operates using the environment's reward function. Alternatively, when the reward function is unavailable, we can learn an approximation of the reward function in the DRR.MACC method. Here, the agent's environment interactions are used to train the approximation of the reward function using supervised learning. In the experiments, we compare the novel DR.MACC method against the MACC method with an individual Q-function and a joint Q-function. The results show that the DR.MACC method can outperform both MACC variants in the different environment configurations.

Keywords: Multi-Agent · Reinforcement Learning · Communication Learning · Difference Return

1 Introduction

Single-agent RL (Reinforcement Learning) [9–11,17,18] has received a lot of attention from the machine-learning community. However, many real-world sys-

F. A. Oliehoek et al. (Eds.): BNAIC/Benelearn 2023, CCIS 2187, pp. 82–100, 2025.
https://doi.org/10.1007/978-3-031-74650-5_5

tems can naturally be described as cooperative multi-agent systems (e.g. industrial robotic or traffic light control [14]). When combining multi-agent systems with RL, we enter the domain of MARL (Multi-Agent Reinforcement Learning). In cooperative MARL systems, the agents need to learn to work together to achieve a common goal. To achieve this, the agents are trained using a shared team reward which encourages cooperative behaviour and prevents the agents from learning any competitive behaviour. In certain environments, the agents need to share information with the other agents to successfully reach their common objective. This inter-agent communication [4,20] can simultaneously be learned while training the action policy (e.g. communication for MARL traffic light control [19]). This allows the agents to learn a custom communication protocol which is specifically created for a certain environment.

A general problem within MARL with or without communication is the credit-assignment problem [1,2,5,20]. This problem is caused by only using a single reward to train a set of cooperative agents which makes it difficult for the agents to extract their impact on the team reward. A common method to handle the credit-assignment problem within cooperative MARL is by using the CTDE (Centralized Training and Decentralized Execution) paradigm [1,4,5,13,20]. Within this paradigm, the agents are trained centralized which allows us to use centralized training structures (like parameter sharing, free communication between the agents, and a centralized critic) while the policies can still be deployed decentralized. This chapter tackles the credit-assignment problem in cooperative MARL with inter-agent communication, using the CTDE paradigm, by presenting the novel DR.MACC (Difference Reward Multi-Agent Counterfactual Communication) and DRR.MACC (Difference Reward with a learned Reward model Multi-Agent Counterfactual Communication) methods. These methods combine the DR.PG method [1] (see Sect. 3.2) and the MACC method [20] (see Sect. 3.3). These methods allow us to learn a discrete action and discrete communication policy, without the need to learn a joint Q-function which has scalability problems, by using or learning a joint reward function.

2 Related Work

An important problem in cooperative MARL is the credit-assignment problem [1,5,20]. This is caused by training a set of cooperative agents using a team reward which makes it difficult for an agent to observe its impact on this reward. A popular method to tackle the credit-assignment problem is by using a centralized critic under the CTDE paradigm. MADDPG [7] is a multi-agent variant of the DDPG (Deep Deterministic Policy Gradient) method [15] where we use a centralized critic allowing it to reduce the credit-assignment problem. However, using the centralized critic requires us to learn a joint Q-function which poses scaling and stability problems for any method that uses a centralized critic. Next, Foerster *et al.*. [5] presented the COMA (Counterfactual Multi-Agent) policy gradients method which also uses a centralized critic. Here the critic creates an agent-specific advantage by subtracting a counterfactual baseline from the joint

Q-value which is then used to train the individual agents. The COMA method shares a similar disadvantage as MADDPG by requiring a joint Q-function. The DR.PG (Difference Reward Policy Gradient) [1] method is an alternative to the COMA method where there is no need to train a joint Q-function. The method uses the environment reward function or a learned approximation to create an agent-specific difference return. This difference return is then used to train the individual agents. Section 3.2 discusses this method in more detail.

Next, we describe the related work of communication learning in MARL. Foerster *et al.*. [4] presented the DIAL (Differentiable Inter-Agent Learning) which uses a differentiable communication channel. This communication channel allows the gradients to flow back from the receiving agents back towards the sending agent (inter-agent backpropagation) and learn a communication protocol between the agents. The action policies of the agents are trained by using independent Q-learning. Sukhbaatar *et al.*. [16] propose a similar method called CommNet which learns a communication protocol by sharing the hidden state of an agent with the other agents. This hidden state is then also trained using inter-agent backpropagation. TarMAC (Targeted Multi-Agent Communication) [3] is a communication learning method where the agents add a signature to each send message which allows the receiving agents to focus on the relevant messages by using an attention mechanism. Similar to the DIAL and CommNet methods, TarMAC also uses a differentiable communication channel to train the communication policy by using inter-agent backpropagation. Additionally, this method uses a centralized critic (joint Q-function) in the policy gradient update for the different agents. Jaques *et al.*. [6] presented a method to learn the social influence between agents in a MARL system. Here they investigate social influence through the actions of the other agents and through learning a communication protocol. The agents are trained to learn their social influence by adding a causal influence reward which models the change in distribution when the agents perform an action or send a message. This distribution is obtained by reasoning about counterfactual actions. Using this method it is not necessary to use a differentiable communication channel. Finally, the MACC [20] method is a communication variant of the COMA method. This method learns the communication policy by using counterfactual reasoning to obtain a policy-specific advantage. In Sect. 3.3, the MACC method is discussed in more detail. However, similar to the COMA method, the method requires us to learn a joint Q-function which again poses scaling and stability problems.

So in this work, we present the DR.MACC method which combines the DR.PG method with the MACC method. This allows us to learn a communication protocol using a counterfactual baseline without the need to learn a joint Q-function.

3 Background

In this section, we describe the background information on the multi-agent Markov decision process, DR.PG (Difference Reward Policy Gradient) [1], and

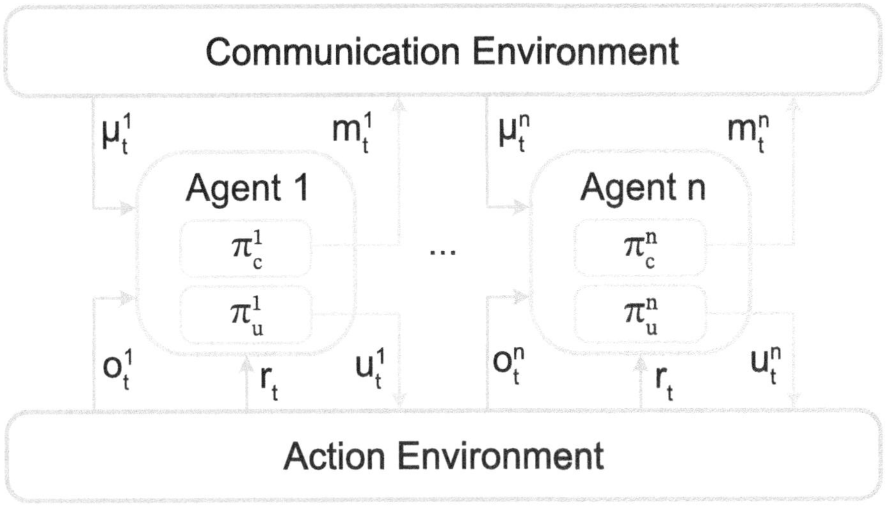

Fig. 1. The Dec-MDP with communication between the agents.

MACC (Multi-Agent Counterfactual Communication) [20]. This section and the following sections use a shared notation where the superscript is used as an agent identifier. Here, a identifies the current agents and $-a$ identifies the group of all the agents without the current agent. The joint variant is indicated by the omission of the superscript. Next, the subscript indicates if the symbol is used for actions (u) or communication (c). Additionally, the subscript is also used to define the current time step t where $t : T$ is used to show the group of times steps from t until the terminal time step T $(s_{t:T} = \cup_{k=0}^{T} s_{t+k})$. Finally, the notation $\mathbb{E}[X; P]$ represents the expected value of X under the distribution P.

3.1 Markov Decision Process

In this work, we use the Dec-MDP (Decentralized Markov Decision Process) [12] framework. Here, n agents are trained using a shared team reward r_t to achieve cooperative behaviour between the agents. At time step t, every agent a selects an action u_t^a based on the action policy of the agent π_u^a using the observation o_t^a and the received messages μ_t^a. Additionally, every agent also includes a communication policy π_c^a which generates an output message m_t^a by using the observation o_t^a and input messages μ_t^a The input messages are created by the communication environment (defined by the communication function M) based on the output messages of the communication policies $\mu_{t+1} = M(m_t)$ (see Fig. 1). A Dec-MDP is a jointly observable environment which means that the global environment state s_t can be uniquely identified by the joint observation o_t. When this property does not hold, we end up in the Decentralized Partially Observable Markov Decision Process [12] framework (see Sect. 4.6 where we describe the DR.MACC equations to use in a Dec-POMDP).

Table 1. The relation between the reward, discounted return, and the expected discounted return.

	Value	Expected Value	Difference Value
Reward	$R(s_t, u_t)$	$\bar{R}(s_t)$	$\Delta R(s_t, u_t)$
Discounted Return	$G(s_{t:T}, u_{t:T})$	$\bar{G}(s_{t:T})$	$\Delta G(s_{t:T}, u_{t:T})$
Expected Discounted Return	$Q(s_t, u_t)$	$V(s_t)$	$A(s_t, u_t)$

3.2 Difference Reward

Castellini *et al.*. [1] described the DR.PG (Difference Reward Policy Gradient) method which is a method that is closely related to the COMA method [5]. Both these methods use the aristocrat utility [21] to create a baseline which enables them to create an agent-specific advantage or difference reward. However, the COMA method requires us to learn a joint Q-function while the DR.PG can use the environment reward function directly when possible or learn a model of the reward function in the DRR.PG (Difference Reward Policy with a learned Reward model Gradient) method. The agent-specific action difference reward ΔR_u^a is the difference between the reward and the expected reward $\bar{R}_u^a$ under policy π_u^a. The expected reward can be calculated by using the reward function R and the policy of the agents (see Eq. 1). Here, the joint action is defined by the concatenation of the actions of the other agents u_t^{-a} and the alternative actions of the current agent $u_t^{\prime a}$.

$$\begin{aligned} \Delta R_u^a(s_t, u_t) &= r_t - \bar{R}_u^a(s_t) \\ &= r_t - \sum_{u_t^{\prime a}} \pi_u^a(u_t^{\prime a} | o_t^a) R(s_t, \langle u_t^{\prime a}, u_t^{-a} \rangle) \end{aligned} \tag{1}$$

The difference return ΔG_u^a is obtained by calculating the discounted difference reward as shown in Eq. 2.

$$\Delta G_u^a(s_{t:T}, u_{t:T}) \triangleq \sum_{k=t}^{T} \gamma^{k-t} \Delta R^a(s_k, u_k) \tag{2}$$

The relation between the reward, discounted return, and the expected discounted return is shown on Table 1. Next, the gradient g_u^a for the action policy is obtained by using the difference return (see Eq. 3). The gradient can then be used to update the parameters of the action policy for agent a.

$$g_u^a = \mathbb{E}\Big[\sum_{t=0}^{T-1} \nabla_{\theta_u^a} \ln \pi_{u,\theta_u^a}^a (u_t^a | o_t^a, \mu_t^a) \Delta G_u^a(s_{t+1:T}, u_{t:T-1}) \Big] \tag{3}$$

Finally, the reward function is not available in every situation, so Castellini *et al.*. [1] also presented the DRR.PG method which learns the reward function after which the previously described DR.PG method is used to train the action policy.

3.3 Multi-Agent Counterfactual Communication

MACC (Multi-Agent Counterfactual Communication), as described by Vanneste *et al.*. [20], learns a centralized action Q-function Q_u that is used to learn both the action policy π_u (similar to COMA) and communication policy π_c by calculating a policy-specific advantage. The communication policy gradient is shown in Eq. 4 which is used to update the parameters of the communication policy.

$$g_c^a = \mathbb{E}\Big[\sum_{t=0}^{T-1} \nabla_{\theta_c^a} \ln \pi_{c,\theta_c^a}^a(m_t^a|o_t^a, \mu_t^a) A_c^a(s_{t+1:T}, m_{t:T-1})\Big] \tag{4}$$

The communication policy advantage A_c^a is used to learn the communication policy and can be obtained by using counterfactual reasoning. These calculations are shown in Eq. 5 and 6.

$$A_c^a(s_{t:t+1}, \boldsymbol{\mu}_t^a, m_t) = Q_c(s_{t:t+1}, m_t) - V_c^a(s_{t:t+1}, \boldsymbol{\mu}_t^a, m_t^{-a}) \tag{5}$$

$$V_c^a(s_{t:t+1}, \boldsymbol{\mu}_t^a, m_t^{-a}) = \sum_{m_t'^a} \Big(Q_c(s_{t:t+1}, \langle m_t'^a, m_t^{-a}\rangle)\pi_c^a(m_t'^a|o_t^a, \boldsymbol{\mu}_t^a)\Big) \tag{6}$$

The communication Q-function Q_c cannot be learned because of the non-stationarity of the communication utility due to the changing policy of the other agents. While the communication Q-function Q_c cannot be learned, it can be calculated using the policies of the other agents and the action Q-function Q_u. To do so, the communication Q-function Q_c is split into the CU (Communication Policy to Action Policy) Q-function Q_{cu} and the discounted CC (Communication Policy to Communication Policy) Q-function Q_{cc} as shown in Eq. 7.

$$Q_c(s_{t:t+1}, m_t) = Q_{\text{cu}}(s_{t:t+1}, m_t) + \gamma_c Q_{\text{cc}}(s_{t:t+1}, m_t) \tag{7}$$

The CU Q-function Q_{cu} is defined as the expected action Q-value under the action policy of the agents given the output messages as shown in Eq. 8. The CC Q-function Q_{cc} can be calculated by using a specialized algorithm for which we refer to the work of Vanneste *et al.*. [20].

$$Q_{\text{cu}}(s_{t:t+1}, m_t) = \mathbb{E}\Big[Q_u(s_{t:t+1}, u_{t+1}'); \pi_u(u_{t+1}'|o_{t+1}, M(m_t))\Big] \tag{8}$$

Vanneste *et al.*. [20] investigate several methods to approximate the CU Q-function Q_{cu} to reduce the computational cost. Based on these results, we use ABS (Agent-Based Sampling) as shown in Eq. 9.

$$\hat{Q}_{\text{cu}}(s_{t:t+1}, m_t) = \frac{1}{n}\sum_{a'=0}^{n} \mathbb{E}\Big[Q_u(s_{t+1}, (u_{t+1}'^{a'}, \widetilde{u}_{t+1}^{-a'})); \pi_u^{a'}(u_{t+1}'^{a'} \mid o_{t+1}^{a'}, M^{a'}(m_t))\Big]$$
$$\text{with: } \widetilde{u}_{t+1}^{-a'} \sim \pi_u^{-a'}(o_{t+1}^{-a'}, M^{-a'}(m_t)) \tag{9}$$

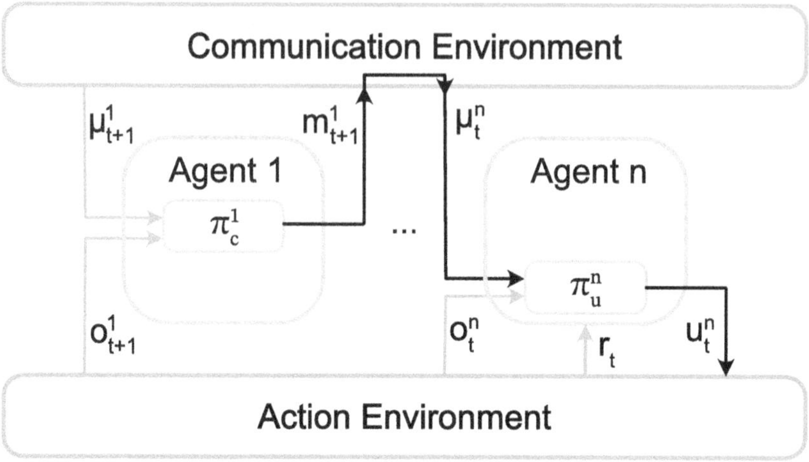

Fig. 2. A visual representation of how a communication policy can interact with the action environment by influencing other action policies.

4 Method

In this section, we describe the novel DR.MACC method. This method is created a centralized critic by combining the ideas of the MACC method [20] and applying it to difference rewards using the DR.PG method [1]. The trained centralized critic is then used to learn the action policy. However, to get a more intuitive understanding of the method, we first describe the implications of the policy and environments architecture from the MACC method.

4.1 Policy and Environment Definition

In this work, we use the same policy and environment definition as Vanneste *et al.*. [20] (see Fig. 1). In this definition, the action and communication policies of an agent are independent. These policies can be split because both policies receive the agent's observation and received messages. This allows other agents to share encoded observation or history information which can assist in reducing the partial observability of an environment (e.g. in a Dec-MDP communication between the agents reduces the problem to an MMDP). Furthermore, there is no theoretical reason to combine the two policies as the communication policy receives the full observation, input messages and can learn the expected action of the action policy to create a message. However, in certain environments it can be useful to combine the two policies using shared preprocessing layers to improve training speed.

Next, when we focus on the environment definition, it is important to note that we make a key assumption by having an independent action and communication environment. Here, we assume that only an action policy can interact with the action environment and a communication policy can only interact with the communication environment. However, the action and communication policies can still observe both environments. This also indicates that a communication policy can never directly use the team reward, which is used to train the action policies, because these policies do not interact with that environment. The only way a communication policy can have an impact on the action environment and the reward function is by influencing an action policy by sending messages. This concept is shown visually in Fig. 2. In Definition 1 this idea is defined formally.

Definition 1. *A set of communication policies* $\pi_c(m_t|o_t, \mu_t)$ *acting in a communication environment* M *can only influence the expected reward by influencing the action policies following equation* $\mathbb{E}[R(s_t, u'_t); \pi_u(u'_t|o_t, M(m_{t-1}))]$.

This definition is then further extended in the MACC method to train the communication policy aiming to improve the expected discounted return. So, Eq. 8, from Sect. 3.3, combines Definition 1 with a joint Q-function to train communication policies that maximize the expected discounted return. In this work, the DR.MACC (Difference Reward Multi-Agent Counterfactual Communication) method combines this definition in combination with the DR.PG method.

4.2 Difference Reward Multi-Agent Counterfactual Communication

In our novel DR.MACC (Difference Reward Multi-Agent Counterfactual Communication) method, the agent-specific communication policy is trained using the agent-specific communication difference reward. The global architecture of the DR.MACC method is shown in Fig. 3. In this architecture, the reward critic creates an action and communication difference return based on the reward function. Next, the communication difference return is used to calculate the gradient g_c^a (see Eq. 10) of the communication policy for agent a which is used to update the neural network parameters θ_c^a.

$$g_c^a = \mathbb{E}\Big[\sum_{t=0}^{T-1} \nabla_{\theta_c^a} \ln \pi^a_{c,\theta_c^a}(m_t^a|o_t^a, \mu_t^a)\Delta G_c^a(s_{t+1:T}, m_{t:T-1})\Big] \tag{10}$$

The agent-specific communication difference return ΔG_c^a is composed of the CU (Communication Policy to Action Policy) difference return ΔG_{cu}^a and the CC (Communication Policy to Communication Policy) difference return ΔG_{cc}^a (see Eq. 11).

$$\Delta G_c^a(s_{t+1:T}, m_{t:T-1}) = \Delta G_{\text{cu}}^a(s_{t+1:T}, m_{t:T-1}) + \gamma_c \Delta G_{\text{cc}}^a(s_{t+1:T}, m_{t:T-1}) \tag{11}$$

First, the CU return G_{cu}^a models the expected difference return of a certain message under the joint action policy of the different agents (see Eq. 12).

$$G_{\text{cu}}(s_{t+1:T}, m_{t:T-1}) = \mathbb{E}\big[G_u(s_{t+1:T}, u'_{t+1:T}); \pi_u(u'_{t+1:T}|o_{t+1:T}, M(m_{t:T-1}))\big] \tag{12}$$

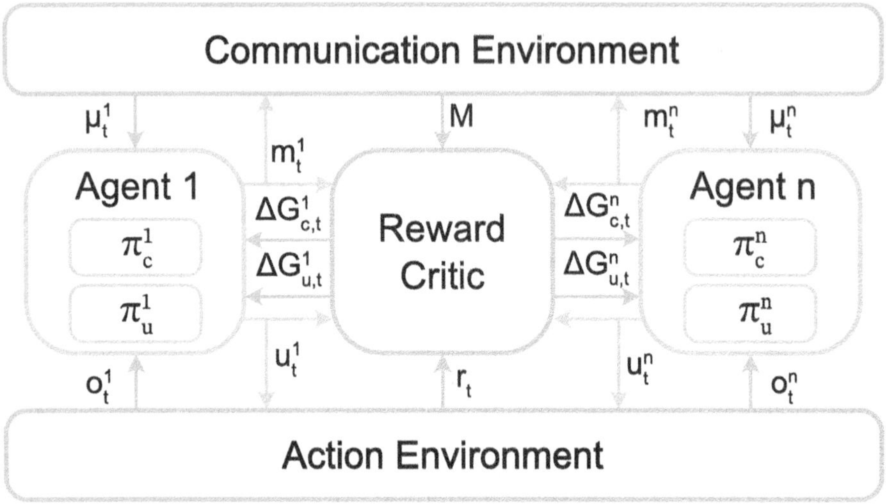

Fig. 3. The DR.MACC architecture where a centralized reward critic calculates a difference reward for the action and communication policies.

This CU return is based on Definition 1 and the CU Q-function from the MACC method as shown in Eq. 8. Intuitively, this CU return represents the impact of a message on the selection of the joint action and how it impacts the expected return. It is important to note that this equation uses the communication function M to determine which messages are received by which agents. Equation 13 shows how we can obtain the CU difference return based on the CU return.

$$\Delta G^a_{\text{cu}}(s_{t+1:T}, m_{t:T-1}) = G_{\text{cu}}(s_{t+1:T}, m_{t:T-1}) - \mathbb{E}\big[G_{\text{cu}}(s_{t+1:T}, \langle m'^a_{t:T-1}, m^{-a}_{t:T-1}\rangle); \pi^a_c(m'^a_{t:T-1}|o_{t+1:T}, \mu^a_{t+1:T})\big] \tag{13}$$

Next, the CC return G_{cc} is the expected CU return under the joint communication policy (see Eq. 14) which is also similar to the CC Q-function from the MACC method. The intuition behind the CC return is to reason about how a communication policy can influence another communication policy. This multi hop communication can be useful in certain communication topologies. When every agent can communicate with every other agents, there is no need for message hopping. In these situations, the CC return can be disabled by setting the communication discount factor γ_c to zero. However, when the communication topology is restrictive and prevents the agents to communicate with certain agents, message hopping may be required by using the CC return.

$$G_{\text{cc}}(s_{t+1:T}, m_{t:T-1}) = \mathbb{E}\big[G_{\text{cu}}(s_{t+2:T}, m'_{t+1:T-1}); \pi_c(m'_{t+1:T-1}|o_{t+1:T-1}, \mu_{t+1:T-1})\big] \tag{14}$$

The CC difference return ΔG_{cc} is the difference between the CC return and the expected CC return over the communication policy (see Eq. 15).

$$\Delta G^a_{\text{cc}}(s_{t+1:T}, m_{t:T-1}) = G_{\text{cc}}(s_{t+1:T}, m_{t:T-1}) - \mathbb{E}[G_{\text{cc}}(s_{t+1:T}, \langle m'^a_{t:T-1}, m^{-a}_{t:T-1}\rangle); \pi^a_c(m'^a_{t:T-1}|o_{t+1:T}, \mu^a_{t+1:T})] \tag{15}$$

Finally, the DR.MACC method uses the same loss function as described in the MACC method. The social loss function (see Eq. 16) is an additional loss function for the action and communication policy to promote social behaviour. In our context more social behaviour results in adapting the action and communication distribution depending on which message is presented. This is achieved by increasing the loss when the distribution does not change when different input messages are presented. This change in distribution is important when learning a communication protocol because when the other agents do not have a change in distribution, the resulting communication difference return will be zero. We refer to the work of Vanneste *et al.*. [20] for a more detailed description of the social loss.

$$\mathcal{L}^s(\theta^i_{\pi^a_u}) = -\frac{\lambda}{k}\sum_{x=0}^{k}\left|\pi^a_u(o^a, \mu, \theta^i_{\pi^a_u}) - \pi^a_u(o^a, (\neg\mu_x, \mu_{-x}), \theta^i_{\pi^a_u})\right| \tag{16}$$

4.3 Memory-Improved Equations for the Communication Returns

Calculating the different returns to obtain the CU difference return can be computationally expensive and memory-intensive. So, we investigated memory-improved equations to acquire the different communication returns. These equations allow us to reuse the action difference returns which are used to train the action policy and discard the action returns after the difference return is obtained. The memory-improved method to calculate the CU difference return is shown in Eq. 17. Here, y is the expected action difference reward given the alternative messages $m'^a_{t:T-1}$. In this equation, the global difference return is created as the sum of the agent-specific difference returns as shown in Eq. 18. This is because the communication policy attempts to improve the difference return for all the agents. However, this assumption is only valid in a cooperative setting and not in a competitive or mixed cooperative-competitive setting.

$$\begin{aligned} \Delta G^a_{\text{cu}}(s_{t:T}, m_t) =& \mathbb{E}\left[y; \pi^a_c(m'^a_{t:T-1}|o^a_{t:T-1}, \mu^a_{t:T-1})\right] \\ y =& -\mathbb{E}\big[\Delta G_u(s_{t+1:T}, u'_{t+1:T}, M(m_{t:T-1})); \\ & \pi_u(u'_{t+1:T}|o_{t+1:T}, M(\langle m'^a_{t:T-1}, m^{-a}_{t:T-1}\rangle))\big] \end{aligned} \tag{17}$$

$$\Delta G_u(s_{t+1:T}, u_{t+1:T}, \mu_{t+1:T}) = \frac{1}{n}\sum_a \Delta G^a_u(s_{t+1:T}, u^a_{t+1:T}, \mu^a_{t+1:T}) \tag{18}$$

Equation 17 can be unintuitive because of the negative sign, so we provide a formal proof for this equation in Theorem 1 which shows how this equation is obtained.

Theorem 1. *The CU difference return ΔG^a_{cu} can be defined as the negative expected action difference return ΔG^a_u.*

Proof.

$$
\begin{aligned}
&\Delta G^a_{\text{cu}}(s_{t:T}, m_t) \\
&\quad = G^a_{\text{cu}}(s_{t:T}, m_t) \\
&\quad\quad - \mathbb{E}[G^a_{\text{cu}}(s_{t:T}, M(\langle m'^a_{t:T-1}, m^{-a}_{t:T-1}\rangle))\pi^a_c(m'^a_{t:T-1}|o^a_{t:T-1}, \mu^a_{t:T-1})] \\
&\quad = \mathbb{E}[G_u(s_{t+1:T}, u''_{t+1:T}); \pi_u(u''_{t+1:T}|o_{t+1:T}, M(m_{t:T-1}))] \\
&\quad\quad - \mathbb{E}[\mathbb{E}[G_u(s_{t+1:T}, u'_{t+1:T}); \pi_u(u'_{t+1:T}|o_{t+1:T}, M(\langle m'^a_{t:T-1}, m^{-a}_{t:T-1}\rangle))]; \\
&\quad\quad \pi^a_c(m'^a_{t:T-1}|o^a_{t:T-1}, \mu^a_{t:T-1})] \\
&\quad = \mathbb{E}[\sum_{k=t+1}^{T} \gamma^{k-t} R(s_k, u''_k); \pi_u(u''_{t+1:T}|o_{t+1:T}, M(m_{t:T-1}))] \\
&\quad\quad - \mathbb{E}[\mathbb{E}[\sum_{k=t+1}^{T} \gamma_c^{k-t} R(s_k, u'_k); \pi_u(u'_{t+1:T}|o_{t+1:T}, M(\langle m'^a_{t:T-1}, m^{-a}_{t:T-1}\rangle))]; \\
&\quad\quad \pi^a_c(m'^a_{t:T-1}|o^a_{t:T-1}, \mu^a_{t:T-1})] \\
&\quad = -\mathbb{E}[\mathbb{E}[\sum_{k=t+1}^{T} \gamma^{k-t}(R(s_k, u'_k) - \mathbb{E}[R(s_k, u''_k); \pi_u(u''_k|o_k, M(m_{k-1}))]); \\
&\quad\quad \pi_u(u'_{t+1:T}|o_{t+1:T}, M(\langle m'^a_{t:T-1}, m^{-a}_{t:T-1}\rangle))]; \pi^a_c(m'^a_{t:T-1}|o^a_{t:T-1}, \mu^a_{t:T-1})] \\
&\quad = -\mathbb{E}[\mathbb{E}[\sum_{k=t+1}^{T} \gamma^{k-t} \Delta R(s_k, u'_k, M(m_{k-1})); \\
&\quad\quad \pi_u(u'_{t+1:T}|o_{t+1:T}, M(\langle m'^a_{t:T-1}, m^{-a}_{t:T-1}\rangle))]; \pi^a_c(m'^a_{t:T-1}|o^a_{t:T-1}, \mu^a_{t:T-1})] \\
&\quad = -\mathbb{E}[\mathbb{E}[\Delta G_u(s_{t+1:T}, u'_{t+1:T}, M(m_{t:T-1}))); \\
&\quad\quad \pi_u(u'_{t+1:T}|o_{t+1:T}, M(\langle m'^a_{t:T-1}, m^{-a}_{t:T-1}\rangle))]; \pi^a_c(m'^a_{t:T-1}|o^a_{t:T-1}, \mu^a_{t:T-1})]
\end{aligned}
\tag{19}
$$

Next, a memory-improved method to calculate the CC difference return is shown in Eq. 20 which shows similar properties to the memory-improved CU difference return calculations by allowing us to discard the CU returns. Here, y is the expected CU return given the communication policies of the agents and the alternative message $m'^a_{t:T-1}$. The proof for this CC difference return equation is shown in Proof 2.

$$
\begin{aligned}
\Delta G^a_{\text{cc}}(s_{t:T}, m_t) = &- \mathbb{E}\Big[y; \pi^a_c(m'^a_{t:T-1}|o^a_{t:T-1}, \mu^a_{t:T-1})\Big] \\
y = &\mathbb{E}\big[\Delta G_{\text{cu}}(s_{t+2:T}, m'_{t+1:T-1}); \\
&\pi_c(m'_{t+1:T-1}|o_{t+1:T-1}, M(\langle m'^a_{t:T-1}, m^{-a}_{t:T-1}\rangle))\big]
\end{aligned}
\tag{20}
$$

Theorem 2. *The CC difference return ΔG^a_{cc} can be defined as the negative expected CU difference return ΔG^a_{cu}.*

Proof.

$$
\begin{aligned}
&\Delta G^a_{\text{cc}}(s_{t:T}, m_t)\\
&\quad= G^a_{\text{cc}}(s_{t:T}, m_t)\\
&\quad\quad - \mathbb{E}[G^a_{\text{cc}}(s_{t:T}, M(\langle m'^a_{t:T-1}, m^{-a}_{t:T-1}\rangle))\pi^a_c(m'^a_{t:T-1}|o^a_{t:T-1}, \mu^a_{t:T-1})]\\
&\quad= \mathbb{E}[G_{\text{cu}}(s_{t+2:T}, m''_{t+1:T-1}); \pi_c(m''_{t+1:T-1}|o_{t+1:T-1}, \mu_{t+1:T-1})]\\
&\quad\quad - \mathbb{E}[\mathbb{E}[G_{\text{cu}}(s_{t+2:T}, m'_{t+1:T-1});\\
&\quad\quad\quad\quad \pi_c(m'_{t+1:T-1}|o_{t+1:T-1}, M(\langle m'^a_{t:T-1}, m^{-a}_{t:T-1}\rangle))];\\
&\quad\quad\quad \pi^a_c(m'^a_{t:T-1}|o^a_{t:T-1}, \mu^a_{t:T-1})]\\
&\quad= -\mathbb{E}[\mathbb{E}[G_{\text{cu}}(s_{t+2:T}, m'_{t+1:T-1}) - \mathbb{E}[G_{\text{cu}}(s_{t+2:T}, m''_{t+1:T-1});\\
&\quad\quad\quad\quad\quad\quad\quad\quad \pi_c(m''_{t+1:T-1}|o_{t+1:T-1}, \mu_{t+1:T-1})];\\
&\quad\quad\quad\quad \pi_c(m'_{t+1:T-1}|o_{t+1:T-1}, M(\langle m'^a_{t:T-1}, m^{-a}_{t:T-1}\rangle))];\\
&\quad\quad\quad \pi^a_c(m'^a_{t:T-1}|o^a_{t:T-1}, \mu^a_{t:T-1})]\\
&\quad= -\mathbb{E}[\mathbb{E}[\Delta G_{\text{cu}}(s_{t+2:T}, m'_{t+1:T-1});\\
&\quad\quad\quad\quad \pi_c(m'_{t+1:T-1}|o_{t+1:T-1}, M(\langle m'^a_{t:T-1}, m^{-a}_{t:T-1}\rangle))];\\
&\quad\quad\quad \pi^a_c(m'^a_{t:T-1}|o^a_{t:T-1}, \mu^a_{t:T-1})]
\end{aligned}
\tag{21}
$$

4.4 Communication Return Approximation

The memory requirements to calculate the communication difference returns have already been reduced by the memory-improved equations. However, calculating the CU and CC difference return can still be very computationally expensive as the expectation is under the joint action and communication policy respectively. This results in a computational complexity of $\#M^a * \prod_{a'}^{\mathcal{A}} \#U^{a'}$ where $\#M^a$ is the number of messages for agent a and $\#U^{a'}$ is the number of actions for agent a'. In the work of Vanneste *et al.*. [20], two approximation methods are compared to the exact method to calculate the CU and CC Q-values with a lower computational complexity. The results showed that the ABS (Agent-Based Sampling) approximation has a good balance between training performance and computational complexity. An adapted version of the CU return calculations, using the ABS approximation, is shown in Eq. 22. The CU Q-value calculations using ABS approximation has a computational complexity of $\#M^a * \sum_{a'}^{\mathcal{A}} \#U^{a'}$.

$$\Delta G^a_{\text{cu}}(s_{t:T}, m_{t:T-1}) =$$
$$\frac{1}{n}\sum_{a'=0}^{n} \mathbb{E}\big[G_u(s_{t+1:T}, \langle u'^{a'}_{t+1:T}, \widetilde{u}^{-a'}_{t+1:T}\rangle); \pi^{a'}_u(u'^{a'}_{t+1:T}|o^{a'}_{t+1:T}, Ma'(m_{t:T-1}))\big]$$
$$\text{with}: \widetilde{u}^{-a'}_{t+1:T} \sim \pi^{-a'}_u(o^{-a'}_{t+1:T}, \mu_{t+1:T}) \tag{22}$$

The memory-improved CU difference return calculations from Eq. 17 can then be combined with Eq. 22. This results in the final CU difference return calculation, as shown in Eq. 23, which is used for the DR.MACC-ABS method.

$$\Delta G^a_{\text{cu}}(s_{t:T}, m_t) =$$
$$-\mathbb{E}\Big[\frac{1}{n}\sum_{a'=0}^{n} \mathbb{E}\big[\Delta G_u(s_{t+1:T}, \langle u'^{a'}_{t+1:T}, \widetilde{u}^{-a'}_{t+1:T}\rangle, M(m_{t:T-1}))\big);$$
$$\pi^{a'}_u(u'^{a'}_{t+1:T}|o^{a'}_{t+1:T}, Ma'(m_{t:T-1}))\big]; \pi^a_c(m'^a_{t:T-1}|o^a_{t:T-1}, \mu^a_{t:T-1})\Big]$$
$$\text{with}: \widetilde{u}^{-a'}_{t+1:T} \sim \pi^{-a'}_u(o^{-a'}_{t+1:T}, \mu_{t+1:T}) \tag{23}$$

The calculations for the CC return have a computational complexity of $\#M^a * \prod_{a'}^{\mathcal{A}} \#M^{a'}$. The computational complexity of the CC return using ABS (see Eq. 24) can be defined as $\#M^a * \sum_{a'}^{\mathcal{A}} \#M^{a'}$.

$$\Delta G_{\text{cc}}(s_{t+1:T}, m_{t:T-1}) =$$
$$\frac{1}{n}\sum_{a'=0}^{n} \mathbb{E}\big[G_{\text{cu}}(s_{t+2:T}, \langle m'^{a'}_{t+1:T-1}, \widetilde{m}'^{-a'}_{t+1:T-1}\rangle); \pi^a_c(m'^{a'}_{t+1:T-1}|o^{a'}_{t+1:T-1}, \mu^{a'}_{t+1:T-1})\big]$$
$$\text{with}: \widetilde{m}'^{-a'}_{t+1:T-1} \sim \pi^{-a'}_c(o^{-a'}_{t+1:T}, \mu_{t+1:T}) \tag{24}$$

Equation 24 is then combined with Eq. 20 to achieve Eq. 25 which is used in the DR.MACC-ABS method to calculate the CC difference reward.

$$\Delta G^a_{\text{cc}}(s_{t:T}, m_t) = -\mathbb{E}\Big[\frac{1}{n}\sum_{a'=0}^{n} \mathbb{E}\big[G_{\text{cu}}(s_{t+2:T}, \langle m'^{a'}_{t+1:T-1}, \widetilde{m}'^{-a'}_{t+1:T-1}\rangle);$$
$$\pi^a_c(m'^{a'}_{t+1:T-1}|o^{a'}_{t+1:T-1}, \mu^{a'}_{t+1:T-1})\big];$$
$$\pi^a_c(m'^a_{t:T-1}|o^a_{t:T-1}, \mu^a_{t:T-1})\Big]$$
$$\text{with}: \widetilde{m}'^{-a'}_{t+1:T-1} \sim \pi^{-a'}_c(o^{-a'}_{t+1:T}, \mu_{t+1:T}) \tag{25}$$

4.5 Learning the Reward Function

The DR.MACC method assumes that we have access to the environment's reward function. However, we cannot always make this assumption. So, similar to the DRR.PG method, we will learn the reward function and use this to calculate the difference reward. When we learn the reward function for the

DR.MACC method, we denote it as the DRR.MACC method. The reward model is trained in a supervised manner using the data generated by the interactions of the agents with the environment. Equation 26 shows the loss function that is used to train the reward function $\bar{R}(s_t, u_t)$. The training of the reward model occurs simultaneously with the training of the agents. It is important to note that learning the reward function is significantly easier than learning a global Q-function which is required for the MACC method. This is because the reward function does not depend on the policy of the other agents when we have access to the joint action.

$$\mathcal{L}(\theta_r) = \mathbb{E}_{s_t, u_t, r_t}\left[\left(r_t - \bar{R}(s_t, u_t, \theta_r)\right)^2\right] \tag{26}$$

4.6 DR.MACC in a Dec-POMDP

Additionally, we also provide the difference return equations which are more suitable for a Dec-POMDP by including a history τ of the past observations and actions. It is important to note that the reward function is only a function of the current state and the current joint action because the reward function is independent of the policy of the agents when we have access to the joint action of the agents.

$$\Delta R^a(o_t, \tau_t, u_t) = r_t - \sum_{u_t'^a} \pi_u^a(u_t'^a|\tau_t^a) R(o_t, \langle u_t'^a, u_t^{-a} \rangle) \tag{27}$$

$$\Delta G_u^a(o_{t:T}, \tau_{t:T}, u_{t:T}) \triangleq \sum_{k=t}^{T} \gamma^{k-t} \Delta R^a(o_k, \tau_k, u_k) \tag{28}$$

These equations can then be used by the memory-improved CU difference return equation as shown in Eq. 29.

$$\begin{aligned} \Delta G_{\text{cu}}^a(o_{t:T}, \tau_{t:T}, m_t) = -\mathbb{E}\Big[\mathbb{E}\big[\Delta G_u(o_{t+1:T}, \tau_{t:T}, u'_{t+1:T}, M(m_{t:T-1})));\\ \pi_u(u'_{t+1:T}|\tau_{t+1:T}, M(\langle m_{t:T-1}'^a, m_{t:T-1}^{-a}\rangle))\big]; \pi_c^a(m_{t:T-1}'^a|\tau_{t:T-1}^a, \mu_{t:T-1}^a)\Big] \end{aligned} \tag{29}$$

Similarly, the memory-improved CC difference return equation can be adapted to include the history as shown in Eq. 30.

$$\begin{aligned} \Delta G_{\text{cc}}^a(o_{t:T}, \tau_{t:T}, m_t) = -\mathbb{E}\Big[\mathbb{E}\big[\Delta G_{\text{cu}}(o_{t+2:T}, \tau_{t+2:T}, m'_{t+1:T-1});\\ \pi_c(m'_{t+1:T-1}|\tau_{t+1:T-1}, M(\langle m_{t:T-1}'^a, m_{t:T-1}^{-a}\rangle))\big]; \pi_c^a(m_{t:T-1}'^a|\tau_{t:T-1}^a, \mu_{t:T-1}^a)\Big] \end{aligned} \tag{30}$$

5 Results

In this section, the DR.MACC and DRR.MACC methods are compared to the Q-variant of MACC [20], using a centralized critic, which we will denote as Q-learning MACC (Q.MACC). Additionally, we also compared with an independent variant of MACC which uses an independent Q-function. Here, every agent uses a decentralized critic based on its observation and action. This variant of the MACC method is denoted as Independent Q-Learning MACC (IQL.MACC). The IQL.MACC variant allows us to compare both the centralized and decentralized critic variants. This variant enables us to demonstrate the importance of a centralized critic in learning to communicate because this is not the case for every environment as described by Lyu *et al.*. [8]. The different methods all use the ABS (Agent-Based Sampling) method [20] to reduce the computational cost. We used the speaker with multiple listener's environment from the work of Vanneste *et al.*. [20] which is based on the speaker listener setting from the Particle environment [7]. In this environment, n listeners need to go towards one of three target landmarks in a 2D world. However, the listeners do not know to which landmark they need to go. This information is only available to the speaker, so it needs to share this information with the listener agents by learning a certain communication protocol. The speaker agent can use two bits of information to share this information with the listener agents. The agents are trained using a shared reward which is the negative average distance of the different listeners to their target landmark. This means that a set of optimal agents can achieve an average return of -15 independently of the number of listeners in the environment. No specific reward is presented to the agents for sharing information between the speaker and listeners, so the agents need to learn a communication protocol to minimize the distance between the listeners and their target landmarks. This environment allows us to easily test the scalability of the different methods by increasing the number of listeners and comparing the average return. We tested the different methods in three different configurations with One, two and four listeners. Additionally, the difference reward variants are also evaluated with eight listeners. In our experiments, we used the same agent configuration and implementation for the different methods and only adapt the method to calculate the advantage or difference reward. The different agents are trained under the CTDE paradigm, so we allowed the agents to share network parameters during training. Every method and number of listeners combination is trained five times after which the results are combined into a training graph and violin graph of the average return of the final episodes. The data of the training graphs are processed to show the interquartile mean and the bootstrapped 90% confidence interval. These results are shown in Figs. 4, 5, 6, and 7.

The results show that the IQL.MACC variant is not able to learn a communication policy for any number of listeners. This is because a decentralized critic is not able to properly estimate the expected discounted reward without the observation of the listener. The Q.MACC can learn a valid communication protocol in the configuration with one listener because an average return of -15 is achieved. However, when the number of listeners is increased to two, the Q.MACC method cannot achieve this. When we increase the number of listeners to four, the Q.MACC method cannot learn a valid action policy and achieves an average return of -400 in the final episodes. The results of the DRR.MACC method, which uses a learned reward function, can outperform the Q.MACC method in every tested configuration. Although the DRR.MACC method achieves bet-

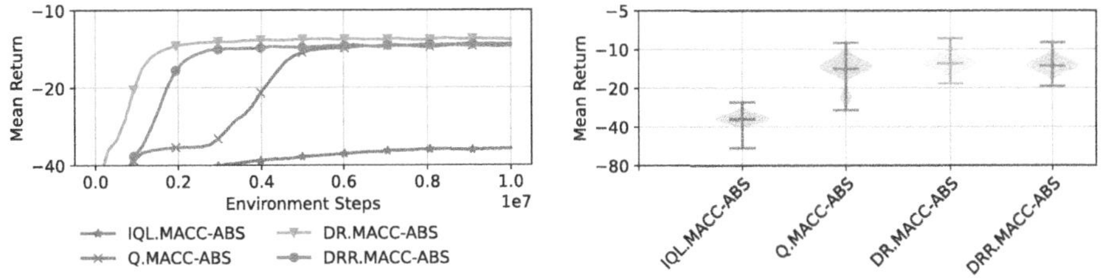

(a) Training Graph (b) Return of the Final Episodes

Fig. 4. Speaker with One Listener.

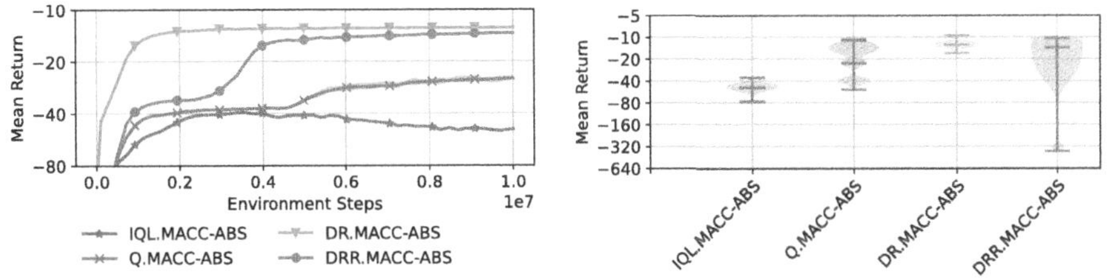

(a) Training Graph (b) Return of the Final Episodes

Fig. 5. Speaker with Two Listeners.

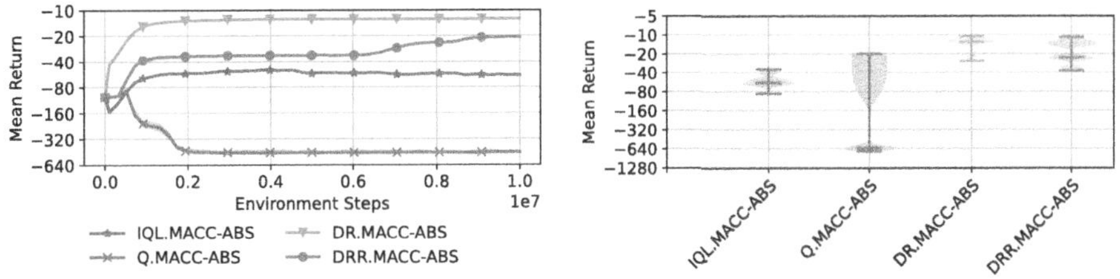

(a) Training Graph (b) Return of the Final Episodes

Fig. 6. Speaker with Four Listeners.

ter results than the Q.MACC method, the method cannot learn a set of valid policies for the configuration with eight listeners where it achieves an average return of -400. The DR.MACC method, which uses the environment's reward function, can learn a valid communication policy for every configuration. These results show that the main factor which determines the agents' performance, is the accuracy of the Q-function or Reward function. Since the reward function is much easier to learn, the DRR.MACC method can learn with a higher number of agents compared to the Q.MACC method. When using the reward function directly, which is perfectly accurate by definition, the DR.MACC method can learn within all the tested configurations.

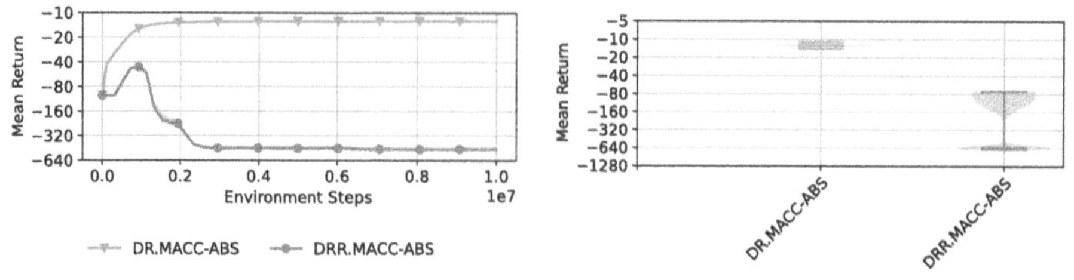

(a) Training Graph (b) Return of the Final Episodes

Fig. 7. Speaker with Eight Listeners.

6 Conclusion

In this work, we presented the DR.MACC and the DRR.MACC methods. These methods combine the benefits of two methods. First, the MACC method [20] enables us to learn a discrete communication policy by using counterfactual reasoning over the policy of the other agents. Next, the DR.PG method [1] allows us to calculate an agent-specific return by the reward function or a trained approximation instead of the more complex Q-function. To reduce the memory requirements of the computations, we provided a set of memory-improved equations for the communication difference return which can reuse the action difference return directly. However, these calculations still depend on the expectation of the joint action and joint communication policy of the agents which is very computationally expensive using the exact method. To reduce this computational cost to a great extent, we used the ABS (Agent-Based Sampling) method from the work of Vanneste *et al.*. [20]. The results show that the IQL.MACC method, using the individual Q-function, is not able to learn a communication protocol because the critic cannot access the observation of the speaker. However, the Q.MACC method can learn a communication protocol for one listener but encounters scalability problems in the configuration with two and four listeners because of the need to learn a joint Q-function. The DRR.MACC method outperforms the Q.MACC method in every tested configuration but cannot learn a set of policies for the eight listener's environment. The DR.MACC method, using the reward function directly, can learn a valid action and communication policy in every tested configuration. In future work, the DR.MACC and DRR.MACC methods could be evaluated in a Dec-POMDP using the adaptions to the difference return as presented in Sect. 4.6. Additionally, other approximation methods to calculate the communication difference return could be investigated.

Acknowledgments. Simon Vanneste and Astrid Vanneste are supported by the Research Foundation Flanders (FWO) under Grant Number 1S94120N and Grant Number 1S12121N respectively.

Disclosure of Interests. The authors have no competing interests to declare that are relevant to the content of this article.

References

1. Castellini, J., Devlin, S., Oliehoek, F.A., Savani, R.: Difference rewards policy gradients (2021)
2. Chang, Y.H., Ho, T., Kaelbling, L.: All learning is local: multi-agent learning in global reward games. In: Advances in Neural Information Processing Systems, vol. 16 (2003)
3. Das, A., et al.: Tarmac: targeted multi-agent communication. In: International Conference on Machine Learning, pp. 1538–1546. PMLR (2019)
4. Foerster, J., Assael, I.A., De Freitas, N., Whiteson, S.: Learning to communicate with deep multi-agent reinforcement learning. In: Advances in Neural Information Processing Systems, vol. 29 (2016)
5. Foerster, J., Farquhar, G., Afouras, T., Nardelli, N., Whiteson, S.: Counterfactual multi-agent policy gradients. In: Proceedings of the AAAI Conference on Artificial Intelligence, vol. 32 (2018)
6. Jaques, N., et al.: Social influence as intrinsic motivation for multi-agent deep reinforcement learning. In: International Conference on Machine Learning, pp. 3040–3049. PMLR (2019)
7. Lowe, R., Wu, Y.I., Tamar, A., Harb, J., Pieter Abbeel, O., Mordatch, I.: Multi-agent actor-critic for mixed cooperative-competitive environments. In: Advances in Neural Information Processing Systems, vol. 30 (2017)
8. Lyu, X., Xiao, Y., Daley, B., Amato, C.: Contrasting centralized and decentralized critics in multi-agent reinforcement learning (2021)
9. Mandhane, A., et al.: Muzero with self-competition for rate control in vp9 video compression. arXiv preprint arXiv:2202.06626 (2022)
10. Mnih, V., et al.: Asynchronous methods for deep reinforcement learning. In: International Conference on Machine Learning, pp. 1928–1937. PMLR (2016)
11. Mnih, V., et al.: Human-level control through deep reinforcement learning. Nature **518**(7540), 529–533 (2015)
12. Oliehoek, F.A., Amato, C.: A Concise Introduction to Decentralized POMDPs. Springer, Cham (2016)
13. Oliehoek, F.A., Vlassis, N.: Q-value functions for decentralized POMDPs. In: Proceedings of the 6th International Joint Conference on Autonomous Agents and Multiagent Systems, pp. 1–8 (2007)
14. Van der Pol, E., Oliehoek, F.A.: Coordinated deep reinforcement learners for traffic light control. In: Proceedings of Learning, Inference and Control of Multi-Agent Systems (at NIPS 2016) (2016)
15. Silver, D., Lever, G., Heess, N., Degris, T., Wierstra, D., Riedmiller, M.: Deterministic policy gradient algorithms. In: International Conference on Machine Learning, pp. 387–395. PMLR (2014)
16. Sukhbaatar, S., Fergus, R., et al.: Learning multiagent communication with backpropagation. In: Advances in Neural Information Processing Systems, vol. 29 (2016)
17. Sutton, R.S., Barto, A.G.: Introduction to Reinforcement Learning, 1st edn. MIT Press, Cambridge (1998)
18. Van Hasselt, H., Guez, A., Silver, D.: Deep reinforcement learning with double q-learning. In: Proceedings of the AAAI Conference on Artificial Intelligence, vol. 30 (2016)
19. Vanneste, S., et al.: Learning to communicate with reinforcement learning for an adaptive traffic control system. In: Barolli, L. (ed.) 3PGCIC 2021. LNNS, vol. 343, pp. 207–216. Springer, Cham (2022). https://doi.org/10.1007/978-3-030-89899-1_21

20. Vanneste, S., et al.: Learning to communicate using counterfactual reasoning. In: Proceedings of the Adaptive and Learning Agents Workshop (ALA 2022). Adaptive and Learning Agents Workshop (ALA 2022) (2022)
21. Wolpert, D.H., Tumer, K.: Optimal payoff functions for members of collectives. Adv. Complex Syst. **4**(02n03), 265–279 (2001)

Forecast Reconciliation for Vaccine Supply Chain Optimization

Bhanu Angam[1], Alessandro Beretta[2], Eli De Poorter[1], Matthieu Duvinage[2], and Daniel Peralta[1](✉)

[1] IDLab, Department of Information Technology, Ghent University - imec, Technologiepark 126, 9052 Gent, Belgium
bhanu.angam@talentguide.com, {eli.depoorter,daniel.peralta}@ugent.de
[2] GSK, Avenue Fleming, 20, 1300 Wavre, Belgium
{alessandro.x.beretta,matthieu.x.duvinage}@gsk.com

Abstract. Vaccine supply chain optimization can benefit from hierarchical time series forecasting, when grouping the vaccines by type or location. However, forecasts of different hierarchy levels become incoherent when higher levels do not match the sum of the lower levels forecasts, which can be addressed by reconciliation methods.

In this paper, we tackle the vaccine sale forecasting problem by modeling sales data from GSK between 2010 and 2021 as a hierarchical time series. After forecasting future values with several ARIMA models, we systematically compare the performance of various reconciliation methods, using statistical tests. We also compare the performance of the forecast before and after COVID. The results highlight Minimum Trace and Weighted Least Squares with Structural scaling as the best performing methods, which provided a coherent forecast while reducing the forecast error of the baseline ARIMA.

Keywords: Time series reconciliation · Hierarchical time series · ARIMA · Time series forecasting · Supply chain optimization · Vaccine

1 Introduction

Forecasting vaccine demand is critical to practitioners; its underestimation lead to loss of customers and profits, whereas its overestimation would cause the expiry of produced vaccines and a waste of resources [2,10]. Vaccine demand forecasting is mostly done by replicating values from previous years [7,15], sometimes combining them with demographic information [9]. However, machine learning techniques become necessary to obtain better solutions to this problem.

Given enough previous data, vaccine demand can be modeled as a time series, that is, a sequence of values measured in fixed time intervals [13]. There are various methods to forecast future values in a time series. Among them, linear methods like ARIMA are still widely used, due to their interpretability and stability. In many domains, time series can be arranged in the form of a hierarchy [14].

F. A. Oliehoek et al. (Eds.): BNAIC/Benelearn 2023, CCIS 2187, pp. 101–118, 2025.
https://doi.org/10.1007/978-3-031-74650-5_6

For instance, sales can be split into geographical regions or product types, where the series at one level corresponds to the sum of the values of the series at the immediately lower level. Each of these time series can be independently forecast; however, the coherency of the time series is lost: the forecast of a higher level does not correspond to the sum of the forecasts of lower levels.

Forecast combination methods ensure the coherency of the forecasts by only forecasting the series at one level (typically the highest or the lowest), and then calculating the forecasts for the rest of the hierarchy [11,12]. Their main limitation is that they use only one level of the hierarchy to compute the forecasts. Forecasting reconciliation aims at obtaining coherent forecasts based on the entire hierarchy [1,12,13]. Several methods have been proposed in the field, such as Ordinary Least Squares [14], Weighted Least Squares [13] and Trace Minimization [17]. Frequently, the values of the time series are limited to a certain range, which is often the positive real or integer numbers. Positive outcomes when forecasting are usually enforced by taking the logarithm of the series; however, when applying the reconciliation in the original space it is possible that some forecasts become negative. Therefore, some methods have been proposed to enforce positive reconciled forecasts [18].

There are a few works in the scientific literature that model vaccine demand as a time series and then forecast future values. In [16], ARIMA was applied to forecast vaccine demand in Indonesia. In [4], a cloud infrastructure used a Long Short-Term Memory (LSTM) to forecast the demand for COVID-19 vaccines. However, none of these works consider hierarchical time series to forecast vaccine demand.

In this paper, we compare several state-of-the-art combination and reconciliation methods to adjust the ARIMA forecast of the vaccine sales of a hierarchy of products across several geographical areas. We also evaluate the impact of COVID-19 on the sales, analyzing how the forecast error increases after COVID-19 due to large unexpected changes in demand patterns. We carry out a series of statistical tests on the obtained results, and come to the conclusion that, for this dataset, Minimum Trace and Weighted Least Squares with Structural scaling were the best performing reconciliation methods, achieving reconciled forecasts while also lowering the forecast error.

The main contributions of this paper are the following:

- Comparison of various combination and reconciliation methods for adjusting the ARIMA forecast of vaccine sales in a hierarchical product structure.
- Evaluation of the impact of COVID-19 on sales and demonstrating an increase in forecast error due to changes in demand patterns.
- Finally, through statistical tests, we conclude that Minimum Trace and Weighted Least Squares with Structural scaling are the best performing and most robust reconciliation methods for the dataset used.

This paper is structured as follows. First, Sect. 2 introduces the topic of forecast recombination and reconciliation in hierarchical time series. Section 3 describes the methodology carried out in this study, including the dataset analyzed and its preprocessing. The results of the experiments are presented and analyzed in Sect. 4. Finally, Sect. 5 presents the conclusions of this study.

2 Background

2.1 Hierarchical Time Series

In a hierarchical time series, the values of a particular level can be expressed as the sum of values at the immediately lower level. A hierarchical time series with n observations, k levels, a total of m series, and m_i series in level i can be expressed as a matrix $\mathbf{Y}_t$ with dimensions $m \times n$, where each row contains one of the time series. Therefore, the hierarchical time series can be expressed as $\mathbf{Y}_t = \mathbf{S}\mathbf{Y}_{k,t}$, where $\mathbf{S}$ is a summing matrix with dimensions $m \times m_k$ and $\mathbf{Y}_{k,t}$ contains the series at the bottom level of the hierarchy. The example hierarchy shown in Fig. 1 can be represented as (1). Note that the bottom m_k rows of $\mathbf{S}$ are the identity matrix $\mathbf{I}_{m_k}$.

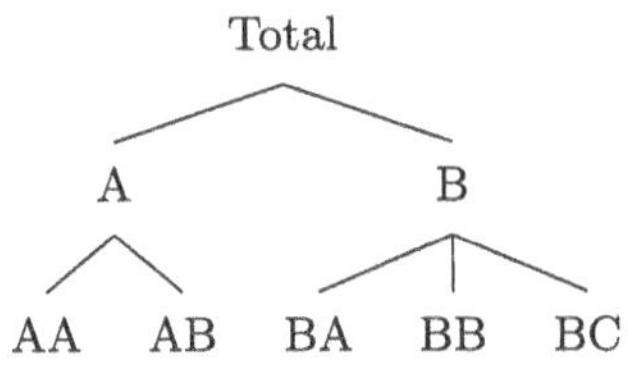

Fig. 1. Example of a simple hierarchy

$$\begin{bmatrix} Y_{T,t} \\ Y_{A,t} \\ Y_{B,t} \\ Y_{AA,t} \\ Y_{AB,t} \\ Y_{BA,t} \\ Y_{BB,t} \\ Y_{BC,t} \end{bmatrix} = \begin{bmatrix} 1\,1\,1\,1\,1 \\ 1\,1\,0\,0\,0 \\ 0\,0\,1\,1\,1 \\ 1\,0\,0\,0\,0 \\ 0\,1\,0\,0\,0 \\ 0\,0\,1\,0\,0 \\ 0\,0\,0\,1\,0 \\ 0\,0\,0\,0\,1 \end{bmatrix} \begin{bmatrix} Y_{AA,t} \\ Y_{AB,t} \\ Y_{BA,t} \\ Y_{BB,t} \\ Y_{BC,t} \end{bmatrix} \tag{1}$$

In general, given h-step-ahead independent forecasts for the base series $\hat{\mathbf{Y}}_n(h)$, a final forecast $\tilde{\mathbf{Y}}_n(h)$ can be estimated for all series as shown in (2), where $\mathbf{G}$ is an $m_k \times m$ matrix.

$$\tilde{\mathbf{Y}}_n(h) = \mathbf{S}\mathbf{G}\hat{\mathbf{Y}}_n(h) \tag{2}$$

2.2 Forecast Combination

Forecast combination methods [5] typically forecast the time series of one hierarchy level, and extrapolate the forecasts via aggregation or proportion. In this way, the coherence of the forecasts is guaranteed.

Bottom-Up (BU). It is arguably the simplest hierarchical forecast method, consisting of forecasting only the base level of the hierarchy, and then aggregating the forecasts using $\mathbf{S}$ for the rest of the hierarchy. The matrix $\mathbf{G}$ is defined as shown in (3), which yields $\mathbf{SG}_{\mathbf{BU}} = \mathbf{S}$.

$$\mathbf{G}_{BU} = \left[\mathbf{0}_{m_k \times (m-m_k)} \; \mathbf{I}_{m_k}\right] \tag{3}$$

Top-Down (TD). It computes forecasts only for the top level of the hierarchy, and then splits the values across all hierarchical levels using factors, which are estimated from previous values of the series. Typically, the proportions of historical averages $\mathbf{p}$ are used [1,3], as shown in (4), in combination with matrix $\mathbf{G}$ (5). A drawback of this approach is that the forecasts are biased, for any $\mathbf{p}$, even if the base forecasts are unbiased [14].

$$p_j = \frac{\sum_{t=1}^{n} Y_{j,t}}{\sum_{t=1}^{n} Y_t}, \quad j = 1, \ldots, m_k \tag{4}$$

$$\mathbf{G}_{TD} = \left[\mathbf{p} \; \mathbf{0}_{m_k \times (m-1)}\right] \tag{5}$$

2.3 Forecast Reconciliation

Forecast reconciliation methods, although sometimes categorized as combination methods, have the particularity that a forecast is computed for every individual time series in the hierarchy, and these forecasts are then adjusted to increase their coherence.

Generalized Least Squares (GLS). The base forecasts can be rewritten as in (6), where $\boldsymbol{\beta}_n(h)$ is the unknown mean of the future values of the bottom level of the hierarchy, and $\boldsymbol{\epsilon}_h$ has zero mean and covariance matrix $\boldsymbol{\Sigma}_h$. Additionally, Hyndman et al. [14] demonstrated that adjusted forecasts (following (2)) are unbiased if and only if constraint (7) is met.

$$\begin{aligned}\hat{\mathbf{Y}}_n(h) &= \mathbf{S}\boldsymbol{\beta}_n(h) + \boldsymbol{\epsilon}_h \\ \boldsymbol{\beta}_n(h) &= E[\mathbf{Y}_{k,n+h} | \mathbf{Y}_1, \ldots, \mathbf{Y}_{m_k}]\end{aligned} \tag{6}$$

$$\mathbf{SGS} = \mathbf{S} \tag{7}$$

Combining these definitions, an unbiased estimate for $\boldsymbol{\beta}_n(h)$ can be obtained by GLS estimation as in (8), where $\boldsymbol{\Sigma}_h^{\dagger}$ is the Moore-Penrose pseudoinverse of $\boldsymbol{\Sigma}_h$. The main difficulty with this formulation is that estimating $\boldsymbol{\Sigma}_h$ and subsequently computing $\boldsymbol{\Sigma}_h^{\dagger}$ can be difficult for large hierarchies. The different reconciliation methods described in the next few subsections use different estimates for $\boldsymbol{\Sigma}_h$.

$$\begin{aligned}\hat{\boldsymbol{\beta}}_n(h) &= (\mathbf{S}'\boldsymbol{\Sigma}_h^{\dagger}\mathbf{S})^{-1}\mathbf{S}'\boldsymbol{\Sigma}_h^{\dagger}\hat{\mathbf{Y}}_n(h) \\ \tilde{\mathbf{Y}}_n(h) &= \mathbf{S}\hat{\boldsymbol{\beta}}_n(h) = \mathbf{S}\mathbf{G}_{GLS}\hat{\mathbf{Y}}_n(h) \\ \mathbf{G}_{GLS} &= (\mathbf{S}'\boldsymbol{\Sigma}_h^{\dagger}\mathbf{S})^{-1}\mathbf{S}'\boldsymbol{\Sigma}_h^{\dagger}\end{aligned} \tag{8}$$

Ordinary Least Squares (OLS). By assuming that the errors are aggregated across the hierarchy in the same way as the series themselves ($\epsilon_h \approx \mathbf{S}\epsilon_{k,h}$), OLS can be applied and $\mathbf{G}$ can be derived as shown in (9) [14]. Interestingly, this optimal value for $\mathbf{G}$ depends exclusively on the summing matrix and not on the data itself.

$$\mathbf{G}_{OLS} = \mathbf{S}(\mathbf{S}'\mathbf{S})^{-1}\mathbf{S}' \tag{9}$$

Minimum Trace (MinT). Wickramasuriya et al. [17] showed that the covariance matrix of the coherent forecast errors follows (10), where $\mathbf{W}_h$ is the covariance matrix of the base forecast errors. In this setting, we want to find the $\mathbf{G}$ that minimizes the error variances, whose sum is the trace of $\mathbf{V}_h$, while respecting the constraint for an unbiased forecast in (7), as shown in (11).

$$\begin{aligned} \mathbf{V}_h &= \mathrm{Var}\left[\mathbf{Y}_{n+h} - \tilde{\mathbf{Y}}_n(h)\right] = \mathbf{S}\mathbf{G}\mathbf{W}_h\mathbf{G}'\mathbf{S}' \\ \mathbf{W}_h &= \mathrm{Var}\left[\mathbf{Y}_{n+h} - \hat{\mathbf{Y}}_n(h)\right] \end{aligned} \tag{10}$$

$$\begin{aligned} \mathbf{G}_{MinT} &= (\mathbf{S}'\mathbf{W}_h^{-1}\mathbf{S})^{-1}\mathbf{S}'\mathbf{W}_h^{-1} \\ \tilde{\mathbf{Y}}_n(h) &= \mathbf{S}(\mathbf{S}'\mathbf{W}_h^{-1}\mathbf{S})^{-1}\mathbf{S}'\mathbf{W}_h^{-1}\hat{\mathbf{Y}}_n(h) \end{aligned} \tag{11}$$

Naturally, $\mathbf{W}_h$ is unknown and has to be estimated from the training data; different estimates yield different reconciliation methods. Note that assuming that $\mathbf{G}$ is independent of the data—and therefore $\mathbf{W}_h = \mathbf{I}_\mathbf{m}$—yields OLS. Also, note that the estimates of $\mathbf{W}_h$ usually include a scaling factor in the original publications [13,17], which is only relevant when computing confidence intervals and is canceled out when applying (11). For the sake of simplicity, in this paper we assume that the constant is 1.

Equation (12) shows a more relaxed assumption: that the error covariance matrices are proportional to each other. This allows us to estimate the matrix for $h = 1$, and derive $\mathbf{W}_h$ from it. In this case, $\mathbf{W}_1$ is estimated based on the sample covariance of the residuals. Throughout this paper, this is the method we will refer to as *MinT*.

$$\mathbf{W}_h = \mathbf{W}_1 \tag{12}$$

Weighted Least Squares with Variance Scaling (WLSV). When $\mathbf{W}_h$ is defined as in (13), where $\mathbf{e}_t$ is an m-dimensional vector containing the residuals of the base models trained on each series, the weights for each series are scaled according to the variance of the residuals of the base forecasts.

$$\begin{aligned} \mathbf{W}_h &= \mathrm{diag}(\hat{\mathbf{W}}_1) \\ \hat{\mathbf{W}}_1 &= \frac{1}{T}\sum_{t=1}^{T}\mathbf{e}_t\mathbf{e}_t' \end{aligned} \tag{13}$$

Weighted Least Squares with Structural Scaling (WLSS). In this case, we define $\mathbf{W}_h$ as in (14). In other words, each value along the diagonal of $\mathbf{W}_h$ corresponds to the sum of the corresponding row in $\mathbf{S}$, which makes it dependent exclusively on the structure of the hierarchy and not on the values of the time series nor the models.

$$\mathbf{W}_h = \text{diag}(\mathbf{S}\mathbf{1}_{m_k}) \tag{14}$$

Non-negative Reconciliation (NNOLS and NNMinT). Previously described methods do not ensure that the reconciled forecasts are non-negative, which is a constraint in many real-life problems. In fact, a sufficient condition for the non-negativity of $\tilde{\mathbf{Y}}_n(h)$ is that vectors $\tilde{\mathbf{b}}_n(h) = \mathbf{G}\hat{\mathbf{Y}}_n(h)$ should be non-negative, as can be derived from (2). In [18], it is demonstrated that this the optimal $\tilde{\mathbf{b}}_n(h)$ is the solution of the quadratic programming problem in (15).

$$\begin{aligned} \tilde{\mathbf{b}}_n(h) = \min_{\mathring{\mathbf{b}}} \frac{1}{2}\mathring{\mathbf{b}}'\mathbf{S}'\mathbf{W}_h^{-1}\mathbf{S}\mathring{\mathbf{b}} - \mathring{\mathbf{b}}'\mathbf{S}'\mathbf{W}_h^{-1}\hat{\mathbf{Y}}_n(h) \\ s.t.\ \mathring{b}_i \geq 0 \quad \forall i \in \{1, \ldots, m\} \end{aligned} \tag{15}$$

3 Forecast Reconciliation of Vaccine Sales

In this paper, we applied classic and state of the art methods to reconcile vaccine sales hierarchical time series. Section 3.1 describes the dataset tackled. Then, Sect. 3.2 describes the preprocessing applied on the dataset, Sect. 3.3 depicts the combination and reconciliation methods that were considered in this study, and Sect. 3.4 describes the model selection prodecure followed to choose the hyperparameters for the forecast.

3.1 Dataset

The dataset used for this study consists of monthly vaccine sales from GSK, between years 2010 and 2021. The time series hierarchy has 5 levels: commercial segment, product family, aggregated product, product type and stock keeping unit. To ensure that the lowest level time series contain sufficient data, we focus on the top 3 levels of the hierarchy (noted as CS, PF and AP respectively), which are composed by 3, 10 and 16 time series, respectively, as shown in Fig. 2. It is noteworthy that some series start later than 2010, typically because they refer to recently developed products.

Because the time series represent sales numbers, their values are, in general, non-negative integers. However, the raw time series collected directly from the sales department also contains corrections done at the end of the year to compensate for registration errors and ensure that yearly totals are correct. This causes some of the time series values to have unexpectedly large or small values, leading to negative values and breaking seasonal patterns, which in turns adds to the complexity of the problem.

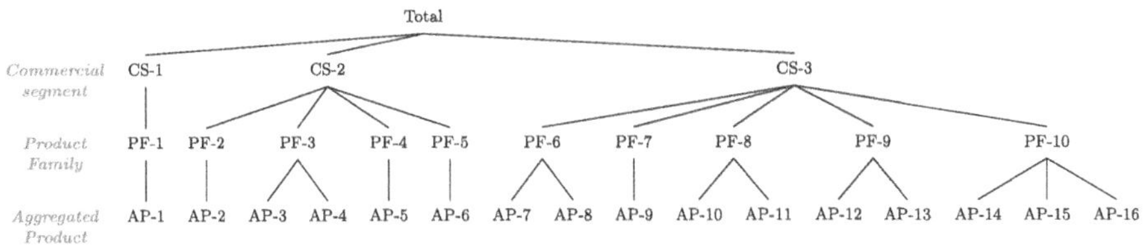

Fig. 2. Hierarchical representation of the dataset

The data was split into training and forecast periods. Due to a potentially different behavior of the time series during the COVID-19 pandemic, two different splits were considered, which either excluded the pandemic period from the data, or included it entirely in the forecast period, as shown in Table 1.

Table 1. Train and forecast period splits of data

Period	Before COVID-19	After COVID-19
Training	2010–2017	2010–2019
Forecasting	2018–2019	2020–2021

3.2 Preprocessing

Negative values in the time series were replaced by a linear interpolation of the preceding and following values, while shifting all the values for that year proportionally, to ensure that the total sales volume for the year remains the same. This was done at the PF level of the hierarchy.

The outlier detection was carried out by first applying a Seasonal and Trend decomposition using Loess decomposition (STL) [8], to extract seasonal, trend and remainder components from the series. Then, values in the remainder that deviate from the quartiles by more than 3 times the inter-quartile range were considered to be outliers, following other works in the field [13]. As an example, Figs. 3 and 4 show the STL decomposition and the corrected outliers of time series PF3, which is clearly seasonal.

3.3 Forecasting

The entire pipeline applied on this problem is shown on Fig. 5. The time series were normalized with a Box-Cox transformation (16), estimating λ via profile likelihood function and goodness of fit tests for normality, and with $\lambda_2 = \min y_i$. After normalization, we train a seasonal ARIMA model for each time series in the hierarchy. Naturally, each of these time series might have a different seasonality

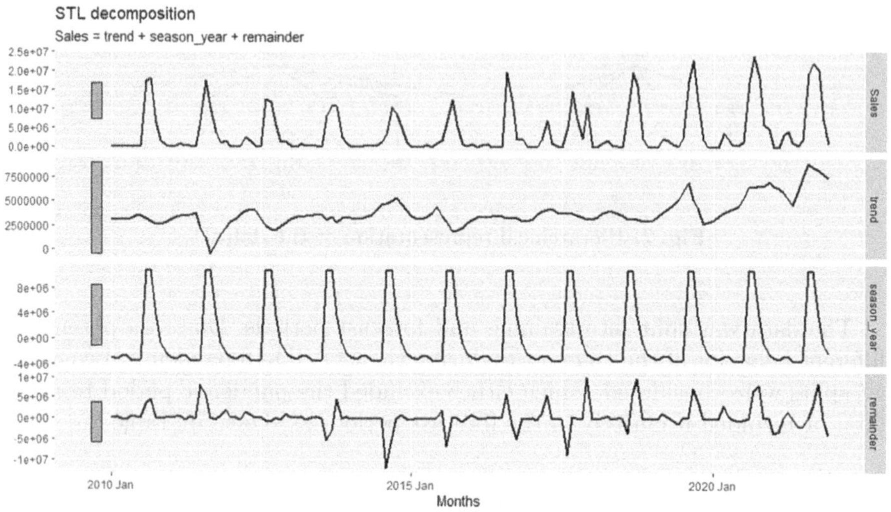

Fig. 3. STL decomposition of PF3

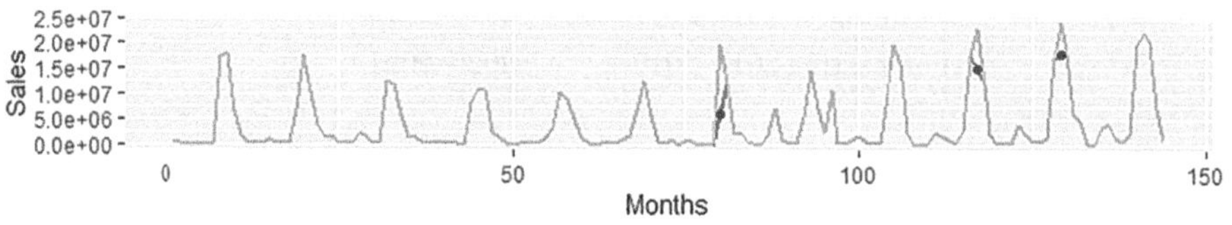

Fig. 4. STL decomposition and outlier detection on the remainder component

and dependencies on lagged values; therefore, a model selection has to be done when training each series.

$$y_i^{(\lambda)} = \begin{cases} \frac{(y_i+\lambda_2)^\lambda - 1}{\lambda} & \text{if } \lambda \neq 0 \\ \ln(y_i + \lambda_2) & \text{if } \lambda = 0 \end{cases} \tag{16}$$

3.4 Model Selection

To compute the baseline forecasts of the time series, Seasonal ARIMA [13] models were trained with 4 different parameters for the seasonality (1, 3, 6 and 12) months. Additionally, the non-seasonal (p, d and q) and seasonal (P, D and Q) parameters of ARIMA must be chosen. The differencing term d was estimated using two tests—Kwiatkowski, Phillips, Schmidt-Shin (KPSS) and Dickey-Fuller (ADF)—and taking the maximum value from both. The seasonal differencing D was estimated by Osborn, Chui, Smith, and Birchenhall (OCSB) test. The remaining parameters were estimated via a grid search within the training set, using Akaike's Information Criterion (AIC) as the optimized metric.

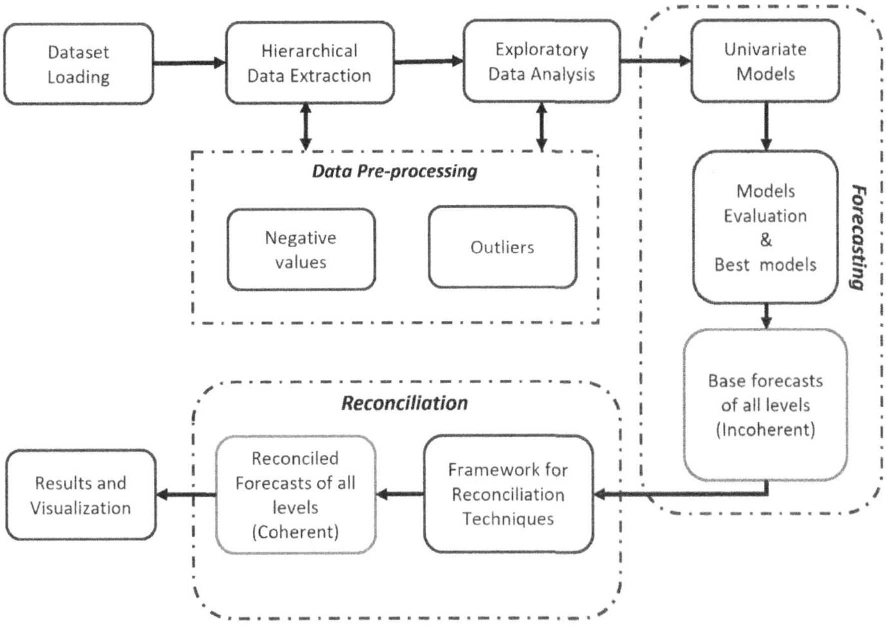

Fig. 5. General workflow of the proposal

After the 6 hyperparameters for each seasonality have been optimized, we must select the seasonal frequency that obtains the best results. This is done by choosing the one that yields the best symmetric mean absolute percentage error (SMAPE). To this purpose, a specific variant of cross-validation is applied (rolling forecasting origin [6]), where the size of the training set is increased for each iteration, and the validation set has a fixed size and always starts immediately after the training set (Fig. 6).

The rolling forecasting origin was performed with a minimum training set size of 28 months, and a validation set size of 2 months, increasing the size of the training set 1 month at a time. As there are a total of 84 months in the entire training set, this yielded 54 pairs of training and validation sets.

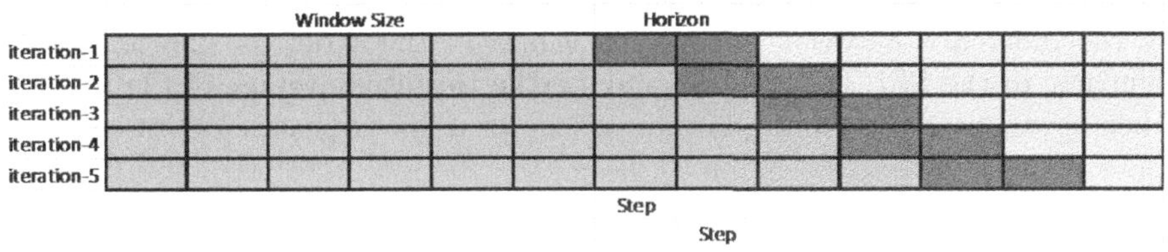

Fig. 6. Cross-validation by rolling origin (training in green, validation in red) (Color figure online)

3.5 Reconciliation

After computing the forecast for all time series, we reconcile the forecasts using the methods described in Sect. 2.3, namely BU, OLS, NNOLS, WLSS, WLSV and MINT.

3.6 Performance Measures

Two measures were used to evaluate the forecasts and their reconciliations.

Sales Forecast Bias (SFB). It measures the tendencies to over- and underforecast along a certain period of length T, rather than at individual points in time. This measure is often used by companies to evaluate sales predictions, because an over-estimation in a certain month can be compensated by an equivalent under-estimation in the following month (or vice-versa). Furthermore, this measurement is robust to the tendency of companies (for instance, in accountancy) to account for errors in a certain month by applying an equivalent correction on a subsequent month, rather than by editing the previously stored value. The SFB of a certain time series i is computed as shown in (17). Therefore, the lower the value of the SFB, the better.

$$SFB_i = \frac{\sum_{s=1}^{T} \left[\hat{Y}_{i,n-s}(h) - Y_{i,n-s}(h)\right]}{\sum_{s=1}^{T} Y_{i,n-s}(h)} \times 100 \tag{17}$$

In this work, we calculated the SFB as a percentage over a period of 6 months ($T = 6$). To aggregate results for multiple time series while avoiding the cancellation of positive and negative errors, we computed the weighted average of the absolute values of SFB for all series (volume-Weighted SFB, WSFB, (18)), where the weight w_i is the sum of all values of a time series:

$$\begin{aligned} WSFB &= \frac{\sum_{i=1}^{m} w_i SFB_i}{\sum_{i=1}^{m} w_i} \\ w_i &= \sum Y_{i,t} \end{aligned} \tag{18}$$

Root Mean Squared Scaled Error (RMSSE). An error measure scaled by the difference between consecutive values in the series as shown in (19). Similarly to the SFB in (18), we compute the weighted average of the RMSSE when aggregating over multiple time series, for a fair comparison between time series.

$$RMSSE = \sqrt{\frac{\frac{1}{h}\sum_{t=n+1}^{n+h}(y_t - \hat{y}_t)^2}{\frac{1}{n-1}\sum_{t=2}^{n}(y_t - y_{t-1})^2}} \tag{19}$$

4 Results

This section describes the results obtained from the experiments. First, baseline results are presented in Sect. 4.1. The results of the different reconciliation methods are shown in Sect. 4.2. Section 4.3 compares the behavior of the results, and finally Sect. 4.4 presents a general discussion of the results.

4.1 Baseline Forecasting

Table 2 and Fig. 7 present an overview of the SFB and RMSSE obtained using the baseline forecast method for each series, at each level of the hierarchy. As expected, it can clearly be seen that the highest level in the hierarchy (Commercial segment) is easier to predict than lower levels, whose series are subject to a higher variability. However, the difference in forecast error between the two lowest levels is very small, and the range of obtained errors differs greatly. Some series are very accurately predicted, while others have a large forecast error.

These observations are due to several factors. First, lower time series have a smaller scale, and therefore are more subject to noise and variability. Second, they can also display very different behaviors (seasonal/non-seasonal, cyclic/non-cyclic, with/without zero values...), which causes that some series are easier to predict than others. When considered aggregately in higher levels of the hierarchy, the time series become more predictable, as the noise becomes smaller in relation to the scale of the values.

Additionally, we observe that the plots also reflect an increase in the errors after COVID-19, despite the fact that the training set becomes larger. This hints at a change in the behavior of the time series at that point.

4.2 Reconciliation

Figure 8 shows the SFB and RMSSE obtained for all time series and reconciliation methods. As was observed in the previous section, we can see that the highest level of the hierarchy is easier to predict than the two lowest levels, a behavior that is consistent across all methods tested.

Although all methods seem to improve on the baseline, MINT and WLSS obtain the lowest SRB and RMSSE in the two tested periods and for all hierarchy levels. However, the boxplots show a large overlap of the error values, which makes it difficult to conclude whether the results of all individual time series are consistently improved by these methods. Figure 9 shows the difference in SFB and RMSSE obtained by each method with respect to the result obtained by the baseline. We also see that most differences are indeed negative, indicating that in a vast majority of the cases the results of the baseline are improved. As expected, the combination method BU doesn't modify the forecast for the base level of thei hierarchy. WLSS and MINT improve the results almost in all cases.

For reference, the complete results are reported in the Tables 6 and 7.

Table 2. Baseline ARIMA results for each level, before and after COVID

	SFB		RMSSE	
Series	Before	After	Before	After
CS1	.0823	.0970	.8500	.8101
CS2	.1040	.1530	.2975	.6108
CS3	.1174	.2020	1.2340	1.8258
PF1	.1200	.1330	1.2514	1.2734
PF2	.1400	.0790	.9094	.8255
PF3	.2200	.2710	1.7796	2.5599
PF4	.0870	.2550	.8804	2.1496
PF5	.2300	.2540	3.2135	2.7705
PF6	.2700	.1210	1.1544	1.5091
PF7	.2890	.3460	.5860	.7630
PF8	.1110	.0970	.4999	.8568
PF9	.1300	.1870	2.3414	2.4231
PF10	.2400	.2820	2.6340	3.7584

	SFB		RMSSE	
Series	Before	After	Before	After
AP1	.0860	.1810	1.7226	2.4580
AP2	.1020	.0410	.8710	.8318
AP3	.1940	.1710	.7796	1.1590
AP4	.1870	.2910	2.5067	3.0681
AP5	.2960	.2760	3.2135	3.0005
AP6	.1210	.1010	.6460	.8516
AP7	.1290	.3980	1.1353	1.2203
AP8	.1830	.0210	1.1544	2.5091
AP9	.3670	.4120	1.1474	2.9291
AP10	.2440	.4630	.4702	1.8843
AP11	.0750	.1000	1.1219	1.9539
AP12	.0710	.0970	.4999	1.8357
AP13	.3990	.3830	1.8604	1.5216
AP14	.2320	.2420	1.9526	2.3568
AP15	.1460	.2820	3.2340	3.3258
AP16	.2500	.3780	1.1624	1.7590

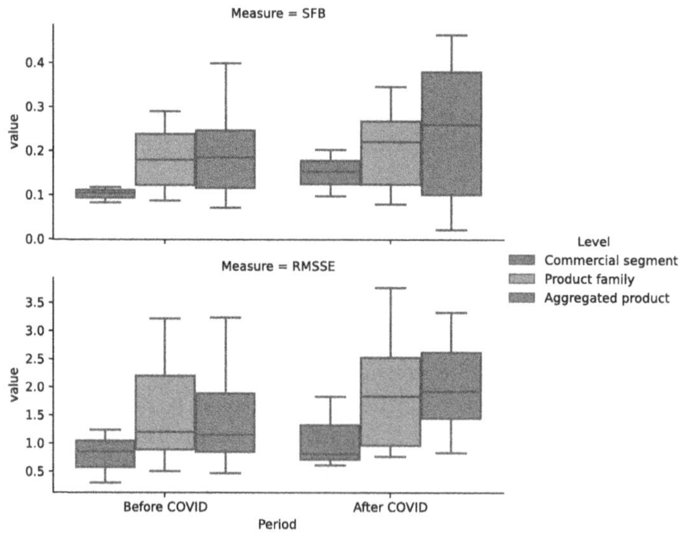

Fig. 7. Distribution of baseline results

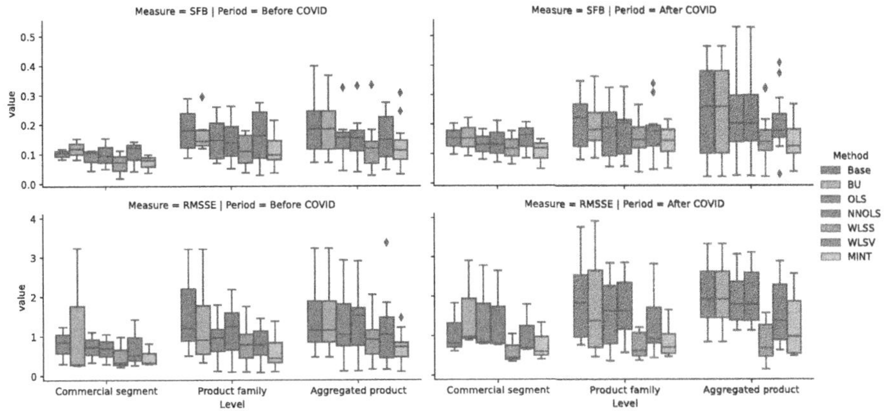

Fig. 8. Distribution of results after reconciliation

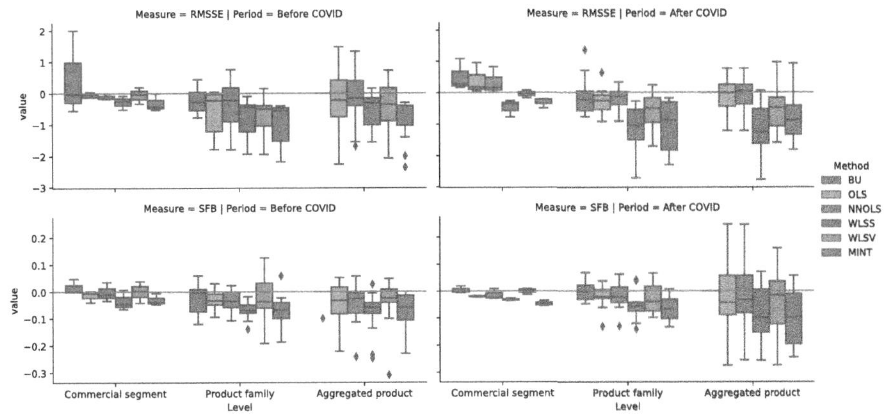

Fig. 9. Distribution of the differences with respect to base forecast

4.3 Comparison Before/after COVID-19

In the previous figures, it could be seen that, in general, the error increased in the period after COVID-19. As initially expected, forecasting the behavior of the series after the start COVID-19 is more difficult, as the test data differs more from the training data. This trend is observed for all methods and levels, but is more accused in the lowest level of the hierarchy, where we can see that some forecasts achieve very large errors, and also that, for some of the series, the reconciliation methods produce forecasts that are worse than the baseline. Only WLSS and MINT seem to escape this trend, having the 75th percentile of the difference in SFB and RMSSE (Fig. 9) below zero for both measures and for all hierarchy levels, indicating that at least 75% of the time series have their forecast improved by these reconciliation methods.

4.4 Discussion

In this section, we carry out a statistical analysis of the results obtained in this experimental study, in order to determine if the differences observed in the results of the different methods are statistically significant or not. First, Table 3 shows the results of the Friedman test to determine whether there is any difference in the distributions of the SFB and RMSSE values obtained by all methods.

Table 3. Friedman test between reconciliation methods

	Statistic	p-value
SFB	108.1	5.081e−21
RMSSE	164.2	7.504e−33

Clearly, there are differences in the distributions, which enables us to apply a Dunn test to evaluate potential differences in the results of every combination and reconciliation method, using the baseline as a reference in every case. Holm's method was applied for p-value adjustment. The results of this test are shown in Table 4. In the table, we can see that WLSS and MINT obtain statistically significant differences with the baseline method. This result is in line with the previous observation that these two algorithms outperformed the rest systematically, for all aggregation levels, both before and after COVID.

It is somewhat surprising that the two methods that consistently outperform others (WLSS and MINT) actually apply different assumptions on the data. While MINT estimates the covariance of the residuals at horizon 1, WLSS uses the diagonal of the hierarchy structure matrix $\mathbf{S}$ to compute $\mathbf{W}_h$. However, the results of WLSV (which uses the variance of the residuals) were less good, which hints that the covariance of the residuals was informative in this case, but not their variance. The common point of WLSS and MINT is that they use information about the relation between the time series in the hierarchy; therefore, this information is relevant for the problem of predicting vaccine sales.

To conclude the study, Table 5 shows the results of Wilcoxon's test to compare the performance of all methods, at all levels, before and after COVID. Clearly, there is a statistically significant performance drop when test values after COVID are considered, despite the use of a larger training set, indicating an important change in the behavior of the time series analyzed.

Table 4. Dunn test with Holm p-value adjustment

	SFB	RMSSE
Base	1	1
BU	1	1
OLS	1	1
NNOLS	1	1
WLSS	0.004067	1.012e−06
WLSV	1	0.06092
MINT	0.001384	1.53e−06

Table 5. Wilcoxon's test with Bonferroni correction between before and after COVID

	Statistic	p-value
SFB	4546	9.988e−11
RMSSE	3488	5.116e−16

5 Conclusion

Vaccine demand prediction is a critical problem in industry, with a large impact on public health and economy. For the first time, we have modeled this problem as a hierarchical time series forecast, establishing a hierarchy based on product families and gathering sales data between 2010 and 2021 in GSK.

Then, we have carried out a comparison of the results of different forecast reconciliation methods for hierarchical time series, applied on a real dataset of vaccine sales containing a 3-level hierarchy over 12 years. The baseline forecast for each level of the hierarchy was computed with ARIMA, and results were computed in a rolled cross-validation scheme.

The analysis has shown that MINT and WLSS obtained the best results for the forecast, a conclusion that is supported by statistical significance o the performed tests, while producing forecasts that are reconciled along the entire hierarchy. Furthermore, we have observed that the algorithms systematically obtain worse forecasts when data during the COVID period is used as test set, despite the use of more years of training data. This indicates a significant change of the behavior of the time series during this period. However, MINT and WLSS are again able to yield better results than the rest of the methods analyzed, palliating the performance drop, indicating their higher robustness to this kind of changes.

Acknowledgement. This work was sponsored by GlaxoSmithKline Biologicals SA.

Appendix: Complete Result Tables

Table 6. SFB after reconciliation, for all levels and methods

Series	Before COVID							After COVID						
	Base	BU	OLS	NNOLS	WLSS	WLSV	MINT	Base	BU	OLS	NNOLS	WLSS	WLSV	MINT
CS1	.0823	.0810	.0430	.0490	.0170	.0410	.0360	.0970	.0920	.0800	.0700	.0638	.0844	.0480
CS2	.1040	.1520	.1060	.0940	.1112	.1420	.0980	.1530	.1520	.1310	.1300	.1175	.1627	.1179
CS3	.1174	.1180	.1120	.1530	.0720	.1211	.0790	.2020	.2210	.1830	.2110	.1760	.2061	.1484
PF1	.1200	.1800	.0690	.0710	.0740	.1120	.0800	.1330	.1410	.1650	.1950	.1710	.1980	.1110
PF2	.1400	.1360	.0990	.0980	.0690	.0780	.0360	.0790	.1470	.0880	.0980	.0370	.0450	.0490
PF3	.2200	.1810	.1960	.1930	.1380	.0280	.0880	.2710	.2950	.2100	.2110	.1500	.1720	.1487
PF4	.0870	.1450	.0800	.0920	.0690	.1360	.1450	.2550	.2100	.2260	.2140	.1940	.1810	.1899
PF5	.2300	.1440	.2600	.2450	.1710	.2750	.1440	.2540	.2390	.2440	.2110	.1120	.1770	.1390
PF6	.2700	.1830	.1750	.1620	.1300	.2050	.0830	.1210	.1430	.1010	.1000	.0610	.0790	.0530
PF7	.2890	.2950	.2070	.1900	.1790	.2670	.2140	.3460	.3620	.3240	.3220	.2660	.3370	.2120
PF8	.1110	.1210	.0700	.0510	.0370	.0570	.0710	.0970	.0840	.0760	.0940	.1380	.1630	.1040
PF9	.1300	.1270	.1180	.1160	.0890	.2550	.1070	.1870	.1520	.0550	.0560	.1440	.1120	.1520
PF10	.2400	.1190	.2520	.2630	.1720	.1890	.1790	.2820	.2350	.3190	.3268	.2287	.3070	.2150
AP1	.0860	.0860	.0430	.0390	.0300	.0460	.0310	.1810	.1810	.1100	.1080	.0870	.1610	.1050
AP2	.1020	.1020	.1200	.1040	.0410	.0730	.0820	.0410	.0410	.0250	.0240	.0210	.0290	.0380
AP3	.1940	.1940	.1570	.1780	.1330	.2400	.0880	.1710	.1710	.2050	.2090	.1130	.2180	.0800
AP4	.1870	.1870	.1620	.1660	.1380	.0900	.0770	.2910	.2910	.2980	.3240	.1470	.1670	.1090
AP5	.2960	.2960	.1700	.1950	.0610	.2750	.1440	.2760	.2760	.1700	.1950	.1610	.2750	.1140
AP6	.1210	.1210	.1110	.1120	.1150	.1260	.1210	.1010	.1010	.1980	.1970	.1720	.1220	.1570
AP7	.1290	.1290	.1810	.1800	.1560	.1440	.0990	.3980	.3980	.2590	.2590	.1400	.1230	.1520
AP8	.1830	.1830	.1550	.1520	.1300	.1550	.1130	.0210	.0210	.1010	.1000	.0510	.1790	.0430
AP9	.3670	.3670	.3250	.3310	.3340	.2660	.3070	.4120	.4120	.3420	.3650	.2140	.2880	.1960
AP10	.2440	.2440	.1370	.1300	.1820	.2410	.2440	.4630	.4630	.2940	.2970	.3220	.3710	.2674
AP11	.0750	.0750	.0912	.0680	.0700	.1230	.0750	.1000	.1000	.1490	.1490	.0960	.1310	.1080
AP12	.0710	.0710	.1000	.0810	.0270	.0570	.0710	.0970	.0970	.2060	.2040	.1380	.1630	.0840
AP13	.3990	.2990	.1770	.1570	.1510	.0900	.1690	.3830	.3830	.2990	.2980	.1960	.1730	.1820
AP14	.2320	.2320	.1520	.1510	.1240	.1910	.1120	.2420	.2420	.1730	.1710	.1360	.2120	.1350
AP15	.1460	.1460	.1820	.2030	.0720	.1890	.1190	.2820	.2820	.5280	.5270	.3190	.4070	.2350
AP16	.2500	.2500	.1560	.1670	.1130	.2190	.1500	.3780	.3780	.1020	.1210	.1330	.1970	.1800

Table 7. RMSSE after reconciliation, for all levels and methods

Series	Before COVID							After COVID						
	Base	BU	OLS	NNOLS	WLSS	WLSV	MINT	Base	BU	OLS	NNOLS	WLSS	WLSV	MINT
CS1	.8500	.2926	.7300	.6899	.3315	.5148	.3210	.8101	.9735	.8432	.8132	.4421	.6427	.5935
CS2	.2975	.2597	.3300	.2905	.2165	.2585	.2890	.6108	.8876	.7900	.7699	.3496	.6863	.3996
CS3	1.2340	3.2340	1.1000	1.0497	.9785	1.4216	.8110	1.8258	2.9028	2.7746	2.6442	1.0441	1.7909	1.3296
PF1	1.2514	.4825	1.1825	1.1919	.8311	.8759	.3725	1.2734	1.0944	.3565	1.3551	.4597	.9080	1.0944
PF2	.9094	.3323	.9508	.9544	.5853	.4715	.3163	.8255	.6468	.5642	.5643	.3686	.4318	.6468
PF3	1.7796	1.8292	1.7885	2.0019	1.2811	.6962	1.3796	2.5599	3.9093	2.4894	2.4858	.7114	.8537	.5480
PF4	.8804	.4432	.8115	1.6368	.7807	1.0321	.4042	2.1496	2.8502	1.7114	1.7196	1.0763	2.3910	.8502
PF5	3.2135	3.2135	1.7466	2.1832	1.7532	1.2741	1.0332	2.7705	2.0253	2.1935	2.1563	1.1665	1.8132	.7529
PF6	1.1544	.7544	1.1373	1.4343	.7931	.6726	.6347	1.5091	.8391	1.5415	1.5402	.4812	.9168	.5391
PF7	.5860	.8680	.1549	.0923	.1073	.0806	.1237	.7630	.4630	1.3916	1.0918	.4882	.6541	.4630
PF8	.4999	.9399	.1111	.1169	.0948	.1510	.0999	.8568	.5991	.5954	.6651	.5117	.7951	.4991
PF9	2.3414	1.6080	.5601	.5533	.4098	1.4517	.4802	2.4231	1.6496	2.2739	2.3967	1.2019	1.3616	1.6496
PF10	2.6340	2.4779	.9798	1.3010	1.1216	1.1588	.9013	3.7584	3.8628	2.8346	2.8464	1.0297	2.8109	1.4563
AP1	1.7226	1.7226	1.0207	1.6699	.9825	1.0449	.8226	2.4580	2.4580	2.7238	2.7099	1.2516	1.3846	1.1081
AP2	.8710	.8710	.7571	.7666	.5767	.5026	.4710	.8318	.8318	1.1283	1.1281	.4200	.6259	.4872
AP3	.7796	.7796	1.9968	1.8277	.7059	.9877	.4796	1.1590	1.1590	1.3443	1.3559	.6043	1.7601	.5480
AP4	2.5067	2.5067	2.9258	2.9010	1.4763	1.6079	1.1067	3.0681	3.0681	1.9185	2.8995	1.4595	2.8748	1.8039
AP5	3.2135	3.2135	1.7466	1.6635	1.6532	3.3697	1.2135	3.0005	3.0005	2.1935	2.1563	1.5665	2.4366	2.0253
AP6	.6460	.6460	.4012	.4044	.3365	.2560	.2460	.8516	.8516	1.5946	1.5943	.3758	.6583	.6329
AP7	1.1353	1.1353	1.5412	1.5380	1.0957	1.0255	.7353	1.2203	1.2203	1.4608	1.4615	1.2796	2.1847	1.4387
AP8	1.1544	1.1544	2.1373	2.1343	.9931	1.5479	.7544	2.5091	2.5091	2.5415	2.5402	.4812	.9168	.8391
AP9	1.1474	1.1474	2.6218	2.4743	1.3002	1.4370	.7474	2.9291	2.9291	3.0567	3.1055	.1419	2.8455	2.4862
AP10	.4702	.4702	.1554	.2553	.1567	.1692	.1002	1.8843	1.8843	1.7840	1.6847	.6024	.7727	.5308
AP11	1.1219	1.1219	1.1889	1.1927	.9676	1.8498	.7219	1.9539	1.9539	1.3540	1.3532	.3079	1.0097	.8235
AP12	.4999	.4999	.1111	.1169	.2948	.1510	.0999	1.8357	1.8357	1.7954	1.8951	.6117	.6951	.4991
AP13	1.8604	1.8604	.7458	.7446	.8582	.7142	1.4604	1.5216	1.5216	2.2831	2.2842	1.2929	2.2325	2.4452
AP14	1.9526	1.9526	1.0600	1.5021	.6333	1.0797	.5526	2.3568	2.3568	1.1362	1.1390	.7425	1.2788	.5336
AP15	3.2340	3.2340	.9798	1.5448	2.0479	1.1599	.8740	3.3258	3.3258	2.9346	2.9464	1.0297	2.4109	2.5628
AP16	1.1624	1.1624	.9668	.8633	.4236	.2642	.4624	1.7590	1.7590	1.3981	1.3792	.8790	1.3590	1.2826

References

1. Abolghasemi, M., Hyndman, R.J., Spiliotis, E., Bergmeir, C.: Model selection in reconciling hierarchical time series. Mach. Learn. **111**, 739–789 (2022). https://doi.org/10.1007/s10994-021-06126-z
2. Andrus, J.K., Sherris, J., Fitzsimmons, J.W., Kane, M.A., Aguado, M.T.: Introduction of human papillomavirus vaccines into developing countries - international strategies for funding and procurement. Vaccine **26**, K87–K92 (2008). https://doi.org/10.1016/J.VACCINE.2008.05.003
3. Athanasopoulos, G., Gamakumara, P., Panagiotelis, A., Hyndman, R.J., Affan, M.: Hierarchical forecasting. Adv. Stud. Theor. Appl. Econometrics **52**, 689–719 (2020). https://doi.org/10.1007/978-3-030-31150-6_21/FIGURES/13
4. Barajas, M., Bhatkande, S., Baskaran, P., Gohel, H., Pandey, B.: Advancing deep learning for supply chain optimization of Covid-19 vaccination in rural communities. In: Proceedings of the 2021 IEEE 10th International Conference on Communication Systems and Network Technologies, CSNT 2021 pp. 690–695 (2021). https://doi.org/10.1109/CSNT51715.2021.9509710

5. Bates, J.M., Granger, C.W.J.: The combination of forecasts. J. Oper. Res. Soc. **20**, 451–468 (1969). https://doi.org/10.2307/3008764
6. Bergmeir, C., Hyndman, R.J., Koo, B.: A note on the validity of cross-validation for evaluating autoregressive time series prediction. Comput. Stat. Data Anal. **120**, 70–83 (2018). https://doi.org/10.1016/J.CSDA.2017.11.003
7. Cernuschi, T., Malvolti, S., Nickels, E., Friede, M.: Bacillus Calmette-Guérin (BCG) vaccine: a global assessment of demand and supply balance. Vaccine **36**, 498–506 (2018). https://doi.org/10.1016/J.VACCINE.2017.12.010
8. Cleveland, R.B., Cleveland, W.S., McRae, J.E., Terpenning, I.J.: STL: a seasonal-trend decomposition procedure based on loess. J. Official Stat. **6**, 3–73 (1990)
9. Debellut, F., et al.: Forecasting demand for the typhoid conjugate vaccine in low-and middle-income countries. Clin. Infect. Dis. **68**, S154–S160 (2019). https://doi.org/10.1093/CID/CIY1076
10. Gilchrist, S.A., Nanni, A.: Lessons learned in shaping vaccine markets in low-income countries: a review of the vaccine market segment supported by the Gavi alliance. Health Policy Plan. **28**, 838–846 (2013). https://doi.org/10.1093/HEAPOL/CZS123
11. Gross, C.W., Sohl, J.E.: Disaggregation methods to expedite product line forecasting. J. Forecast. **9**, 233–254 (1990). https://doi.org/10.1002/FOR.3980090304
12. Hollyman, R., Petropoulos, F., Tipping, M.E.: Understanding forecast reconciliation. Eur. J. Oper. Res. **294**, 149–160 (2021). https://doi.org/10.1016/J.EJOR.2021.01.017
13. Hyndman, R., Athanasopoulos, G.: Forecasting: Principles and Practice, 3rd edn. OTexts (2021)
14. Hyndman, R.J., Ahmed, R.A., Athanasopoulos, G., Shang, H.L.: Optimal combination forecasts for hierarchical time series. Comput. Stat. Data Anal. **55**, 2579–2589 (2011). https://doi.org/10.1016/j.csda.2011.03.006
15. Mueller, L.E., et al.: The impact of implementing a demand forecasting system into a low-income country's supply chain. Vaccine **34**, 3663–3669 (2016). https://doi.org/10.1016/J.VACCINE.2016.05.027
16. Sahisnu, J.S., Natalia, F., Ferdinand, F.V., Sudirman, S., Ko, C.S.: Vaccine prediction system using Arima method. ICIC Express Lett. Part B Appl. **11**, 567–575 (2020). https://doi.org/10.24507/ICICELB.11.06.567
17. Wickramasuriya, S.L., Athanasopoulos, G., Hyndman, R.J.: Optimal forecast reconciliation for hierarchical and grouped time series through trace minimization. J. Am. Stat. Assoc. **114**, 804–819 (2019). https://doi.org/10.1080/01621459.2018.1448825
18. Wickramasuriya, S.L., Turlach, B.A., Hyndman, R.J.: Optimal non-negative forecast reconciliation. Stat. Comput. **30**, 1167–1182 (2020). https://doi.org/10.1007/S11222-020-09930-0/TABLES/8

Machine Learning Applications in Route Planning for Attended Home Delivery

Thomas R. Visser(✉), Ruggiero Seccia, Wouter Merkx, Wouter Kool, and Leendert Kok

ORTEC B.V., Houtsingel 5, 2719 EA Zoetermeer, The Netherlands
{thomas.visser,wouter.kool,leendert.kok}@ortec.com
https://www.ortec.com/

Abstract. In the attended home delivery industry, customers order products online, which are then delivered to their home within a time slot of their choice. Given the nature of the products, e.g., groceries or appliances, the customer must be at home to receive the goods. Therefore, on-time delivery is of key importance. Due to the inherent variability of various planning factors, such as uncertain travel times and time to deliver an order, gaps appear between route planning and execution of the delivery routes. Additionally, during the planning process additional customers may order and choose new time slots. This fuels the need for data-driven approaches that can account for these uncertainties. In this paper, we present an overview of ORTEC applications that use machine learning combined with route planning, to create accurate, yet efficient and robust route plans. To validate the impact of the proposed approaches in practice, the machine learning models are trained and tested on real-world data. Simulation experiments highlight the impact and value created by such approaches for home delivery companies.

Keywords: Attended Home Delivery · Machine Learning Applications in Industry · Vehicle Routing

1 Introduction

The home delivery industry has recently seen a massive growth in popularity, fueled even more by the COVID19 pandemic [12]. Together with narrow profit margins and high customer service requirements, it is important for home delivery companies to use routes that are efficient, yet consider real-world uncertainties, to minimize cost and ensure customer satisfaction through on-time delivery. To this end, this paper investigates various applications of machine learning combined with route optimization, used at ORTEC to improve the overall accuracy, efficiency and robustness of the route schedule throughout the planning process.

Wouter Merkx and Ruggiero Seccia — no longer work for ORTEC, Work done while at ORTEC.

F. A. Oliehoek et al. (Eds.): BNAIC/Benelearn 2023, CCIS 2187, pp. 119–134, 2025.
https://doi.org/10.1007/978-3-031-74650-5_7

1.1 Problem Description

The problem considered in this paper is an extension to the In the (theoretical) vehicle routing problem with time windows (VRPTW) [10]. In the VRPTW, a set of customers needs to be visited or *serviced* using a number of available vehicles, which start and end their routes at a depot. Each vehicle has a capacity and the total demand of customers serviced by a vehicle cannot exceed the capacity. Additionally, service of each customer may take a certain amount of *service time* (e.g. to unload goods) and should start within a certain *time window.* The goal is to minimize the total time or distance for all vehicles, each one starting and returning at the depot. In the real-world setting considered in this paper, we also take into account several additional practical constraints such as time-dependent travel times and duration constraints (see e.g., [23]) and break rules (see e.g., [16]).

In the VRPTW, service and travel times are considered fixed. In practice, this is rarely the case. For example, service times may depend on the type of building, parking availability, etc., whereas travel times may vary depending on traffic, weather, etc. This means that 1) these values need to be estimated and 2) the actual values can differ from the estimates, introducing a *gap* between the planned and the realized route schedule (see Fig. 1). This means that there is uncertainty that needs to be accounted for.

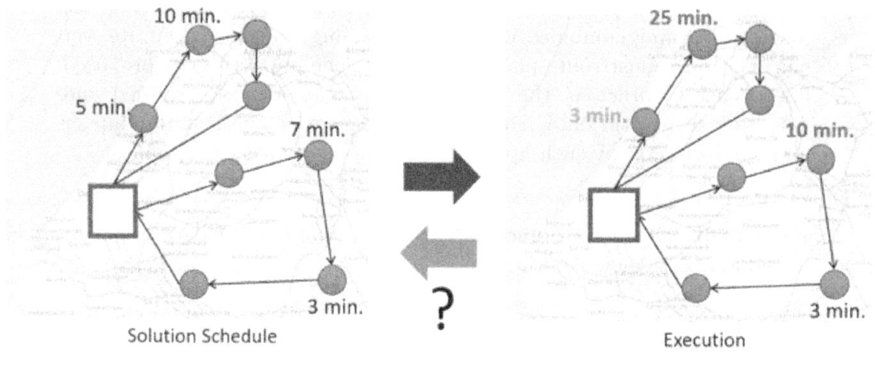

Fig. 1. Example of realized service times taking longer than planned, which may result in time window violations for subsequent customers. Section 2 of this paper explores how to use realization data to improve future service time estimations

Gaps between planned and realized service and travel times can lead to several problems. Routes taking longer than expected may result in missing customer time windows or overtime for the driver, negatively affecting customer and driver satisfaction and potentially incurring additional costs for operational recovery. On the other hand, routes taking shorter than expected result in wasted capacity as more orders could have been planned, negatively affecting route efficiency and transportation costs. Therefore, improving service and travel time estimates improves both customer and driver satisfaction and reduces operational costs through improved route accuracy and efficiency. The approach we take in this paper is to use data from realized routes to train machine learning models to predict service times (Sect. 2) and travel times (Sect. 3).

While travel and service times are clearly uncertain, even demand and time windows are uncertain as customers may update their orders during the planning process. In the setting we consider, time windows are chosen by the customer, but from a set of *time slots* offered by the supplier, typically selected to ensure feasibility and efficiency of the final route plan. The problem of offering time slots, known as *time slot management* [2], is a challenge as 1) feasible options need to be determined in real-time while 2) feasibility may depend on future orders which are uncertain and 3) it is uncertain which time slot the customer will actually choose from the set of options. Therefore, Sect. 4 explores fast predictions of feasible time slots using machine learning and Sect. 5 considers the problem of learning customer behavior from previously selected time slots.

In the following, each section focuses on one of the problems described above, outlining the methodology implemented and the main results obtained. Simulations were performed to estimate the impact of using these models in real scenarios. Finally, we would like to stress that the models described hereafter can be easily integrated (and are being integrated) into our solutions, empowering our clients to enhance their estimations of service time and travel time, as well as improve their time slotting methodologies.

2 Learning for Service Time Predictions

In this section, we use supervised learning to predict the service times of individual customer orders.

2.1 Methodology

We consider both Lasso [22] and Random Forest regression models [14], trained on a data set of order features and realized service times, measured by the actual start and finish times of the delivery. To estimate the operational impact of the improved service time predictions, we run a set of simulation experiments.

2.2 Data Preparation

The data consist of approximately 2.5 million deliveries from a main US-based retail company, spanning a duration of 8 months. For each delivery in our data, we have information about the number of items, the time of day, and the location of the delivery. To estimate the impact of including extra features into our models, we categorize features into two sets: a *basic* set encompassing 5 basic features such as the amount to deliver and basic location-related information; an *advanced* set including 20 extra features that could enhance the predictive accuracy of the model such as weather information, population density, and time window information.

The dataset was split into 75% training and 25% testing data and a rigorous data cleaning process was undertaken to replace outliers and missing values with the mean values observed in the training data. Finally, features encoding was also implemented to enable models to consider categorical and cyclical features correctly.

2.3 Learning Procedure

In order to gain insights into the main factors impacting service durations, we explore interpretable methods, specifically Lasso [22] and Random Forests (RF) [14], which exhibited the most promising performance among multiple boosting and ensemble methods. For tuning the models' hyperparameters, a Halving Random Search cross-validation [15] was employed while minimizing the Mean Absolute Error (MAE). In Table 1 we report the MAE and Mean Absolute Percentage Error (MAPE) on the test set obtained by the baseline (i.e., the values supplied by the company themselves and obtained via some expert knowledge decision rule) and the trained models when using the two sets of features.

Table 1. Results of the models' performance on the test set

Model	Features	MAE	MAPE
Baseline		212.2	0.53
Lasso	*basic*	193.4	0.47
RF	*basic*	193.1	0.46
Lasso	*advanced*	191.0	0.46
RF	*advanced*	183.7	0.44

Both Lasso and RF models consistently demonstrated significant improvements in all the metrics for both sets of features, indicating their superiority over the baseline approach. Moreover, using more advanced models and more features leads to better performance. In particular, compared to the baseline, using an RF with the *basic* set of features reduces the MAE by 9.0%, while using the *advanced* features leads to a further 4.4% improvement on MAE. While analyzing the importance of features for the RF model, we found that the delivery amount and the population density of the delivery zipcode are the most prominent. Other location- and time-related features play an important role, while weather-related features show a relatively low correlation with the output.

2.4 Simulations Experiments

Finally we investigated the impact on the operational key performance indicators (KPIs) derived by using the improved service time predictions defined by the best RF model obtained above. To this end, we considered 300 schedules not available at training time, we updated the planned service times of their orders using the values returned by the RF trained on the *advanced* features set, and we optimized the schedules again by using the ORTEC route optimizer (which solves the problem by using advanced optimization heuristics). The execution of these newly planned schedules was subsequently simulated using the *actual* realized service times, and the efficiency (realized total cost) and service level (percentage of missed time windows) KPIs were computed and compared with the KPIs obtained when using the baseline service time prediction model.

Overall, there is a trade-off between realized costs and time window violations: planning with lower service times enables a more efficient schedule (more stops per route) at planning time but also results in more time window violations during execution, and vice versa. This trade-off can be controlled by multiplying all service time estimates by a constant scaling factor, representing the *risk appetite* of the home delivery company. Thus, for both the baseline approach and the RF model, we run simulations by varying the scaling factor between 0.9 (optimistic case) and 1.2 (conservative case) and plot the results as a trade-off curve in Fig. 2. When we consider the service time predictions returned by the model without any multiplication factor, i.e., the multiplication factor is equal to 1, the Random Forest approach improves cost efficiency by 1.3% but increases time window violations from 2.6% to 3.9% compared to the baseline, suggesting that the baseline is more conservative. Nevertheless, as we consider the curves defined when including the multiplication factors, the Random Forest approach (in red) strictly dominates the baseline approach (in blue) by consistently leading to lower total costs and time window violations.

3 Learning for Travel Time Predictions

This section presents a deep learning approach that improves the efficiency and reliability of solutions for the VRPTW by refining travel time estimations. Similar to service time estimates (Sect. 2), improved travel time estimates lead to more robust and efficient routes.

Solving a routing problem requires the availability of a travel duration matrix, i.e. pairwise travel durations between all depots and customers that require a delivery. ORTEC applies Customizable Route Planning [8] to compute large duration matrices. Current travel durations often lack precision, leading to inefficiencies and, consequently, customer dissatisfaction. In this section, we aim at leveraging realization GPS data coming from our customers and deep learning techniques to make travel time predictions more reliable, similar to related work [9,24,29].

3.1 Methodology

We propose the application of a Deep Feedforward Neural Network [18] to predict durations for individual road edges and turns by exploiting GPS realization data.

Once the model has been trained, the new edge and turn durations are used to compute new pairwise travel durations for the VRPTW. Finally, to validate the model, we compare the old baseline travel durations and the new travel durations with the realized ones.

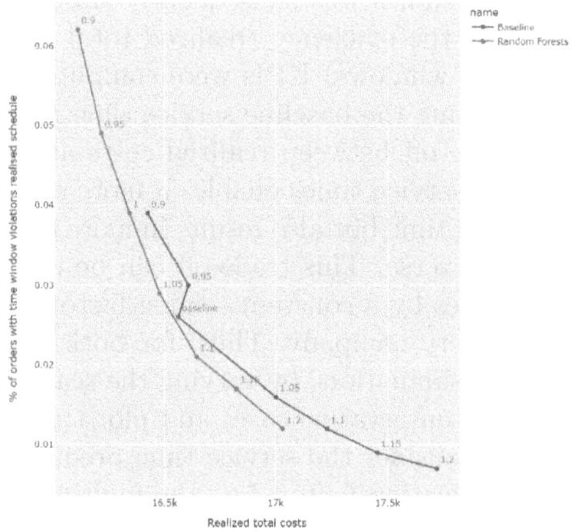

Fig. 2. Impact on realized operational KPIs with different multiplication factors (reported in orange) for both the service times currently planned (curve in blue) and the predictions returned by an RF trained with features from the *advanced* features set (curve in red) (Color figure online)

The decision of using Deep Neural Networks for this learning problem derives from the structure of the available data. While information regarding the duration between successive GPS observations is available, the specific time taken to traverse individual road segments and turns remains unknown. Thus, in order to avoid the introduction of subjective human biases, such as predetermined allocation of time intervals between GPS observations to each road segment and turn, we let the model make this decision by learning the problem in a *end-to-end* fashion. In this way, by leveraging the available data without any human input, the model learns how to split time between road segments and turns. This approach would have not been viable with conventional Machine Learning models (e.g. Random Forests or Support Vector Machines), while, given their flexibility and modelling capabilities, Deep Neural Networks were well suited to tackle this end-to-end learning problem.

3.2 Data Preparation

Overall, we considered more than 1 million travels done between July 2021 and March 2022, where a travel is defined as the time between two consecutive stops without considering the parking time. Data consists of GPS observations with 1 min frequency of delivery vans performing deliveries in the North-East US area.

After a first data cleaning procedure to remove faulty observations, we used a *map-matching* procedure to recover the *most likely* path travelled by each van. Indeed, since we want to predict the travel time for every single edge of the road network, but we know the location of each van only once per minute, we need to reconstruct the most likely path that was travelled by each van during their route. Finally, we also filtered out all those GPS observations not really related to travel time but more related to parking/service time. In Fig. 3 we report a visualization of the cleaning procedure to define a travel.

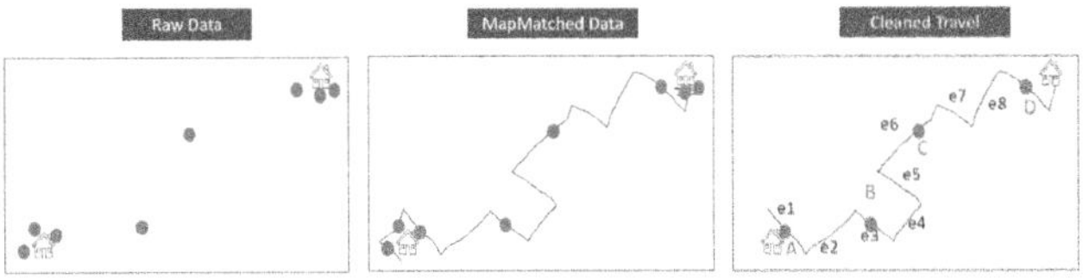

Fig. 3. Data preparation procedure: given the raw GPS observations, we first map-match them to obtain a likely route travelled by the vans. Then, we remove all the GPS observations that we detect are not related to traveling times, e.g., parking time, service time and break time

For each road edge, relevant features such as the number of lanes, the road type, and the speed limit are extracted and turning features such as turn angles and the number of left/right incoming roads are computed. Thus, each edge/turn is characterized by approximately 200 features, including edge features, next-edge features, and turn features.

3.3 Learning Procedure

Travels were split into training-validation (80%) and test sets (20%). The deep neural network architecture consists of several fully connected linear layers with non-linear activation functions. For each edge, the model predicts its speed and the time needed to perform each possible turn (i.e., the time needed to move from that edge to any other adjacent edge).

During the training, we used the capped Symmetric Mean Absolute Percentage Error (capped-SMAPE) [20] as loss function because we want to treat errors on long and short travels similarly and we want similar magnitude of errors for under/overpredictions. SMAPE values were capped at 1.2 to reduce the impact of faulty observations in the training data such as errors when computing the most-likely path to connect two GPS observations or undetected breaks/stops.

3.4 Results and Discussion

The models' performance is validated on approximately 320,000 travels from the test set and its performance are compared with the performance obtained by the current baseline model, which is a non-linear regression model based on the free flow speed of each edge and other similar features. For each travel, the origin and destination are extracted, and a new route is computed using the baseline and the NN-based model (i.e., for each origin-destination pair we solved the shortest path problem on the graph defined by the baseline and the new model). These estimated durations of the new routes are then compared against the realized duration of the actual route.

When moving from the baseline to the new NN-based model, we remarkably observed a SMAPE decrease from 29.12% to 21.22%. This performance enhancement is illustrated in Fig. 4. Error distribution with the model predicted travel times (in red) is less spread and more centered in 0, while the baseline approach (in blue) overpredicts the actual travel time and has higher variability. The new learned model thus improves the predicted travel time accuracy for the VRPTW, leading to more accurate and efficient route plannings.

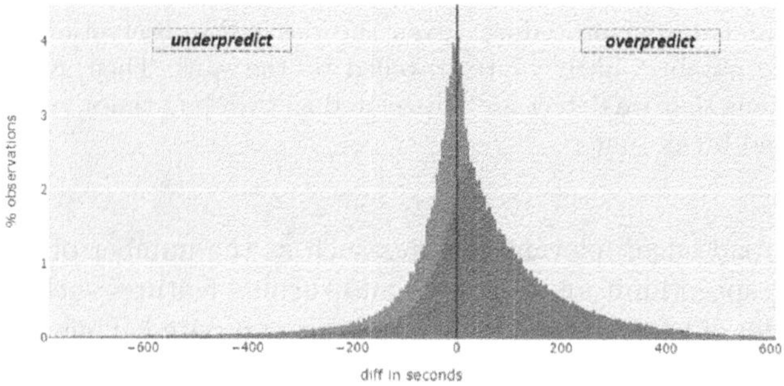

Fig. 4. Error distribution between predicted and realized values for the baseline approach (blue) and the new learning-based approach (red) (Color figure online)

Differently from Sect. 2, where we can assume that realized service times are independent from the route schedule, simulating the operational impact of the new travel times estimation model is very challenging due to potential changes in route schedules resulting in travels without observed realisations. However, employing this model at the company, with added slack time to diminish time window violations, exhibited a 40% decrease in time window violations and a 3% reduction in transportation cost per order.

4 Learning for Time Slot Feasibility Predictions

This section focuses on *time slot management* [2], i.e., the problem of offering time slots to customers placing their order during the ordering process. Here, the goal is to offer time slots that not only meet customer preferences but also align with the capabilities of the existing fleet of delivery vehicles, considering all currently scheduled customer orders. Effective time slot management strategies are key to balance route efficiency and customer satisfaction. Conceptually, this involves solving for each time slot a VRPTW containing the set of already booked customer orders and the new arriving customer with that time slot. The main challenge is determining these feasible time slots quickly since customers are not willing to wait for long during the ordering process [3]. Given the NP-Hardness of the VRPTW [10], most approaches in the literature use cheapest insertion heuristic-based methods [25]. However, learning approaches might be able to leverage offline learning for fast and good-quality online predictions. This section highlights the main methodology and outcomes of the recently published work [13] on a supervised learning approach to predict time slot feasibility to which the interested reader is referred for further details.

4.1 Methodology

A data set of representative VRPTW instances, e.g., instances containing representative customer orders and their time slots encountered during the ordering process, is generated and these problems are solved to assess feasibility, e.g., determine if all customer orders can be feasibly serviced by the given fleet of delivery vehicles. This data is then used to train a classification model to predict feasibility of a VRPTW instance. The resulting model is then used online, i.e., during the ordering process, to predict the feasibility of each time slot for an incoming customer order. Note that this requires one feasibility prediction per time slot, as each time slot will correspond to a different VRPTW instance to access. Only time slots with predicted feasibility higher than a certain threshold are offered to the customer.

4.2 Data Preparation and Learning Procedure

In this study, we consider a data set containing 144,000 VRPTW instances with feasibility, obtained from 120 simulated runs of the ordering process with 400 arriving customers with varying geographic distributions and delivery fleet sizes. The VRPTW instances were solved using the ORTEC route optimization software, employing advanced optimization heuristics.

Motivated by their consistent performance on a variety of high-dimensional binary classification data sets [6], Random Forests, Gradient Boosted Trees, and Neural Networks based classification models were considered. All models were trained via a five-fold cross-validation and a Neural Network, with one hidden layer and 100 neurons, yielded the highest accuracy. Multiple sets of VRPTW instance features were investigated. Interestingly, models using a set of aggregated features, consisting of the number of orders, number of orders per time slot, total demand, total vehicle capacity, and number of vehicles, outperformed those using a more raw set of features, consisting of number of vehicles, capacity per vehicle, depot location coordinates, service time at customer and each customer location coordinates. Probably the set of raw features grows prohibitively large, with many symmetries between them, as the number of booked customer orders increases.

4.3 Comparing Feasibility Estimators

To benchmark the learning procedure against commonly used feasibility methods found in the literature, the best neural network model method (ML) is compared with: a cheapest insertion heuristic (IH), a continuous approximation approach (CA) (e.g., like [17]), a simple order thresholds (OT) and order thresholds per time slot (OTTS) approaches (e.g., [5,11]). To compare the accuracy of the methods, another set of 28,800 simulated VRPTW feasibility instances were used, with 54.6% of the instances belonging to the negative class, and the remaining to the positive class.

Table 2. Results of the methods' performance on a validation set

Method	Accuracy	TP	FP	FN	TN
IH	90.8	36.2	0.0	9.2	54.6
ML	94.5	44.9	5.0	0.5	49.6
CA	86.3	32.8	1.1	12.6	53.5
OT	93.9	39.7	0.4	5.7	54.1
OTTS	89.1	34.6	0.0	10.9	54.6

Table 2 reports the accuracy of the methods, as percentage compared to the feasibility obtained via the ORTEC route optimizer, together with the percentage of true positives (TP), false positives (FP), false negatives (FN) and true negatives (TN). With an accuracy of 94.5%, the Neural Network (ML) classifies outperformed the other methods, mainly because of its low false negative rate. Furthermore, we highlight that the Neural Network classifier is slightly more optimistic than the other methods in predicting which instances are still feasible, with an FP rate around 5.0%.

4.4 Simulations Experiments

After comparing the accuracies of the different methods, we investigated if the applicability of ML to offer time slots would also translate into more booked customers during a time slot management process. Overall, 24 time slot management processes were simulated. The methods of above were used to define the time slots to offer to each (simulated) arriving customer, and each customer picking a time slot among the offered ones according to an ordered preference list. This subset of time slots is randomly generated for each customer. If none of the time slots in the preference list are offered, the customer decides to not place an order. At the end of each time slotting simulation, the ORTEC route optimizer is used to generate the final route schedule. As most methods are predicting feasibility, it can happen that not all booked customer orders can be actually planned using the available fleet of delivery vehicles. In that case, a *surplus* of customer orders is observed.

Table 3. Results of the methods used in an ordering process simulation

Method	# customers			Computation Time (ms)
	Booked	Scheduled	Surplus	
IH	156.6	156.6	0.0	294
ML	185.7	182.3	3.4	20
CA	143.0	142.1	0.9	0
OT	160.0	158.7	1.3	0
OTTS	150.0	150.0	0.0	0

Table 3 shows the number of booked, scheduled and surplus customers and online computation times, averaged over the simulation runs. The learning method (ML) resulted in the most booked and scheduled customers among the different methods. However, this method also returned the largest amount of surplus customers, e.g., which could not be scheduled feasibly in the final schedule. This probably connects with the relatively high percentage of false positives (FP) we observed earlier in Table 2. As a last point, we would like to underline how the learning method required on average much less online computation time for the predictions compared to the insertion heuristic, resulting in a faster and more effective tool for supporting time slot management operations.

5 Learning for Customer Choice Predictions

Section 4 explored the selection of feasible time slots from the perspective of the home delivery company. On the other hand, from the perspective of the customer, a smooth ordering process, including the availability of a preferred delivery time slot, is an important driver for customer satisfaction [7]. However, only focusing on maximizing customer satisfaction will lead to inefficient delivery routes. Therefore, beyond ensuring feasibility, home delivery companies may reduce the set of offered time slots to maximize efficiency without excessively compromising customer satisfaction. Additionally, customers may be nudged to select, or to not select, a particular time slot using, for instance, differentiated delivery fees, which enhances the delivery route efficiency [2].

A clear understanding of customer behavior is essential to balance the trade-off between customer satisfaction and route efficiency. In this section, we aim to learn the choice of the customer, who either selects a time slot, or decides not to book at all. This section summarizes an early exploration done at ORTEC on the predictability of customer behavior in the form of time slot selections [19], to which the interested reader is referred for further details.

While out of scope for this paper, a successful customer choice model could be incorporated in the time slotting offer strategy, for example to balance the preference and efficiency of the offered slots, or to offer discounts on efficient but less desirable slots. In this way, customer satisfaction level could be improved, while still maintaining high route efficiency.

5.1 Methodology

In this work, three different customer choice models are considered: a simple model predicting the most frequent chosen time slot in the past (Baseline); a Multinomial Logit Model (MNL); and a multi-layer Neural Network (NN) model. The first model will set the baseline to beat, while the MNL model is frequently used in the customer choice modeling literature (see e.g., [1,28] and [27]) and the NN model is chosen because of its great ability in modeling interactions between variables.

5.2 Data Preparation

We consider five weeks of data from an online grocery retailer in 2022. During that period, around 75,000 requests for time slots were received, of which around 25,000 could be matched to a resulting order booking, while the others could be considered as *lost sales*. Once requests and orders were matched, some feature engineering and enriching the data with external information was performed to create a meaningful set of features. The main features for each prediction model are shown in Fig. 5.

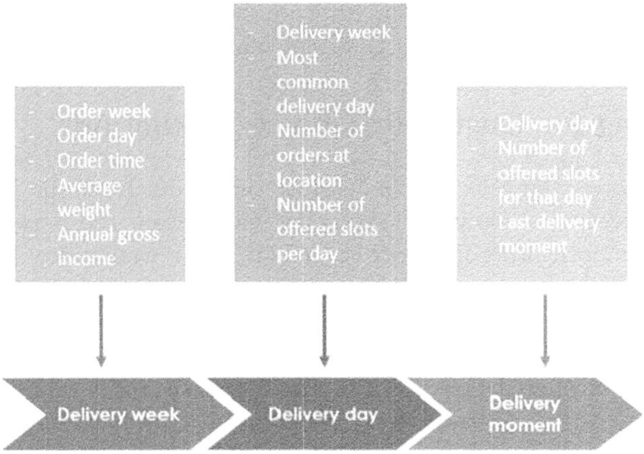

Fig. 5. Feature sets of the subsequent prediction model

5.3 Results and Discussion

Models performed the best when applied in a sequential approach that divides the prediction into three subsequent steps: 1) predict the delivery week, 2) predict the delivery day within the week, and 3) predict the delivery moment of the day.

In each of the three multi-class classification problems data were highly unbalanced with some classes strongly under-represented. Table 4 reports the percentage of observations per class per each of the three learning problems.

Table 4. Percentage of observations per class for the three learning problems considered

Delivery week	Perc.	Delivery day	Perc.	Part of the delivery day	Perc.
44	12.0	Monday	5.2	Early morning	22.0
45	19.4	Tuesday	4.6	Morning	46.3
46	18.1	Wednesday	3.7	Noon	15.3
47	19.0	Thursday	3.9	Eve	15.2
48	19.1	Friday	5.5	Night	1.2
49	7.1	Saturday	4.8		
50	1.5	Sunday	4.8		
51	3.6	Lost order	67.5		
52	0.2				

To prevent models from disregarding the minority class (as mentioned above, only one out of 3 requests could be matched to a successful order), classes were weighted differently in the loss function and the best model configurations were selected via hyperparameter tuning. The F1-score is used to measure the models' performance, and is determined via a sampling method from the models' output probabilities. The results are shown in Table 5. The baseline model has the lowest score for all of the subsequent prediction steps, while the more advanced models are able to better identify customer choice behavior. Even though the NN models perform slightly better than the MNL models, the F1 scores for the models predicting the part of the delivery day are still relatively low indicating the increased difficulty of predicting which part of day a customer will choose compared to the delivery day prediction.

Table 5. F1-scores of the customer choice models

	Baseline	MNL	NN
Delivery week	0.420	0.521	0.695
Delivery day	0.123	0.743	0.797
Part of the delivery day	0.127	0.333	0.368

Analysis of the feature importance of the NN and MNL models shows that features containing information about previously placed orders of a customer have a significant impact. To further validate this conclusion, in Table 6 we report the F1 scores obtained when considering only customers who have already placed orders in the past. This suggests that gathering and including more historical customer information would likely increase the accuracy of the models as well.

Table 6. F1-scores of the customer choice models with historical data customers only

	Baseline	MNL	NN
Delivery day	0.210	0.733	0.801
Part of the delivery day	0.166	0.500	0.549

6 Conclusions

In this paper, we demonstrated the advantages of machine learning methods in refining service and travel time predictions for efficient yet customer-satisfying attended home delivery operations. Next, we explored machine learning approaches for time slot feasibility and customer preference predictions in the context of time slot management for home delivery.

Machine learning models trained on large datasets with service and travel time realizations showed significant improvements in accuracy compared to the baselines. Simulations showed that improved service time predictions can lead to better route schedules both in terms of efficiency and customer service level. The deep neural network developed for travel times yields significant improvements in travel time accuracy compared to the baseline. Machine learning models trained for time slot managements were shown to be capable of predicting time slot feasibility with high accuracy while keeping the computation times low, and to be able to recover customer time slot preferences, especially for returning customers.

In future research, we plan to consider Graph Neural Networks [4,26] to include the spatial/geographical context of the predictions in detail and including the learning of congestion factors for travel time estimations. Additionally, since service time and travel time estimates interact in the overall route schedule timing computation, we plan to combine the training of both models end-to-end. For time slot management, we would like to generalize predicting time slot feasibility into predicting time slot efficiency, and explore the integration with customer preference predictions in the time slot offer strategy. This would enable to quickly score options in terms of efficiency and desirability, and for example offer a discount on efficient but (slightly) less preferred options. As the actual customer preference for such options is unknown, we would like to validate such an approach in a real setting, and experiment with iteratively updating the model based on feedback, as in a reinforcement learning [21] setting.

Disclosure of Interests. We acknowledge that all authors of this article are affiliated with ORTEC, which might introduce a potential conflict of interest. We have made every effort to ensure the objectivity and integrity of the research conducted and here reported. We want to highlight that most of the research reported was conducted in collaboration with universities, further ensuring the high quality and impartiality of the results reported.

References

1. Agatz, N., Fan, Y., Stam, D.: The impact of green labels on time slot choice and operational sustainability. Prod. Oper. Manag. **30**(7), 2285–2303 (2021)
2. Agatz, N., Campbell, A.M., Fleischmann, M., Savels, M.: Challenges and opportunities in attended home delivery. In: Golden, B., Raghavan, S., Wasil, E. (eds.) The Vehicle Routing Problem: Latest Advances and New Challenges. ORCS, vol. 43, pp. 379–396. Springer, Boston (2008). https://doi.org/10.1007/978-0-387-77778-8_17
3. Akamai: Akamai Online Retail Performance Report: Milliseconds Are Critical (2017). https://www.akamai.com/uk/en/about/news/press/2017-press/akamai-releases-spring-2017-state-of-online-retail-performance-report.jsp
4. Bogaerts, T., Masegosa, A.D., Angarita-Zapata, J.S., Onieva, E., Hellinckx, P.: A graph CNN-LSTM neural network for short and long-term traffic forecasting based on trajectory data. Transp. Res. Part C: Emerg. Technol. **112**, 62–77 (2020)
5. Campbell, A.M., Savelsbergh, M.W.P.: Decision support for consumer direct grocery initiatives. Transp. Sci. **39**(3), 313–327 (2005)
6. Caruana, R., Karampatziakis, N., Yessenalina, A.: An empirical evaluation of supervised learning in high dimensions. In: International Conference on Machine Learning (2008)
7. Consumer Panel Services GfK: Shopping behavior 2022: of shocks and accelerators. https://discover.gfk.com/story/shopping-behavior-2022/page/4/3. Accessed 24 Aug 2023
8. Delling, D., Goldberg, A.V., Pajor, T., Werneck, R.F.: Customizable route planning. In: Pardalos, P.M., Rebennack, S. (eds.) SEA 2011. LNCS, vol. 6630, pp. 376–387. Springer, Heidelberg (2011). https://doi.org/10.1007/978-3-642-20662-7_32
9. Derrow-Pinion, A., et al.: ETA prediction with graph neural networks in Google maps. In: Proceedings of the 30th ACM International Conference on Information & Knowledge Management, pp. 3767–3776 (2021)
10. Desaulniers, G., Madsen, O.B., Ropke, S.: The vehicle routing problem with time windows. In: Toth, P., Vigo, D. (eds.) Vehicle Routing: Problems, Methods, and Applications, MOS-SIAM Series on Optimization, 2nd edn., vol. 18, pp. 119–159. SIAM - Society for Industrial and Applied Mathematics, Philadelphia (2014)
11. Ehmke, J.F., Campbell, A.M.: Customer acceptance mechanisms for home deliveries in metropolitan areas. Eur. J. Oper. Res. **233**(1), 193–207 (2014)
12. Forbes: E-commerce sales grew 50 (2022). https://www.forbes.com/sites/jasongoldberg/2022/02/18/e-commerce-sales-grew-50-to-870-billion-during-the-pandemic/
13. van der Hagen, L., Agatz, N., Spliet, R., Visser, T.R., Kok, L.: Machine learning–based feasibility checks for dynamic time slot management. Transp. Sci. **58**(1), 94–109 (2024)
14. Ho, T.K.: Random decision forests. In: Proceedings of 3rd International Conference on Document Analysis and Recognition, vol. 1, pp. 278–282. IEEE (1995)
15. Jamieson, K., Talwalkar, A.: Non-stochastic best arm identification and hyperparameter optimization. In: Gretton, A., Robert, C.C. (eds.) Proceedings of the 19th International Conference on Artificial Intelligence and Statistics. Proceedings of Machine Learning Research, vol. 51, pp. 240–248. PMLR, Cadiz (2016). https://proceedings.mlr.press/v51/jamieson16.html

16. Kok, A.L., Meyer, C.M., Kopfer, H., Schutten, J.M.J.: A dynamic programming heuristic for the vehicle routing problem with time windows and European community social legislation. Transp. Sci. **44**(4), 442–454 (2010)
17. Köhler, C., Haferkamp, J.: Evaluation of delivery cost approximation for attended home deliveries. Transp. Res. Procedia **37**, 67–74 (2019)
18. LeCun, Y., Bengio, Y., Hinton, G.: Deep learning. Nature **521**(7553), 436–444 (2015)
19. Middelweerd, M.: Investigating different models that can be used to define the characteristics that influence customer behaviour in the online grocery sector. Master's thesis, Department Maritime and Transport Technology of Faculty Mechanical, Maritime and Materials Engineering of Delft University of Technology (2023)
20. Morley, S.K., Brito, T.V., Welling, D.T.: Measures of model performance based on the log accuracy ratio. Space Weather **16**(1), 69–88 (2018)
21. Sutton, R.S., Barto, A.G.: Reinforcement Learning: An Introduction. MIT Press, Cambridge (2018)
22. Tibshirani, R.: Regression shrinkage and selection via the lasso. J. R. Stat. Soc. Ser. B Stat Methodol. **58**(1), 267–288 (1996)
23. Visser, T.R., Spliet, R.: Efficient move evaluations for time-dependent vehicle routing problems. Transp. Sci. **54**(4), 1091–1112 (2020)
24. Wang, D., Zhang, J., Cao, W., Li, J., Zheng, Y.: When will you arrive? Estimating travel time based on deep neural networks. In: Proceedings of the AAAI Conference on Artificial Intelligence, vol. 32 (2018)
25. Waßmuth, K., Köhler, C., Agatz, N., Fleischmann, M.: Demand management for attended home delivery–a literature review. Eur. J. Oper. Res. **311**(3), 801–815 (2023)
26. Wu, Z., Pan, S., Chen, F., Long, G., Zhang, C., Philip, S.Y.: A comprehensive survey on graph neural networks. IEEE Trans. Neural Netw. Learn. Syst. **32**(1), 4–24 (2020)
27. Yang, X., Straus, A.K.: An approximate dynamic programming approach to attended home delivery management. Eur. J. Oper. Res. **263**(3), 935–945 (2017)
28. Yang, X., et al.: Choice-based demand management and vehicle routing in e-fulfillment. Transp. Sci. **50**(2), 473–488 (2016)
29. Zhang, H., Wu, H., Sun, W., Zheng, B.: DeepTravel: a neural network based travel time estimation model with auxiliary supervision. arXiv preprint arXiv:1802.02147 (2018)

Laser Learning Environment: A New Environment for Coordination-Critical Multi-agent Tasks

Yannick Molinghen[1(✉)], Raphaël Avalos[2], Mark Van Achter[4], Ann Nowé[2], and Tom Lenaerts[1,2,3]

[1] Machine Learning Group, Université Libre de Bruxelles, Brussels, Belgium
yannick.molinghen@ulb.be
[2] AI Lab, Vrije Universiteit Brussel, Brussels, Belgium
[3] Center for Human-Compatible AI, UC Berkeley, Berkeley, USA
[4] KU Leuven, Leuven, Belgium

Abstract. We introduce the Laser Learning Environment (LLE), a collaborative multi-agent reinforcement learning environment where coordination is key. In LLE, agents depend on each other to make progress (*interdependence*), must jointly take specific sequences of actions to succeed (*perfect coordination*), and accomplishing those joint actions does not yield any intermediate reward (*zero-incentive dynamics*). The challenge of such problems lies in the difficulty of escaping state space bottlenecks caused by interdependence steps since escaping those bottlenecks is not rewarded. We test multiple state-of-the-art value-based MARL algorithms against LLE and show that they consistently fail at the collaborative task because of their inability to escape state space bottlenecks, even though they successfully achieve perfect coordination. We show that Q-learning extensions such as prioritised experience replay and n-steps return hinder exploration in environments with zero-incentive dynamics, and find that intrinsic curiosity with random network distillation is not sufficient to escape those bottlenecks. We demonstrate the need for novel methods to solve this problem and the relevance of LLE as cooperative MARL benchmark.

Keywords: Reinforcement Learning · Multi-Agent · Cooperative

1 Introduction

Many problems, ranging from societal to technological, are inherently multi-agent and often require coordination (or cooperation) among the agents to achieve individually and collectively defined goals (Cao et al., 2013, Klima et al. 2018). While evolution has provided humans with the skills to deal with such tasks, researchers and engineers have to train the artificial agents in a much shorter time span to also manage such tasks.

F. A. Oliehoek et al. (Eds.): BNAIC/Benelearn 2023, CCIS 2187, pp. 135–154, 2025.
https://doi.org/10.1007/978-3-031-74650-5_8

We are interested in Reinforcement Learning (Sutton and Barto 2018, RL) as one of the branches of Machine Learning that holds the promise of training such agents by interacting with their environment. Deep RL has made dazzling progress in recent years with deep Q-learning, showing human or superior to human performance in a wide range of single-agent situations (Mnih et al., 2015), and this progress influenced Multi-Agent Reinforcement Learning (Panait and Luke, 2005, MARL).

In comparison to single-agent RL, centralised MARL faces the issue of the exponential growth of state and joint action spaces with the number of agents, making this approach intractable even for relatively small problems. Decentralised MARL approaches avoid the exponential growth of the action space at the cost of nonstationarity Laurent et al. (2011): Since multiple learning agents update their policy over time, each agent continuously has to adapt to the changing policy of the other agents, making it more challenging to acquire robust and general policies. To mitigate that effect, Oliehoek et al. (2008a) introduced the paradigm of Centralised Training with Decentralised Execution (CTDE) that has demonstrated how successful it can be in complex cooperative multi-agent tasks (Sunehag et al., 2018, Rashid et al., 2018, Avalos et al., 2022).

In the last seven years, a variety of environments have been developed for cooperative MARL. Among others, the Multi-agent Particle Environment (Lowe et al., 2017, Mordatch and Abbeel, 2017, MPE) the StarCraft Multi-Agent Challenge (Samvelyan et al., 2019, SMAC) the Hanabi Learning Environment (Bard et al., 2020, HLE) and Overcooked Wu et al. (2021) respectively aim at studying different aspects of cooperative multi-agent problem-solving such as the ability to infer the intentions of other agents or the emergence of basic compositional language.

Contributions. In this work, we focus on fully cooperative multi-agent problems where agents optimise a single shared reward. We identify a category of such problems that is not well studied, introduce the Laser Learning Environment (LLE) that fits in that category and test state-of-the-art CTDE methods against it[1]. To the best of our knowledge, LLE exhibits a unique combination of three properties: 1) *perfect coordination*: failing to coordinate can be fatal; 2) *interdependence*: agents need each other to make progress; 3) *zero-incentive dynamics*: key steps toward success are not rewarded. We then show how agents successfully achieve perfect coordination but are unable to overcome the zero-incentive dynamics and escape state space bottlenecks, even when using Q-learning extensions such as prioritised experience replay (Schaul et al., 2016), n-steps return (Watkins, 1989) and intrinsic curiosity with Random Network Distillation (Burda et al., 2018). Together, our results demonstrate that LLE is a relevant benchmark for future work and aim to point researchers in new relevant directions of cooperative MARL research.

[1] The code is available at https://github.com/yamoling/bnaic-2023-lle.

2 Background

2.1 Multi-agent Markov Decision Process

A Multi-agent Markov Decision Process (Boutilier, 1996, MMDP) is described as a tuple $\langle n, S, A, T, R, s_0, s_f, \gamma \rangle$ where n is the number of agents, S is the set of states, $A \equiv A_1 \times \cdots \times A_n$ is the set of joint actions and A_i is the set of actions of agent i, $T \colon S \times A \to \Delta_S$ is a function that gives the probability of transitioning from state s to state s' by taking action a, $R : S \times A \times \mathrm{S} \to \mathbb{R}$ is the function that gives the reward obtained by transitioning from s to s' by performing joint action $\boldsymbol{a}$, $s_0 \in S$ is the initial state, s_f is the final state and $\gamma \in [0, 1)$ is a discount factor.

A transition is defined as $\tau = \langle s, \boldsymbol{a}, r, s' \rangle$ with $s, s' \in S, \boldsymbol{a} \in A, r \in \mathbb{R}$. An episode of length l is a sequence of transitions $\tau_1, \ldots, \tau_l$ such that $\tau_1 = \langle s_0, \boldsymbol{a}, r, s' \rangle$ and $\tau_l = \langle s_{l-1}, \boldsymbol{a}, r, s_f \rangle$. Each agent i acts according to a policy $\pi_i \colon S \to \Delta_{A_i}$ and their objective is to find the joint policy $\boldsymbol{\pi} = \langle \pi_1, \ldots, \pi_n \rangle$ that maximises their expected discounted reward $\mathbb{E}\left[\sum_{t=0}^{\infty} \gamma^t R_t | s = s_0, \boldsymbol{\pi}\right]$. The action-value function of a policy measures the expected return obtained by taking action $\boldsymbol{a}$ is state s by following policy $\boldsymbol{\pi}$. In particular, we define the joint action-value function $Q^{\pi} : S \times \boldsymbol{A} \to \mathbb{R}$.

Scenarios where agents receive individual observations of the state instead of the full state are referred to as Decentralised Partially Observable Markov Decision Processes (Oliehoek and Amato 2016).

2.2 Q-Value factorisation

Laurent et al. (2011) showed that multi-agent systems suffer from a non-stationarity problem Tuyls and Weiss (2012) also refer to it as the multi-agent moving target problem) because learning agents perceive the other learning agents as part of the environment. Claus and Boutilier (1998) have shown that naive implementations of Independent Q-Learning (IQL) were often unsuccessful, even for very simple tasks, partly because of this non-stationarity.

To tackle this non-stationarity problem, Sunehag et al. (2018) introduce Value Decomposition Network (VDN), an algorithm based on the concept of Q-value factorisation (Oliehoek et al., 2008b) in which each agent i has its own utility function $Q_i : S \times A_i \to \mathbb{R}$. VDN decomposes the joint Q-value into a simple sum of the agents' utility.

This factorisation allows for decentralised execution thanks to the Individual Global Max property (Son et al., 2019, IGM) that ensures consistency in action selection between the centralised training and the decentralised execution. QMIX (Rashid et al., 2018) extends VDN by allowing more complex factorisation using a monotonically increasing hyper network conditioned on the state.

2.3 Cooperative Multi-agent Environments

In the last few years, several cooperative multi-agent environments have emerged to study different aspects of the cooperative multi-agent problem and we give here an overview of popular environments with discrete action spaces.

The StarCraft Multi-agent Challenge. (Samvelyan et al., 2019, SMAC) comes with a wide range of maps and offers a complex cooperative partially observable problem where individual agents of the same team have to defeat the opponent team in a short skirmish. This environment has been introduced to study whether agents could learn complex behaviours such as kiting.

Overcooked. (Wu et al., 2021) is a cooperative environment in which multiple agents receive recipes and have to cook them before serving them on a plate. On top of spatial movements, this environment has been introduced to study the ability of agents to infer the hidden intentions of others as well as the ability of agents to learn when to split the tasks amongst themselves (divide and conquer) and when to work on the same task (cooperate).

Hanabi Learning Environment. (Bard et al., 2020, HLE) is an environment that comes from a board game with the same name. In Hanabi, every player plays one after the other and has to decide whether to play a card or give a clue to a teammate. This environment is well suited to study reasoning, beliefs and intentions of other players.

The Multi-agent Particle Environment. (Lowe et al., 2017, Mordatch and Abbeel, 2017, MPE) is a set of cooperative and competitive 2D tasks with a dense reward signal. It has both partially and fully observable variants and offers scenarios that involve communication. This environment has been introduced to study the emergence of a basic compositional language.

3 The Laser Learning Environment

We introduce here the Laser Learning Environment (LLE), a grid world populated with agents of different colours (see Fig. 1) and with different types of tiles: floor, start, wall, laser, laser source, gem, and exit tiles. The main objective in LLE is for each agent to reach an exit tile, while additional points can be gathered by collecting gems along the way. The game is cooperative since agents must help each other to pass laser beams: if an agent's colour doesn't match the colour of a laser beam, this agent dies and the game ends. However, when an agent of matching colour stands in line with a beam, it blocks the laser and allows other agents to reach areas of the map that they could not access by themselves.

LLE comes with six predefined levels presented in Appendix D and can generate random solvable maps of arbitrary sizes based on multiple parameters (number of agents, number of gems, number of lasers and wall density). Randomly generated maps can also be constrained to some degree of difficulty depending

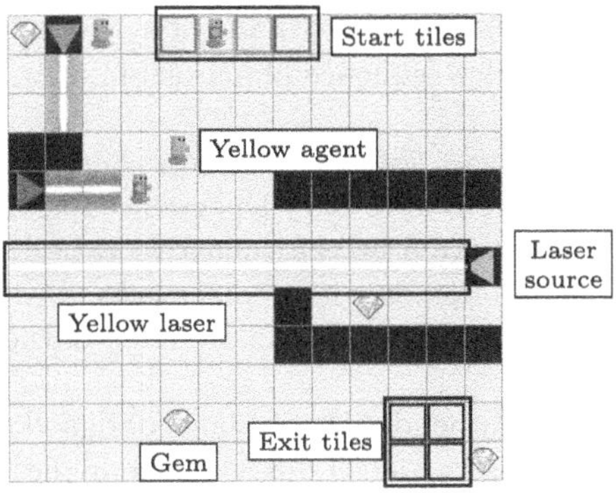

Fig. 1. Level 6 of LLE, which has 4 agents, 3 lasers and 4 gems. Agent red is blocking the red laser, making it possible for the other agents to pass to the lower part of the grid world. Additional blocking of the yellow laser is required for all of them to pass and reach the exit tiles (Color figure online)

on how many steps of *perfect coordination* (see Sect. 3.1) are required to complete the level. While future work will address the issue of curriculum learning (Parker-Holder et al., 2022), in this work, we focus on the configuration visualised in Fig. 1.

3.1 Motivations

As explained in Sect. 2.3, there already exist several multi-agent cooperative environments that are suitable for studying various fields of MARL. However, LLE aims at studying a new range of problems that require coordinated exploration in hazardous situations. To the best of our knowledge, LLE introduces new complexities in the study of cooperative problem solving due to a combination of three properties: *perfect coordination*, *interdependence* and *zero incentive dynamics*.

Perfect coordination is defined as the property of a policy in which agents simultaneously take a specific sequence of actions such that any agent that singlehandedly deviates from this policy in state s_t would directly lead to a penalty in state s_{t+1} and the failure of the collaborative task.

Unlike all the environments presented in Sect. 2.3, LLE requires agents to achieve perfect coordination when blocking lasers. Focusing on agents red and yellow in Fig. 1, it requires perfect coordination for agent yellow to cross the red laser: if agent yellow goes down and agent red releases the laser, agent yellow would die and the game would terminate with a punishment. Although Hanabi has the comparable property of directly punishing agents that fail to coordinate, the environment is such that agents play one after the other. For that reason, Hanabi does not require *perfect coordination*.

Interdependence expresses how much a set of agents relies on another set of agents to perform a particular sequence of actions in order to make progress in the collective task.

Interdependence introduces *bottlenecks in the state space* in the steps that require coordination. A high level of interdependence means that from the start state, the end state that maximises the collective expected discounted return is located beyond such interdependence bottlenecks. Inversely, a low level of interdependence means that agents can explore most of the state space without relying on each other.

The maps presented in Appendix D have been designed with increasing levels of interdependence in mind, with level 6 having the highest level of interdependence. In comparison, SMAC, MPE and HLE challenge agents with situations where any agent can explore the state space, sometimes even finish the game, regardless of its teammates' actions.

Overcooked explicitly uses the concept of sub-tasks in the form of recipes that also enclose the reachable state space until the current sub-task is solved. However, agents can most of the time accomplish those sub-tasks by themselves and are therefore not interdependent. Arguably, there is *interdependence* in completely split maps where agents do not have access to every kitchen tool (e.g.: full-divider map) and must pass items over the counter to the other to complete recipes.

Zero-incentive dynamics defines the property of an environment in which overcoming state space bottlenecks is not rewarded. Intuitively, an environment with zero-incentive dynamics does not reward agents for succeeding at key (cooperative) dynamics.

As detailed in Sect. 3.4, blocking lasers in LLE does not provide any reward, and laser-blocking are state space bottlenecks caused by interdependence. Consequently, LLE has zero-incentive dynamics. Overcooked on the other hand provides rewards for finishing recipes and therefore does not have zero-incentive dynamics, even in the full-divider map that does have interdependence. We discuss in Sect. 4.1 that the combination of interdependence and zero-incentive dynamics makes it difficult for agents to escape regions surrounded by lasers during the training process, which makes LLE a challenging exploration task.

We distinguish zero-incentive dynamics from temporal credit assignment (Sutton, 1984), which is related to the ability of a policy to determine which action takes credit for some later reward, and not a property of the environment.

3.2 States

The state of LLE encodes the location of grid-world elements layer by layer as illustrated in Fig. 2. These items are namely agents, walls, lasers, laser sources, gems and exits locations. There is one layer per agent and one layer per laser colour. This representation has the advantage of being very generic as long as the size of the map and the number of agents remain constant, allowing future

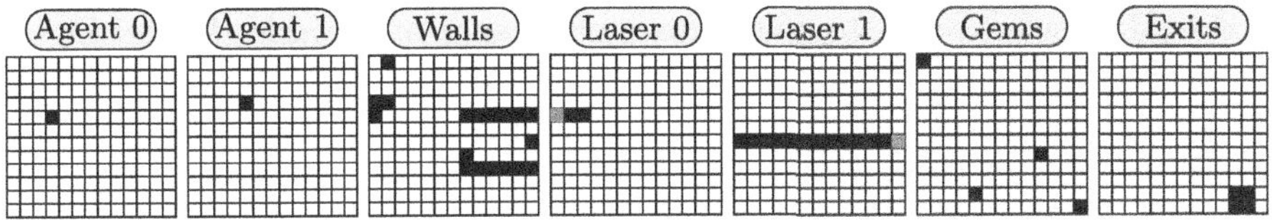

Fig. 2. Representation of the state shown in Fig. 1. Layers "Agent 2", "Agent 3", "Laser 2" and "Laser 3" were omitted for the sake of conciseness. Each layer encodes the location of a specific type of object of the grid world (lasers, agents, walls, ...). White, black and grey squares respectively encode 0s, 1s and -1s

work in the field of generalisation and curriculum learning (Parker-Holder et al., 2022).

3.3 Actions

The action space of LLE is discrete and the possible actions are `NORTH`, `EAST`, `SOUTH`, `WEST` and `STAY`, which is required for laser-blocking purposes. Actions are identical for all agents.

LLE prevents agents from entering invalid tiles by providing the set of available actions for each agent at each time step. An agent cannot enter a wall, move beyond the grid boundaries nor enter a tile that is currently occupied by another agent. This prevents multiple types of conflicts that can occur in grid world problems such as edge, following and swapping conflicts (Stern et al., 2017). Additionally, once an agent enters an exit tile, it cannot leave it anymore and the only action allowed is `STAY`.

Vertex conflicts – when two or more agents enter the same tile – can unfortunately not be prevented with information on action availability. As a result, when two or more agents provoke a vertex conflict by trying to move to the same tile, their actions are replaced by `STAY`.

3.4 Rewards

The reward function of LLE has a single scalar output as the team reward, which is the result of the joint action of the agents at a given time step. Collecting a gem or entering an exit tile provides a collective reward of $+1$. Finishing the game, i.e. when all agents are on an exit tile, also provides an additional reward of $+1$. However, if an agent dies at a time step, the episode ends and the reward is set to -1 times the number of agents that have died.

3.5 Metrics

Two metrics are used here to evaluate the performance of the LLE agents: the score and the exit rate.

Score. The score refers to the undiscounted sum of rewards throughout an episode. This is metric is close to the one the agents are trained to maximise, i.e. the *discounted* sum of rewards over the course of an episode, but does not give insight on the time taken to achieve the task. The maximal score of an LLE environment can be calculated as follows: given a map with n agents and g gems, we can compute the maximum score as maximum score $= n + g + 1$. In Fig. 1, the maximal score is $4 + 4 + 1 = 9$.

Exit Rate. The exit rate is defined as the proportion of agents that reach an exit tile at the end of an episode. Since the objective in every LLE is to exit the level, this metric gives an estimation of how close agents are to the objective. An exit rate of 1 means that all agents have successfully exited the level.

The combination of those two metrics gives insight into the agents' behaviour. As long as the exit rate is below 1, it means that the agents are not able to finish the level. If the exit rate is 1, then analysing the score allows us to know if agents have collected all the gems.

4 Experiments

We analyse the score and exit rate on level 6 shown in Fig. 1 with Independent deep Q-Learning (Mnih et al., 2015, IQL) Value Decomposition Network (Sunehag et al., 2018, VDN) and QMIX (Rashid et al., 2018). Then, we discuss in Sect. 5 the results with regard to perfect coordination, interdependence and zero-incentive dynamics.

In their respective papers, VDN and QMIX have been introduced in the scope of partially observable environments while LLE is fully observable. We treat the fully observable case as a special case of the partially observable one (Dec-POMDP) where individual observations are equal to the state. We motivate the usage of QMIX by the fact that it has demonstrated its superior representational capability in comparison to VDN with a fully observable example referred to as *Two-Step game* (Rashid et al., 2018). Therefore, we use a feed-forward neural network instead of a recurrent one.

Experimental Setup. In our experiments, agents interact with the environment for one million time steps and policies are updated every 5 steps on a batch of 64 transitions. Agents use an ϵ-greedy policy linearly annealed from 1 to 0.05 over 500k time steps and use a replay memory of 50k transitions. We use Double Q-learning (Van Hasselt et al., 2016) for all algorithms. The target network is updated via soft updates with $\tau = 0.01$ (Lillicrap et al., 2016) which has experimentally provided better results than periodic hard updates of the target network. A complete table of hyperparameters can be found in Appendix A.

The utility values Q_i of each agent $i \in \{1, \dots, n\}$ are estimated with a convolutional neural network (LeCun et al., 1998) to take advantage of the spatial nature of the layered observations. Since observations are designed such that every *pixel* gives information, the stride of the convolutions is 1. Appendix B.1 provides a more detailed description of the neural network architecture. Since

LLE is fully observable and agents share the same neural network, we concatenate the flattened output of the CNN with a one-hot encoding of the agent id. This allows the shared neural network to output different Q_i-values for each agent.

We set the maximal duration of an episode to $\lfloor \frac{width \times height}{2} \rceil$ steps, after which the episode is truncated. This heuristic value allows the agents to discover a lot of dynamics of the environment without polluting the replay memory with too many useless transitions. For instance, in level 6, if agents red and yellow reach the exit tiles but did not open the way for blue and green, then the remaining time steps of the episode would just be the latter two waiting behind the beam.

Note that by definition, the value of a terminal state is zero (Sutton and Barto, 2018). Here, we distinguish *done* episodes whose last transition is a terminal state (death of an agent or reaching the exit tiles) from *truncated* episodes whose last state is not terminal and whose value must in turn be estimated by the target network in the optimization process.

Foreanalysis. Level 6 (Fig. 1) is of size 12×13 and has 4 agents and 4 gems. The maximal score achievable is hence $4 + 4 + 1 = 9$ as explained in Sect. 3.5. The optimal policy in level 6 is the following: **i)** Agent green should collect the gem in the top left corner; **ii)** Agent red should block the red laser and wait for every other agent to cross; **iii)** Agent yellow should cross the red laser and collect the gem that only he can collect near the yellow source; **iv)** Agent yellow should block the laser for every agent to cross; **v)** Agents should collect the remaining gems on the bottom half; **vi)** Agents should go to the exit tiles. The length of such an episode is ≈ 30 time steps, well below the time limit of $\lfloor \frac{12 \times 13}{2} \rceil = 78$ steps.

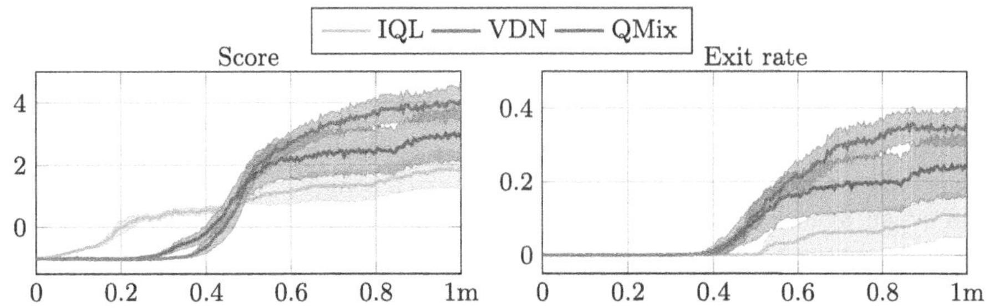

Fig. 3. Training score and exit rate over time for IQL, VDN and QMIX on level 6 (Fig. 1). The maximal achievable score is 9. Results are averaged on 20 different seeds and shown with 95% confidence intervals

4.1 Baseline Results

Figure 3 shows the mean score and exit rate over the course of training on level 6 (Fig. 1). Note that none of the algorithms ever reach the highest possible score of 9 and at most half of the agents ever reach the exit tiles.

VDN performs best on this map, then QMIX, then IQL. Although there is no clear explanation to why QMIX performs worse than VDN in this case, we measured that unlike VDN and IQL, QMIX overestimates Q-values by up to 5 orders of magnitude in the early stages of the learning process before stabilising later on. In previous work on single-agent deep RL, van Hasselt et al. (2018) show that this soft-divergence phenomenon correlates with poor performance and is more likely to happen when the size of the neural network increases. In our case, QMIX indeed has a bigger neural network than VDN and IQL.

Looking into the results, the best policy learned only completes items i), iii) and v) discussed in the foreanalysis. Agents red and yellow escape the top half of the map, collect gems on the bottom half and reach the exit, while agents green and blue are not waited for. This policy yields a score of 6 and an exit rate of 0.5. We could introduce reward shaping in order to drive the agents towards a better solution but reward shaping is notoriously difficult to achieve properly and can drive agents towards unexpected and likely undesired behaviours (Amodei et al., 2016). Moreover, changing the reward function would modify the problem instead of solving it.

4.2 Results with Q-Learning Extensions

When a policy is not successful enough, there exists a few common approaches to try and improve the learning of the policy. We extend both VDN and QMIX with Prioritised Experience Replay (Schaul et al., 2016, PER) n-step return (Watkins, 1989) and intrinsic curiosity (Schmidhuber, 1991) and analyse the impact of these methods on the learning process.

Prioritised Experience Replay is a technique used in off-policy reinforcement learning to enhance learning efficiency by prioritising experiences and sampling them based on their informativeness. The intuition is to sample past experiences whose Q-values are poorly estimated with a higher probability and hope that when agents discover a better policy than their current one, this policy would be prioritised. In our setting, we hope that if agents ever complete the level, this experience would be prioritised.

As Schaul et al. suggest, we use the temporal difference error as the priority. We have performed a hyperparameter search with VDN on α and β that respectively control the exponential scale of priorities and the exponential scale of importance sampling weights with values ranging from 0.3 to 0.8 and have found the best values to be $\alpha = 0.6$ and $\beta = 0.5$, where β is annealed from 0.5 to 1 on the course of the training (1 m steps).

Figure 4 shows that prioritised sampling performs worse than uniform sampling with both VDN and QMIX. We hypothesise that PER hinders exploration

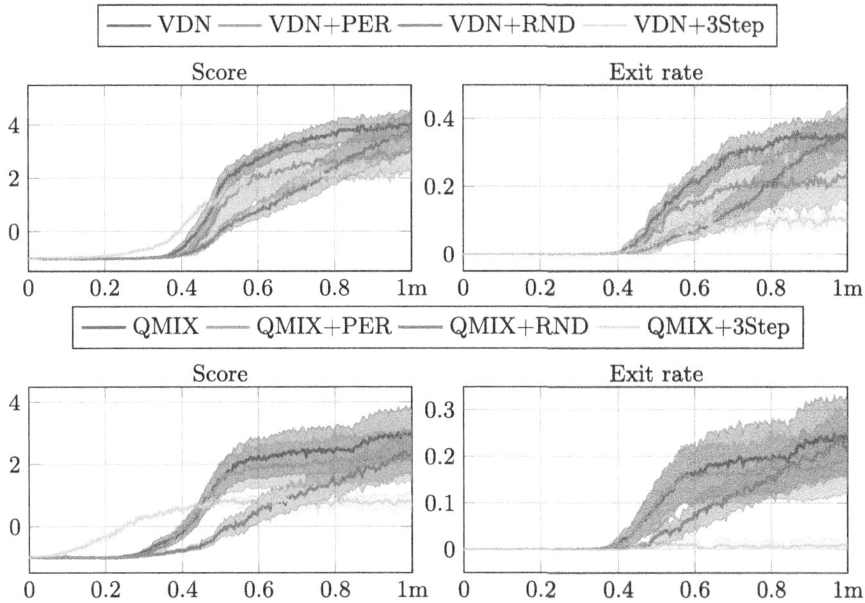

Fig. 4. Training score and exit rate over training time on level 6 with PER, RND and 3-step return. The maximal achievable score is 9. Results are averaged on 20 different seeds and shown with 95% confidence intervals

in the early stages of the training because of the zero-incentive dynamics of the game and discuss this further in Sect. 5.2 and Sect. 5.3 with regard to interdependence and zero-incentive dynamics respectively.

***N*-step return** is a technique that aims at speeding up the bootstrapping process (Sutton and Barto, 2018) by propagating rewards up to n-steps into the past. In the scope of LLE, the idea here is to propagate the reward for collecting gems faster to the step of laser blocking. We have tried values for $n \in \{3, 5, 7, 9\}$ with VDN and found $n = 3$ to give the highest score on average.

Figure 4 shows that 3-step return yields worse results than any other variant with both VDN and QMIX. We relate this poor performance to the high probability of dying from lasers while exploring, resulting in agents learning more conservative policies. We relate this phenomenon to the zero-incentive dynamics of the game and discuss this topic further in Sect. 5.3.

Intrinsic curiosity aims at introducing bias in the learning process to encourage agents to explore unknown states. In the learning phase, intrinsic curiosity adds an extra reward referred to as the intrinsic reward, thereby altering the updates of the Q-function. With this method, we hope that agents would learn faster about laser-blocking and therefore allow them to escape state space bottlenecks.

Intrinsic curiosity with Random Network Distillation (Burda et al., 2018, RND) has proven to work well in single-agent environments with zero-incentive dynamics such as Montezuma's Revenge, where the agent must first collect a torch (unrewarded) to be able to light up a dark room (unrewarded) and in the end, collect a treasure (rewarded). Similarly, in LLE, the objective of using RND is to quicken the discovery of the laser-blocking dynamic and encourage agents to explore the state space. The layout of the random network can be found in Appendix B.1. We scale the intrinsic reward by a factor μ linearly annealed from 2 to $\frac{2}{3}$ over the course of the training.

Figure 4 shows that QMIX+RND performs similarly to the QMIX baseline and does not enable the agents to escape more state space bottlenecks and therefore to learn significantly better policies. With VDN+RND, we can see that agents take more time to reach the same score and exit rate as the VDN baseline but achieve the same score and exit rate after 1 m time steps. Unlike other variants, the metrics of VDN+RND do not seem to stabilise after 1 m time steps, which suggests that more training may yield better results.

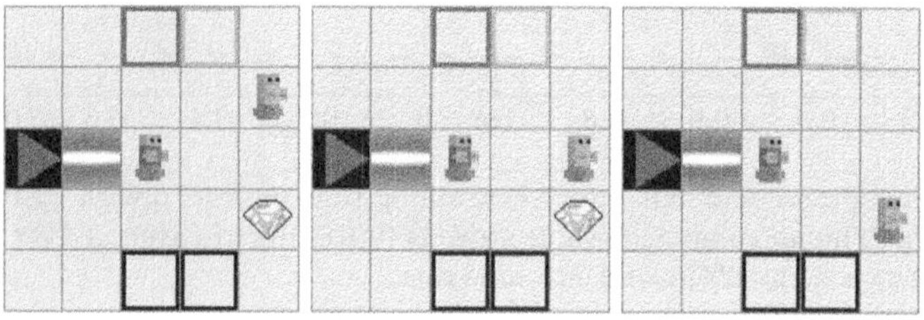

(a) (b) (c)

Fig. 5. Four consecutive states of an episode. Agent red blocks the laser for agent yellow and waits for the latter to leave the range of the blocked beam (Color figure online)

Table 1. Q_i-values from the successive states depicted in Fig. 5. The highest Q_i-values are in bold

State	Agent	North	South	West	East	Stay
Figure 5a	Red	-1.29	-0.97	2.52	2.53	**2.56**
	Yellow	0.78	**0.94**	0.67	0.91	0.85
Figure 5b	Red	1.44	1.51	1.48	1.51	**1.56**
	Yellow	1.77	**2.13**	1.18	1.41	1.45
Figure 5c	Red	1.15	**1.36**	1.16	1.19	1.25
	Yellow	0.71	1.42	**1.49**	1.42	1.41

5 Discussion

5.1 Perfect Coordination

We analyse the policy that agents learn with the VDN baseline and show their ability to achieve perfect coordination. VDN has been chosen over QMIX for interpretability reasons and because it has been the most successful algorithm in our tests.

Level 6. Analysing the policy of the four agents after training for 1 m steps, we can see that the agents understand the laser dynamics: they learn low Q_i-values for walking into deadly lasers and for releasing a laser beam on another agent (killing it). Agents red and yellow also learn to cooperate and block lasers for each other in order to reach the bottom half of the map, collect the gems and reach the exit tiles. We argue that agents learn perfect coordination and illustrate that behaviour in a simpler toy example illustrated in Fig. 5, where agents must also coordinate and block a laser.

Toy Example. Consider the toy example depicted in Fig. 5 with one laser and two agents. We train the agents for 160k steps with VDN and then analyse the Q_i-values during the steps concerned by perfect coordination in Table 1.

Starting with step 5a, the red agent understands that releasing the laser beam has a much lower value than the other actions because it would likely kill agent yellow. The Q_i-values suggest that the *credit* for killing an agent is assigned to the one releasing the beam, not to the one walking in the laser span. At step 5b, the Q_i-values of agent yellow show that the yellow agent has a clear preference for the south action to collect a gem and close the gap with the exit. Meanwhile, agent red keeps blocking the laser as long as agent yellow stands in the range of the laser beam. With such behaviour similar to the one of level 6 for agent red and yellow, we conclude that agents achieve perfect coordination successfully.

5.2 Interdependence

As discussed in Sect. 3.1, agent interdependence introduces bottlenecks in the state space, making such environments challenging exploration tasks. We hypothesise that this difficulty of randomly stumbling on good policies contributes to the failure of PER: if agents never come across good policies, PER can never prioritise it. Across the 20 seeded runs with PER on level 6, we checked that at no single point in time, any episode ever reached an exit rate above 0.5.

With RND however, agents occasionally reached an exit rate higher than 0.5. This occasional high exit rate combined with the fact that VDN+RND did not seem to stabilise after 1 m time steps (as shown in Fig. 4) suggest that methods based on intrinsic motivation could at least partially answer the question of agent interdependence.

5.3 Zero-Incentive Dynamics

We argue that the zero-incentive dynamics of LLE have a detrimental effect on n-step return and on PER because they stress the punishment of dying from lasers each in their own way.

With regard to PER, since walking into a laser either yields no reward or a punishment (as the definition of zero-incentive dynamics implies), PER is likely to give a higher priority to transitions where punishment has occurred rather than to transitions with a null reward. As a result, we hypothesise that in the early stages of the game, PER emphasises the fact that lasers can be deadly which results in agents being more reluctant to walk into lasers overall.

Looking into the poor performance of n-step return, we observe that agents are very likely to die by walking into a laser in their exploration phase. It is also very likely that this punishment is the only non-null reward signal within the n last steps because of the reward sparsity and the zero-incentive dynamics of the environment. Consequently, when this "bad" experience (caused by a poor policy or by random exploration) is then sampled from the replay buffer, the agents learn that the n last actions eventually lead to punishment and their policy is therefore updated to be "safer". Our experimental results in Appendix C support this explanation, as the mean score and exit rate decrease when n increases.

6 Conclusion

In this paper, we introduced the Laser Learning Environment (LLE), a new cooperative multi-agent grid world with a focus on hazardous coordinated exploration. To the best of our knowledge, LLE exhibits a unique combination of three properties: *perfect coordination*, *interdependence* and *zero-incentive dynamics*. We discussed that the interdependence property induces state space bottlenecks that are difficult to explore and that both perfect coordination and zero-incentive dynamics make this exploration hazardous.

We tested IQL, VDN and QMIX against LLE and showed that those algorithms were unable to complete the cooperative task. Our experiments demonstrated that agents successfully achieve perfect coordination but also showed that agents failed at long-term coordination due to interdependence and zero-incentive dynamics and thus never complete the task. We highlighted that prioritised experience replay and n-steps return hinder the agents' performance because of the zero-incentive dynamics of the environment. Although intrinsic curiosity with random network distillation occasionally yielded higher exit rates than their baselines, it did not provide enough incentive to escape state space bottlenecks and did not enable agents to learn significantly better policies on average.

Overall, our experiments demonstrated that current state-of-the-art value-based methods fail in LLE and reveal that new benchmarks are needed in cooperative Multi-Agent Reinforcement Learning. This is why we look forward to seeing how the MARL community will approach the Laser Learning Environment and use it to tackle the challenges discussed in this paper and other topics such as generalisation, curriculum learning and inter-agent communication.

Acknowledgements. Raphaël Avalos is supported by the FWO (Research Foundation – Flanders) under the grant 11F5721N. Tom Lenaerts is supported by an FWO project (grant nr. G054919N) and two FRS-FNRS PDR (grant numbers 31257234 and 40007793). His is furthermore supported by Service Public de Wallonie Recherche under grant no 2010235-ariac by digitalwallonia4.ai. Ann Nowé and Tom Lenaerts are also suported by the Flemish Government through the AI Research Program and TAILOR, a project funded by EU Horizon 2020 research and innovation programme under GA No 952215.

A Hyperparameters

A hyperparameter search has been performed with VDN on a combination of batch sizes (32, 64 and 128 transitions), memory sizes (50k, 100k and 200k transitions) and training intervals (1 and 5). Then, we performed a hyperparameter search for prioritised experience replay on a combination of α (0.3, 0.4, 0.5, 0.6, 0.7, 0.8) and β (0.3, 0.4, 0.5, 0.6, 0.7, 0.8). For random network distillation, we have explored update ratios $p \in \{0, 0.25, 0.5, 0.75\}$.

Table 2. Hyperparameters used across all the experiments

Parameter	Value	Comment
Memory size	50 000	Transitions
Batch size	64	Transitions
Train interval	5 time steps	The policy is optimised every 5 time steps.
Optimiser	Adam	
α (Learning rate)	0.0005	For both Q-network and mixer
Grad norm clipping	10	Clips both Q-network and mixer
γ	0.95	Discount factor
τ	0.01	Soft update rate
ϵ_{start}	1	
ϵ_{min}	0.05	
ϵ annealing	500k time steps	Linearly annealed
α	0.6	PER
β	$0.5 \rightarrow 1$	PER, linearly increases over 1 m time steps
TD error clipping	5	PER
p	0.25	RND error masking probability
μ	$2 \rightarrow \frac{2}{3}$	RND multiplier, linearly annealed over 1 m steps

B Neural Networks Architectures

B.1 Q-Network

The Q-network is made of two parts with an interconnection: a convolutional neural network of three layers, an interconnect that flattens the CNN, and finally a neural network of three linear layers. This is depicted in Table 3.

Table 3. Q-network architecture

Layer type	Activation	Output shape	Stride	Kernel
Input		$11 \times 13 \times 15$		
Conv2D	ReLU	$32 \times 11 \times 13$	1	3×3
Conv2D	ReLU	$64 \times 9 \times 11$	1	3×3
Conv2D	ReLU	$32 \times 7 \times 9$	1	3×3
Flatten		2016		
Concat with agent id		2020		
Linear	ReLU	64		
Linear	ReLU	64		
Linear		5		

B.2 Random Network Distillation

The random network used for the intrinsic reward computation is a convolutional one similar to the Q-network and is depicted in Table 4. The frozen random network (the target) consists in the first part of the table with an output of size 512. The optimised network (the predictor) has an additional tail with one ReLU activation and one linear layer.

Table 4. Random network architecture

Layer type	Activation	Output shape	Stride	Kernel
Input		11 × 13 × 15		
Conv2D	ReLU	32 × 11 × 13	1	3 × 3
Conv2D	ReLU	64 × 9 × 11	1	3 × 3
Conv2D	ReLU	32 × 7 × 9	1	3 × 3
Flatten		2016		
Concat with agent id		2020		
Linear	ReLU	64		
Linear	ReLU	64		
Linear		512		
Predictor only				
	ReLU	512		
Linear		512		

C Results of n-Steps Returns with VDN

We plot in Fig. 6 the score and exit rate over the course of the training on level 6 illustrated in Fig. 1. The agents are trained on VDN with n-steps return and with the hyperparameters shown in Table 2. These results show that a higher value of n yield worse results, as discussed in Sect. 5.3.

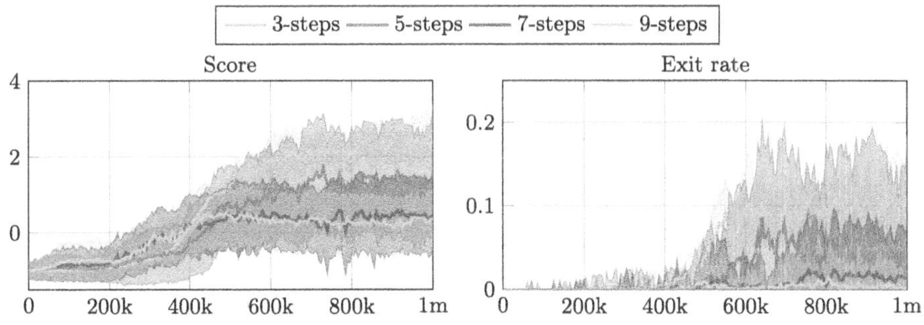

Fig. 6. Scores and exit rates for different values of n in n-steps return. Results are averaged on 10 different seeds and shown ± standard deviation

D Maps Provided by LLE

LLE comes with six predefined levels illustrated in Fig. 7.

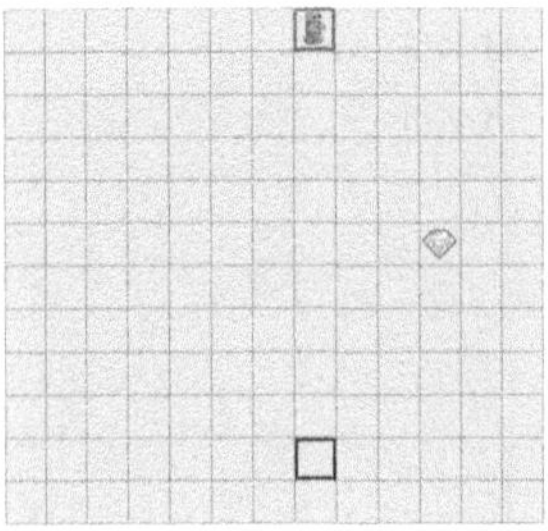

(a) Level 1 for debugging purposes.

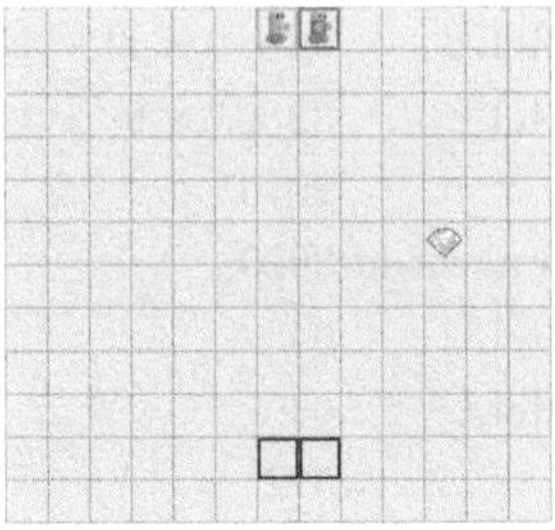

(b) Level 2, first step into multi-agent problems, almost no interdependence.

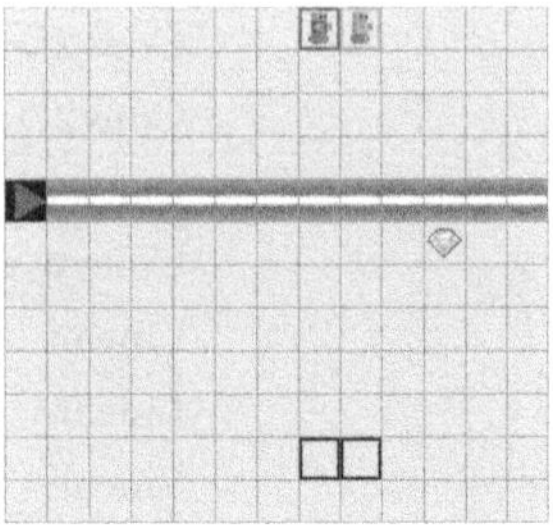

(c) Level 3, introduces the dynamic of laser-blocking, which increases interdependence.

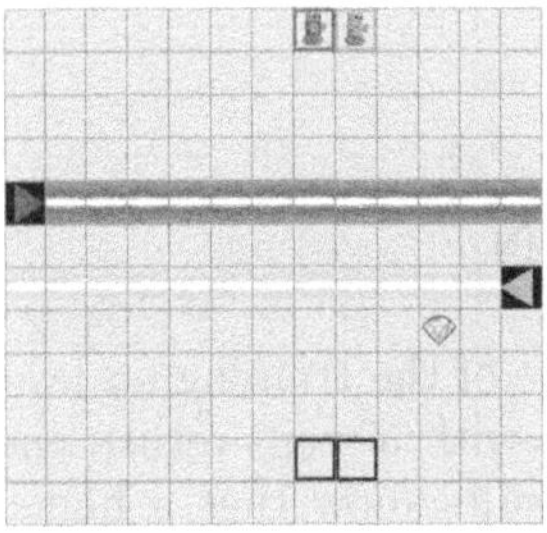

(d) Level 4 introduces two lasers such that each agent successively has to block it for the other for even more interdependence.

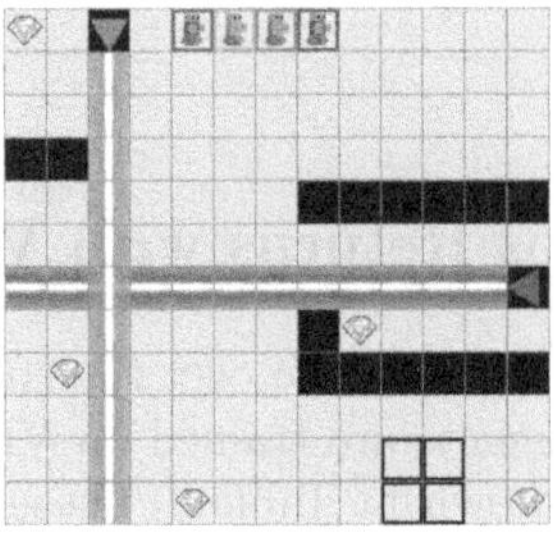

(e) Level 5 also has 2 lasers but has 4 agents, which increases interdependence.

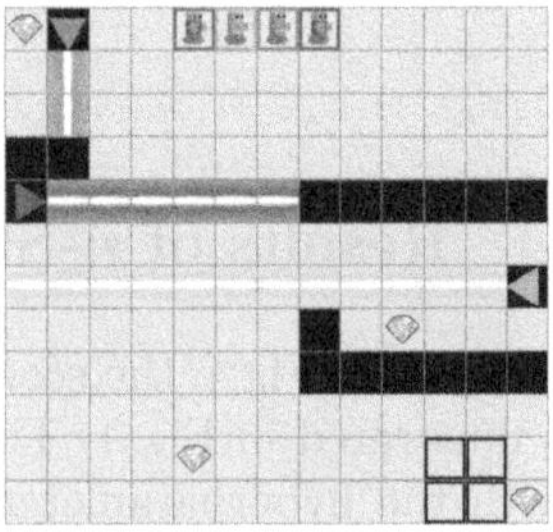

(f) Level 6, four agents and three lasers, the most difficult level introduced with the highest level of interdependence.

Fig. 7. Six standard levels of LLE. The levels have been designed with incremental level of interdependence in mind. Level 6 is the main level studied in this work

References

Amodei, D., Olah, C., Steinhardt, J., Christiano, P.F., Schulman, J., Mané, D.: Concrete problems in AI safety. CoRR, abs/1606.06565 (2016)

Avalos, R., Reymond, M., Nowé, A., Roijers, D.M.: Local advantage networks for cooperative multi-agent reinforcement learning. In: AAMAS 2022: Proceedings of the 21st International Conference on Autonomous Agents and MultiAgent Systems (Extended Abstract) (2022)

Bard, N., et al.: The hanabi challenge: a new frontier for AI research. Artif. Intell. **280**, 103216 (2020). ISSN: 00043702

Boutilier, C.: Planning, learning and coordination in multiagent decision processes. In: Proceedings of the 6th Conference on Theoretical Aspects of Rationality and Knowledge, pp. 195–210 (1996)

Burda, Y., Edwards, H., Storkey, A., Klimov, O.: Exploration by random network distillation (2018)

Cao, Y., Wenwu, Yu., Ren, W., Chen, G.: An overview of recent progress in the study of distributed multi-agent coordination. IEEE Trans. Ind. Inf. **9**(1), 427–438 (2013)

Claus, C., Boutilier, C.: The dynamics of reinforcement learning in cooperative multiagent systems. In: Proceedings of the Fifteenth National Conference on Artificial Intelligence and Tenth Innovative Applications of Artificial Intelligence Conference, AAAI 1998 (1998)

Klima, R., et al.: Space debris removal: learning to cooperate and the price of anarchy. Front. Robot. AI **5**, 54 (2018). ISSN: 2296-9144

Laurent, G.J., Matignon, L., Le Fort-Piat, N.: The world of independent learners is not Markovian. Int. J. Knowl.-Based Intell. Eng. Syst. **15**(1), 55–64 (2011). ISSN: 18758827, 13272314

LeCun, Y., Bottou, L., Bengio, Y., Ha, P.: Gradient-based learning applied to document recognition (1998)

Lillicrap, T.P., et al.: Continuous control with deep reinforcement learning. In: Bengio, Y., LeCun, Y. (eds.) ICLR (2016)

Lowe, R., Wu, Y., Tamar, A., Harb, J., Abbeel, P., Mordatch, I.: Multi-agent actor-critic for mixed cooperative-competitive environments. In: Neural Information Processing Systems (NIPS) (2017)

Mnih, V., et al.: Human-level control through deep reinforcement learning. Nature **518**(7540), 529–533 (2015). ISSN: 1476-4687

Mordatch, I., Abbeel, P.: Emergence of grounded compositional language in multi-agent populations. arXiv preprint arXiv:1703.04908 (2017)

Oliehoek, F.A., Amato, C.: A Concise Introduction to Decentralized POMDPs. SpringerBriefs in Intelligent Systems, Springer, Cham (2016). https://doi.org/10.1007/978-3-319-28929-8. ISBN: 978-3-319-28929-8

Oliehoek, F.A., Spaan, M.T.J., Vlassis, N.: Optimal and approximate Q-value functions for decentralized POMDPs. J. Artif. Intell. Res. **32**, 289–353 (2008a). ISSN: 1076-9757

Oliehoek, F.A., Spaan, M.T.J., Whiteson, S.: Exploiting locality of interaction in factored Dec-POMDPs. In: International Joint Conference on Autonomous Agents and Multi-Agent Systems, pp. 517–524 (2008b)

Panait, L., Luke, S.: Cooperative multi-agent learning: the state of the art. Auton. Agents Multi-Agent Syst. **11**(3), 387–434 (2005). ISSN: 1573-7454

Parker-Holder, J., et al.: Evolving curricula with regret-based environment design. In: International Conference on Machine Learning, pp. 17473–17498. PMLR (2022)

Rashid, T., Samvelyan, M., De Witt, C.S.: QMIX: monotonic value function factorisation for deep multi-agent reinforcement learning (2018)

Samvelyan, M., et al.: The StarCraft multi-agent challenge. CoRR, abs/1902.04043 (2019)

Schaul, T., Quan, J., Antonoglou, I., Silver, D.: Prioritized experience replay. In: 4th International Conference on Learning Representations, ICLR 2016 - Conference Track Proceedings, pp. 1–21 (2016)

Schmidhuber, J.: A possibility for implementing curiosity and boredom in model-building neural controllers. In: Meyer, J.-A. (ed.) From Animals to Animats, pp. 222–227. The MIT Press (1991). International Conference on Simulation Adaptive Behavior: From Animals to Animats Edition. ISBN: 978-0-262-25667-4

Son, K., Kim, D., Kang, W.J., Hostallero, D.E., Yi, Y.: QTRAN: learning to factorize with transformation for cooperative multi-agent reinforcement learning (2019)

Stern, R., et al.: Multi-agent pathfinding: definitions, variants, and benchmarks (2017)

Sunehag, P., et al.: Value-decomposition networks for cooperative multi-agent learning based on team reward. In: Proceedings of the International Joint Conference on Autonomous Agents and Multiagent Systems, AAMAS, vol. 3, pp. 2085–2087 (2018). ISSN: 15582914. ISBN: 9781510868083

Sutton, R.S., Barto, A.G.: Reinforcement learning: an introduction (2018)

Sutton, R.S.: Temporal credit assignment in reinforcement learning. Ph.D. thesis, University of Massachusetts Amherst (1984). AAI8410337

Tuyls, K., Weiss, G.: Multiagent learning: basics, challenges, and prospects. AI Mag. **33**(3), 41 (2012). ISSN: 2371-9621, 0738-4602

Van Hasselt, H., Guez, A., Silver, D.: Deep reinforcement learning with double q-learning (2016). ISBN: 9781577357605

van Hasselt, H., Doron, Y., Strub, F., Hessel, M., Sonnerat, N., Modayil, J.: Deep reinforcement learning and the deadly triad (2018)

Watkins, C.: Learning from delayed rewards. Ph.D. thesis, University of Cambridge (1989)

Wu, S.A., Wang, R.E., Evans, J.A., Tenenbaum, J.B., Parkes, D.C., Kleiman-Weiner, M.: Too many cooks: coordinating multi-agent collaboration through inverse planning. Topics in Cognitive Science (2021)

Deep Learning Classifiers to Reduce False Positives in Osteolytic Lesion Segmentation Results from Low-Dose CT Scans of Multiple Myeloma

Martijn P. van Leeuwen[1], Munirdin Jadikar[1], Thijs van Oudheusden[2], Sebastiaan Oei[2], Bastiaan Steunenberg[2], Rik Kint[2], Erik R. Ranschaert[3], Gerlof P. T. Bosma[2], Gorkem Saygili[1], and L. L. Sharon Ong[1](✉)

[1] Department of CSAI, Tilburg University, Tilburg, The Netherlands
{m.p.vanleeuwen,m.jadikar,g.saygili,l.l.ong}@tilburguniversity.edu
[2] Elisabeth-TweeSteden Ziekenhuis, Tilburg, The Netherlands
{t.vanoudheusden,b.oei,b.steunenberg,r.kint,gpt.bosma}@etz.nl
[3] St. Nikolaus Hospital, Eupen and Ghent University, Ghent, Belgium
erik.ranschaert@ugent.be

Abstract. Multiple myeloma (MM) is a hematological malignancy with a low survival rate if not diagnosed in an early stage. A common symptom of MM is the development of osteolytic lesions, which are often visualized using low-dose CT imaging. Finding one lesion with a diameter of 5 mm or more is enough to support the diagnosis of MM. However, the evaluation of whole-body CT scans (WBCT) is time-consuming and susceptible to errors. We developed an automated lesion segmentation algorithm to assist in the detection and segmentation of such lesions. Although providing adequate detection results, this model returned false positive predictions which hampers the application of the method in the clinic. This work utilized various deep learning classifiers to categorize the segmentation outputs into true positives or false positives. A dataset comprising patches containing osteolytic lesions, and image patches containing regular bone tissue was constructed. After training on this dataset, the results showed that the best-performing model, a fine-tuned ResNet50 model, achieved an F1 score of 0.83 on the test set. To further test generalizability, radiologists labeled a collection of segmentation results as true or false positives, creating a separate holdout test set. The model achieved an F1 score of 0.68 a False Positive Rate (FPR) of 0.47 and a False Negative Rate (FNR) of 0.24 on the holdout test set. Our results show the number of false positive segmentations can be reduced 53% while still detecting 76% of the lesions. Implementing our proposed model into the segmentation pipeline can reduce the number of false positive segmentation, leading to a more refined and reliable system. However, further research is required to optimize the model performance.

M. P. van Leeuwen and M. Jadikar—These authors contributed equally to this work.

F. A. Oliehoek et al. (Eds.): BNAIC/Benelearn 2023, CCIS 2187, pp. 155–173, 2025.
https://doi.org/10.1007/978-3-031-74650-5_9

Keywords: False positive reduction · Osteolytic lesion segmentation · Convolutional Neural Networks

1 Introduction

Multiple myeloma (MM) is a hematological malignancy that leads to an uncontrolled proliferation of plasma cells [7]. Patients with MM frequently exhibit indications like hypercalcemia and anemia and are susceptible to the development of osteolytic lesions [7]. Up to 80% of MM, patients develop these lesions during their disease [17].

One of the imaging methods that is commonly used to examine osteolytic lesions is low-dose Computed Tomography (CT) imaging of the whole body [27]. Osteolytic lesions are small and can be found in multiple locations in the body. Due to interpretation errors ranging between 20% and 30% in cross-sectional imaging [14], there is a possibility that radiologists may overlook certain lesions when evaluating a patient's CT scan. According to the International Myeloma Working Group (IMWG), a patient can be diagnosed with MM if at least one lesion with a diameter $\geq 5\ mm$ is present [15]. Due to the difficulty of diagnosing MM, it is often detected in its later stages [4]. Such a late-stage diagnosis is often made after a skeletal-related event involving lytic disease or a fracture and has a 5-year survival rate of 48% [4]. Detecting MM in an earlier stage increases this 5-year survival rate from 48% to 71% [4]. However, only 5% of the MM diagnoses are made in such an early stage. Deep learning tools that help detect MM in an early stage of the disease can therefore significantly increase the patient 5-year survival rate.

There already exist several deep learning tools that focus on the automated detection of osteolytic lesions [5,27]. Similar to this previous research, our group has developed a deep learning model that segments osteolytic lesions in low-dose CT scans. However, due to the similarity of osteolytic lesions with other hypodense regions in bone tissue, the developed segmentation model was prone to produce false positive predictions. Figure 1 shows some examples of false positive predictions found by this segmentation model. The highlighted regions depict segmentation results confirmed as false positives by radiologists.

To improve the reliability and adoption of a lesion detection/segmentation algorithm, we propose a post-processing strategy to reduce the number of false positive predictions. By classifying the output of the segmentation results as lesions or non-lesions, we aim to determine whether a potential lesion site is an actual lesion or a false positive prediction. This post-processing model was developed by fine-tuning pre-trained classification models on 96 low-dose CT scans acquired at Elisabeth-TweeSteden Hospital (ETZ) in Tilburg.

This study is the first to investigate a classification model as a post-processing step to reduce false positive predictions in osteolytic lesion segmentation results. We demonstrate the effectiveness of this classification model using two distinct test sets: one where the negative class was generated automatically from bone masks, and another where this class was derived from expert labeling of segmentation results. In addition, we created a graphical user interface that enabled

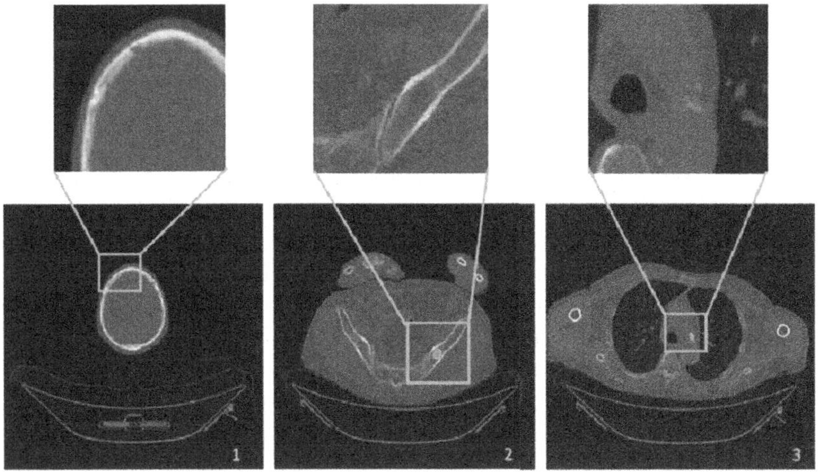

Fig. 1. False positive osteolytic lesion segmentations. The detected structures were labeled by radiologists as granulation (1), yellow bone marrow (2) and calcified aorta (3). (Color figure online)

radiologists to label false positive segmentations for the separate hold-out test dataset. The inclusion of this hold-out dataset in this study highlights the importance of evaluating a medical AI model, trained on automatically generated image patches, on real instances on which the model will eventually be applied.

2 Related Work on False Positive Reduction in Medical Image Analysis

Reduction of false positives has been a crucial task in medical applications. Setio et al. [21] proposed a novel computer-aided detection system for pulmonary nodule detection using multi-view convolutional networks to reduce false positive predictions. In a similar vein, Teramoto et al. [25] suggested employing a convolutional network to decrease false positive detections of solitary pulmonary nodules in PET/CT images, successfully eliminating nearly half of the false positives. Some studies aim to reduce the false positives in pulmonary nodule detection using connected component analysis rather than a CNN [20]. Applied to a different task, Zhang et al. [30] implemented fully convolutional networks to segment breast lesions on ultrasound scans while aiming to reduce false positives via data augmentation and using different loss functions. Yamamoto et al. [28] and Hiramatsu et al. [11] also proposed separate false-positive reduction algorithms based on support vector machine and CNN. These studies emphasize the relevancy of reducing false positives in various tasks.

A survey on the state-of-the-art lung nodule detection methods performed by Gu et al.[8] showed that there are also studies that deploy additional classification models to reduce the number of false positive predictions [1,12]. Some techniques involve the utilization of features extracted through radiomics analysis to classify the detected or segmented regions using machine learning models [3], while others use CNN structures to classify the suspected nodule region [21].

One of the best-performing methods in classifying lung nodules is the ResNet architecture [26]. This method, when compared to other neural networks such as VGG16 and InceptionV3, showed a better performance in terms of accuracy and false positive rate [26]. There is no known previous work on classifying osteolytic lesion segmentations to reduce the number of false positive segmentations using these types of classification models. The primary objective of this study is therefore to explore to what extent false positive predictions can be removed by applying these post-processing classification models.

3 Experimental Setup

Figure 2 illustrates the experimental configuration employed in this paper, wherein four pre-trained models-VGG16, InceptionV3, ResNet50, and EfficientNetB7- were tested. A description of these models and the preprocessing applied for each model is presented in Appendix A. The first step in training these models is the preprocessing of the data. This step generated image patches containing either osteolytic lesions or regular bone tissue. Due to the limited number of labeled data, data augmentation (horizontal and vertical flipping)

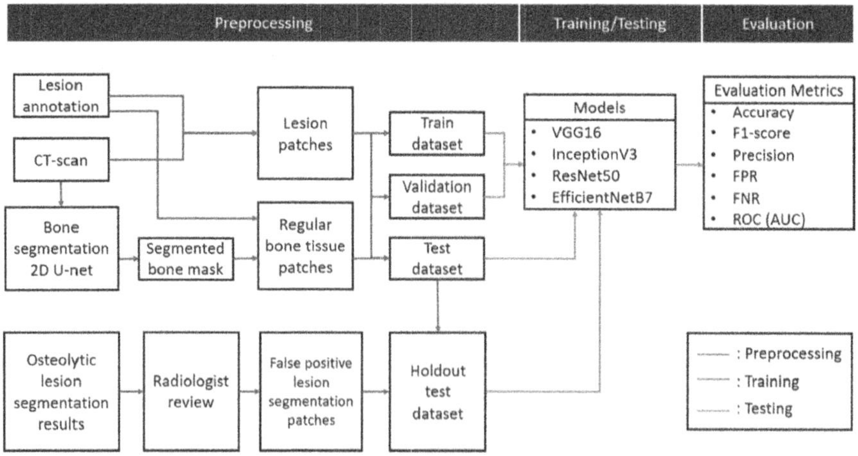

Fig. 2. Experimental procedure: Initially, image patches were generated for training, validation, and testing, followed by the evaluation of four finetuned models. Finally, the models were tested on a holdout test set, created from segmentation results that were reviewed by radiologists.

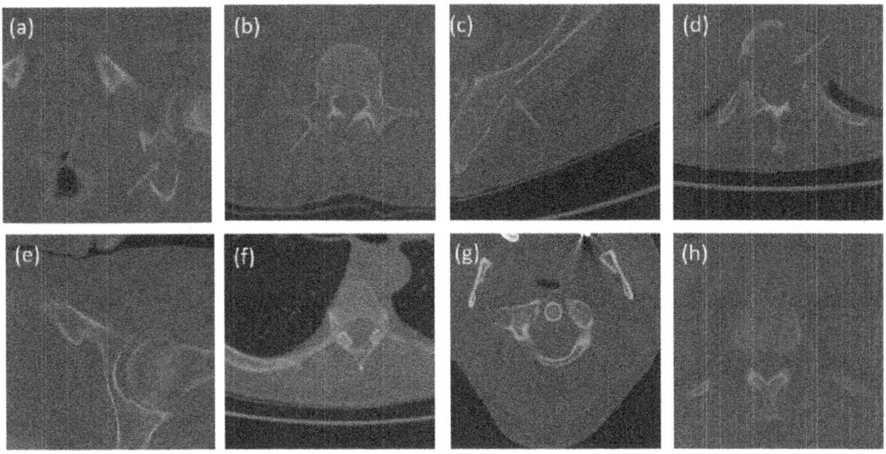

Fig. 3. Examples of positive patches of size 224 × 224, containing osteolytic lesions in the hip (a-c) and vertebrae (b-d) and negative patches of regular bone tissue in the hip (e) and vertebrae (f-h). For visualization purposes, the lesions are indicated with a red arrow.

was applied to increase the training dataset size. The pre-trained models were fine-tuned on the augmented dataset and afterward, all models were evaluated on a test set and a separate holdout test set.

3.1 Dataset and Data Preparation

The dataset consisted of 96 CT scans from 79 patients diagnosed with multiple myeloma from Elisabeth-TweeSteden Hospital (ETZ) in Tilburg in which all demographic information has been anonymized. Each patient had a full body scan or a combination of an upper and lower body scan, with axial resolutions of either 512 × 512 pixels or 768 × 768 pixels, and a slice thickness of 2.5 mm or 3 mm. The lesions were annotated by radiologists and radiology residents from the ETZ hospital by creating segmentation masks using 3D Slicer [6]. In the 96 low-dose CT scans, a total of 665 lesions were annotated, and 2D patches of 224×224 pixels were created by randomly cropping around each lesion's centroid. The extracted patches were split (subject-wise) into a training, validation, and test set as shown in Table 1.

The classifiers were trained to distinguish between tissues with lesions and those without. Since these lesions are predominantly present in bone tissue, patches of regular bone tissue were selected as a negative class. However, extracting a lesion-free patch at a random location in the CT scan could result in a patch in which no bone tissue was present. To ensure that bone tissue is present in these patches, a bone tissue mask was made for each scan using a 2D U-Net segmentation model [19], trained on the CT-ORG dataset [18]. The bone masks were then used to randomly generate patches in which at least 10% of the patch

Table 1. Overview of image patches and patient counts in each dataset. Lesion patches were created from radiologist-annotated segmentation masks. Training, validation, and test datasets' non-lesion patches were generated using bone masks, while the holdout test set's non-lesion patches comprised false positive lesion segmentation results labeled by radiologists.

Dataset	No. Lesion patches	No. Non-lesion patches	No. Patients
Training data	5267	5267	59
Validation data	710	710	10
Test data	705	705	10
Holdout test data	277	277	4 (from test set)

consisted of bone tissue while ensuring that no annotated lesions were included in the patch. Some examples of lesions with and without lesions are shown in Fig. 3.

Holdout Test Set. The holdout test set was created using a 2D U-Net segmentation model which was trained on the lesion masks that were annotated by the ETZ radiologists. This model was trained on patches of 192×192 pixels and tested on several low-dose CT scans using a sliding window approach [16]. These results were then evaluated by a group of radiologists who labeled the results as true positives or false positives. This labeled data will be referred to as the holdout test set throughout this paper. To balance this holdout test set, positive lesion patches were randomly sampled from the positive patches in the original test set to ensure a 1:1 ratio. Table 1 shows an overview of the number of patches/patients in each dataset.

3.2 Model Design

The standard procedure for applying transfer learning involves the removal of the final classification layers of a pre-trained model and replacing it with a self-designed classifier. This pre-trained model called the base model, acts as a feature extractor for the new classifier. The base model is commonly followed by a global average pooling (GAP) layer or a flatten layer. Due to the susceptibility of overfitting when using a flatten layer, particularly when the amount of training data is limited [13], a GAP layer was selected to link the base model to the classifier. After removing the final classification layer, a GAP layer, a dense layer, and a final output layer with a sigmoid activation function were added to the pre-trained models. Before training, the weights of these pre-trained models were unfrozen to tailor the feature extraction to the characteristics of this domain. A schematic overview of this design is included in Appendix B.

Hyperparameter optimization was conducted on the validation dataset. The final hyperparameters were selected based on the best-performing model. An overview of the hyperparameters and their evaluated ranges are included in Appendix C.

3.3 Evaluation Metrics

To evaluate the trained models, the accuracy, precision, and F1 score were calculated for each model. As the focus lies on the removal of false positives, the false positive rate (FPR) and false negative rate (FNR) were also calculated as defined below in Eq. 1 and Eq. 2.

$$FPR = \frac{FP}{FP + TN} \tag{1}$$

$$FNR = \frac{FN}{FN + TP} \tag{2}$$

To visualize the trade-off between true and false positives, we computed ROC curves illustrating how varying the classification threshold affects the balance between false positives and true positives. The overall evaluation of a ROC curve is computed by assessing the area under the curve (AUC) that gives an impression of how well the model can differentiate between the classes [2]. AUC values above 0.8 are generally considered clinically useful, whereas models with AUC values below 0.8 are often seen as less clinically significant [2].

4 Results

This section will report the performance of the classification models on the test set and the holdout test set.

4.1 Evaluation of Models on Test Set

Table 2 shows the test accuracy for each model. The results indicated that the fine-tuned ResNet50 model outperformed the other models, achieving a test accuracy of 0.84, a precision score of 0.86, an F1 score of 0.83, an FPR of 0.12, and an FNR of 0.20. Figure 4 illustrates the confusion matrix and ROC curve of ResNet5, demonstrating a relatively low FPR (0.12) and FNR (0.20), with the ROC curve indicating a high AUC (0.91). The confusion matrices and ROC curves for the VGG16, InceptionV3, and EfficientNetB7 can be found in Appendix D.

Table 2. The results of fine-tuned models on the test set when a classification threshold of 0.5 is used.

Models	Accuracy	Precision	F1-score	FPR	FNR
VGG16	0.83	0.81	0.84	0.20	0.14
InceptionV3	0.81	0.80	0.81	0.21	0.18
ResNet50	**0.84**	**0.86**	**0.83**	**0.12**	**0.20**
EfficientNetB7	0.77	0.83	0.75	0.14	0.31

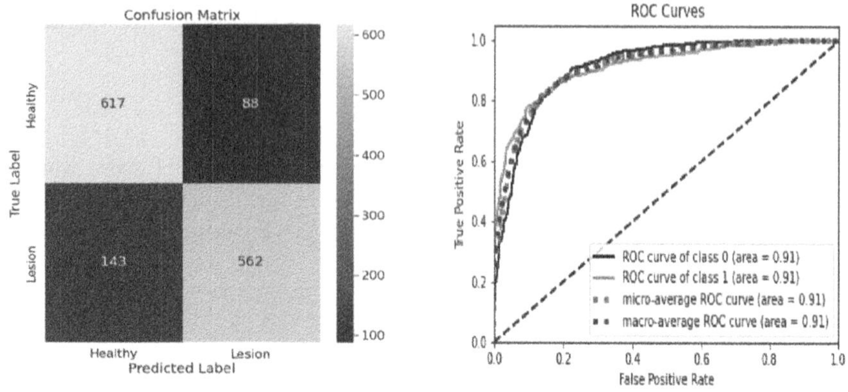

Fig. 4. Confusion Matrix and ROC curve of ResNet50 on the test dataset when a classification threshold of 0.5 is used.

Table 3. The results of fine-tuned models on the holdout test set when a classification threshold of 0.5 is used.

Models	Accuracy	Precision	F1-score	FPR	FNR
VGG16	0.60	0.56	0.67	0.64	0.17
InceptionV3	0.64	0.60	0.70	0.55	0.16
ResNet50	**0.64**	**0.62**	**0.68**	**0.47**	**0.24**
EfficientNetB7	0.58	0.57	0.61	0.51	0.33

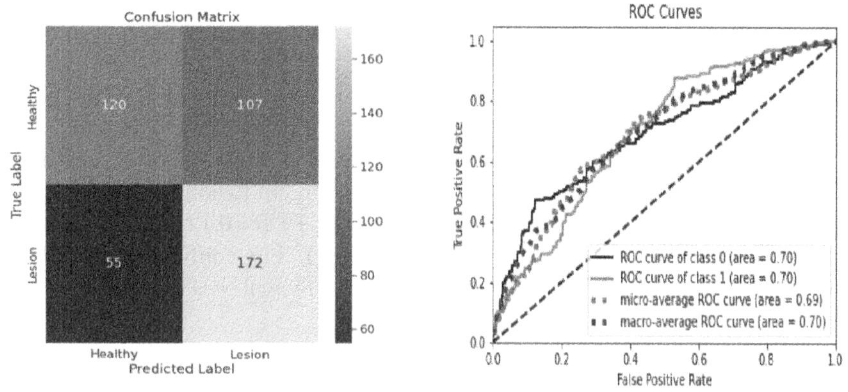

Fig. 5. Confusion matrix and ROC curve of ResNet50 on the holdout test set when a classification threshold of 0.5 is used.

4.2 Generalization on Holdout Test Set

Table 3 displays the final result of the four models on the holdout test set. Overall, ResNet50 and InceptionV3 outperformed VGG16 and EfficientNetB7, consistent

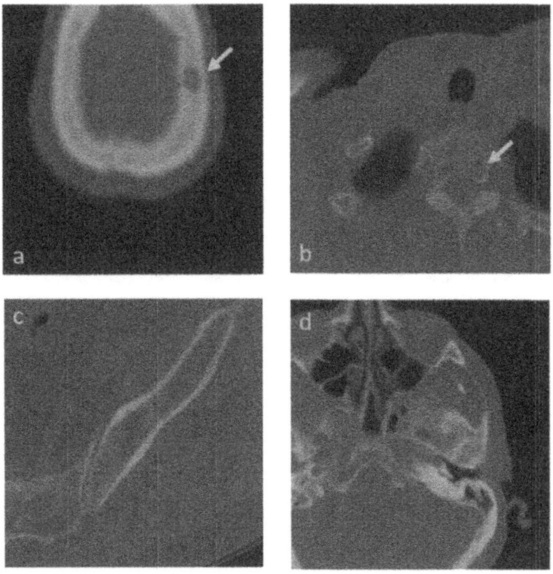

Fig. 6. Example images which ResNet50 correctly classified as true positives (top) and true negatives (bottom). Patch *a* and *b* show a lesion in the skull and a vertebra respectively, which were both correctly classified by ResNet50. Patch *c* shows a hypodense region in the pelvis which was correctly identified as regular bone tissue, and also the complex bone tissue in the skull shown in patch *d* was correctly labeled as regular bone tissue.

with the initial test set findings. The ResNet50 model was the best-performing model with an accuracy of 0.64, a precision of 0.62, and an F1-score of 0.68. However, classification performance decreased on the holdout test set compared to the performance on the standard test set.

Figure 5 shows the confusion matrix and ROC curves for the ResNet50 model. The results show that 107 out of 227 non-lesions were still classified as lesions. The ROC curves in Fig. 5 also show an AUC of 0.70 which is lower than the earlier observed 0.91 in Fig. 4. Overall, the model on the holdout test set did not perform as well as it did on the test set that contained automatically generated regular bone tissue patches.

Figure 6 shows examples of correct classifications made by ResNet50 on the holdout test set. It shows a correctly classified lesion in the skull and vertebra and regular bone tissue in the pelvis and skull. The images in Fig. 7 show some misclassifications made by ResNet50. The top two images contain osteolytic lesions mistaken for regular bone tissue, and the bottom two images display regular bone tissues misclassified as osteolytic lesions.

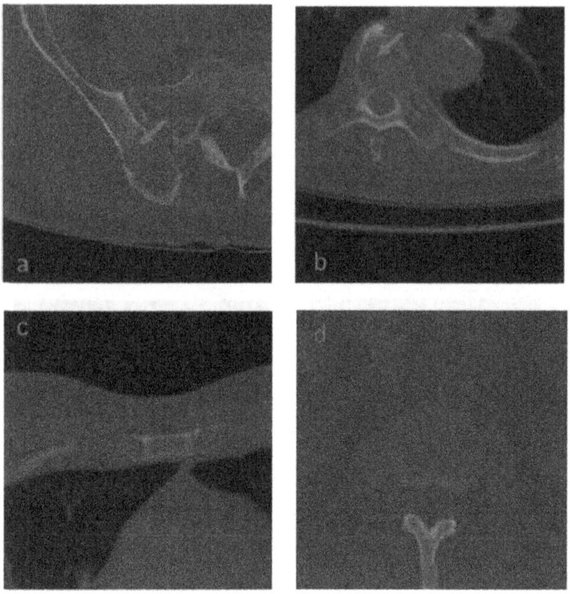

Fig. 7. Example images which ResNet50 misclassified as false negatives (top) and false positives (bottom). Patch *a* and patch *b* both contain a lesion but were incorrectly labeled as regular bone tissue by ResNet50. Patch *a* shows a lesion in the pelvis and patch *b* displays a lesion in the vertebra. Patch *c* displays costal cartilage between the sternum and the ribs and patch *d* shows an intervertebral disc. Both these regions in image *c* and *d* have similarities with osteolytic lesions which is presumable the reason why these are classified as lesions by ResNet50

5 Discussion

There exists literature on classification models that reduce false positive predictions [1,8,12], yet no previous studies on applying such methods to classifying osteolytic lesion segmentation results. This paper tested to what extent these methods could be used to reduce the number of false positive segmentations of an osteolytic lesion segmentation model.

The proposed method performed well in distinguishing automatically generated regular bone tissue patches from patches that contained osteolytic lesions. However, the model performance dropped when applied to a dataset composed of false positive osteolytic lesion segmentation results. The AUC on the hold-out test set (0.70) was lower than the AUC found in the original test set (0.91). As previously mentioned, a clinically significant model should typically achieve an AUC greater than 0.80 [2]. This criterion is met when the model is applied to the automatically generated patches, but not achieved when evaluated on the holdout test set that contained false positive segmentations.

The different performance between the two datasets could be partially attributed to the method in which the training, validation, and test datasets were generated. We expect that the model performance will increase when the model is trained with false positive segmentation predictions as negative patches.

A major limitation of this study is the limited availability of annotated data. Nevertheless, this paper demonstrated that the results obtained are still adequate, even with a small dataset. Out of the 227 false positive segmentation patches in the hold-out test set, 120 patches were correctly identified as healthy tissue, resulting in a 53% reduction in false positive segmentations when applying a classification threshold of 0.5. At this threshold, the FNR (0.24) observed in this dataset indicates that the classifier correctly identified 76% of the lesions. To enhance this work, additional feedback on segmentation results should be collected and used to train the classifiers, ensuring that the training data more closely resembles the inference data.

There are no existing studies that assess the clinical impact of these models. In the future, a reader study should be conducted to compare our pipeline against the performance of radiologists in detecting osteolytic lesions.

6 Conclusion

This paper is the first to demonstrate the potential of classification models in minimizing false positive osteolytic lesion segmentations. For training and assessing the classifiers, a dataset consisting of image patches with osteolytic lesions and image patches of regular bone tissue was created. The results showed that the best-performing model, a fine-tuned ResNet50 model, achieved an F1 score of 0.83 on the test set. A team of radiologists annotated several false-positive osteolytic lesion segmentation results to create a holdout test set. These false positives were used as the negative class in this binary classification task. The model achieved an F1 score of 0.68 an FPR of 0.47 and an FNR of 0.24 on this holdout test set. By integrating our proposed model into the original segmentation pipeline, we can reduce the number of false positive segmentations by 53%, while still detecting 76% of the lesions. These results suggest that it is possible to train osteolytic lesion classifiers to minimize false positive segmentations. However, the final results show that the model is not yet sufficiently robust and requires further research.

Acknowledgements. This study was funded by the WeCare research program, a collaboration between Elisabeth-TweeSteden Ziekenhuis and Tilburg University and a starter grant from NWO.

Disclosure of Interests. The authors declare no competing interests relevant to the content of this article.

A Models for Transfer Learning

With limited data, we applied transfer learning for classification. Four different, well-known pre-trained models were explored; VGG16, InceptionV3, ResNet50, and EfficientNetB7, described below.

A.1 VGG16

The VGG16 model consists of 13 convolutional layers with 3×3 filters. The convolutional layers can be divided into five blocks, followed by a max pooling layer. The final max pooling layer is connected to a flatten layer followed by three dense layers. The final dense layers have 1000 output nodes with sigmoid activation functions. TL tasks without a modified VGG16 model require an input image shape of 224×224 [22]. When its final dense layers are removed, it can be modified with different dense layers with different input image shapes. Compared to many other models, the VGG16 has a shallow structure and requires less computational power [29].

A.2 InceptionV3

The inceptionV3 architecture contains multiple inception modules (Fig. 8), stacked upon each other [23]. We chose to explore this model for classification as it is robust against overfitting with limited data. Compared to previous inception models, the filters are smaller (3 × 3), requiring less computational power. Computation is also reduced with asymmetric convolution filters[23].

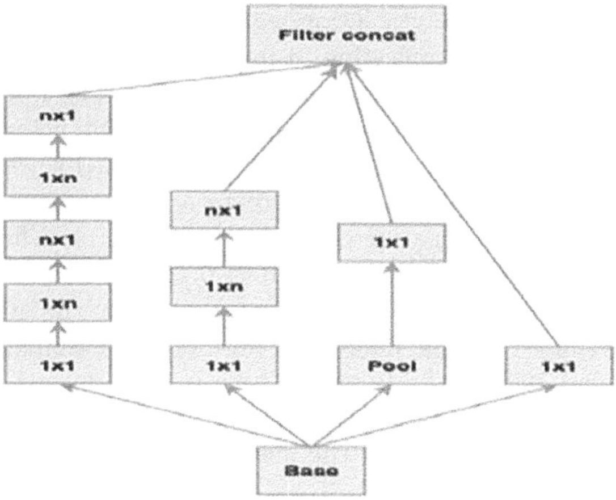

Fig. 8. Inception module with n × n convolution. Adapted from [23]

A.3 ResNet50

The Resnet50 model consisted of 50 layers [9] with residual network architectures. Many deep learning structures suffer from gradient vanishing or exploding problems. Residual networks overcome this problem by allowing for deeper model architectures. In Resnet50, the residual block contains three convolutional layers with 1×1, 3×3, and 1×1 filters, with the 1×1 filter reducing the trainable parameters [9]. Despite the deeper structure of Resnet50, it has fewer floating point operations (FLOPs) than shallow models such as VGG16.

A.4 EfficientNetB7

EfficienNetB7 is one of the new versions of the EfficientNet model family. This model is designed based on a new way to scale model dimensions like depth, width, and resolution [24]. First, the relationship of different scaling dimensions is searched based on the grid search to find an optimal value for the compound scaling method. Then, the model is scaled up according to the compound coefficient, balancing the network dimensions optimally (Figure 9). This model is relatively new, and there is limited study on EfficientNetB7 in medical image classification. However, it is a relatively large model with more than 66 million parameters and is expected to achieve very high accuracy in image classification [10].

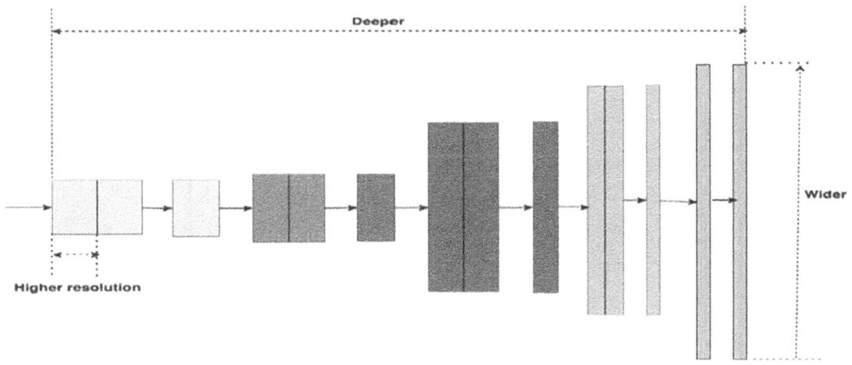

Fig. 9. Model scaling methods in EfficientNetB7. Adapted from [24]

A.5 Requirements for Preprocessing Images in Pre-Trained Models

The pre-trained models employed in this study were trained on different image input shapes. Omitting the fully connected layers at the model's top enables different input shapes for the osteolytic lesion classification. Furthermore, each pre-trained model necessitated a specific method for processing the input images 4. These preprocessing methods allow the pre-trained models to achieve the best performance. The TensorFlow framework offers a built-in preprocessing approach for each pre-trained model. These models were trained on ImageNet and subsequently fine-tuned to enhance their performances.

Table 4. Preprocessing requirements of pre-trained models

Model name	Pre-trained image shape	Preprocessing method
VGG16	224 × 224	Converted to BGR and zero-centered.
InceptionV3	299 × 299	[–1, 1]
Resnet50	224 × 224	Converted to BGR and zero-centered.
EfficienNetB7	224 × 224	[0, 255]

B Pre-training Models

Due to the limited dataset size, pre-trained models are used to classify the osteolytic lesion segmentations. To tailor these models to this classification task, some additional layers must be added so that the pre-trained models can function as feature extractors. An overview of the added layers is shown below in Fig. 10.

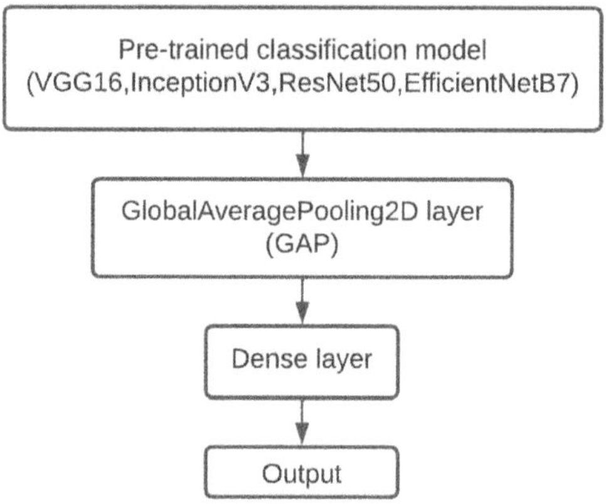

Fig. 10. Model design using transfer learning with base model.

C Hyperparameter Tuning

A total of eight different hyperparameters with varying values were considered for each pre-trained model (Table 5). The models were trained with pre-trained weights and fine-tuned by unfreezing the trainable layers.

Table 5. Tested hyperparameters with selected value

Hyper parameter	Value range	Selected Value
Learning Rate		
Connecting Layer to TL model	Flattened, GAP	GAP
Nodes in Dense layer	[32,64,128,512]	64
Batch size	[4,8,15,32,64]	32
Optimizers	Adam, Nadam	Adam
Loss function	Binary cross-entropy Categorical cross-entropy	Binary cross-entropy
Epochs	[10,20,100]	100 (Early stopping ended it earlier)
Freeze layers	True,False	True

D Results for All Models

This section shows the results for the VGG16, InceptionV3, and EfficientNetB7 models.

D.1 VGG16

Figure 11 and Fig. 12 show the performance of the VGG16 model on the standard and the holdout test dataset.

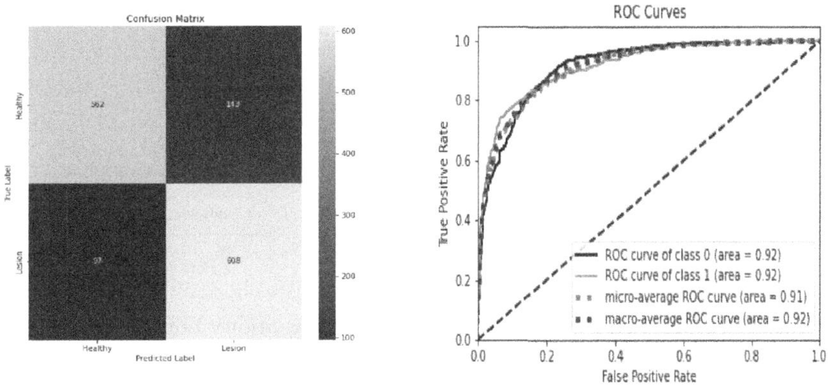

Fig. 11. Confusion matrix and ROC curve of VGG16 on the test set

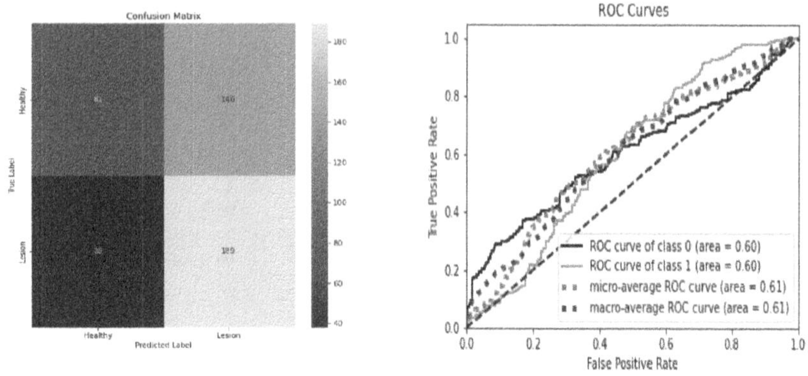

Fig. 12. Confusion matrix and ROC curve of VGG16 on the holdout test set

D.2 InceptionV3

Figure 13 and Fig. 14 show the performance of the InceptionV3 model on the standard and the holdout test dataset.

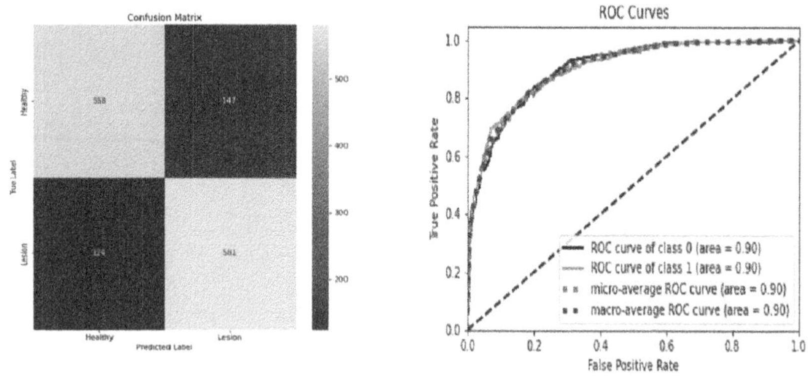

Fig. 13. Confusion matrix and ROC curve of InceptionV3 on the test set

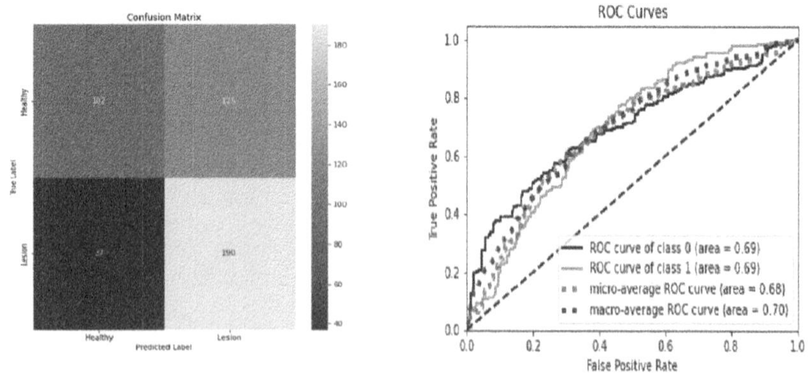

Fig. 14. Confusion matrix and ROC curve of InceptionV3 on the holdout test set

D.3 EfficientNetB7

Figure 15 and Fig. 16 show the performance of the InceptionV3 model on the standard and the holdout test dataset.

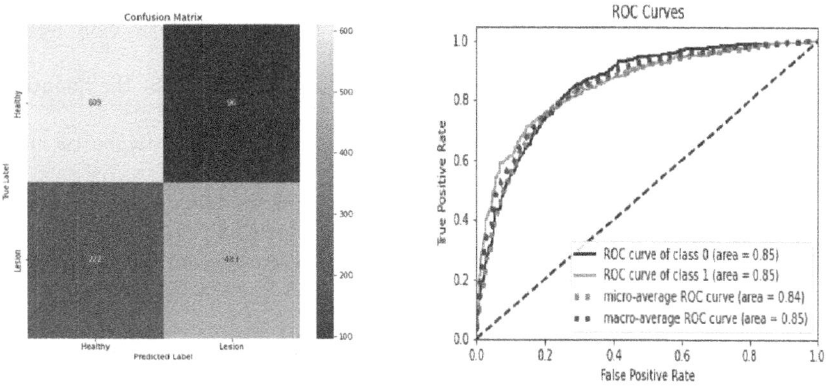

Fig. 15. Confusion matrix and ROC curve of EfficientNetB7 on the test set

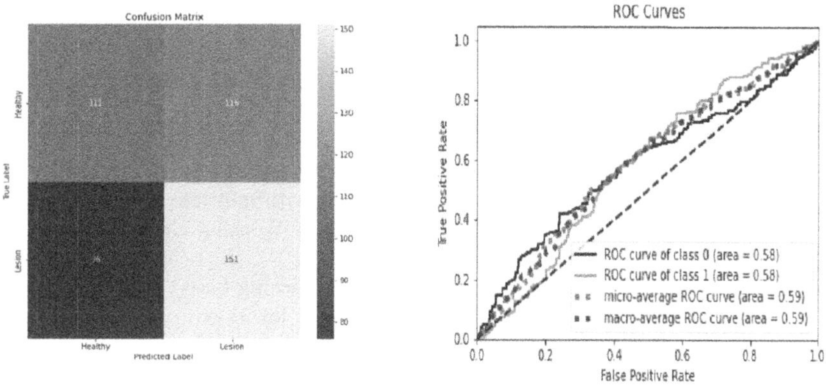

Fig. 16. Confusion matrix and ROC curve of EfficientNetB7 on the holdout test set

References

1. Chen, Y., Hou, X., Yang, Y., Ge, Q., Zhou, Y., Nie, S.: A novel deep learning model based on multi-scale and multi-view for detection of pulmonary nodules. J. Digit. Imaging **36**(2), 688–699 (2023)
2. Çorbacıoğlu, ŞK., Aksel, G.: Receiver operating characteristic curve analysis in diagnostic accuracy studies: a guide to interpreting the area under the curve value. Turk. J. Emerg. Med. **23**(4), 195 (2023)

3. Daliri, M.R.: A hybrid automatic system for the diagnosis of lung cancer based on genetic algorithm and fuzzy extreme learning machines. J. Med. Syst. **36**, 1001–1005 (2012)
4. Dao, A., McDonald, M.M., Savage, P.B., Little, D.G., Schindeler, A.: Preventing osteolytic lesions and osteomyelitis in multiple myeloma. J. Bone Oncol. 100460 (2022)
5. Faghani, S., et al.: A deep learning algorithm for detecting lytic bone lesions of multiple myeloma on ct. Skeletal Radiol. **52**(1), 91–98 (2023)
6. Fedorov, A., et al.: 3D slicer as an image computing platform for the quantitative imaging network. Magn. Reson. Imaging **30**(9), 1323–1341 (2012)
7. Filho, A.G., et al.: Whole-body imaging of multiple myeloma: diagnostic criteria. Radiographics **39**, 1077–1097 (2019)
8. Gu, D., Liu, G., Xue, Z.: On the performance of lung nodule detection, segmentation and classification. Comput. Med. Imaging Graph. **89**, 101886 (2021)
9. He, K., Zhang, X., Ren, S., Sun, J.: Deep residual learning for image recognition. In: 2016 IEEE Conference on Computer Vision and Pattern Recognition (CVPR), pp. 770–778 (2016)
10. He, Y., et al.: Deep learning-based classification of primary bone tumors on radiographs: A preliminary study. EBioMedicine **62**, 103121 (2020)
11. Hiramatsu, Y., Muramatsu, C., Kobayashi, H., Hara, T., Fujita, H.: Automated detection of masses on whole breast volume ultrasound scanner: false positive reduction using deep convolutional neural network. In: Medical Imaging 2017: Computer-Aided Diagnosis, vol. 10134, pp. 717–722. Spie (2017)
12. Jin, H., Li, Z., Tong, R., Lin, L.: A deep 3d residual cnn for false-positive reduction in pulmonary nodule detection. Med. Phys. **45**(5), 2097–2107 (2018)
13. Lin, M., Chen, Q., Yan, S.: Network in network. In: International Conference on Learning Representations (ICLR) (2014)
14. Maskell, G., Frcp, F.: Commentary error in radiology-where are we now? (2019)
15. Moulopoulos, L.A., et al.: Recommendations for acquisition, interpretation and reporting of whole body low dose CT in patients with multiple myeloma and other plasma cell disorders: a report of the IMWG Bone Working Group. Blood Cancer J. **8**, 95 (2018)
16. Ong, L.S., Martijn van Leeuwen, G.S.: A deep learning-based approach to detect and segment osteolytic bone lesions in whole-body, low-dose ct imaging of multiple myeloma patients. In: EuSoMII Annual Meeting 2022 (2022)
17. Rajkumar, S.V., Kumar, S.: Multiple myeloma: diagnosis and treatment. Mayo Clinic Proc. **91**, 101–119 (2016)
18. Rister, B., Yi, D., Shivakumar, K., Nobashi, T., Rubin, D.L.: Ct-org, a new dataset for multiple organ segmentation in computed tomography. Sci. Data **7** (2020)
19. Ronneberger, O., Fischer, P., Brox, T.: U-net: convolutional networks for biomedical image segmentation. In: Navab, N., Hornegger, J., Wells, W.M., Frangi, A.F. (eds.) MICCAI 2015. LNCS, vol. 9351, pp. 234–241. Springer, Cham (2015). https://doi.org/10.1007/978-3-319-24574-4_28
20. Sahu, S.P., Londhe, N.D., Verma, S., Agrawal, P., Banchhor, S.K.: False positives reduction in pulmonary nodule detection using a connected component analysis-based approach. Int. J. Biomed. Eng. Technol. **39**(2), 131–148 (2022)
21. Setio, A.A.A., et al.: Pulmonary nodule detection in ct images: false positive reduction using multi-view convolutional networks. IEEE Trans. Med. Imaging **35**(5), 1160–1169 (2016)

22. Simonyan, K., Zisserman, A.: Very deep convolutional networks for large-scale image recognition. In: International Conference on Learning Representations (ICLR) (2015)
23. Szegedy, C., Vanhoucke, V., Ioffe, S., Shlens, J., Wojnaw, Z.: Rethinking the inception architecture for computer vision. In: IEEE Conference on Computer Vision and Pattern Recognition (CVPR), pp. 2818–2826 (2016)
24. Tan, M., Le, Q.V.: EfficientNet: rethinking model scaling for convolutional neural networks. In: Proceedings of the 36th International Conference on Machine Learning (ICML), vol. 97, pp. 6105–6114 (2019)
25. Teramoto, A., Fujita, H., Yamamuro, O., Tamaki, T.: Automated detection of pulmonary nodules in pet/ct images: ensemble false-positive reduction using a convolutional neural network technique. Med. Phys. **43**(6Part1), 2821–2827 (2016)
26. Wu, P., et al.: Classification of lung nodules based on deep residual networks and migration learning. Comput. Intell. Neurosci. **2020** (2020)
27. Xu, L., et al.: Automated whole-body bone lesion detection for multiple myeloma on 68 ga-pentixafor pet/ct imaging using deep learning methods. Contrast Media Molec. Imaging **2018** (2018)
28. Yamamoto, D., et al.: Computer-aided detection of multiple sclerosis lesions in brain magnetic resonance images: false positive reduction scheme consisted of rule-based, level set method, and support vector machine. Comput. Med. Imaging Graph. **34**(5), 404–413 (2010)
29. Yan, K., Wang, X., Lu, L., Summers, R.M.: Deeplesion: automated mining of large-scale lesion annotations and universal lesion detection with deep learning. J. Med. Imaging **5**, 1 (2018)
30. Zhang, S., Al Zoubi, A., Du, H.: Fully convolutional network for breast lesion segmentation in ultrasound image: towards false positive reduction. In: Multimodal Image Exploitation and Learning 2022, vol. 12100, pp. 65–79. SPIE (2022)

Explaining Boolean Classifiers with Non-monotonic Background Theories

Tjitze Rienstra(✉)

Department of Advanced Computing Sciences, Maastricht University, Maastricht, The Netherlands
t.rienstra@maastrichtuniversity.nl

Abstract. Understanding why a classifier makes a certain prediction is crucial in high-stakes applications. It is also one of the central problems studied in the field of Explainable AI. To accurately explain predictions of a classifier, it is essential to take information about relationships between features into account. Many approaches, however, ignore this information. We address this problem in the context of symbolically encoded boolean classifiers. Darwiche and Hirth proposed the notion of *sufficient reason* (also called *PI explanation* or *abductive explanation*) to explain predictions of such classifiers. We show that sufficient reasons may be inaccurate and overly verbose, as they ignore information about relationships between features. We propose to represent this information using preferential models, which we use to encode hard as well as soft constraints between features. Preferential models define non-monotonic consequence relations that encode statements such as "birds typically fly" and "penguins typically don't fly". We introduce a number of ways to define reasons in the presence of background knowledge about the feature space, and we analyse these notions by means of general principles that characterise their behaviour.

Keywords: Explainable AI · Non-monotonic Reasoning · Machine Learning

1 Introduction

Understanding why a classifier makes a certain prediction is crucial in high-stakes applications. It is also one of the central problems studied in the field of Explainable AI. So called post-hoc explanation techniques such as LIME and SHAP treat a classifier as a 'black box' and generate explanations for decisions by perturbing the values of the input instance [13,17]. Explanation techniques based on logic and formal methods of reasoning have been proposed as well [3,8,9,14,15]. In this paper we focus on the approach proposed by Darwiche and Hirth [3], where a boolean classifier with boolean-valued input features is represented symbolically by a propositional formula whose models are the instances that are classified

F. A. Oliehoek et al. (Eds.): BNAIC/Benelearn 2023, CCIS 2187, pp. 174–188, 2025.
https://doi.org/10.1007/978-3-031-74650-5_10

as positive. This formula can be extracted from a classifier that was learned from data, and captures the same input-output behaviour. The benefit of this approach is that it allows us to reason about the behaviour of a classifier using formal methods of logic and reasoning. This includes explaining why the classifier makes a particular decision for a given input; they define the notion of *sufficient reason* (also called *PI-explanation* [18] or *abductive explanation* [9]) as justifications for a decision, based on the prime implicants of the classifier formula. This logic-based approach provides a theory of explanation with provable guarantees concerning correctness and minimality.

Every classification task involves a *feature space*, which is the set of possible input instances. We use the term *background knowledge* to refer to knowledge about the (relative) plausibility of different input instances. Background knowledge plays an important role when generating explanations. For instance, Slack et al. [19] show that SHAP and LIME may generate misleading explanations if background knowledge is ignored. The reason is that these approaches rely on perturbations of the instance that is being explained but ignore, in their standard formulation, the question of whether these perturbations represent plausible input instances. The same problem affects Darwiche and Hirth's notion of sufficient reason. Gorji and Rudin [7] show that, if background knowledge is ignored, sufficient reasons may be unnecessarily long. They propose a generalisation of the notion of sufficient reason in order to take *hard constraints* into account of the form *all input instances satisfy* ϕ. We further generalise this approach and also consider *soft constraints*. of the form *instances that satisfy* ϕ *typically also satisfy* ψ. We represent these constraints using *preferential models* consisting of a plausibility ordering of the set of possible instances [11]. A preferential model defines a *non-monotonic consequence relation*, which encodes defeasible conditionals of the form "if ϕ then typically ψ".

The focus of this paper is mostly theoretical, and we leave computational aspects for future work. We address the question of how the notion of sufficient reason can be adapted to deal with soft constraints. To gain insights into how these adapted notions behave, we define general principles that express desirable properties of explanations in the presence of background knowledge. These principles validate our definitions and characterise the difference between the various types of explanations that we define.

The plan of this paper is as follows. In Sect. 2 we present a number of preliminary definitions, and recall Darwiche and Hirth's notion of sufficient reason. In Sect. 3 we discuss an example of a classification scenario involving background knowledge, and show that sufficient reasons are inadequate in this scenario. In Sect. 4 we discuss the theory of preferential models and non-monotonic consequence relations that we rely on. We then define the notion of *minimal reason* in Sect. 5, which represents our first proposal to explaining decisions in the presence of background knowledge. We then analyse this notion in terms of a number of formally defined general principles including *succinctness* (Sect. 6) and *coherence* (Sect. 7). Based on this analysis we define two further types of explanations:

minimally coherent reasons (Sect. 8) and *ideal* reasons (Sect. 9). We summarise our results, discuss future work and conclude this paper in Sect. 10.

2 Preliminaries

In this section we present notation and definitions that will be used throughout this paper. We use uppercase letters $(A, B, C, \ldots)$ to denote atoms. Given a set At of atoms we denote by $\mathscr{L}(At)$ the propositional language that includes At and is closed under the usual logical connectives. A *literal* is an atom or the negation of an atom. A *term* is a conjunction of literals. We also treat terms as sets of literals. For example, given two terms τ and τ', we write $\tau \subseteq \tau'$ to say that every literal that appears in τ also appears in τ'. When denoting terms we sometimes omit conjunction symbols and use overlines for negation. For example, $A\overline{BC}$ denotes the term $A \wedge \neg B \wedge \neg C$.

A *valuation* of At is a function $v : At \longrightarrow \{0, 1\}$ assigning a truth value to each atom (0 for false, 1 for true). We also denote valuations by their corresponding terms. For example, $A\overline{BC}$ denotes the valuation that assigns 1 to A and 0 to B and C. We extend v to assign truth values to the elements of $\mathscr{L}(At)$ in the usual way, and say that v is a *model* of ϕ iff $v(\phi) = 1$. Given a formula $\phi \in \mathscr{L}(At)$ we denote by $[\phi]$ the set of valuations of At that are models of ϕ. Given formulas $\phi, \psi \in \mathscr{L}(At)$, we say that ϕ *entails* ψ (written $\phi \vdash \psi$) iff $[\phi] \subseteq [\psi]$.

Following Darwiche and Hirth [3] we represent a boolean classifier with input features At by a propositional formula $\Delta \in \mathscr{L}(At)$. The input instances for this classifier are the valuations of At. We use $\alpha, \beta, \ldots$ to denote instances. The models of Δ representing the positive instances, and the non-models of Δ representing negative instances. A *characteristic* of an instance α is a literal satisfied by that instance (e.g., A and $\neg B$ are characteristics of the instance $A\overline{BC}$). A *property* of an instance is a term satisfied by that instance (e.g., $A \wedge \neg B$ is a property of the instance $A\overline{BC}$). Given an instance α we use $\Delta(\alpha)$ to denote the decision made by Δ for instance α: $\Delta(\alpha) = 1$ if $\alpha \in [\Delta]$, and $\Delta(\alpha) = 0$ if $\alpha \models \neg\Delta$. We define Δ_α as follows: $\Delta_\alpha = \Delta$, if $\Delta(\alpha) = 1$, and $\Delta_\alpha = \neg\Delta$, if $\Delta(\alpha) = 0$.

Darwiche and Hirth [3] proposed the notion of *sufficient reason* to represent justifications for decisions made by a boolean classifier. Sufficient reasons are based on *prime implicants*. A term τ is an *implicant* of a formula ϕ if $\tau \vdash \phi$. A term τ is a *prime implicant* of a formula ϕ if τ is an implicant of ϕ and there is no $\tau' \subset \tau$ that is an implicant of ϕ. Sufficient reasons are defined as follows.

Definition 1. *A sufficient reason for decision $\Delta(\alpha)$ is a term $\tau \subseteq \alpha$ that is also a prime implicant of Δ_α.*

One of the examples used by Darwiche and Hirth is the following [3]. Consider an admission classification task with features E (entrance exam passed), F (first time applicant), G (high GPA score), and X (has work experience). Suppose we are classifying individuals according to whether they will be admitted, and that we are dealing with a classifier Δ defined by $\Delta = E \wedge (\neg \text{ F} \vee G \vee X)$. Suppose Greg passed the entrance exam, is not a first-time applicant, does not have a high GPA but does have work experience: $E\overline{FG}X$. According to classifier Δ, Greg will be admitted: $\Delta(E\overline{FG}X) = 1$. This decision has two sufficient reasons: $E \wedge \neg F$ (passed the entrance exam and is not a first-time applicant) and $E \wedge X$ (passed the entrance exam and has work experience).

3 The Problem with Sufficient Reasons

The following toy example demonstrates the inadequacy of sufficient reasons if we take background knowledge into account.

Example 1. Suppose we are classifying animals into whether or not they have the ability to fly. Among the features we use are B (the animal is a bird), P (the animal is a penguin) and S (the animal is supernatural). An animal flies if it is a bird but not if it is a penguin. There is one exception to this rule: penguins that are supernatural do have the ability to fly. We therefore use the classifier $\Delta = B \wedge (P \rightarrow S)$. The table below shows three instances along with their decisions and sufficient reasons.

α	$\Delta(\alpha)$	Sufficient Reasons
$B\overline{PS}$	1	$(B \wedge \neg P)$
$BP\overline{S}$	0	$(P \wedge \neg S)$
BPS	1	$(B \wedge S)$

Let us evaluate these sufficient reasons under the assumption that we have the following background knowledge about the feature space.

(1) All penguins are birds.
(2) A bird is typically not a penguin (penguins are rare among birds).
(3) A penguin is typically not supernatural (supernaturalness is rare among penguins).

Note that fact (1) is a hard constraint. It states that every instance that satisfies P also satisfies B. Facts (2) and (3) are soft constraints. For instance, fact (2) states that instances that satisfy B typically do not satisfy P, without ruling out the existence of instances satisfying B and P.

Let us look at the sufficient reasons for decision $\Delta(B\overline{PS})$. This instances is classified as flying ($\Delta(B\overline{PS}) = 1$), the unique sufficient reason being $(B \wedge \neg P)$. However, since we know that birds are typically not penguins we can argue that $\neg P$ is redundant. We could extend our example with other rare conditions that prevent a bird from flying, such being an ostrich, a kiwi, a newly hatched chick, and so on. The sufficient reason would include the negation of *all* of these properties. A similar problem arises with the instance $BP\overline{S}$, which is classified as non-flying with reason $(P \wedge \neg S)$. We know that penguins are typically not supernatural, and hence $\neg S$ can be regarded as redundant. The instance BPS, representing a supernatural penguin, is classified as flying. The unique sufficient reason for this decision is $(B \wedge S)$. The problem with this reason is that we know that penguins are birds. Therefore, $P \wedge S$ is just as good an explanation as $B \wedge S$. Moreover, $P \wedge S$ may be preferred over $B \wedge S$ on grounds of specificity. That is, given our background knowledge, $P \wedge S$ implies $B \wedge S$ while the converse is not true. However, the reason $P \wedge S$ is not among the sufficient reasons for this decision.

Our aim is to define alternatives to sufficient reasons that take background knowledge about the feature space into account. We will first address the question of how we represent this background knowledge.

4 Non-monotonic Consequence Relations and Preferential Models

We will assume that background knowledge about the feature space is represented by a *non-monotonic consequence relation*. This is a relation $\mid\sim$ between propositional formulas that encodes a set of conditional assertions: if $\phi \mid\sim \psi$ then ϕ *typically implies* ψ. As is common, we use the $\mid\sim$ symbol rather than the classical $\vdash$ to emphasise that we are dealing with a relation that, unlike $\vdash$, violates Monotony:

(Monotony) If $\phi \mid\sim \psi$ then $\phi \wedge \chi \mid\sim \psi$.

Common sense reasoning often exhibits non-monotonicity. A typical example is the following. We may believe that a bird is an animal that flies ($B \mid\sim F$) but retract this conclusion if we learn that the bird in question is a penguin ($B \wedge P \not\mid\sim F$). Monotony, however, would force us to maintain this conclusion ($B \wedge P \mid\sim F$). The approach to non-monotonic reasoning that we use is often referred to as the *KLM approach*, after the authors Kraus, Lehmann and Magidor [11,12]. This approach defines a semantics for non-monotonic consequence relations in terms of preferential models, which are strict partial orderings of possible worlds according to their relative plausibility. A preferential model defines a consequence relation using the rule that $\phi \mid\sim \psi$ holds if the most plausible worlds that satisfy ϕ also satisfy ψ.

Definition 2. *A* preferential model *is a triple* $W = (S, \prec, l)$*, where* S *is a finite set of* possible worlds, $\prec$ *is a strict partial order over* S*, and* l *is a function mapping every possible world* $s \in S$ *to a valuation. We define* $\widehat{\phi}$ *by* $\widehat{\phi} = \{s \in S \mid l(s) \models \phi\}$*. A state* $s \in X$ *is said to be* $\prec$-preferred *in a set* X *iff there is no* $s' \in X$ *such that* $s' \prec s$*. The consequence relation* $\mid\sim^W$ *is defined by the following rule:*

$$\phi \mid\sim^W \psi \textit{ iff for all } s \prec\textit{-preferred in } \widehat{\phi} \textit{ we have that } l(s) \models \psi.$$

A *ranked model* is a specific type of preferential model where the ordering of possible worlds corresponds to a numerical ranking.

Definition 3. *A* ranked model *is a preferential model* $(S, \prec, l)$ *such that there exists some mapping* $R : S \rightarrow \mathbb{N}$ *such that* $s \prec s'$ *iff* $R(s) < R(s')$.

In our setting, the possible worlds S are input instances, and $\prec$ encodes the relative plausibility of these input instances. The assertion $\phi \mid\sim_W \psi$ can be thought of as a soft constraint on the feature space: instances that satisfy ϕ typically also satisfy ψ. We can also represent hard constraints: the fact that every instance satisfies ϕ is represented by the assertion $\neg\phi \mid\sim_W \bot$, which holds if and only if all members of S satisfy ϕ [12].

A *preferential consequence relation* is any consequence relation that satisfies the following set of axioms. These axioms characterise the class of consequence relations defined by a preferential model [11], and will be useful in proving various properties of the reasons we define in this paper.

(Reflexivity) $\phi \mid\sim \phi$.
(Left Logical Equivalence) If $\phi \equiv \psi$ and $\phi \mid\sim \chi$ then $\psi \mid\sim \chi$.
(Right Weakening) If $\phi \mid\sim \psi$ and $\psi \models \chi$ then $\phi \mid\sim \chi$.
(Or) If $\phi \mid\sim \chi$ and $\psi \mid\sim \chi$ then $\phi \vee \psi \mid\sim \chi$.
(Cautious Monotony) If $\phi \mid\sim \psi$ and $\phi \mid\sim \chi$ then $\phi \wedge \psi \mid\sim \chi$.
(Cut) If $\phi \mid\sim \psi$ and $\phi \wedge \psi \mid\sim \chi$ then $\phi \mid\sim \chi$.

Definition 4. *A consequence relation* $\mid\sim$ *satisfying the above set of properties is called a* preferential *consequence relation.*

Theorem 1. *A consequence relation* $\mid\sim$ *is preferential iff it is defined by some preferential model [11].*

Two interesting axioms are Cautious Monotony and Cut. Cautious Monotony is a weakening of Monotony and states that strengthening a premise with something that typically follows from that premise does not lead to the retraction of conclusions. Cut states that weakening a premise with something that typically follows from that premise does not lead to the retraction of consequences. For a more detailed discussion of these axioms we refer the reader to [11]. The *Rational Monotony* axiom defined below represents a strengthening of cautious monotony. Let us say that ψ is *exceptional* with respect to ϕ if $\phi \mid\sim \neg\psi$. Rational Monotony states that strengthening a premise with something that is not exceptional with respect to that premise does not lead to the retraction of consequences.

(Rational Monotony) If $\phi \not\mid\sim \neg\psi$ and $\phi \mid\sim \chi$ then $\phi \wedge \psi \mid\sim \chi$.

The axioms of preferential consequence relations, supplemented with Rational Monotony, define the class of *ranked* consequence relations. These axioms characterise the class of consequence relations defined by a ranked model [12].

Definition 5. *A preferential consequence relation* $\mid\sim$ *that satisfies Rational Monotony is called a* rational *consequence relation.*

Theorem 2. *A consequence relation* $\mid\sim$ *is rational iff it is defined by some ranked model [12].*

In the following example we define a ranked model that will serve to represent the background knowledge described in Example 1.

Example 2. Let $W = (S, \prec, l)$ be the ranked model where S contains the instances shown in the table below; l is the identity function; and $\prec$ is defined by the function R that maps every instance s to the number $R(s)$ (see Definition 3) shown in the header of the column in which s resides in the table below. We can think of these numbers as degrees of implausibility: the higher the number, the more implausible the instance. Thus, $\overline{BPS}$ and $B\overline{PS}$ are more plausible than $BP\overline{S}$, $\overline{BP}S$ and $B\overline{P}S$, which are in turn more plausible than BPS.

$R(s)$	0	1	2
s	$\overline{BPS}$ $B\overline{PS}$	f $BP\overline{S}$ $\overline{BP}S$ $B\overline{P}S$	BPS

We will use this ranked model to represent the background knowledge in our running example. The conditional assertions entailed by this model include:

- $P \wedge \neg B \mid\!\sim_W \bot$ (All penguins are birds).
- $B \mid\!\sim_W \neg P$ (Bird are typically not penguins).
- $P \mid\!\sim_W \neg S$ (Penguins are typically not supernatural).

5 Minimal Reasons

We now define a new type of reason for decisions made by boolean classifiers in the presence of background knowledge about the feature space. We assume that a classifier over a set At of boolean features is represented by a formula $\Delta \in \mathscr{L}(At)$. In addition, we assume that our background knowledge is represented by a consequence relation $\mid\!\sim \subseteq \mathscr{L}(At) \times \mathscr{L}(At)$. In our running example, we will use the consequence relation $\mid\!\sim_W$ defined by the ranked model W defined in Example 2.

A $\mid\!\sim$*-reason* for a decision $\Delta(\alpha)$ is any property of α that consistently and typically entails the decision formula Δ_α.

Definition 6. *A* $\mid\!\sim$-reason *for decision* $\Delta(\alpha)$ *is a term* $\tau \subseteq \alpha$ *such that* $\tau \not\mid\!\sim \bot$ *and* $\tau \mid\!\sim \Delta_\alpha$.

Not every $\mid\!\sim$-reason represents a reasonable explanation for a decision. We will propose a number of selection criteria to pick out $\mid\!\sim$-reasons that are in some sense reasonable. Our first selection criterion picks out the minimal ones.

Definition 7. *A* $\mid\!\sim$*-reason* τ *for* $\Delta(\alpha)$ *is* minimal *if there exists no* $\mid\!\sim$*-reason* τ' *for* $\Delta(\alpha)$ *such that* $\tau' \subset \tau$.

Example 3. Consider again the classifier $\Delta = B \wedge (P \rightarrow S)$ introduced in Example 1. Let our background knowledge be represented by the ranked model W defined in Example 2. Table 1 shows three instances along with their decisions, sufficient reasons, $\mid\!\sim_W$-reasons and minimal $\mid\!\sim_W$-reasons.

Table 1. Three decisions and their sufficient and (minimal) $\mid\!\sim_W$-reasons.

α	$\Delta(\alpha)$	Sufficient Reasons	$\mid\!\sim_W$-reasons	Minimal $\mid\!\sim_W$-reasons
$B\overline{PS}$	1	$(B \wedge \neg P)$	$(B \wedge \neg P \wedge \neg S), (B \wedge \neg S), B, (B \wedge \neg P)$	B
$BP\overline{S}$	0	$(P \wedge \neg S)$	$(B \wedge P \wedge \neg S), (P \wedge \neg S), P, (B \wedge P)$	P
BPS	1	$(B \wedge S)$	$(B \wedge P \wedge S), (P \wedge S), (B \wedge S), B$	$(P \wedge S), B$

- Row 1: The unique minimal $\mid\!\sim_W$-reason for decision $\Delta(B\overline{PS}) = 1$ is B. In words, a non-penguin, non-supernatural bird flies, the reason being it is a bird. Unlike the sufficient reason $(B \wedge \neg P)$, this reason does not include $\neg P$ since this fact is redundant given our background knowledge $(B \mid\!\sim_W \neg P)$.
- Row 2: Likewise, the minimal $\mid\!\sim_W$-reason for decision $\Delta(BP\overline{S}) = 0$ is P. In words: a non-supernatural bird penguin does not fly, the reason being it is a penguin. Unlike the sufficient reason $(P \wedge \neg S)$, this reason does not include $\neg S$ since this fact is redundant given our background knowledge $(P \mid\!\sim_W \neg S)$.
- Row 3: The minimal $\mid\!\sim_W$-reasons for decision $\Delta(BPS) = 1$ are $(P \wedge S)$ and B. In words: a supernatural bird penguin flies, the reasons being that (1) it is a supernatural penguin, and (2) it is a bird.

Let us look at some basic features of (minimal) $\mid\!\sim$-reasons. First, note that we can plug any consequence relation into the definition above. This includes the classical monotonic relation $\vdash$, which can be regarded as encoding no background knowledge. In this case we recover the standard notion of sufficient reason. Minimal $\mid\!\sim$-reasons include, in this sense, sufficient reasons as a special case.

Proposition 1. *The sufficient reasons for a decision are the minimal $\vdash$-reasons for that decision.*

An important feature of sufficient reasons is that every decision has at least one sufficient reason [3]. If we assume that $\mid\!\sim$ is preferential then the same holds for minimal $\mid\!\sim$-reasons, provided the instance being explained is consistent with respect to the background knowledge.

Proposition 2. *If $\mid\!\sim$ is preferential then every decision $\Delta(\alpha)$ such that $\alpha \not\mid\!\sim \bot$ has a minimal $\mid\!\sim$-reason.*

Proof. Consider decision $\Delta(\alpha)$ where $\alpha \not\mid\!\sim \bot$. Then $\alpha \vdash \Delta_\alpha$. Using Reflexivity and Right Weakening we get $\alpha \mid\!\sim \Delta_\alpha$. Thus, α is a $\mid\!\sim$-reason for Δ_α. By definition of minimal $\mid\!\sim$-reason, it follows that either α is a minimal $\mid\!\sim$-reason for Δ_α, or there is another reason $\tau' \subset \tau$ that is a minimal $\mid\!\sim$-reason for Δ_α.

Another important property of sufficient reasons is that they identify characteristics of an instance that justify the decision in the sense that *the reason entails the decision even if other characteristics were different* [3]. We will refer to this as the *robustness* principle, and formalise it as follows.

Definition 8. *A $\mid\!\sim$-reason τ for decision $\Delta(\alpha)$ is* robust *if for every $\tau' \supseteq \tau$ we have that $\tau' \mid\!\sim \Delta_\alpha$.*

Robustness follows directly from the monotony property of the consequence relation.

Proposition 3. *If $\mid\!\sim$ satisfies Monotony then every $\mid\!\sim$-reason is robust.*

Since $\vdash$ satisfies Monotony it follows that sufficient reasons (i.e., minimal $\vdash$-reasons) are robust. However, if $\mid\!\sim$ is non-monotonic, then $\mid\!\sim$-reasons, even the minimal ones, may violate robustness. To see why, let Δ and W be defined as in Example 3. The unique minimal $\mid\!\sim_W$-reason for decision $\Delta(B\overline{PS}) = 1$ is B. If this reason were robust then we would have $B \wedge$ P $\mid\!\sim_W \Delta$, but this is false.

The *rational* and *cautious* robustness principles characterise weaker forms of robustness that are satisfied by $\mid\!\sim$-reasons. In words, a reason τ for decision $\Delta(\alpha)$ is rationally robust if the reason typically entails the decision even if other characteristics were different, *as long as these characteristics are not exceptional with respect to* τ. A reason τ for decision $\Delta(\alpha)$ is cautiously robust if the reason typically entails the decision even if other characteristics were different, *as long as these characteristics typically follow from* τ. Rational and cautious robustness follow directly from, respectively, the rational and cautious monotony properties of the consequence relation.

Definition 9. *Let τ be an $\mid\!\sim$-reason for decision $\Delta(\alpha)$. Then τ is:*

- rationally robust *if for every $\tau' \supseteq \tau$ such that $\tau \not\mid\!\sim \neg(\tau' \setminus \tau)$, we have that $\tau' \mid\!\sim \Delta_\alpha$.*
- cautiously robust *if for every $\tau' \supseteq \tau$ such that $\tau \mid\!\sim \tau' \setminus \tau$, we have that $\tau' \mid\!\sim \Delta_\alpha$.*

Proposition 4. *If $\mid\!\sim$ satisfies Rational Monotony then every $\mid\!\sim$-reason is rationally robust.*

Proposition 5. *If $\mid\!\sim$ satisfies Cautious Monotony then every $\mid\!\sim$-reason is cautiously robust.*

Most of the minimal $\mid\!\sim$-reasons provided in Example 3 appear reasonable. For instance, the unique minimal $\mid\!\sim_W$-reason for decision $\Delta(B\overline{PS}) = 1$ is B. Unlike the sufficient reason $(B \wedge \neg P)$, this reason does not include $\neg P$ since this fact is redundant $(B \mid\!\sim_W \neg P)$. In the Sect. 6 we will formalise the principle that reasons do not contain redundant properties, and will prove that minimal $\mid\!\sim$-reasons satisfy this principle. The minimal $\mid\!\sim_W$-reasons for decision $\Delta(BPS) = 1$ in the example above are $(P \wedge S)$ and B. The latter reason can be questioned on two grounds. Firstly, between the two reasons $(P \wedge S)$ and B, the reason $(P \wedge S)$ is more specific in the sense that $(P \wedge S) \mid\!\sim B$ and $B \mid\!\sim (P \wedge S)$. More specific reasons may be preferred since they provide more information. We can thus say that B should be rejected in favour of $(P \wedge S)$. Secondly, while being a bird indeed a reason for why an animal flies, this is not a good reason for why this particular animal flies, since this creature is also a penguin, and this 'invalidates' the reason (a bird that is a penguin typically does *not* fly). In Sect. 7 we formalise the idea that reasons are not invalidated by other properties of the instance, and we consider ways in which we can enforce this principle.

6 Succinctness

We want to ensure that reasons do not contain properties that are redundant with respect to our background knowledge. The *succinctness* principle formalises this idea. We regard a property of a reason as redundant if it typically follows from the other properties of that reason.

Definition 10. *A $\mid\!\sim$-reason τ for decision $\Delta(\alpha)$ is* succinct *if there are no two terms τ', τ'' such that $\tau' \cup \tau'' = \tau$, $\tau' \cap \tau'' = \emptyset$, $\tau'' \neq \emptyset$ and $\tau' \mid\!\sim \tau''$.*

Not every $\mid\!\sim$-reason is succinct. For instance, the decision $\Delta(B\overline{PS}) = 1$ in Example 3 has, among its $\mid\!\sim_W$-reasons, the reason $(B \wedge \neg P)$. This reason is not succinct because we have $B \mid\!\sim_W \neg P$. Every minimal $\mid\!\sim$-reason, however, is succinct.

Proposition 6. *If $\mid\!\sim$ is preferential then every minimal $\mid\!\sim$-reason is succinct.*

Proof. Suppose τ is a minimal $\mid\!\sim$-reason for decision $\Delta(\alpha)$. Assume, towards a contradiction, that τ is not succinct. Then let τ', τ'' be terms such that $\tau' \cup \tau'' = \tau$, $\tau' \cap \tau'' = \emptyset$, $\tau'' \neq \emptyset$ and $\tau' \mid\!\sim \tau''$. We then have $\tau' \cup \tau'' \mid\!\sim \Delta_\alpha$. Cut then implies that $\tau' \mid\!\sim \Delta_\alpha$. Since $\tau' \subset \tau$ this implies that τ is not a minimal $\mid\!\sim$-reason reason for $\Delta(\alpha)$, which contradicts our assumption. It thus follows that τ is succinct.□

7 Coherence

The next principle can be seen as a variant of the robustness (Definition 8). We call it *coherence.* It states that a reason typically entails the decision *even if other characteristics would be the way they are according to the instance that is explained.* This appears to be an intuitive principle; it means that the reason is not 'invalidated' by any of the other characteristics of the instance whose decision is being explained.

Definition 11. *A $\mid\!\sim$-reason τ for decision $\Delta(\alpha)$ is* coherent *if, for every term τ' such that $\tau \subseteq \tau' \subseteq \alpha$, τ' is a $\mid\!\sim$-reason for $\Delta(\alpha)$.*

Unfortunately, minimal $\mid\!\sim$-reasons are not in general coherent, even if $\mid\!\sim$ is a rational consequence relation. The reason B for decision $\Delta(BPS)$ shown in the third row of Table 1 is a counterexample. While we do have $B \mid\!\sim_W \Delta_{BPS}$ and $B \wedge P \wedge \mathrm{S} \mid\!\sim_W \Delta_{BPS}$, we do not have $B \wedge \mathrm{P} \mid\!\sim_W \Delta_{BPS}$. In other words, the reason B for decision $\Delta(BPS)$ is invalidated by the characteristic P.

8 Minimally Coherent Reasons

We have now established that minimal reasons are sufficient but not coherent. If we wish to obtain reasons are coherent, we can use minimality among the coherent reasons as a selection criterion. Like minimal reasons (see Proposition 2), these *minimally coherent* reasons are guaranteed to exist, provided that the instance being explained is consistent with respect to the background knowledge.

Definition 12. *A* $\mid\!\sim$*-reason* τ *for decision* $\Delta(\alpha)$ *is* minimally coherent *if* τ *is coherent and there is no coherent* $\mid\!\sim$*-reason* τ' *for* $\Delta(\alpha)$ *such that* $\tau' \subset \tau$.

Proposition 7. *If* $\mid\!\sim$ *is preferential then every decision* $\Delta(\alpha)$ *such that* $\alpha \not\mid\!\sim \bot$ *has a minimally coherent* $\mid\!\sim$*-reason.*

Proof. Similar to the proof of Proposition 2.

Table 2. Three decisions and their sufficient, minimal, and minimally coherent reasons.

α	$\Delta(\alpha)$	Suff. Reasons	Minimal $\mid\!\sim_W$-reasons	Minimally coherent $\mid\!\sim_W$-reasons
$B\overline{PS}$	1	$(B \wedge \neg P)$	B	B
$BP\overline{S}$	0	$(P \wedge \neg S)$	P	P
BPS	1	$(B \wedge S)$	$(P \wedge S), B$	$(P \wedge S), (B \wedge S)$

Example 4. Let Δ and W be defined as in Example 3. Table 2 shows the minimally coherent reasons for the three decision $\Delta(B\overline{PS})$, $\Delta(BP\overline{S})$ and $\Delta(BPS)$. Here we see that the minimally coherent reasons coincide with the minimal reasons for the decisions $\Delta(B\overline{PS})$ and $\Delta(BP\overline{S})$. In Sect. 7 we saw that the minimal reason B for decision $\Delta(BPS)$ is not coherent. The minimally coherent reasons replace B with $(B \wedge S)$. If we use specificity as an additional selection criterion, then $(P \wedge S)$ is selected in favour of $(B \wedge S)$, since we have $(P \wedge S) \mid\!\sim_W (B \wedge S)$ and $(B \wedge S) \not\mid\!\sim_W (P \wedge S)$.

While the minimally coherent reasons in Table 2 are also succinct, the following example demonstrates that this not the case in general. Thus, if we use minimally coherent reasons then we have to give up on the guarantee that reasons are succinct.

Example 5. Consider a classification task with input features A, B and C. Let $\Delta = A \wedge B$ and let the ranked model W be as shown below.

R	0	1
ω	$AB\overline{C}$ $\overline{ABC}$	All other instances

The instance ABC is classified as positive: $\Delta(ABC) = 1$. This decision has two minimal $\mid\!\sim_W$-reasons A and B. These reasons are not coherent as we have $A \wedge C \not\mid\!\sim_W \Delta_\alpha$ and $B \wedge C \not\mid\!\sim_W \Delta_\alpha$. The unique minimally coherent $\mid\!\sim_W$-reason is $(A \wedge B)$. However, we have $A \mid\!\sim_W B$, and hence this reason is not succinct.

9 Ideal Reasons

In Sect. 7 we saw that minimal reasons are succinct but may violate coherence. In Sect. 8 we defined minimally coherent reasons, which are coherent but may violate succinctness. This raises the question of whether we can somehow obtain reasons that are both coherent and succinct. The answer is yes. We will prove that every decision has at least one reason that is both coherent and succinct.

Proposition 8. *If* $\mathrel{|\!\sim}$ *is preferential then every decision* $\Delta(\alpha)$ *such that* $\alpha \mathrel{|\!\not\sim} \bot$ *has a* $\mathrel{|\!\sim}$*-reason that is both coherent and succinct.*

Proof. Suppose $\mathrel{|\!\sim}$ is preferential. Let $\tau_0 = \alpha$ and assume that $\alpha \mathrel{|\!\not\sim} \bot$. Then, since $\alpha \mathrel{|\!\not\sim} \bot$, τ_0 is an $\mathrel{|\!\sim}$-reason for $\Delta(\alpha)$ and, using Reflexivity, it follows that $\tau_0 \mathrel{|\!\sim} \alpha$. For $i > 0$, let $\tau_i \subsetneq \tau_{i-1}$ be a $\mathrel{|\!\sim}$-reason for $\Delta(\alpha)$ such that $\tau_i \mathrel{|\!\sim} \alpha$. Lemma 1 implies that τ_i exists if τ_{i-1} is not succinct. Since α is finite and $\tau_i = \emptyset$ implies that τ_i is succinct, it follows that there must be an n such that τ_n is succinct. Lemma 2 furthermore implies that τ_n is coherent.

Lemma 1. *If* $\mathrel{|\!\sim}$ *satisfies Cut then for every* $\mathrel{|\!\sim}$*-reason* τ *for* $\Delta(\alpha)$ *such that* $\tau \mathrel{|\!\sim} \alpha$ *and* τ *is not succinct, there exists a* $\mathrel{|\!\sim}$*-reason* $\tau' \subset \tau$ *for* $\Delta(\alpha)$ *such that* $\tau' \mathrel{|\!\sim} \alpha$.

Proof. Let τ be a $\mathrel{|\!\sim}$-reason for $\Delta(\alpha)$ such that $\tau \mathrel{|\!\sim} \alpha$ and τ is not succinct. Since τ is not succinct there are terms τ', τ'' such that $\tau' \cup \tau'' = \tau$, $\tau' \cap \tau'' = \emptyset$, $\tau'' \neq \emptyset$ and $\tau' \mathrel{|\!\sim} \tau''$. Then $\tau \mathrel{|\!\sim} \Delta_\alpha$ and $\tau' \mathrel{|\!\sim} \tau''$ imply, using Cut, that $\tau' \mathrel{|\!\sim} \Delta_\alpha$. Furthermore, $\tau \mathrel{|\!\sim} \alpha$ and $\tau' \mathrel{|\!\sim} \tau''$ imply, using Cut, that $\tau' \mathrel{|\!\sim} \alpha$. Hence τ' is a $\mathrel{|\!\sim}$-reason for $\Delta(\alpha)$ such that $\tau' \subset \tau$ and $\tau' \mathrel{|\!\sim} \alpha$.

Lemma 2. *If* $\mathrel{|\!\sim}$ *satisfies Right Weakening and Cautious Monotony then for every* $\mathrel{|\!\sim}$*-reason* τ *for* $\Delta(\alpha)$ *such that* $\tau \mathrel{|\!\sim} \alpha$*, it holds that* τ *is coherent.*

Proof. Let τ be a $\mathrel{|\!\sim}$-reason for $\Delta(\alpha)$ such that $\tau \mathrel{|\!\sim} \alpha$. To prove that τ is coherent, let τ' be a term such that $\tau \subseteq \tau' \subseteq \alpha$. We will prove that $\tau' \mathrel{|\!\sim} \Delta_\alpha$. Using Right Weakening, $\tau \mathrel{|\!\sim} \alpha$ implies $\tau \mathrel{|\!\sim} \tau'$. Since τ is a $\mathrel{|\!\sim}$-reason for $\Delta(\alpha)$ it follows that $\tau \mathrel{|\!\sim} \Delta_\alpha$. Using Cautious Monotony, $\tau \mathrel{|\!\sim} \tau'$ and $\tau \mathrel{|\!\sim} \Delta_\alpha$ imply $\tau' \mathrel{|\!\sim} \Delta_\alpha$. It thus follows that τ is coherent.

Having established that reasons that are both coherent and succinct are guaranteed to exist, we refer to the minimal among them as the *ideal* reasons for the decision.

Definition 13. *An* ideal $\mathrel{|\!\sim}$-reason *for decision* $\Delta(\alpha)$ *is a term* τ *such that* τ *is a coherent and succinct* $\mathrel{|\!\sim}$*-reason for* $\Delta(\alpha)$*, and there is no coherent and succinct* $\mathrel{|\!\sim}$*-reason* τ' *for* $\Delta(\alpha)$ *such that* $\tau' \subset \tau$.

The minimally coherent reasons for the decisions discussed in Example 4 (see Table 2) coincide with the ideal reasons for these decisions. The situation in Example 5 is different, however.

Example 6 (Continued from Example 5). The instance ABC is classified as positive: $\Delta(ABC) = 1$. This decision has two minimal $\mid\!\sim_W$-reasons A and B, and a unique minimally coherent $\mid\!\sim_W$-reason $(A \wedge B)$. In Example 5 we saw that A and B are not coherent, and that $(A \wedge B)$ is not succinct. The unique ideal reason for decision $\Delta(ABC) = 1$ is $A \wedge B \wedge C$. This reason is both succinct and coherent.

10 Discussion and Future Work

Table 3 summarises the main results that we obtained. It shows that sufficient reasons satisfy all the principles that we have defined: robustness, cautious/rational robustness, succinctness and coherence. Note that in the case of sufficient reasons, cautious/rational robustness and coherence follow directly from robustness, while succinctness is satisfied trivially, since $\vdash$ encodes no background knowledge with respect to which succinctness can be violated. If we move on to minimal $\mid\!\sim$-reasons then we lose robustness but retain the weaker cautious/rational robustness principles. We furthermore lose coherence but retain succinctness. Note here that rationally robustness applies only if $\mid\!\sim$ is a rational consequence relation (indicated by a *). If we move to minimally coherent $\mid\!\sim$-reasons reasons, we gain coherence but lose succinctness. Finally, ideal $\mid\!\sim$-reasons combine succinctness and coherence.

Table 3. Summary of results, assuming $\mid\!\sim$ is a preferential consequence relation.

Selection Criterion	Robust	Cautiously Robust	Rationally Robust	Succinct	Coherent
Sufficient reasons	yes	yes	yes	yes	yes
Minimal $\mid\!\sim$-reasons	no	yes	yes*	yes	no
Minimally coherent $\mid\!\sim$-reasons	no	yes	yes*	no	yes
Ideal $\mid\!\sim$-reasons	no	yes	yes*	yes	yes

We have not obtained a definite answer to the question of how reasons should be explained in the presence of background knowledge. If violation of coherence is acceptable, then minimal reasons can be used. If coherence is required but succinctness is not, then minimally coherent reasons can be used. We have shown that specificity can be used as an additional selection criterion. We have seen that ideal reasons, which combine succinctness and coherence, are guaranteed to exist. Ideal reasons may, as Example 6 shows, be considered as too verbose. In future work we plan a more detailed analysis of the notions developed in this paper, including a study of additional principles and more realistic examples.

There are a number of important questions that we did not address in this paper. One question is: Where does the background knowledge for a given classification scenario come from? In other words: how do we obtain a suitable rational consequence relation, or a ranked model that defines such a relation? One way is to transform the empirical probability distribution of the training data (or a probabilistic model of the data generating process) into a ranked model. Algorithms to perform such transformations are described in [2] and [5]. Another possibility is to manually specify background knowledge in a declarative way. Here we can use Pearl's System Z, which allows one to compute rational consequences on the basis of a knowledge base of conditional statements [16]. Alternatives to System Z such as [6,10,20] may also be applicable. Worth mentioning in this context is also work on belief revision, much of which is essentially about the revision of ranked models (see, e.g., [4]).

Darwiche and Hirth did not only define sufficient reasons for boolean classifiers. They also defined *complete reasons*, *necessary reasons* and *decision counterfactuals*. They furthermore determined conditions under which a boolean classifier is biased with respect to a protected feature. In future work we plan to investigate these aspects in to context of our setting as well. The approach of Darwiche and Hirth has also been generalised in order to deal with variables with any discrete domain, including continuous features can be discretized into intervals [1]. We believe our theory can be generalised in a similar way.

References

1. Choi, A., Shih, A., Goyanka, A., Darwiche, A.: On symbolically encoding the behavior of random forests. CoRR arxiv:2007.01493 (2020)
2. Darwiche, A., Goldszmidt, M.: On the relation between kappa calculus and probabilistic reasoning. In: UAI, pp. 145–153. Morgan Kaufmann (1994)
3. Darwiche, A., Hirth, A.: On the reasons behind decisions. In: De Giacomo, G., et al. (eds.) ECAI 2020, vol. 325 of Frontiers in Artificial Intelligence and Applications, pp. 712–720. IOS Press (2020)
4. Darwiche, A., Pearl, J.: On the logic of iterated belief revision. Artif. Intell. **89**(1–2), 1–29 (1996)
5. Giang, P.H., Shenoy, P.P.: On transformations between probability and spolinian disbelief functions. In: UAI, pp. 236–244. Morgan Kaufmann (1999)
6. Goldszmidt, M., Morris, P.H., Pearl, J.: A maximum entropy approach to nonmonotonic reasoning. IEEE Trans. Pattern Anal. Mach. Intell. **15**(3), 220–232 (1993)
7. Gorji, N., Rubin, S.: Sufficient reasons for classifier decisions in the presence of domain constraints. In: AAAI, pp. 5660–5667. AAAI Press (2022)
8. Ignatiev, A., Narodytska, N., Asher, N., Marques-Silva, J.: From contrastive to abductive explanations and back again. In: Baldoni, M., Bandini, S. (eds.) AIxIA 2020. LNCS (LNAI), vol. 12414, pp. 335–355. Springer, Cham (2021). https://doi.org/10.1007/978-3-030-77091-4_21
9. Ignatiev, A., Narodytska, N., Marques-Silva, J.: Abduction-based explanations for machine learning models. In: AAAI, pp. 1511–1519. AAAI Press (2019)
10. Kern-Isberner, G., Eichhorn, C.: Structural inference from conditional knowledge bases. Stud. Logica. **102**(4), 751–769 (2014)
11. Kraus, S., Lehmann, D.J., Magidor, M.: Nonmonotonic reasoning, preferential models and cumulative logics. Artif. Intell. **44**(1–2), 167–207 (1990)

12. Lehmann, D.J., Magidor, M.: What does a conditional knowledge base entail? Artif. Intell. **55**(1), 1–60 (1992)
13. Lundberg, S.M., Lee, S.I.: A unified approach to interpreting model predictions. CoRR arxiv:1705.07874 (2017)
14. Marques-Silva, J., Gerspacher, T., Cooper, M.C., Ignatiev, A., Narodytska, N.: Explanations for monotonic classifiers. In: ICML, vol. 139 of Proceedings of Machine Learning Research, pp. 7469–7479. PMLR (2021)
15. Marques-Silva, J., Ignatiev, A.: Delivering trustworthy AI through formal XAI. In: AAAI, pp. 12342–12350. AAAI Press (2022)
16. Pearl, J.: System Z: a natural ordering of defaults with tractable applications to nonmonotonic reasoning. In: TARK, pp. 121–135. Morgan Kaufmann (1990)
17. Ribeiro, M.T., Singh, S., Guestrin, C.: why should I trust you?": explaining the predictions of any classifier. In: KDD, pp. 1135–1144. ACM (2016)
18. Shih, A., Choi, A., Darwiche, A.: A symbolic approach to explaining bayesian network classifiers. In: IJCAI, pp. 5103–5111. ijcai.org (2018)
19. Slack, D., Hilgard, S., Jia, E., Singh, S., Lakkaraju, H.: Fooling LIME and SHAP: adversarial attacks on post hoc explanation methods. In: Markham, A.N., Powles, J., Walsh, T., Washington, A.L. (eds.) AIES '20: AAAI/ACM Conference on AI, Ethics, and Society, New York, NY, USA, 7–8 February 2020, pp. 180–186. ACM (2020)
20. Weydert, E.: System JLZ - rational default reasoning by minimal ranking constructions. J. Appl. Log. **1**(3–4), 273–308 (2003)

Maximum Entropy Logistic Regression for Demographic Parity in Supervised Classification

Flore Vancompernolle Vromman(✉), Sylvain Courtain, Pierre Leleux, Constantin de Schaetzen, Eve Beghein, Alexia Kneip, and Marco Saerens

LouRIM & ICTEAM, Université catholique de Louvain, Louvain-la-Neuve, Belgium
flore.vancompernolle@uclouvain.be

Abstract. Discrimination and segregation have become major societal concerns while the increasing use of algorithms in various domains raises interest in their fairness and transparency. In this context, this paper presents a new approach to improve fairness in supervised classification, built on previous work. The proposed method uses the maximum-entropic formulation of logistic regression allowing for the easeful addition of linear (fairness) constraints directly on the probabilistic outputs of the model. We investigate the particular case of fairness problems, but the same technique could be applied to other situations requiring linear constraints on the outputs. In addition, we introduce a fairness-aware stepwise selection technique that gradually reduces the number of features according to their impact on demographic parity to further decrease discrimination. Experiments on five different datasets and comparisons with two competing models show that the proposed approach significantly reduces discrimination in terms of demographic parity, as well as in terms of two new measures of fairness described in this paper (the area under the demographic parity curve, and the F1 demographic parity) while maintaining a high level of accuracy on the investigated datasets.

Keywords: Fairness · Demographic parity · Supervised classification · Maximum entropy

1 Introduction

1.1 General Introduction

Over the last decades, society has become increasingly concerned about the discrimination and segregation displayed towards groups of citizens. Some groups are said to undergo unjustified treatment disparities when compared to others. However, 'unjustified' depends heavily on the situation and the overall objectives within the institution, or the society as a whole, which often leads to stormy public debates. At the same time, interest in fairness and transparency of algorithms

F. A. Oliehoek et al. (Eds.): BNAIC/Benelearn 2023, CCIS 2187, pp. 189–208, 2025.
https://doi.org/10.1007/978-3-031-74650-5_11

is growing given that these are used in many domains and may have a significant impact on people's lives when it relates to, for example, hiring, lending, justice, or healthcare, to name a few [4,45,48]. A well-known example in classification is the case of COMPAS. The COMPAS algorithm was used in the USA to assess early release from prison depending on the recidivism computed risk. In 2016, a study by ProPublica [2] claimed that African-Americans were discriminated against by the algorithm because they were more likely to be labeled as high-risk, even when their criminal history was the same as the one of Caucasians. This led to a huge debate with hundreds of articles on that issue.

Our goal here is not to discuss when discrimination occurs, but instead how to define and set up mechanisms that can guarantee or improve fair treatment (in terms of demographic parity) in data science algorithms and, more precisely, supervised classification. To do so, we propose the use of the maximum-entropic formulation of logistic regression [5,37,55] with additional constraints improving fairness. The main advantage of the maximum-entropic formulation is that, as we show later, it provides a way of controlling the impact of each feature on the output of the classification model, in terms of fairness and accuracy. It also allows applying fairness constraints directly on the probabilistic predictions of the model. Moreover, it is not only applicable to fairness concerns – it can also be generalized for other situations requiring linear constraints on the predicted outputs.

In addition, a fairness-aware stepwise feature selection technique, reducing gradually the number of features based on the computation of the minimum achievable covariance (a proxy of demographic parity; see Sect. 2), is also developed in order to possibly provide additional improvements to the fairness objective. Experiments performed on five datasets show that the proposed mechanism can reduce significantly the discrimination in terms of demographic parity while still observing a high level of accuracy.

1.2 Related Work

In this subsection, we first discuss how biases and unfairness may appear in the outputs of algorithms related to data science. Then, we briefly describe the concept of fairness in algorithms and a well-known operational metric used to measure it. Afterwards, we depict how to incorporate fairness in supervised classification models and describe more precisely the in-processing models of Donini et al. [16] and Zafar et al. [53] that are the most related to our work.

Biases in Algorithms. Unfairness and biases may be present in the outputs of algorithms for many reasons. A first one concerns the presence of unrepresentative training samples in the data. Indeed, in some cases, the dataset includes fewer samples from the protected group, which is then called a minority group. Therefore, the algorithm may not have enough information to provide accurate predictions for the minority group, or its prevalence might not reflect reality, leading to biased outcomes [40,41,48]. Furthermore, results may be biased if data is aggregated from different sources without an accurate reflection about their characteristics [40], while omitted variables can lead to unfair predictions because the model may overlook crucial aspects that impact the outcome [40,45]. Additionally, 'proxy' attributes of protected variables can cause undesirable algorithmic bias. Indeed, when protected variables such as ethnicity or gender are not included in the algorithm, other related features may still have an impact on fairness [45]. For instance, zip codes are often a proxy for race or socioeconomic status, leading to 'biased', discriminatory, outcomes. Another source of unfairness is related to historically vulnerable categories. Even when data accurately represent reality, historical patterns may be biased due to racism and sexism already present in society; see for example [40,41,45]. Finally, how an algorithm is designed may add bias. Algorithm designers may overlook the impact their design choices will have on different groups, resulting in algorithmic biases that perpetuate existing disparities [40,41].

Fairness Definitions, Metrics, and Notation. Fairness is a complex concept that can be viewed either from an individual perspective (similar individuals should be treated similarly) or from a group perspective (individuals are grouped according to one or more protected variables and each group should be treated similarly) [46]. In our work, we focus on group fairness, which is probably the most studied regarding algorithmic fairness [49], although debatable as it considers fairness at the level of the whole group. Protected variables, also called sensitive attributes, vary depending on the study case; they can for instance be gender, ethnicity, age, religion, etc.

However, for a long time, the goal of supervised classification has mainly been to maximize the accuracy of predictions. At the same time, more and more recent studies have focused on defining operational measures of fairness and modeling fair algorithms according to these metrics. Most often, researchers try to balance a trade-off between accuracy and fairness measure [31] because fairness constraints usually decrease the accuracy of the model, which could even become completely useless. It is therefore important to be able to control this trade-off in the model.

Several metrics co-exist to measure fairness in classification problems (see, e.g., [4,9,18,40] for details). More specifically, in a binary classification problem, let $Y \in \{0,1\}$ be the binary class membership, $\hat{Y} \in [0,1]$ the probabilistic class membership predicted by the model, $\hat{Y}^d \in \{0,1\}$ the predicted class after decision (usually, $\hat{Y}^d = 1$ when $\hat{Y} > 0.5$), and Z a binary protected variable. The protected group (i.e. the group that is normally disadvantaged/discriminated against) will be associated with $Z = 1$.

In this work, we mainly concentrate on the **demographic**, or **statistical, parity** measure. This measure is widely used and recognized in practice, and it was among the first studied in supervised classification [7,9,11], even if one could argue that it is too simple in most situations [4]. For instance, it can be misleading when a categorical feature is associated both with the target variable and the protected variable [27]. We will investigate other measures [9,11,27] in future work. Demographic parity requires that the probability of belonging to the favorable, positive, class ($\hat{Y}^d = 1$; being selected for a grant for instance) should be the same for each group, regardless of whether the person is in the protected group or not [9,21,40]. It can be translated operationally by imposing

$$\mathbb{E}[\hat{Y}^d | Z = 0] = \mathbb{E}[\hat{Y}^d | Z = 1] \tag{1}$$

but we usually allow for some predefined tolerance level $\left|\mathbb{E}[\hat{Y}^d|Z = 0] - \mathbb{E}[\hat{Y}^d|Z = 1]\right| \leq \epsilon$ with $\epsilon > 0$, which is the demographic parity measure that will be used in this work.

Fairness in Classification. Three main techniques allow addressing fairness in supervised classification: pre-processing, in-processing, and post-processing [30,40,46]. Pre-processing involves transforming the training data before fitting the model to mitigate underlying biases or discrimination in the data. In-processing consists in modifying existing learning algorithms to improve fairness during the model fitting process. Usually, this technique aims at incorporating changes into the objective function of a training algorithm (for instance through regularization terms) or imposing fairness constraints. Post-processing techniques modify the predictions of the classifier after training.

Our work focuses on in-processing techniques. Several related techniques have already been developed in the literature for supervised classification [22,50]. Some methods incorporate fairness on naive Bayes classifiers [8], others on neural networks [36,39], while other methods apply adversarial learning [34,54]. Our work focuses more precisely on in-processing techniques in the context of logistic regression models, which have already been studied in [1,6,16,53].

The method of Agarwal et al. [1] is based on a logistic regression focusing not only on demographic parity but also on another fairness goal (i.e. bounded group loss). Berk et al. [6] incorporate fairness in a logistic regression with a hybrid measure between individual and group fairness, whereas we are focusing only on group fairness. Therefore we will not compare our work to those two, given that fairness goals are different.

The models closest to ours are those proposed by Donini et al. [16] and especially Zafar et al. [53], also using a logistic regression. Moreover, those models are presented as benchmarked publications in the survey of Hort et al. [22]. Therefore, we will compare our in-processing method to these two methods. Zafar et al. [53] have developed a model maximizing the standard log-likelihood objective function under a fairness constraint (see Eq. 6 in [53]). The fairness constraint takes the form of the covariance between the protected variable and the linear predictions of logistic regression, thus before the nonlinear logistic function is computed. Their model is therefore closely related to the technique presented in this work, with the important difference that, in our model, the covariance constraints are directly applied to the probabilistic predictions, which looks more natural.

Indeed, the maximum entropy formulation of logistic regression straightforwardly allows for the introduction of linear constraints on the probabilistic outputs of the model, which makes it well-suited for our goal. Compared to the model of Zafar et al., our model allows to add more linear constraints on the probabilistic predictions in it, which could be interesting if for example we would like to consider several sensitive variables instead of only one, or to incorporate situations other than fairness that can be written as linear constraints.

The in-processing technique of Donini et al. [16] (see Eq. 10 in their paper) minimizes a loss function of errors with a fairness constraint. More precisely, the authors add a fairness constraint which is an approximation of the equal opportunity matching the first-order moments. Furthermore, the authors show that, for linear models, this constraint results in a simple pre-processing technique.

1.3 Contributions and Content

This paper contributes to (1) the development of two original measures of fairness, called the area under the demographic parity curve (AUDPC) and the F1 demographic parity (F1DP), (2) the analysis of the relationships between demographic parity and sample covariance, (3) the introduction of a logistic regression model directly incorporating fairness constraints on the probabilistic class memberships of the model, coupled with (4) a stepwise feature selection method possibly improving further demographic parity, and (5) experimental comparisons with the methods developed by Zafar et al. [53] and Donini et al. [16] on five datasets.

The paper is organized as follows. First, Sect. 2 shows that demographic parity is closely related to the sample covariance between the predicted values provided by the model (probabilistic class memberships) and the binary protected variable. Then, in Sect. 3, inspired by [16,21] and building upon [53], we take advantage of the maximum-entropic formulation of logistic regression to add fairness constraints to the model to improve demographic parity. Finally, Sect. 4 presents our experiments on five datasets and comparisons with models from [16] and [53].

2 Covariance as a Proxy for Demographic Parity

The covariance measure is well-known to be closely related to demographic parity (see, e.g., [26,53]). Indeed, covariance is often used to de-correlate the output of a model from the protected variable, as a first step towards independence. After a brief reminder in Subsect. 2.1 of the sample covariance concept, Subsect. 2.2 shows that the sample covariance between a binary categorical protected variable Z and the probabilistic predictions $\hat{Y}$ of a classification model is a direct relaxation of the demographic parity measure. Therefore, it further justifies the use of covariance to mitigate discrimination between groups.

2.1 Sample Covariance: a Brief Reminder

Recall that the sample, or empirical, covariance between the n measurements of two random variables, X, Y, gathered in a sample (or training) set $\mathcal{T}$ can be computed[1] [3,38] by

[1] Note that the factor $1/n$ could also be used, instead of $1/(n-1)$, as the empirical definition of the covariance [20], which slightly simplifies the results.

$$\text{cov}(\mathbf{x}, \mathbf{y}) = \frac{1}{n-1} \sum_{i \in \mathcal{T}} (x_i - \bar{x})(y_i - \bar{y}) = \frac{1}{n-1} \sum_{i \in \mathcal{T}} [\mathbf{Hx}]_i [\mathbf{Hy}]_i = \frac{1}{n-1} \mathbf{x}^\mathsf{T} \mathbf{Hy} \quad (2)$$

where $\mathbf{H} = \left(\mathbf{I} - \frac{1}{n}\mathbf{e}\mathbf{e}^\mathsf{T}\right)$ is the centering matrix [38], $\mathbf{e}$ is a $n \times 1$ column vector containing 1's and $[\mathbf{x}]_i$ is element i of column vector $\mathbf{x}$. Indeed, $\mathbf{H}$ centers any vector, $\mathbf{Hx} = \mathbf{x} - \bar{x}\,\mathbf{e}$ with $\bar{x}$ being the average of $\mathbf{x}$. Note that $\mathbf{HH} = \mathbf{H}$.

2.2 Covariance with a Categorical, Protected, Variable

Let us now instigate how the covariance with a binary categorical variable Z, representing a protected group, can be interpreted in the context of demographic parity and a binary classification problem. The protected variable is coded as $\{0, 1\}$ meaning that $z_i = 1$ when observation i belongs to group $\mathcal{C}_1^Z$ (which is the protected group) and $z_i = 0$ if i belongs to group $\mathcal{C}_0^Z$ (the complement of $\mathcal{C}_1^Z$). Thus $\mathcal{C}_0^Z$ and $\mathcal{C}_1^Z$ are mutually exclusive and define a partition of the training set $\mathcal{T}$. The predicted target variable $\hat{Y}$ is assumed to be numerical and is usually interpreted as the a posteriori probability of membership to the class $Y = 1$ predicted by the model (the model is calibrated).

Accordingly, we consider that a sample of Z and $\hat{Y}$ is observed. Let us denote as $\pi_1^Z = \hat{\mathbb{P}}(Z = 1)$ and $\pi_0^Z = \hat{\mathbb{P}}(Z = 0) = 1 - \pi_1^Z$, the proportions of samples in each, protected or non-protected, group. The sample mean of Z is $\bar{z} = \frac{1}{n}\sum_{i \in \mathcal{T}} z_i = |\mathcal{C}_1^Z|/n = \pi_1^Z$ and the predictions mean is $\bar{\hat{y}} = \frac{1}{n}\sum_{i \in \mathcal{T}} \hat{y}_i$. Then, the covariance in Eq. 2 can be decomposed as

$$\begin{aligned}
\text{cov}(\mathbf{z}, \hat{\mathbf{y}}) &= \frac{n}{n-1}\left(\frac{1}{n}\sum_{i \in \mathcal{C}_1^Z}(z_i - \bar{z})(\hat{y}_i - \bar{\hat{y}}) + \frac{1}{n}\sum_{i \in \mathcal{C}_0^Z}(z_i - \bar{z})(\hat{y}_i - \bar{\hat{y}})\right) \\
&= \frac{n}{n-1}\left(\frac{1}{n}\sum_{i \in \mathcal{C}_1^Z}(1 - \pi_1^Z)(\hat{y}_i - \bar{\hat{y}}) + \frac{1}{n}\sum_{i \in \mathcal{C}_0^Z}(0 - \pi_1^Z)(\hat{y}_i - \bar{\hat{y}})\right) \\
&= \frac{n}{n-1}\left(\pi_0^Z \frac{|\mathcal{C}_1^Z|}{n} \frac{1}{|\mathcal{C}_1^Z|}\sum_{i \in \mathcal{C}_1^Z}(\hat{y}_i - \bar{\hat{y}}) - \pi_1^Z \frac{|\mathcal{C}_0^Z|}{n} \frac{1}{|\mathcal{C}_0^Z|}\sum_{i \in \mathcal{C}_0^Z}(\hat{y}_i - \bar{\hat{y}})\right) \\
&= \frac{n}{n-1}\pi_0^Z \pi_1^Z \underbrace{\left(\frac{1}{|\mathcal{C}_1^Z|}\sum_{i \in \mathcal{C}_1^Z}\hat{y}_i - \frac{1}{|\mathcal{C}_0^Z|}\sum_{i \in \mathcal{C}_0^Z}\hat{y}_i\right)}_{\hat{\mathbb{E}}[\hat{Y}|Z=1] - \hat{\mathbb{E}}[\hat{Y}|Z=0]} \qquad (3)
\end{aligned}$$

which is proportional to the relaxed (in the sense that probabilistic predictions $\hat{Y}$ are used instead of binary decisions $\hat{Y}^d$) demographic parity[2], as defined before in Eq. 1. This means that imposing $\text{cov}(\mathbf{z}, \hat{\mathbf{y}}) = 0$ in the case where the protected variable Z is categorical remains meaningful and is closely related to the demographic parity. Indeed, Eq. 3 shows that, for a given dataset, the absolute value of the covariance is proportional to a relaxation of the demographic parity measure based on the predicted probabilities instead of binary decisions.

[2] In Eq. 3, $\hat{\mathbb{E}}[\cdot]$ is the sample average (empirical expectation).

Now, if both variables Z and Y are categorical, by using the simplified form of the covariance,

$$\begin{aligned}\operatorname{cov}(\mathbf{z}, \mathbf{y}) &= \frac{1}{n-1} \sum_{i \in \mathcal{T}} (z_i - \bar{z})(y_i - \bar{y}) \\ &= \frac{n}{n-1} \left(\frac{1}{n} \sum_{i \in \mathcal{T}} z_i y_i - \bar{z}\bar{y} \right) \\ &= \frac{n}{n-1} (\pi_{11}^{ZY} - \pi_1^Z \pi_1^Y) \end{aligned} \tag{4}$$

where $\pi_{11}^{ZY} = \frac{1}{n} \sum_{i \in \mathcal{T}} z_i y_i$ is the proportion of observations for which both $z_i = 1$ and $y_i = 1$ in the sample. Thus, the covariance quantifies in some way the departure from independence between Z and Y observed in the sample. Once again, the covariance should be equal to zero in case of equal treatment.

3 Fairness-Aware Maximum Entropy Formulation of Logistic Regression

The maximum entropy formulation of logistic regression model appears to be quite convenient to add new constraints to the predictions of the model (see for instance [19] in the context of classifier's predictions fusion by taking their 'correlations' into account). This allows us to impose fairness constraints in the form of (relaxed) demographic parity (see Eq. 3) or, equivalently, covariance constraints between the class predictions and the values of the protected variable. In this section, we first introduce the well-known maximum-entropic form of logistic regression, then develop our model taking the protected variable into account and, finally, introduce a backward stepwise procedure.

3.1 Maximum Entropy Formulation of Logistic Regression Model

Let us first briefly introduce the logistic regression model from a maximum entropy [12,25] argument (see, e.g., [5,37,55] and, more generally, for the exponential family [43]). We consider an $n \times m$ data matrix $\mathbf{X} = (x_{if})$ whose element x_{if} contains the measurement of feature/variable f on sample i of the training set. Thus, there are m features, including a constant $+1$ feature for the intercept term of the regression. Categorical variables are represented by binary indicator variables as usual (one-hot encoding). The observed target values are recorded in the $n \times q$ target matrix $\mathbf{Y} = (y_{ik})$ where q is the number of different classes and y_{ik} encodes the observed class membership of each individual i. As it is assumed that classes are mutually exclusive, the y_{ik} are also binary indicator variables, $y_{ik} = 1$ if sample i is categorized in class k and $y_{il} = 0$ for all $l \neq k$. The predicted a posteriori probabilities of belonging to each class, provided by the supervised classification model, are $\hat{y}_{ik}$ with $\sum_{k=1}^{q} \hat{y}_{ik} = 1$, and are recorded in $\hat{\mathbf{Y}}$.

With this in mind, the maximum entropy problem defined on the training set can be stated[3] as follows (ignoring the very last constraint for now),

$$\left|\begin{array}{lll} \underset{\{\hat{y}_{ik}\}}{\text{maximize}} & -\sum_{i=1}^{n}\sum_{k=1}^{q} \hat{y}_{ik}\log\hat{y}_{ik} & \\ \text{subject to} & \frac{1}{n}\sum_{i=1}^{n}\hat{y}_{ik}x_{if} = \frac{1}{n}\sum_{i=1}^{n} y_{ik}x_{if} & \text{for all } f,k \\ & \sum_{k=1}^{q}\hat{y}_{ik} = 1 & \text{for all } i \\ & \hat{y}_{ik} \geq 0 & \text{for all } i,k \\ & \left|\frac{1}{n-1}\sum_{i=1}^{n}\hat{y}_{ik}\tilde{z}_i\right| \leq \epsilon & \text{for the constrained classes } k \end{array}\right. \quad (5)$$

It simply aims to find the maximum entropic predictions under the requirement that the co-moments between the features and the model predictions $\hat{y}_{ik}$ match exactly the co-moments between the features and the observed outputs y_{ik} on the training set (linear constraints) – these co-moments are preserved when computing the predictions. Various algorithms can be used to estimate the Lagrange parameters of the model and to compute the predictions, notably, iterative scaling [5,23] but, in the experiments, we used the CVXPY convex optimization library implemented in Python [15].

3.2 Logistic Regression Formulation Including Demographic Parity Constraints

This section shows how to introduce (relaxed) demographic parity constraints to the maximum entropic formulation of logistic regression. Basically, it aims at adding linear de-correlation constraints to the initial model of Eq. 5. Recall that $\mathbf{z}$ is the $n \times 1$ column vector of measurements of the protected variable. We want to impose that some $n \times 1$ prediction vectors $\hat{\mathbf{y}}_k$ (column k of the prediction matrix $\hat{\mathbf{Y}}$), corresponding to classes k, are (partly) de-correlated with this protected variable $\mathbf{z}$. Therefore, we require that the sample covariance in absolute value between the prediction vector and the protected variable should be no larger than a given threshold[4] $\epsilon \geq 0$ (tolerance level), $|\text{cov}(\hat{\mathbf{y}}_k, \mathbf{z})| \leq \epsilon$. Therefore, from Eq. 2, $\left|\frac{1}{n-1}\mathbf{z}^{\mathsf{T}}\mathbf{H}\hat{\mathbf{y}}_k\right| \leq \epsilon$, and after defining $\tilde{\mathbf{z}} = \mathbf{H}\mathbf{z}$ (the centered protected variable on the training set), the constraint becomes $\left|\frac{1}{n-1}\tilde{\mathbf{z}}^{\mathsf{T}}\hat{\mathbf{y}}_k\right| \leq \epsilon$. Thus, a partial de-correlation is achieved by introducing linear inequality constraints in the maximum entropy formulation, $\left|\frac{1}{n-1}\sum_{i=1}^{n}\hat{y}_{ik}\tilde{z}_i\right| \leq \epsilon$; see the last constraint of Eq. 5, which corresponds to the concave optimization problem to be solved. Notice that this model can easily be extended to multi-class problems, to several protected variables, and to numerical protected variables.

As already stated in Subsect. 1.2, this formulation is close to the one used in [53]. The primary difference is the fact that the maximum entropy formulation applies the constraint directly on the predicted values (the outputs of the

[3] The $0 \cdot \log 0 = 0$ convention applies here.

[4] We consider here that the fairness-aware algorithm should not discriminate the unprotected class, as an adverse effect.

model) whereas, in [53], the constraint is applied to the linear output of logistic regression, before applying the sigmoid function, which is somewhat less natural.

However, in some situations, it happens that the linear constraints (co-moment and fairness constraints) are not compatible; in that case, the problem is infeasible and the model cannot be fitted properly. In order to avoid this delicate situation, we recommend pre-computing the best achievable de-correlation to know a priori the lowest value of ϵ that can be reached while still considering perfect co-moments fitting.

3.3 Computing a Lower Bound on the Covariance with the Protected Variable

The simpler linear programming problem (6)[5], aiming at computing the best achievable de-correlation of the class predictions, is therefore solved first, which provides the lowest covariance ϵ (after taking the absolute value) that can be reached on the training set while still fitting a model preserving the co-moments. As an alternative, the lowest (relaxed) demographic parity could be computed instead of covariance by following Eq. 3.

$$
\begin{array}{lll}
\underset{\{\hat{y}_{ik}\}}{\text{maximize}} & \frac{1}{n-1}\sum\limits_{i=1}^{n} \hat{y}_{ik}\tilde{z}_i & \text{find the covariance closest to 0} \\
\text{subject to} & \frac{1}{n}\sum_{i=1}^{n} \hat{y}_{ik}x_{if} = \frac{1}{n}\sum_{i=1}^{n} y_{ik}x_{if} & \text{for all } f, k \\
& \frac{1}{n-1}\sum_{i=1}^{n} \hat{y}_{ik}\tilde{z}_i \leq 0 & \text{for the constrained classes } k \\
& \sum_{k=1}^{q} \hat{y}_{ik} = 1 & \text{for all } i \\
& \hat{y}_{ik} \geq 0 & \text{for all } i, k
\end{array}
\tag{6}
$$

Then, in order to have a safety barrier, in practice, we set ϵ to 1.05 times[6] the obtained lower bound. The problem (6) is easier and much quicker to solve than the maximum-entropic problem (5) itself. Our algorithm offers the advantage of adjusting epsilon based on specific fairness requirements, allowing to tailor the level of fairness implementation to the application. Later on, this technique will also be used in order to evaluate the further increase of demographic parity that can be obtained when relaxing some co-moment constraints and, thus, evaluating the impact of gradually decreasing the effect of the features. This is the core idea behind the stepwise selection procedure, further improving demographic parity, described in Sect. 3.5. Thus, before de-correlating the output of logistic regression thanks to Eq. 5, the problem (6) is first solved in order to find the ϵ value that will be used in the maximum entropy problem (5). This step is important because experiments have shown that the problem (5) often becomes unfeasible on some training folds when ϵ becomes close to 0, leading to a loss in time and results.

[5] Recall that the covariance between the protected variable and the model prediction for class k should be negative; otherwise there is no discrimination with respect to the protected group and there is no need to impose fairness constraints.

[6] This threshold is chosen (admittedly somewhat arbitrarily) in order to be close to the best achievable solution.

3.4 Optimality Conditions and Predicted Class Memberships

With the introduction of the de-correlation constraints (assuming that they are present for each class k), the Lagrange function obtained from the problem defined in Eq. 5 is

$$\begin{aligned}\mathscr{L}(\hat{\mathbf{Y}}) = &-\sum_{i=1}^{n}\sum_{k=1}^{q}\hat{y}_{ik}\log\hat{y}_{ik} + \sum_{f=1}^{m}\sum_{k=1}^{q}\lambda_{kf}\left(\sum_{i=1}^{n}(\hat{y}_{ik}x_{if} - y_{ik}x_{if})\right)\\ &+\sum_{k=1}^{q}\nu_k\left(\tfrac{1}{n-1}\sum_{i=1}^{n}\hat{y}_{ik}\tilde{z}_i + \epsilon\right) + \sum_{k=1}^{q}\varphi_k\left(-\tfrac{1}{n-1}\sum_{i=1}^{n}\hat{y}_{ik}\tilde{z}_i + \epsilon\right)\\ &+\sum_{i=1}^{n}\mu_i\left(\sum_{k=1}^{q}\hat{y}_{ik} - 1\right)\end{aligned} \tag{7}$$

where a Lagrange parameter is associated with each constraint. Note that there is no need to take the non-negativity constraints on the predictions into account because the solution will automatically be non-negative[7]. After computing the partial derivative with respect to the predictions $\hat{y}_{ik}$ and setting the result to 0, the following expression is obtained [5,12],

$$\hat{y}_{ik} = \frac{\exp\left(\sum_{f=1}^{m}\lambda_{kf}x_{if}\right)\exp\left(\frac{(\nu_k - \varphi_k)\tilde{z}_i}{n-1}\right)}{\sum_{l=1}^{q}\exp\left(\sum_{f=1}^{m}\lambda_{lf}x_{if}\right)\exp\left(\frac{(\nu_l - \varphi_l)\tilde{z}_i}{n-1}\right)} \quad \text{for all } i, k \tag{8}$$

depending on the Lagrange parameters obtained during the optimization. This last equation is used in order to compute class predictions on new data.

3.5 Stepwise Procedure Improving Demographic Parity

Here is a brief description of the backward stepwise procedure used in order to sequentially remove the feature leading to the highest decrease in (absolute) covariance with the protected variable. This procedure is started, if needed (i.e. if we are not satisfied with the reached demographic parity level), after having initially solved the de-correlation procedure (see Eq. 5) with all features included. More precisely, we proceed as follows:

1. Initially, we compute the lower bound on the covariance[8] with the protected variable, ϵ^*, by solving the problem in Eq. 6, as well as the corresponding correlation[8] γ^*. If the obtained lower bound ϵ^* is not satisfactory (we used 10^{-5} in our experiments), we try to decrease it further by relaxing one co-moment constraint, which is equivalent to deleting this feature.

[7] This is a standard property of most maximum entropy problems based on the Shannon entropy; see for instance [12,28].

[8] Here, we always consider the absolute value of the covariance and the correlation.

2. Then, as in a backward stepwise approach, we solve the problem of Eq. 6 after removing each feature in turn to obtain all lower bounds on the correlation[9] between the predicted target values and the protected variable, denoted as $\gamma_{(-f)}$; thus without using the feature f.
3. After that, we select and remove the feature with the smallest resulting correlation, $\gamma = \min_f(\gamma_{(-f)})$, but only if the difference between the correlation of the previous model γ^* and the obtained γ is significant enough (in our experiments, we used larger than 10^{-5}). In this case, we update γ^* accordingly, $\gamma^* \leftarrow \gamma$.
4. The steps 2 and 3 are repeated until no additional feature can be removed.
5. The maximum-entropic problem of Eq. 5 is then solved with the remaining set of features $\mathcal{F}^*$.

For details, see Algorithm 1.

4 Experiments

In this section, we compare the performance of the method introduced in Sect. 3 with the methods proposed by Zafar et al. [53] and Donini et al. [16], as well as with a standard logistic regression (baseline) through fairness-aware classification tasks. Notice however that in [16], the authors use a variant of equal opportunity instead of demographic parity as a fairness measure, so their results are not directly comparable to those obtained by the other two models.

The section is structured as follows. First, the investigated datasets are introduced in Subsect. 4.1. Then, Subsect. 4.2 outlines the details of the experimental methodology. Finally, Subsect. 4.3 presents and discusses the results of the experiments.

4.1 Datasets

To assess our method, we selected from [35] a collection of five datasets already used in several fairness-aware machine learning problems [13,17,33]. All these datasets contain observations of a set of feature variables $\{X_f\}$, a binary protected variable Z, and a binary target variable Y. Note that we perform the same preprocessing, variable selection, and protected variable choice as in [35] for all but two datasets (the differences are explained below). Moreover, we standardize each continuous variable. The number of samples and features obtained after preprocessing and a summary of the main characteristics of each dataset, notably the initial demographic parity of the dataset, are reported in Table 1. The collection is composed of the following datasets:

[9] Note that we use here the correlation with the protected variable (easily computed from the obtained covariance) because it is bounded between −1 and +1, which makes it more interpretable than the covariance.

Algorithm 1. Stepwise feature selection using backward elimination.

Input:
- The set of features ($\mathcal{F}$), together with their observed values.
- The vector of observed values of the protected variable ($\mathbf{z}$).
- The vector of observed values of the target variable ($\mathbf{y}$).

Output:
- The truncated feature set ($\mathcal{F}^*$).
- The lower bound of the absolute correlation using the truncated set (γ^*).
- The corresponding absolute covariance (ϵ^*).

$\gamma^*, \epsilon^* \leftarrow \text{abs}(\text{LowerBound}(\mathcal{F}, \mathbf{z}, \mathbf{y}))$ ▷ Get the correlation and covariance lower bounds for $\mathcal{F}$ by solving problem in Eq. 6.
$\mathcal{F}^* \leftarrow \mathcal{F}$ ▷ Initialization of the feature set before feature eliminations.
if ($\epsilon^* < 10^{-5}$) **then** ▷ Check if the stepwise procedure is necessary.
  return $\mathcal{F}^*, \gamma^*, \epsilon^*$
end if
while $\gamma^* > 10^{-5}$ **do**
  $\gamma \leftarrow \infty$
  for $f \in \mathcal{F}^*$ **do** ▷ Loop on the current set of features.
    $\gamma_{(-f)}, \epsilon \leftarrow \text{abs}(\text{LowerBound}(\mathcal{F}^* \setminus f, \mathbf{z}, \mathbf{y}))$ ▷ Compute the lower bounds when feature f is removed (Eq. 6).
    if $\gamma_{(-f)} < \gamma$ **then** ▷ Search for the feature whose removal reduces most the lower bound.
      $\gamma \leftarrow \gamma_{(-f)}$
      $\mathcal{F}' \leftarrow \mathcal{F}^* \setminus f$
    end if
  end for
  if ($\gamma^* - \gamma > 10^{-5}$) **then** ▷ Check if the improvement (10^{-5}) is sufficient.
    $\mathcal{F}^* \leftarrow \mathcal{F}'$ ▷ Remove the feature.
    $\gamma^*, \epsilon^* \leftarrow \gamma, \epsilon$ ▷ Update the lower bounds.
  else
    break ▷ Exit the loop if the improvement is insufficient.
  end if
end while
return $\mathcal{F}^*, \gamma^*, \epsilon^*$ ▷ Return the feature set and its correlation and covariance lower bounds.

- The *Adult*, or *Census Income*, dataset [29,32] is composed of 45,222 instances represented by 13 features. As an additional step to the preprocessing proposed by [35], we simplify the 'native-country' variable by grouping countries by continent to avoid the curse of dimensionality [24]. The protected variable is the gender of the individual ('Female', $Z = 1$) and the target variable is the income of the individual, specifically whether it exceeds 50,000 USD ('≥50K', $Y = 1$).
- The *Bank marketing* dataset [29,42] comes from phone call marketing campaigns of a Portuguese banking institution and includes 45,211 instances described by 17 features. The classification aims to determine whether a client will subscribe to a term deposit ('Yes', $Y = 1$). The protected variable is the

age of the client, which is transformed into a binary variable by separating clients under 25 or over 60 from those between 25 and 60 ('25–60', $Z = 1$).
- The *COMPAS* dataset released by ProPublica [2,47] is a sample of results provided by the COMPAS algorithm that predicts recidivism risk for defendants. We selected the same set of features as [35] except for the 'Age' variable which is redundant with the 'Age_cat' variable. In addition, as suggested by other studies [2,13], we only keep the defendants of Caucasian or African-American descent, because other ethnicities are much less represented. Therefore, the cleaned dataset contains 6,150 instances and 11 features. The protected variable is the ethnicity of the defendant ('African-American', $Z = 1$) and the target is to predict whether the defendant will re-offend within two years ('Non-recidivist', $Y = 1$).
- The *German credit* dataset [29] is composed of 1,000 instances of bank account holder information described by 22 features. The goal is to predict whether it is hazardous or not to extend credit to a bank account holder ('Good', $Y = 1$). The protected variable is the age of the bank account holder, which is transformed into a binary variable by separating those over 25 from the others ('≤25', $Z = 1$).
- The *Law school* dataset [51] comes from a survey conducted by the Law School Admission Council across 163 law schools in the United States and includes 20,798 instances represented by 12 features. The protected variable is the ethnicity of the student ('Non-white', $Z = 1$) and the target variable is whether the student will pass the bar exam on the first try ('Pass', $Y = 1$).

Table 1. Main characteristics of the datasets used in the experiments.

Dataset name	#Samples	#Features	Target variable Y	Positive target level $Y = 1$	Protected variable Z	Protected variable level $Z = 1$	Demographic parity
Adult	45,522	13	Income	≥50K	Gender	Female	0.1338
Bank marketing	45,211	17	Subscribe	Yes	Age	25–60	0.2490
COMPAS	6,150	11	Two_year_recid	Non-recidivist	Race	African-American	0.1207
German credit	1,000	22	Class_label	Good	Age	≤25	0.1494
Law school	20,798	12	Pass_bar	Yes	Race	Non-white	0.1131

4.2 Experimental Methodology

To evaluate the performance of the methods, we rely on five measures: the accuracy (ACC), the demographic parity computed from binary decisions (DPD) and predicted probabilities (DPP), and two new measures, the area under the demographic parity curve (AUDPC) and the F1 demographic parity (F1DP). Finally, we assess all the methods through a standard five-fold cross-validation procedure to limit the variability in the results. We decided to apply a five-fold cross-validation as suggested in [52] for datasets between 1000 and 50,000 instances, which is our case. Results are averaged on all test sets of the cross-validation.

The demographic parity curve is obtained by plotting demographic parity for different decision thresholds on a graph where the x-axis represents the thresholds and the y-axis the demographic parity values for these threshold levels. Indeed, most of the time, the decision threshold corresponds to 0.5, which means that if $\hat{y}_i > 0.5$, then class 1 is assigned to instance i. However, depending on the study case, the decision makers could have tight constraints on the number of candidates to be selected, which requires changing this threshold. Therefore, computing the area under the demographic parity curve (AUDPC) takes demographic parity into account for all possible situations.

The F1 demographic parity is a straightforward modified version of the F1-measure [10] based on the accuracy (ACC) and the demographic parity (DPD). This measure is defined as

$$F1DP = 2 * \frac{ACC * (1 - |DPD|)}{ACC + (1 - |DPD|)} \tag{9}$$

where we ensure that ACC and DPD evolve in the same direction by taking 1 − |DPD|. In contrast to the other fairness measures used, the F1 demographic parity allows us to consider the trade-off between ACC and DPD. Intuitively, the best model should have high ACC with low DPD, which is reflected by this measure.

Comparisons are performed with the models proposed in [53] (Zafar) and [16] (Donini). Regarding the Zafar method, we use the algorithm presented in Subsect. 3.2 of [53] with the code provided by the authors, adapted to Python 3[10] For the Donini method, we combine the data pre-processing method developed in [16][11] (see Eq. 15 in [16]) for (generalized) linear models with a sklearn logistic regression (solver = lbfgs and max_iter = 10,000) [44]. In addition, we keep the same hyperparameters for all logistic regression models.

4.3 Results and Discussion

The results of our experiments are presented in Table 2 for the five datasets in the following format: mean of the measure across the five folds ± the standard deviation. For clarity, we highlighted the highest ACC, F1DP, lowest DPD, DPP, and AUDPC, in boldface for each dataset. From Table 2, we can observe that our method as well as those of Donini and Zafar all manage to decrease DPD, DPP, and AUDPC by sacrificing in general some accuracy compared to a standard logistic regression baseline. Regarding the F1DP measure, all methods obtain higher results than the logistic regression baseline, with the exception of Zafar method on the Compas dataset. Indeed, we can observe that on the Compas dataset, the Zafar method manages to reduce DPD, but at the cost of a significant decrease in ACC, explaining the lower F1DP value. Furthermore, the

[10] Code Python 2 is available at https://github.com/mbilalzafar/fair-classification.

[11] Python 3 code is available at https://github.com/jmikko/fair_ERM..

Table 2. Mean of classification accuracy (ACC), F1 demographic parity (F1DP), demographic parity computed from decisions (DPD) as well as from predicted probabilities (DPP), and area under the demographic parity curve (AUDPC) with their standard deviations (±) for the various models, obtained on the five datasets. The best performing method is highlighted in boldface for each dataset and measure.

Measure →: Method ↓:	ACC	F1DP	DPD	DPP	AUDPC
			Adult		
Baseline	**0.8451 ± 0.0053**	0.8856 ± 0.0033	0.0698 ± 0.0049	0.1173 ± 0.0039	0.1173 ± 0.0039
Our method	0.8318 ± 0.0061	0.8929 ± 0.0058	0.0364 ± 0.0062	**0.0047 ± 0.0021**	**0.0502 ± 0.0032**
Zafar	0.8429 ± 0.0071	0.9020 ± 0.0107	0.0295 ± 0.0272	0.0625 ± 0.0423	0.0669 ± 0.0386
Donini	0.8436 ± 0.0060	**0.9026 ± 0.0034**	**0.0294 ± 0.0062**	0.0980 ± 0.0055	0.0988 ± 0.0050
			Bank		
Baseline	0.9013 ± 0.0026	0.8708 ± 0.0144	0.1573 ± 0.0276	0.1795 ± 0.0157	0.1795 ± 0.0157
Our method	0.8989 ± 0.0016	**0.9428 ± 0.0024**	**0.0089 ± 0.0056**	**0.0104 ± 0.0084**	**0.0187 ± 0.0078**
Zafar	0.8993 ± 0.0029	0.9367 ± 0.0072	0.0225 ± 0.0160	0.0225 ± 0.0121	0.0303 ± 0.0107
Donini	**0.9016 ± 0.0029**	0.8852 ± 0.0118	0.1302 ± 0.0243	0.1504 ± 0.0180	0.1504 ± 0.0180
			Compas		
Baseline	**0.6789 ± 0.0061**	0.7163 ± 0.0162	0.2413 ± 0.0313	0.1227 ± 0.0110	0.1228 ± 0.0110
Our method	0.6628 ± 0.0110	**0.7810 ± 0.0131**	0.0490 ± 0.0259	0.0133 ± 0.0070	0.0302 ± 0.0061
Zafar	0.5502 ± 0.0167	0.7017 ± 0.0157	**0.0313 ± 0.0158**	**0.0027 ± 0.0024**	**0.0104 ± 0.0026**
Donini	0.6681 ± 0.0104	0.7666 ± 0.0180	0.1002 ± 0.0383	0.0313 ± 0.0123	0.0399 ± 0.0103
			German		
Baseline	**0.7450 ± 0.0302**	0.8055 ± 0.0250	0.1188 ± 0.0661	0.0932 ± 0.0185	0.0986 ± 0.0180
Our method	0.7440 ± 0.0312	0.8292 ± 0.0213	0.0626 ± 0.0177	0.0293 ± 0.0070	0.0449 ± 0.0081
Zafar	0.7380 ± 0.0401	**0.8336 ± 0.0287**	**0.0405 ± 0.0275**	**0.0215 ± 0.0076**	**0.0369 ± 0.0182**
Donini	0.7380 ± 0.0350	0.8310 ± 0.0262	0.0476 ± 0.0313	0.0254 ± 0.0063	0.0426 ± 0.0117
			Law		
Baseline	**0.9520 ± 0.0019**	0.9489 ± 0.0035	0.0541 ± 0.0072	0.1103 ± 0.0080	0.1103 ± 0.0080
Our method	0.9431 ± 0.0016	0.9679 ± 0.0006	0.0059 ± 0.0018	0.0043 ± 0.0044	0.0086 ± 0.0025
Zafar	0.9500 ± 0.0014	**0.9741 ± 0.0008**	**0.0005 ± 0.0004**	**0.0036 ± 0.0016**	**0.0046 ± 0.0016**
Donini	0.9504 ± 0.0022	0.9677 ± 0.0026	0.0144 ± 0.0059	0.0271 ± 0.0067	0.0275 ± 0.0066

Donini method managed to slightly improve the fairness measures while increasing the accuracy on Bank dataset, relative to the logistic regression baseline, which appears somewhat counter-intuitive.

To analyze more thoroughly our results, we perform two nonparametric Friedman-Nemenyi statistical tests followed by multiple Wilcoxon signed-rank tests at a level of confidence of 95% ($\alpha = 0.05$) [14] on the results computed from the cross-validation test folds. Note that we limit our analysis to the two new measures introduced, AUDPC and F1DP, because they encompass ACC, DPD, and DPP. The p-values of the Friedman tests are respectively 1.2×10^{-12} and 8.9×10^{-6} for AUDPC and F1DP, which is inferior to our α meaning that the results of at least one method are significantly different from the others for each measure. As the results of the two Friedman tests are positive, we perform

Nemenyi tests to identify the methods that obtain different results from each other. The results of the Nemenyi tests are illustrated in Fig. 1.

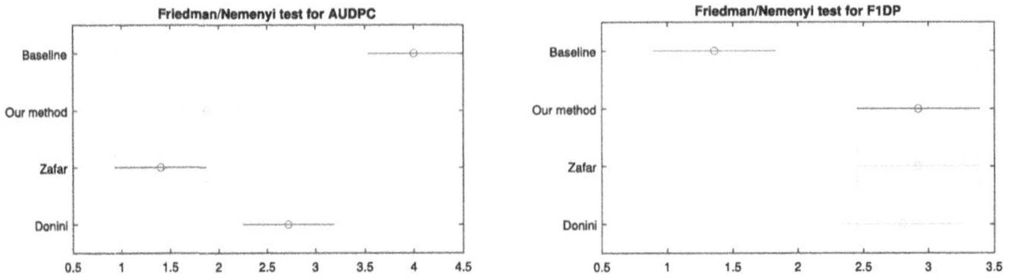

(a) AUCDP (b) F1DP

Fig. 1. Mean ranks and 95% Nemenyi confidence intervals for the AUDPC (a) and F1DP (b) measures. Two methods are considered as significantly different if their confidence intervals do not overlap. The x-axis unit is the average rank of the methods. The lower the rank, the better the method in terms of AUDPC while the higher the rank, the better the method in terms of F1DP. The best methods highlighted in blue are Zafar for AUDPC and ours on par with Zafar for F1DP. (Color figure online)

From this Fig. 1, we can see that the baseline method is outperformed by the other three methods for both AUDPC and F1DP. The tests also show that the Zafar method obtains results significantly superior to those of the Donini method for AUDPC. Moreover, the Wilcoxon signed-rank tests highlight that our method performs significantly better than the Donini method for AUDPC (p-value $= 9.0 \times 10^{-5}$). In addition – and this is also an interesting result – we note that Zafar and the maximum entropy methods provide close results. Therefore, contrary to our initial conjecture, the performance of Zafar's method does not seem to be impacted by the fact that fairness constraints are applied before the sigmoid function (which is not the case for the maximum entropy method directly constraining the outputs).

In summary, all methods, Zafar, Donini, and ours, manage to reduce significantly the demographic parity measures while maintaining a high level of accuracy. However, the Zafar method and ours obtain better results than the Donini method in terms of AUDPC. Moreover, we observed that the main differences between these three methods are mainly due to the class shift of a small part of the observations.

5 Conclusion and Future Work

In this paper, we have presented a novel approach for addressing discrimination and bias in supervised classification problems in terms of demographic parity. A fist contribution includes the development of two original fairness measures for supervised classification problems – area under the demographic parity curve (AUDPC) and F1 demographic parity (F1DP). Moreover, our work unveils intimate relationships between demographic parity and sample covariance, offering insights into fairness in classification problems. The proposed approach involves incorporating fairness constraints on the predictions of a logistic regression model with the use of covariance as a relaxed proxy for demographic parity, as well as the study of a stepwise approach. We have demonstrated its effectiveness through experiments on five datasets.

Looking ahead, there are several promising directions for future research in this area. To address a wider range of classification challenges, we could easily extend the use of covariance in fairness constraints to continuous protected variables, such as age, instead of only focusing on binary protected variables. We also plan to consider multi-class problems as well as the extension to several protected variables. Another interesting contribution would be to develop a dedicated algorithm for solving the maximum entropy problem of Eq. 5 instead of relying on a general convex optimization solver, which would allow scaling to larger datasets. In addition, other techniques, incorporating fairness in classification, could be compared on a larger collection of datasets, especially post-processing techniques. Finally, we could also change the constraints by incorporating other fairness measures in it, while maintaining the formulation of those constraints linear. Specifically, we propose introducing conditional demographic parity [27] into the constraints of our model, deviating from the classical demographic parity. The conditional demographic parity consists of conditioning the demographic parity on a specific variable (other than the sensitive and the target ones) which is highly dependent on the sensitive variable and explains the result. As described in the work of [27], it aims to mitigate the challenges posed by Simpson's paradox, in which a relation observed within distinct groups undergoes a reversal by combining groups. Our model can also be used to add linear constraints other than fairness constraints, enabling it to be applied to other problems.

Acknowledgements. We thank Professor Gianluca Bontempi (Université Libre de Bruxelles) for reading the paper and providing useful remarks as well as future work suggestions.

References

1. Agarwal, A., Dudík, M., Wu, Z.S.: Fair regression: quantitative definitions and reduction-based algorithms. In: Proceedings of the 36th International Conference on Machine Learning (ICML 2019), pp. 120–129. PMLR (2019)
2. Angwin, J., Larson, J., Mattu, S., Kirchner, L.: Machine bias. In: Ethics of Data and Analytics, pp. 254–264. Auerbach Publications (2016)
3. Arnold, S.: Mathematical Statistics. Prentice Hall, Hoboken (1990)
4. Barocas, S., Hardt, M., Narayanan, A.: Fairness and Machine Learning: Limitations and Opportunities. MIT Press, Cambridge (2023)
5. Berger, A., Della Pietra, S.A., Della Pietra, V.J.: A maximum entropy approach to natural language processing. Comput. Linguist. **22**(1), 39–71 (1996)
6. Berk, R., et al.: A convex framework for fair regression. arXiv preprint arXiv:1706.02409 (2017)

7. Calders, T., Kamiran, F., Pechenizkiy, M.: Building classifiers with independency constraints. In: Proceedings of the 9th IEEE International Conference on Data Mining (ICDM 2009), pp. 13–18 (2009)
8. Calders, T., Verwer, S.: Three Naive Bayes approaches for discrimination-free classification. Data Min. Knowl. Disc. **21**, 277–292 (2010)
9. Castelnovo, A., Crupi, R., Greco, G., Regoli, D., Penco, I.G., Cosentini, A.C.: A clarification of the nuances in the fairness metrics landscape. Sci. Rep. **12**(1), 1–21 (2022)
10. Christen, P., Hand, D.J., Kirielle, N.: A review of the f-measure: its history, properties, criticism, and alternatives. ACM Comput. Surv. **56**(3), 1–24 (2023)
11. Corbett-Davies, S., Gaebler, J.D., Nilforoshan, H., Shroff, R., Goel, S.: The measure and mismeasure of fairness. J. Mach. Learn. Res. **24**(1) (2024)
12. Cover, T., Thomas, J.: Elements of Information Theory, 2nd edn. Wiley, Hoboken (2006)
13. Delobelle, P., Temple, P., Perrouin, G., Frénay, B., Heymans, P., Berendt, B.: Ethical adversaries: towards mitigating unfairness with adversarial machine learning. ACM SIGKDD Explor. Newsl. **23**(1), 32–41 (2021)
14. Demšar, J.: Statistical comparisons of classifiers over multiple data sets. J. Mach. Learn. Res. **7**, 1–30 (2006)
15. Diamond, S., Boyd, S.: CVXPY: a Python-embedded modeling language for convex optimization. J. Mach. Learn. Res. **17**(83), 1–5 (2016)
16. Donini, M., Oneto, L., Ben-David, S., Shawe-Taylor, J.S., Pontil, M.: Empirical risk minimization under fairness constraints. In: Proceedings of the 32nd Neural Information Processing Systems Conference (NIPS 2018) (2018)
17. Fish, B., Kun, J., Lelkes, A.D.: A confidence-based approach for balancing fairness and accuracy. In: Proceedings of the 16th SIAM International Conference on Data Mining (SDM 2016), pp. 144–152 (2016)
18. Foggo, V., Villasenor, J., Garg, P.: Algorithms and fairness. Ohio State Technol. Law J. **17**, 123 (2021)
19. Saerens, M., Fouss, F.: Yet another method for combining classifiers outputs: a maximum entropy approach. In: Roli, F., Kittler, J., Windeatt, T. (eds.) MCS 2004. LNCS, vol. 3077, pp. 82–91. Springer, Heidelberg (2004). https://doi.org/10.1007/978-3-540-25966-4_8
20. Hardle, W., Simar, L.: Applied Multivariate Statistical Analysis, 4th edn. Springer, Heidelberg (2015). https://doi.org/10.1007/978-3-662-45171-7
21. Hardt, M., Price, E., Srebro, N.: Equality of opportunity in supervised learning. In: Proceedings of the 29th Neural Information Processing Systems Conference (NIPS 2016) (2016)
22. Hort, M., Chen, Z., Zhang, J.M., Harman, M., Sarro, F.: Bias mitigation for machine learning classifiers: a comprehensive survey. ACM J. Responsible Comput. **1**(2), 1–52 (2023)
23. Huang, F.L., Hsieh, C.J., Chang, K.W., Lin, C.J.: Iterative scaling and coordinate descent methods for maximum entropy models. J. Mach. Learn. Res. **11**(2), 815–848 (2010)
24. Izenman, A.: Modern Multivariate Statistical Techniques. Springer, New York (2008). https://doi.org/10.1007/978-0-387-78189-1
25. Jaynes, E.T.: Information theory and statistical mechanics. Phys. Rev. **106**, 620–630 (1957)
26. Jiang, H., Nachum, O.: Identifying and correcting label bias in machine learning. In: Proceedings of the 23rd International Conference on Artificial Intelligence and Statistics (AISTATS 2020), pp. 702–712 (2020)

27. Kamiran, F., Žliobaitė, I., Calders, T.: Quantifying explainable discrimination and removing illegal discrimination in automated decision making. Knowl. Inf. Syst. **35**, 613–644 (2013)
28. Kapur, J.N., Kesavan, H.K.: Entropy Optimization Principles with Applications. Academic Press, New York (1992)
29. Kelly, M., Longjohn, R., Nottingham, K.: The UCI machine learning repository. https://archive.ics.uci.edu
30. Kim, J.Y., Cho, S.B.: An information theoretic approach to reducing algorithmic bias for machine learning. Neurocomputing **500**, 26–38 (2022)
31. Kleinberg, J., Ludwig, J., Mullainathan, S., Rambachan, A.: Algorithmic fairness. In: Proceedings of 113th Annual Meeting of the American Economic Association (AEA 2018), pp. 22–27 (2018)
32. Kohavi, R.: Scaling up the accuracy of Naive-Bayes classifiers: a decision-tree hybrid. In: Proceedings of the 2nd International Conference on Knowledge Discovery and Data mining (KDD 1996), pp. 202–207 (1996)
33. Krasanakis, E., Spyromitros-Xioufis, E., Papadopoulos, S., Kompatsiaris, Y.: Adaptive sensitive reweighting to mitigate bias in fairness-aware classification. In: Proceedings of the 28th International Conference on World Wide Web (WWW 2018), pp. 853–862 (2018)
34. Lahoti, P., et al.: Fairness without demographics through adversarially reweighted learning. In: Proceedings of the 33rd Neural Information Processing Systems Conference (NIPS 2020), pp. 728–740. MIT Press (2020)
35. Le Quy, T., Roy, A., Iosifidis, V., Zhang, W., Ntoutsi, E.: A survey on datasets for fairness-aware machine learning. Wiley Interdisc. Rev. Data Mining Knowl. Discov. **12**(3), 1–59 (2022)
36. Luong, B.T., Ruggieri, S., Turini, F.: K-NN as an implementation of situation testing for discrimination discovery and prevention. In: Proceedings of the 17th ACM SIGKDD International Conference on Knowledge Discovery and Data Mining (KDD 2011), pp. 502–510 (2011)
37. Malouf, R.: A comparison of algorithms for maximum entropy parameter estimation. In: Proceedings of the 6th International Conference on Natural Language Learning (CoNLL 2002), pp. 49–55 (2002)
38. Mardia, K.V., Kent, J.T., Bibby, J.M.: Multivariate Analysis. Academic Press, New York (1979)
39. Martinez, N., Bertran, M., Sapiro, G.: Minimax pareto fairness: a multi objective perspective. In: Proceedings of the 37th International Conference on Machine Learning (ICML 2020), pp. 6755–6764. PMLR (2020)
40. Mehrabi, N., Morstatter, F., Saxena, N., Lerman, K., Galstyan, A.: A survey on bias and fairness in machine learning. ACM Comput. Surv. **54**(6), 1–35 (2021)
41. Mitchell, S., Potash, E., Barocas, S., D'Amour, A., Lum, K.: Algorithmic fairness: choices, assumptions, and definitions. Annu. Rev. Stat. Appl. **8**, 141–163 (2021)
42. Moro, S., Cortez, P., Rita, P.: A data-driven approach to predict the success of bank telemarketing. Decis. Support Syst. **62**, 22–31 (2014)
43. Murphy, K.: Probabilistic Machine Learning: Advanced Topics. MIT Press, Cambridge (2023)
44. Pedregosa, F., et al.: Scikit-learn: machine learning in Python. J. Mach. Learn. Res. **12**, 2825–2830 (2011)
45. Pessach, D., Shmueli, E.: A review on fairness in machine learning. ACM Comput. Surv. **55**(3), 1–44 (2022)
46. Pitoura, E., Stefanidis, K., Koutrika, G.: Fairness in rankings and recommendations: an overview. Very Large DataBases J. 1–28 (2022)

47. ProPublica: Compas recidivism risk score data and analysis (2023). https://www.propublica.org/datastore/dataset/compas-recidivism-risk-score-data-and-analysis
48. Romei, A., Ruggieri, S.: A multidisciplinary survey on discrimination analysis. Knowl. Eng. Rev. **29**(5), 582–638 (2014)
49. Verma, S., Rubin, J.: Fairness definitions explained. In: Proceedings of the 1st International Workshop on Software Fairness (FairWare 2018), pp. 1–7 (2018)
50. Wan, M., Zha, D., Liu, N., Zou, N.: In-processing modeling techniques for machine learning fairness: a survey. ACM Trans. Knowl. Discov. Data **17**(3), 1–27 (2023)
51. Wightman, L.F.: LSAC national longitudinal bar passage study. LSAC Research Report Series, pp. 1–112 (1998)
52. Yadav, S., Shukla, S.: Analysis of k-fold cross-validation over hold-out validation on colossal datasets for quality classification. In: Proceedings of the IEEE 6th International Conference on Advanced Computing (IACC 2016), pp. 78–83. IEEE (2016)
53. Zafar, M.B., Valera, I., Rogriguez, M.G., Gummadi, K.: Fairness constraints: mechanisms for fair classification. In: Proceedings of the 20th International Conference on Artificial Intelligence and Statistics (AISTATS 2017), pp. 962–970 (2017)
54. Zhang, B.H., Lemoine, B., Mitchell, M.: Mitigating unwanted biases with adversarial learning. In: Proceedings of the 1st AAAI/ACM Conference on AI, Ethics, and Society (AIES 2018), pp. 335–340 (2018)
55. Zhu, S., Ji, X., Xu, W., Gong, Y.: Multi-labelled classification using maximum entropy method. In: Proceedings of the 28th International ACM SIGIR Conference on Research and Development in Information Retrieval (SIGIR 2005), pp. 274–281 (2005)

Identifying Good Donor Datasets for Transfer Learning Scenarios in Motor Imagery BCI

Pierre Guetschel(✉) and Michael Tangermann

Donders Institute for Brain, Cognition and Behaviour, Radboud University, Nijmegen, Netherlands
{pierre.guetschel,michael.tangermann}@donders.ru.nl

Abstract. We present a simple deep learning-based framework commonly used in computer vision and demonstrate its effectiveness for cross-dataset transfer learning in mental imagery decoding tasks that are common in the field of Brain-Computer Interfaces (BCI). We use this framework to characterize the compatibility for transfer learning between twelve motor-imagery datasets.

Challenges. Deep learning models typically require long training times and are data-hungry, which impedes their use for BCI systems that have to minimize the recording time for (training) examples and are subject to constraints induced by experiments involving human subjects. A solution to both issues is transfer learning, but it comes with its own challenge, i.e., substantial data distribution shifts between datasets, subjects and even between subsequent sessions of the same subject.

Approach. For every pair of pre-training (donor) and test (receiver) datasets, we first train a model on the donor dataset before training merely an additional new linear classification layer based on a few receiver trials. Performance of this transfer approach is then tested on other trials of the receiver dataset. We compile these results in a table characterizing the compatibility between the different datasets.

Significance. Our characterisation of compatibility between datasets can be used as a reference for future researchers to make informed donor choices. To strengthen this claim, we present an applied example of such usage. Finally, we lower the threshold to use transfer learning between motor imagery datasets: the overall framework is extremely simple and nevertheless obtains decent classification scores.

Keywords: EEG · BCI · Motor Imagery · Deep Learning · Transfer Learning · Cross-Dataset

F. A. Oliehoek et al. (Eds.): BNAIC/Benelearn 2023, CCIS 2187, pp. 209–235, 2025.
https://doi.org/10.1007/978-3-031-74650-5_12

1 Introduction

Electroencephalography (EEG) offers a non-invasive modality for capturing the electrical activity of the brain. Utilizing machine learning techniques, specific brain activities can be decoded in single trial. Event-related potentials (ERPs), for instance, signify the brain's response to the occurrence of an awaited and attended event [1] compared to ignored events. ERP's differ between attended and ignored stimulus events, and can be evoked by visual [1], auditory [2] and haptic [3] stimuli. Event-related (de-)synchronization describes a decrease (ERD) or increase (ERS) of oscillatory sources, which can be observed over sensorimotor cortices and as a result of either executing, attempting or merely imagining a task such as moving a limb, mental calculation or mental navigation. In Brain-Computer Interface (BCI) systems [4], the decoded brain activity has been explored for different purposes, among them the monitoring of brain states [5], to guide behavioural experiments [6], to shape human-robot interaction [7], to support rehabilitation after stroke [8,9] or when mapped to computer commands, to drive software [10] or hardware applications [11] without requiring the BCI user to show overt behaviour. Among these, the use of direct control commands for communication is the dominating application type. In the context of this work, we will focus on BCI protocols based on ERD/ERS effects, which are observed as a result of motor imagery tasks and have been used for multiple application types.

In a typical setting, each BCI session starts with an initial phase where the user is prompted to produce predefined outputs. This is typically called the *calibration phase* and may require up to an hour for motor imagery tasks. The acquired labelled data enables the supervised training of a decoding model. Only afterwards, the user can interact freely with the BCI application. This productive phase is typically called the *online phase*. The calibration phase can be a tedious and less motivating period for a BCI user, even though the following online application phase is the interesting part that should start as quickly as possible.

Specifically for BCIs which make use of motor imagery tasks, the tedious calibration process prompts the consideration of Transfer Learning (TL) methods. They leverage information, e.g., in the form of data or even pre-calibrated models from various sources, such as earlier sessions of the same user, from other users, or datasets obtained under slightly different experimental conditions, to reduce the need for calibration data samples collected during the ongoing session. In the most rudimentary approach to TL, a model is trained on a dataset we will call *donor*, and tested on another one we will call *receiver*. The necessity for TL becomes even more pronounced in the context of deep learning, given its inherent requirements for large training datasets and their substantial training time which would further delay the online phase [12]. However, TL presents its own challenges, with the biggest being that not every historic motor imagery dataset is suitable as a data donor to pre-train a model for a novel user or session. The reason for the incompatibility of some donor/receiver pairs is a difference in the feature distributions across datasets, subjects, or even sessions. They can be attributed to factors like different brain morphology, but also variations of the experimental protocol, of users' strategies, the concrete EEG recording system used, and different levels of fatigue or medication, among others [13]. While TL has been widely studied in BCI, the focus has been mostly on cross-session transfer [14], cross-subject transfer [15,16], or both [17]. However, cross-dataset transfer learning has been a relatively underexplored domain. The recent BEETL competition [18] has begun to fill this void by drawing attention to the challenges and opportunities cross-dataset transfer represents for BCI. Notably, the top three winning methods in this competition were based on deep learning models. More recently, Xie and colleagues proposed to apply techniques developed for cross-subject transfer to a cross-dataset transfer scenario [19]. Furthermore, it was recently suggested to use cross-dataset transfer to evaluate the structure of cognitive tasks [20].

Upon starting a new study, session or recording, a researcher aiming to leverage TL often poses the question: *"Which dataset could be a suitable donor?"*. To find an answer efficiently, a quick test for compatibility between a few examples from a novel distribution and the much larger collection of pre-existing datasets is required. In this study, we introduce a framework for such quick tests. It follows similar principles as the ImageNet linear evaluation protocol [21], a wildly-adopted approach in the field of computer vision. This framework is simple and requires only the training of a linear classifier on the receiving dataset, which makes it highly computationally efficient. Its primary objective is not to achieve state-of-the-art performance, but rather to allow the evaluation of many combinations of donors and receivers. We use twelve motor imagery datasets of the MOABB collection [22], both as receivers for evaluation purposes and as potential donors for future studies. We investigate the one-to-one transfer between these datasets. To this end, we use our framework to create compatibility tables for each dataset and provide them open access along with the corresponding pre-trained models. These resources are designed to aid future researchers in identifying a suitable donor for their application. For an example application, we demonstrate how the resources can be used.

The problem will be broken down into three sub-questions:

1. Can we design a fast and flexible framework which allows us to characterize datasets concerning their transferability?
2. Which MOABB datasets are generally good donors?
3. Which MOABB datasets are good receivers, which are challenging ones?

In Sect. 2, the article begins by detailing the neural network architecture and datasets utilized in the study. Subsequently, Sect. 3 thoroughly describes the transfer learning framework employed. Section 4 presents the experimental results. Additionally, Sect. 5 provides the example application illustrating how the obtained results can be applied to select suitable donor datasets. Finally, Sect. 6 critically discussed the results and concludes the article. Comprehensive results and additional information are available in Appendix A. Furthermore, supplementary materials, including source code, and pre-trained models, are available online[1,2].

2 Materials

2.1 Neural Network Architecture: EEGNet

We used EEGNet [23] as neural network architecture to conduct our experiments. It consists of an initial temporal convolutional layer that captures temporal correlations in EEG signals. This is followed by a depthwise spatial convolution layer that accounts for spatial correlations across electrodes. The network concludes with a separable convolution for dimensionality reduction before reaching the linear classification layer.

Our choice of EEGNet as the neural network architecture is motivated by three primary factors. First, its versatility is demonstrated through proficient performance across multiple BCI paradigms [23]. Second, its simplicity and computational efficiency make it particularly lightweight. Third, EEGNet has earned widespread community acceptance for EEG decoding, as evidenced by several studies [14,24–28].

2.2 Data: Motor Imagery

We conducted our experiments on EEG-based motor imagery (MI) datasets. They are constituted of EEG recordings capturing subjects as they either imagine or execute specific motor tasks. These motor tasks can range from imagined actions such as squeezing a fist to wiggling toes. In each dataset, multiple motor imagery tasks are represented and the classification problem is to determine which task was imagined/executed in each example, which typically consists of a few seconds of EEG recordings called a trial.

Description of Datasets. In this study, we included all the Motor Imagery datasets available with the MOABB library [22]. However, three datasets were excluded due to technical limitations such as missing electrode names and technical obstacles which prevented the downloading of the data. The complete list of datasets that were included along with their respective descriptions can be found in Table 1. In the Appendix A.1, we provide links to further details, separately per dataset. The column "No. examples" designates for each dataset the number of examples/trials contained for each combination of subject, session and class. The imagined tasks which form the class label information in each dataset are described using the following abbreviations:

[1] Source code: https://gitlab.com/PierreGtch/motor_embedding_benchmark.

[2] Pre-trained models, and results: https://huggingface.co/PierreGtch/EEGNetv4.

Table 1. Summary of Datasets Evaluated in the Study.

Dataset	Classes	No. classes	No. subjects	No. sessions	No. examples
AlexMI [29]	*f, r, rh.*	3	8	1	20
BNCI2014001 [30]	*f, lh, rh, t.*	4	9	2	72
BNCI2014004 [31]	*lh, rh.*	2	9	5	72
BNCI2015001 [32]	*f, rh.*	2	13	3 (subj. 8-11),2 (others)	100
BNCI2015004 [33]	*f, n, rh, s, wa.*	5	9	2	39
Cho2017 [34]	*lh, rh.*	2	53	1	101
Lee2019_MI [31]	*lh, rh.*	2	55	2	200
Ofner2017 [35]	*r, ree, ref, rhc,* rho, rp, rs.	7	15	1	60
PhysionetMI [36]	*bh, f, lh, r, rh.*	5	109	1	23
Schirrmeister2017 [37]	*f, lh, r, rh.*	4	14	1	241
Weibo2014 [38]	*bh, f, lh, lhrf,* r, rh, rhlf.	7	10	1	79
Zhou2016 [39]	*f, lh, rh.*	3	4	3	50

- *bh*: both hands
- *f*: both feet
- *lh*: left hand
- *lhrf*: left hand right foot
- *n*: navigation
- *r*: rest
- *ree*: right elbow extension
- *ref*: right elbow flexion
- *rh*: right hand
- *rhc*: right hand close
- *rhlf*: right hand left foot
- *rho*: right hand open
- *rp*: right hand pronation
- *rs*: right hand supination
- *s*: subtraction
- *t*: tongue
- *wa*: word association

It is noteworthy that the datasets included in this study employ diverse imagination strategies. For example, the Lee2019 dataset required subjects to imagine grasping with the appropriate hand. In contrast, the Cho2017 dataset instructed subjects to imagine moving their fingers from the index to the little finger. The Schirrmeister2017 dataset contains executed instead of imagined movements, where subjects engaged in sequential finger-tapping. Of particular note is the Ofner2017 dataset, which includes *single* instances of both executed and imagined movements, diverging from other datasets that sustain or repeat the imagination tasks over several seconds. Some authors did not report the explicit instructions they gave on the imagination strategies and might have left it to the discretion of the subjects.

Pre-processing. The pre-processing protocol we used for all the datasets involved setting the trial windows to 0 to 3 s post-cue. We strongly limited the EEG channels used to channels C3, C4, and Cz, which are placed over the sensorimotor cortices. The data was resampled at a frequency of 128 Hz, aligning with EEGNet's default setting. A bandpass filter with the range 0.5 to 40 Hz was applied to the data.

3 Methods

In the current study, we employ the transfer learning framework previously proposed in [40]. However, a salient distinction is that, unlike the prior study which focused solely on cross-subject transfer, the present study extends this to cross-dataset transfer. A schematic representation of this methodology is encapsulated in Fig. 1. This transfer framework has two phases: a pre-training phase using the donor dataset and a fine-tuning phase using the receiver dataset.

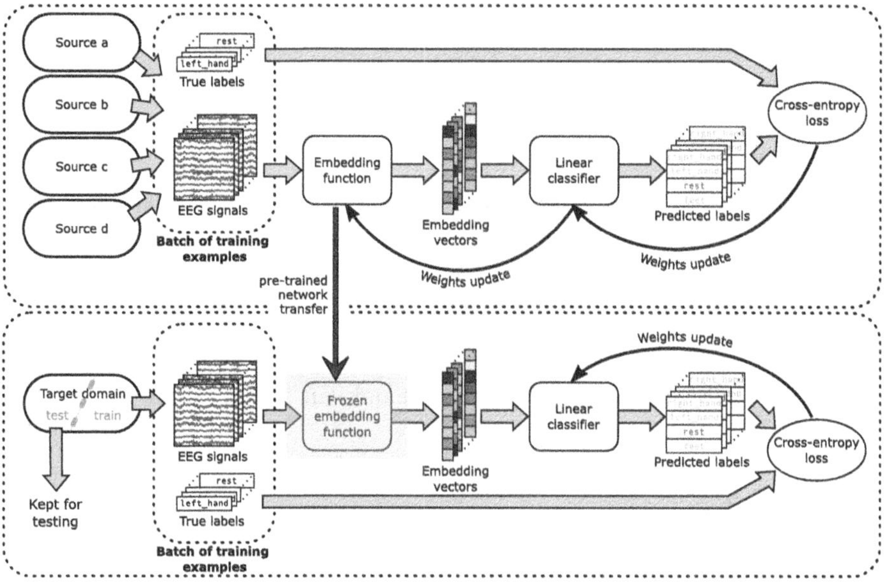

Fig. 1. Schematic representation of the transfer learning framework introduced in [40] and here extended to cross-dataset transfer. The upper block describes the pre-training phase. The lower block describes the fine-tuning phase.

Pre-training Phase. During the pre-training phase, a neural network architecture is trained from scratch on a set of source datasets, or donors. The aim is to categorize the motor task being imagined in each example/trial. To maintain a simple framework, the hyperparameters chosen are consistent with those recommended by the authors of EEGNet for cross-subject training [23]. Upon completion of this phase, the network's classification head is discarded, and the rest of the architecture is frozen, i.e., the remaining parameters will stay unchanged in the following phase.

Fine-Tuning Phase. In the subsequent fine-tuning phase, the pre-trained network is utilized as a feature extractor, wherein its parameters are frozen. A following linear classification layer is then trained from scratch to categorize the embeddings produced by the feature extractor. This classification layer is trained and tested using examples from the same session, i.e. the receiver dataset, adopting a within-session cross-validation (CV) approach through multiple random shuffles of the examples. Importantly, during the fine-tuning phase, only the linear classification layer is subject to training, while the rest of the architecture remains static. This approach offers the distinct advantage of an exceptionally computationally efficient fine-tuning phase, while preserving the ability to adapt to receiver datasets with varying distributions [41]. The examples used to train the linear classification layer will be called *calibration examples*. The dataset employed for this fine-tuning is interchangeably termed as the *receiver dataset*, *test dataset* or *calibration dataset*, given that both fine-tuning and testing are executed within the same session of a single dataset, even though using separate examples.

Leveraging the Compatibility Tables and Pre-trained Models. The end-products of this study are transfer learning compatibility tables between twelve motor imagery datasets contained in MOABB, accompanied by the corresponding pre-trained models (refer to Subsect. 4.2). These resources are designed to assist future researchers in identifying suitable donors for transfer learning applications for, e.g., the following two use cases:

The first use case is the benchmarking of a novel decoding algorithm. In this scenario, it may be valuable to know about the compatibility of datasets such that specifically simple or difficult combinations can be tested. To determine the optimal donor dataset for a specific receiver among the twelve MOABB datasets evaluated in this study, the procedure is straightforward. By consulting the compatibility tables provided in Subsect. A.2 of the appendix, one can effortlessly identify the donor that achieves the highest or lowest score for every receiver. A practical demonstration of this use-case is provided in Sect. 5.

The second use case is at the time point of starting a novel study. Here the goal may be to select a good donor for the novel data collected in the study. Please note, that only a small number of trials of the novel dataset may be accessible at this time point. The process would involve the following steps:

1. Download the 12 pre-trained models generated by our study[3].
2. For each pre-trained donor model, compute the embedding vectors of the few examples contained in the new dataset.
3. For every donor model, evaluate the performance of the embedding vectors by cross-validation of a linear classifier.
4. Select the donor(s) that obtain the best results on the new dataset.

[3] Pre-trained models: https://huggingface.co/PierreGtch/EEGNetv4.

4 Results

4.1 Experimental Design

Pre-training Phase. In this phase, a distinct EEGNet architecture was trained for each dataset, utilizing the entire dataset and all available classes therein. Consequently, a total of 12 pre-trained neural network architectures were generated.

Fine-Tuning Phase. During fine-tuning, we systematically examined varying numbers of calibration examples-specifically 1, 2, 4, 8, 16, 32 (where applicable), and 64 (where applicable) per class-across each session for every subject in the test datasets. Three distinct analyses were conducted: left hand vs. right hand (*lh-rh*), right hand vs. feet (*rh-f*), and an all-classes classification. The classes specified for each analysis, are the only ones from the receiver used during the fine-tuning phase. The ROC-AUC (area under the receiver operating characteristic curve [42]) metric was adopted for *lh-rh* and *rh-f* classification scores, while accuracy metrics were used for the all-classes scenario. The first two binary classification analyses allow for a fair comparison between datasets, whereas the classification with all classes is a fallback case in which the chance level varies with the number of classes. We specifically focussed our analysis on the *lh-rh* and *rh-f* class pairs, as they are the most ubiquitously represented across the various datasets. The number of folds for within-session CV is set to 16. While this may appear excessive, it is crucial to mitigate the significant impact that the selection of just one or two calibration examples can have on the classification performance metrics.

4.2 Interpretation of Results

Data Volume and Analysis. The three analyses culminated in an extensive set of 871,488 scores, derived from the different CV folds, number of calibration examples, sessions, subjects, test datasets, and pre-trained models.

Tabulated Scores. For ease of interpretation, scores were averaged across CV folds, sessions, and subjects. This resulted in three **compatibility tables** that are provided in the Appendix A.2, corresponding to each of the three analytical scenarios (right hand vs feet, right hand vs left hand and all classes together). Each table contains an average score for every unique combination of pre-training dataset, test dataset, and number of calibration examples.

Graphical Representations. Line plots showing test scores with respect to the number of calibration examples per class were generated from tabulated results, averaged either across test datasets in Fig. 2 or pre-training datasets in Fig. 3. Notably, in the averaged line plots, the datasets, even with disparate subject counts, hold equal weight.

Specific Observations and Cautions. The discrete height levels of the blue line on the right-hand y-axis of Fig. 2 denote the number of test datasets included in each average. Its fluctuation is attributed to the variable number of examples across test datasets which does not allow to include all the datasets when using 32 or 64 calibration examples. Consequently, the average curves' progressions should be interpreted only when the dataset count remains constant. When the number of test datasets included in the average decreases, an increase or decrease in score can respectively be explained by the disappearance of a "difficult" or an "easy" dataset.

In contrast, when averaging across pre-training datasets, i.e. Figure 3, the termination of each test dataset line is evident, and in some instances, extrapolation can provide insights into future trends.

It should be noted that scores obtained from the all-classes analyses require cautious interpretation due to varying class numbers across test datasets, which consequently alter the chance levels of accuracy scores.

4.3 Datasets as Donors

Referring to Fig. 2, which illustrates averages across test datasets, the model pre-trained on Ofner2017 consistently performed at chance level. This outcome aligns with the dataset's distinct characteristics, as elaborated in Sect. 2.2. Across the three classification scenarios, models pre-trained on the donor datasets AlexMI, BNCI2015004, or on Cho2017 underperformed. For the *rh-f* classification task, no single model emerged as a clear frontrunner. However, models pre-trained on the donor datasets PhysionetMI, Schirrmeister2017, BNCI2014001, Zhou2016, Lee2019, or BNCI2015001 constituted the leading group. In the *lh-rh* classification task, the model pre-trained on Lee2019 demonstrated a distinct advantage.

Scores incorporating all classes from the test datasets are delicate to interpret and are presented primarily for informational purposes.

4.4 Datasets as Receivers

Turning our attention to Fig. 3, which displays averages across pre-training datasets, we observe the following:

f-rh Analysis. Schirrmeister2017 emerges as the most straightforward dataset to classify, followed by Zhou2016 and then BNCI2014001. On the contrary, BNCI2015004 and PhysionetMI proved to be the most challenging, with performance nearing chance levels for BNCI2015004.

rh-lh Analysis. Zhou2016 demonstrated greater ease of classification relative to other datasets, succeeded by BNCI2014004 and then BNCI2014001. The most challenging datasets for this task are Weibo2014, followed by Lee2019, Cho2017, and Schirrmeister2017.

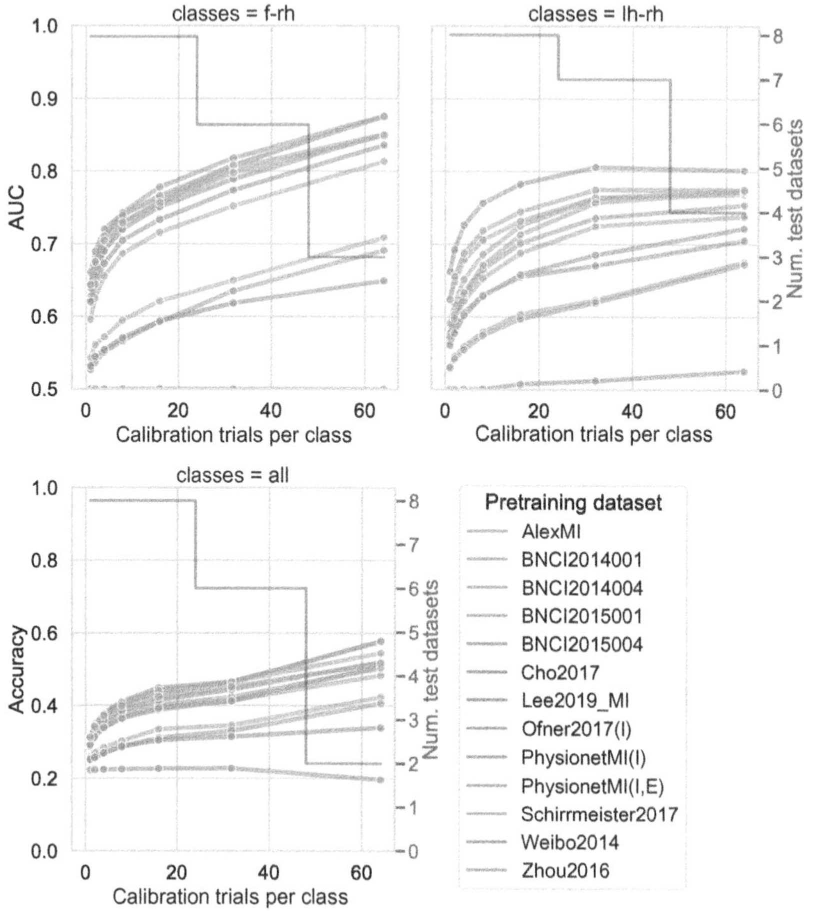

Fig. 2. Characterization of pre-training (donor) datasets. The subplots indicate, which combination of classes was considered. Per subplot, the left y-axis provides scores averaged across test (receiver) datasets, while the x-axis denotes the number of calibration trials per class of the receiver dataset, which were used for the fine-tuning. Please note that 32 and 64 trials per class were available only for a subset of the receiving datasets, as indicated by the blue y-axis on the right-hand side.

All-Classes Analysis. In this context, Zhou2016 and Schirrmeister2017 were the easiest datasets to classify. Notably, none of the pre-trained models supplied features conducive to classifying Ofner2017 and BNCI2015004, with performance for both hovering at chance level.

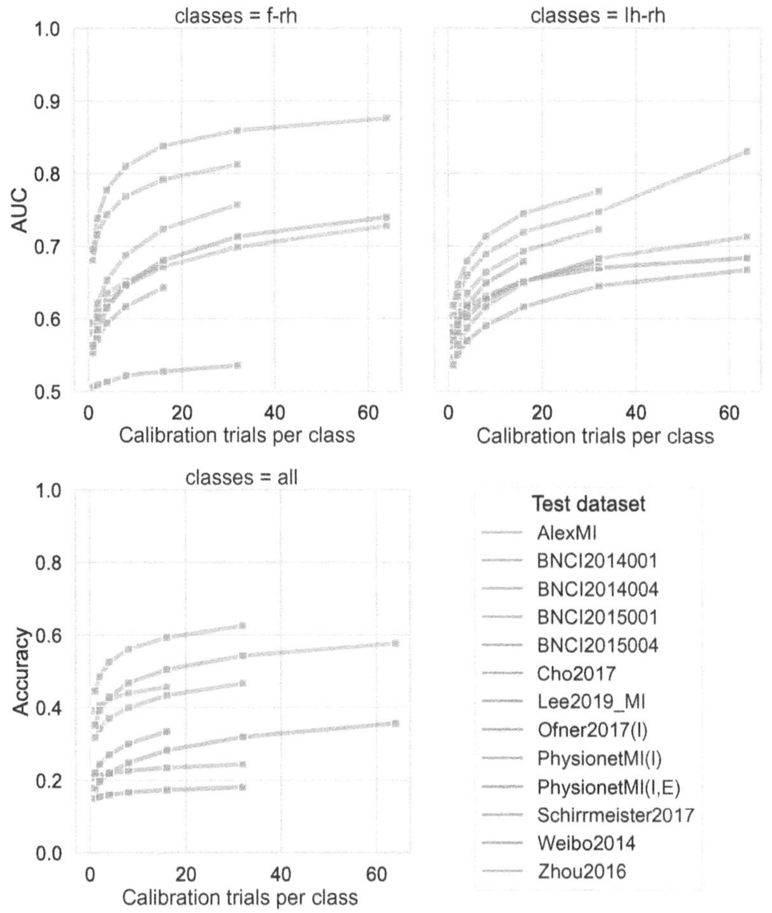

Fig. 3. Characterization of the test (receiver) datasets. The subplots indicate, which combination of classes was considered. Per subplot, the left y-axis provides scores averaged across pre-training (donor) datasets, while the x-axis denotes the number of calibration trials per class of the receiver dataset, which were used for the fine-tuning. Please note, that 32 and 64 trials per class were available only for a subset of the receiving datasets, as indicated by the length of the respective curves.

5 Example Application: Making an Informed Donor Choice

In this section, we exemplify how our results provided in the compatibility tables of Appendix A.2 can be used to make an educated choice of a donor dataset in a transfer learning scenario for a given receiving dataset.

For this purpose, we chose the approach by Xie and colleagues [19] who investigated one-to-one transfer learning between motor imagery datasets. This choice was primarily driven by the fact that it is one of the only studies that explored transfer between motor imagery datasets at the moment. Their transfer learning procedure consists of a pre-training of their network based on a donor dataset before fine-tuning it on a different receiver dataset. They compare four fine-tuning schemes, ranging from only fine-tuning the final classification layer to fine-tuning the entire neural network. Additionally, they investigated how their models would perform when fine-tuned on a small fraction of the receiver data only. They utilized three public datasets, all available in MOABB, namely BNCI2014001, BNCI2014004, and Schirrmeister2017 (referred to as BCIIV 2a, BCIIV 2b, and HGD in their article, respectively), along with one unpublished private dataset.

To investigate the benefit of our proposed educated choice of the donor, we reproduced one of their experiments, focusing on the fourth fine-tuning scheme of Xie and colleagues, i.e., pre-training and fine-tuning the entire neural network, and with the EEGNet architecture. In that scenario, the fine-tuning uses the whole data of one subject. Additional details on the experiment we reproduced can be found in Appendix A.3.

To assess, if an informed donor selection following our framework is beneficial over the original ones used by Xie and colleagues, we use a one-sided Wilcoxon signed-rank test [43] with a Benjamini-Hochberg correction for multiple testing [44].

Using our framework, we identify that PhysionetMI emerges as the optimal donor for both, the Schirrmeister2017 and BNCI2014001 receiver datasets when considering all classes. Conversely, Lee2019 emerges as the most suitable donor for the receiver BNCI2014004.

The average performances of different donor datasets are presented in Fig. 4. This figure also presents, in red, the p-values of the statistical tests (one-sided Wilcoxon signed rank test with Benjamini-Hochberg correction). Except for the receiving dataset BNCI2014_001, the different donors resulted in similar average accuracies. However, the proposed informed choices of donors (PhysionetMI for Schirrmeister2017 and BNCI2014_001, Lee2019 for BNCI2014_004) showed significantly improved average performances for each of the three receiving datasets compared to using the donors proposed by Xie and colleagues.

The benefit of an informed choice for donor datasets is visualized also in Fig. 5. For each receiver dataset, it compares the number of cross-validation folds, for which each of the competing donor datasets reaches the best (first rank), second best (second rank), or lowest (third rank) accuracy values. This rank analysis illustrates the statistical results obtained (see Fig. 4). As an example, the donor dataset Lee2019_MI is by far the best choice for the receiver BNCI2014001, as it obtains the first rank in 64% of the cross-validation folds. The framework's recommendations for the receivers Schirrmeister2017 and BNCI2014_004 are also reproduced by the rank analysis in Fig. 5, however, the donors are more equally distributed on the first rank, i.e., PhysionetMI reaching 41% first ranks for Schirrmeister2017, and Lee2019_MI reaching 46% for BNCI2014_004.

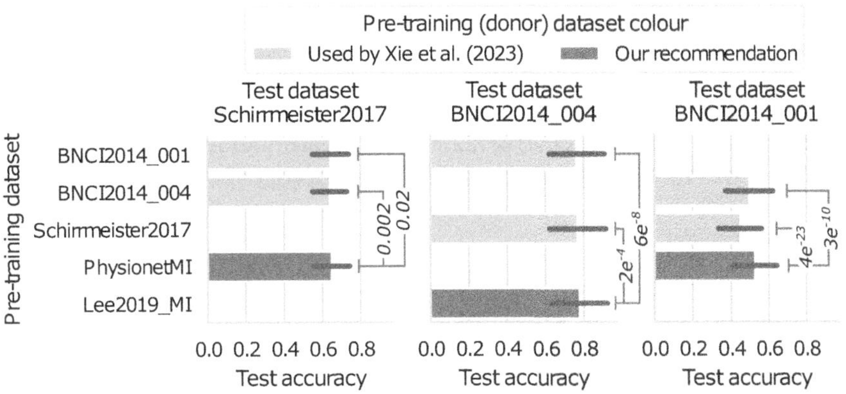

Fig. 4. Bar plots comparing the scores obtained when reproducing the results of Xie and colleagues [19] and when using our recommended pre-training dataset. The title of each sub-figure indicates which test dataset the results correspond to. The thick colored bars indicate the average accuracy across the runs of a given donor - receiver pair. Each run corresponds to one fold within the data of one subject of the test dataset. The thin black horizontal bars indicate their standard deviations. The p-values of the different tests are indicated on the right side of each subplot in red.

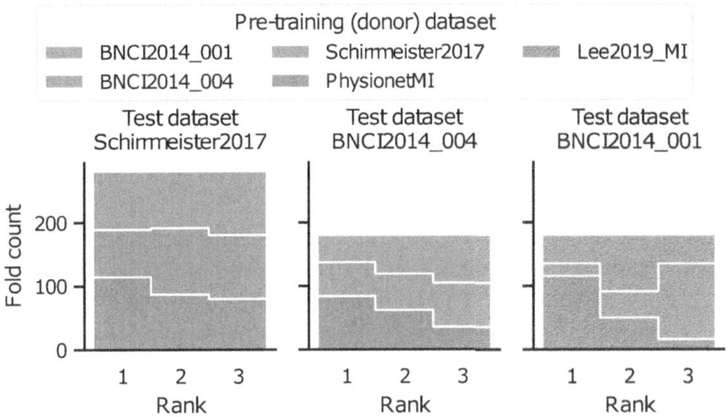

Fig. 5. Evaluation of five donor datasets on three receiver datasets. Left: Receiver Schirrmeister evaluated with 280 cross-validation folds, middle: BNCI2014_004 evaluated with 180 folds, right: BNCI2014_001 with 180 folds. Running 20 folds per subject leads to different fold counts over the three receiver datasets. For each cross-validation fold, the three donor datasets were ranked according to their accuracy scores, with 1 indicating the best donor, and 3 the worst. The height of a coloured block denotes, how often a specific donor dataset has obtained either the first, second or third rank.

6 Discussion

The field of BCI has a tradition of organizing data analysis competitions [30,45–47], and with the availability of the data collections and default analysis pipelines like those provided by MOABB [22,48] the benchmarking of novel decoding approaches was facilitated substantially. Our work contributes to these activities by providing, for the first time, a comprising characterization of datasets in the context of transfer learning.

6.1 Characteristics of Datasets

The simple transfer learning scheme consisting of one donor and one receiver dataset was sufficient to reveal the transfer characteristics of those 12 MOABB datasets which are sufficiently well-documented for this purpose and comprise data from imagery protocols. The resulting compatibility tables in the Subsect. A.2 in the appendix thus are a main contribution of our work. The following datasets showed specifically interesting characteristics:

The Lee2019 dataset emerges as a highly favourable option for pre-training models for a simple *lh-rh* paradigm. Remarkably, even our rudimentary model attains competent classification scores across diverse datasets with very few calibration examples. This is likely attributable to its substantial number of subjects and examples.

PhysionetMI can serve as an interesting benchmark dataset. Its low ranking as a receiver when averaged across pre-training datasets implies inherent challenges. Moreover, its large number of subjects (109) implies also a large diversity. Furthermore, its positive performance as a donor for pre-training suggests that the imagery tasks performed in it are not overly divergent from those in other datasets.

For the same reasons, also Cho2017 and Lee2019 in the receiver role can both serve as challenging benchmarks, but they are limited to the *lh-rh* classes. Conversely, Zhou2016 and BNCI2014001 appear to be relatively uncomplicated benchmarks, consistently ranking among the top-performing receivers.

The Schirrmeister2017 dataset distinguishes itself as both a good donor and receiver. Its performance as a receiver can likely be attributed to the fact that it contains executed motor tasks, which for EEG and ECoG recordings have been reported to express event-related (de-)synchronization features stronger compared to using corresponding imagery tasks but also that it can be trained up to match the level obtained under motor execution [49,50]. A potentially higher information content was also reported for motor execution compared to imagery fNIRS data, with motor execution resulting in higher activation levels, a faster response, and a different spatial distribution [51,52]. The strong performance of the Schirrmeister2017 dataset as a donor is probably due to the higher number of examples available per subject, which sets it apart from other datasets in the study.

The consistent chance-level performance observed with the Ofner2017 dataset, both as a donor and receiver, aligns with expectations given its marked divergence from the dataset pool, as outlined in Sect. 2.2. The observed class-informative motor-related features reported by its authors are dominated by motor-related potentials, which are more closely resemble event-related potentials than the oscillatory desynchronization or synchronization features typically observed for (motor) imagery tasks, and which may need a different decoding approach.

6.2 Making Informed Choices for Donor Datasets

Building upon the work by Xie and colleagues [19] we have exemplified how the compatibility tables (see Appendix A.2) provided by our framework can be used to select a suitable donor dataset for a specific receiver dataset. Its utilization proved to be straightforward: first, we identified the most compatible donors for the receiver datasets used by Xie and colleagues. Subsequently, we replaced their donors with our suggested ones, which was sufficient to yield small, but significant score improvements.

As described in Sect. 3, this approach can also be applied to new receiver datasets, absent from the compatibility table, by using the pre-trained models we published. Given the lightweight nature of each of the pre-trained models (1538 parameters, resulting in a size of approximately 15 kB only) and their fast inference times (in the range of milliseconds per forward pass once the data is loaded to the memory), along with negligible computational overhead for training the linear model, this procedure is entirely feasible for any new motor imagery dataset.

However, it is important to acknowledge the challenge of repeatability. Despite our best efforts to accurately replicate the experiments of Xie and colleagues, we were not able to reproduce the authors' reported results. The absence of published source code and the omission of certain details in the publication hindered our replication efforts. Consequently, we were compelled to make assumptions during our reproduction attempts. Detailed information regarding our attempt to reproduce their results, as well as our code, is available in Appendix A.3.

6.3 Contributions Made by the Proposed Transfer Learning Framework

The proposed transfer learning scheme has been motivated by similar schemes that already are widely utilized in the computer vision domain [21]. The framework we propose is characterized by its simplicity, particularly in its use of a minimal fine-tuning strategy and by the absence of assumptions about the receiver when pre-training on the donor dataset. Indeed, the only fine-tuning conducted is training a new classification layer, which becomes necessary when transferring between datasets with differing classes; however, the rest of the architecture remains frozen.

Because of its simplicity, we would not expect this framework to be competitive with state-of-the-art transfer learning strategies in most situations, except for instances where data scarcity is exceptionally severe. Nonetheless, its simplicity renders it highly computationally efficient. Indeed, the computationally heavy pre-training phase is required only once per donor, so the pre-trained models can subsequently be re-used on all receivers. Furthermore, during fine-tuning, no gradient descent is needed to optimize a linear classification layer.

The efficiency of our framework made it possible to perform an expansive analysis yielding 871,488 individual scores. Moreover, our framework holds particular relevance for evaluating transferability between domains. Assuming the pre-training phase was conducted appropriately, the features of the last hidden layer should optimally represent the examples of the donor dataset for the donor's classification task. Because in our framework all the layers up to the classification layer remain frozen during fine-tuning, the computation of features remains unchanged. Consequently, the score of the new classification layer on the receiver data provides insight into the compatibility of this feature computation method with the receiver's data distribution and classification task.

Nonetheless, despite its simplicity, our framework accomplishes motor-imagery cross-dataset transfer learning, which is known as a difficult problem. Our results, which are proximal to state-of-the-art algorithms[4] and despite using fewer calibration examples from the receiver, attest to this. Naturally, there is a maximal dissimilarity between datasets beyond which a transfer becomes impossible. With our approach, we found that limit with the Ofner2017 dataset.

The swiftness of our fine-tuning strategy could make it suitable for online scenarios, without necessitating prolonged waiting periods for subject-specific model training as only a linear classification layer needs to be trained, which can be done in a few seconds on any recent CPU.

The modular nature of the two-phased framework allows for independent enhancements, facilitating the seamless incorporation of emerging deep learning techniques in both the embedding and fine-tuning stages. Because of the current simplicity of all its steps, we can expect large performance enhancement from improvements at any level. A first straightforward improvement would be to include additional EEG channels.

Finally, our framework demonstrates a pathway for utilizing deep learning models for BCI decoding. This approach effectively mitigates two challenges inherent to deep learning techniques: the extensive requirement for data and lengthy training durations.

6.4 Design Decisions and Limitations

In our framework, we have opted for a one-to-one transfer scenario between datasets, as this scenario allowed us to conduct a clear donor-receiver analysis. However, pre-training a model on multiple datasets concurrently may yield unexpected, and potentially improved results, e.g., two donor datasets that each

[4] For a comprehensive understanding of the state-of-the-art, the reader is advised to consult the MOABB benchmark [48], in conjunction with its forthcoming 2024 update.

have shown suboptimal results in a one-to-one transfer, might complement each other when used in combination.

By using a relatively shallow architecture and a straightforward training procedure that did not include additional hyperparameter tuning, we avoided overfitting. However, large datasets might benefit from more complex architectures and explicit tuning of hyperparameters. While we have observed the largest datasets of our study (PhysionetMI, Schirrmeister2017, and Lee2019) to be generally preferred donors, our simple approach may still have underestimated their performances.

Lastly, as most datasets use different channel sets, which is a significant challenge for cross-dataset transfer in BCI, we opted for restricting our analysis to the three most common channels (C3, C4, and Cz) shared across all datasets. These channels can be expected to carry information about typical motor (imagery) tasks. This limitation to such a sparse, shared channel subset might in the future be tackled by recently proposed channel set invariant architectures [53]. Conducting a similar analysis with such an architecture could yield valuable insights.

6.5 Conclusion

Our contributions can be summarized as follows: we have introduced a straightforward and computationally efficient transfer learning framework that still demonstrates robust performance. Leveraging this framework, we have systematically characterised the compatibility for transfer learning between twelve motor imagery datasets available in the MOABB collection. We present an analytical investigation into the suitability of these datasets for TL, serving as a valuable resource for future research in pre-training or benchmarking models. Finally, through an example application, we have showcased how the results of this compatibility characterisation and our framework can be used to make an informed donor selection.

The proposed framework was applied to datasets of motor (imagery) protocols only, as this data is considered more difficult to decode than datasets based on evoked potentials for which recently substantial performance improvements have been obtained [54–57]. In order to support novel developments for transfer learning also in the ERP feature domain, future work could target to provide a compatibility table also for ERP datasets.

Acknowledgement. This work is in part supported by the Donders Center for Cognition (DCC) and is part of the project Dutch Brain Interface Initiative (DBI2) with project number 024.005.022 of the research programme Gravitation which is (partly) financed by the Dutch Research Council (NWO).

A Appendix

A.1 Description of the Datasets

Below, we provide the list of datasets we used in this study together with a link to a concise online description on the MOABB website. For the full description of each dataset, we recommend the reader to refer to the corresponding original publications cited in Table 1.

AlexMI http://moabb.neurotechx.com/docs/generated/moabb.datasets.AlexMI.html#moabb.datasets.AlexMI
BNCI2014001 http://moabb.neurotechx.com/docs/generated/moabb.datasets.BNCI2014_001.html#moabb.datasets.BNCI2014_001
BNCI2014004 http://moabb.neurotechx.com/docs/generated/moabb.datasets.BNCI2014_004.html#moabb.datasets.BNCI2014_004
BNCI2015001 http://moabb.neurotechx.com/docs/generated/moabb.datasets.BNCI2015_001.html#moabb.datasets.BNCI2015_001
BNCI2015004 http://moabb.neurotechx.com/docs/generated/moabb.datasets.BNCI2015_004.html#moabb.datasets.BNCI2015_004
Cho2017 http://moabb.neurotechx.com/docs/generated/moabb.datasets.Cho2017.html#moabb.datasets.Cho2017
Lee2019 MI http://moabb.neurotechx.com/docs/generated/moabb.datasets.Lee2019_MI.html#moabb.datasets.Lee2019_MI
Ofner2017 http://moabb.neurotechx.com/docs/generated/moabb.datasets.Ofner2017.html#moabb.datasets.Ofner2017
PhysionetMI http://moabb.neurotechx.com/docs/generated/moabb.datasets.PhysionetMI.html#moabb.datasets.PhysionetMI
Schirrmeister2017 http://moabb.neurotechx.com/docs/generated/moabb.datasets.Schirrmeister2017.html#moabb.datasets.Schirrmeister2017
Weibo2014 http://moabb.neurotechx.com/docs/generated/moabb.datasets.Weibo2014.html#moabb.datasets.Weibo2014
Zhou2016 http://moabb.neurotechx.com/docs/generated/moabb.datasets.Zhou2016.html#moabb.datasets.Zhou2016

A.2 Detailed compatibility tables

The AUC scores for the **feet vs. right-hand** classification task for 1, 2, 4, 8, 16, 32, and 64 calibration trials per class can respectively be found in Tables 2a, 3a, 4a, 5a, 6a, 7a, and 8a. The AUC scores for the **left-hand vs. right-hand** classification task can be found in Tables 2b, 3b, 4b, 5b, 6b, 7b, and 8b. Finally, the accuracy scores on **all the classes** from the test dataset can be found in Tables 2c, 3c, 4c, 5c, 6c, 7c, and 8c.

We present here the tables in which we collected our results. These results can be used to estimate the compatibility for transfer learning between the different motor imagery datasets we analysed. Due to editorial reasons, the compatibility tables had to be split according to the number of calibration trials per class and needed to be provided in black and white. A colour and un-split version of these tables is available online[5].

Table 2. Compatibility tables when using 1 calibration example per class. Boldface values indicate the best score in each column.

(a) *f-rh* - AUC score

Test dataset / Pretraining dataset	AlexMI	BNCI2014001	BNCI2015001	BNCI2015004	PhysionetMI(I)	Schirrmeister2017	Weibo2014	Zhou2016
AlexMI	58	55	51	51	51	62	51	51
BNCI2014001	62	**67**	58	50	55	77	55	73
BNCI2014004	60	56	58	51	53	71	57	66
BNCI2015001	**65**	65	**65**	51	**59**	76	**64**	79
BNCI2015004	50	53	52	49	52	59	50	52
Cho2017	53	52	52	51	53	56	50	54
Lee2019_MI	59	61	59	51	57	69	60	78
Ofner2017(I)	50	50	50	50	50	50	50	50
PhysionetMI(I,E)	64	65	61	49	58	78	60	72
Schirrmeister2017	64	61	64	48	56	**84**	59	75
Weibo2014	64	61	58	**52**	56	74	54	73
Zhou2016	60	61	64	49	57	73	61	**85**

(b) *lh-rh* - AUC score

Test dataset / Pretraining dataset	BNCI2014001	BNCI2014004	Cho2017	Lee2019_MI	PhysionetMI(I)	Schirrmeister2017	Weibo2014	Zhou2016
AlexMI	51	55	57	51	54	54	48	51
BNCI2014001	65	59	59	56	58	54	53	66
BNCI2014004	61	**75**	58	60	57	57	55	72
BNCI2015001	60	60	56	56	55	53	55	57
BNCI2015004	53	56	56	51	53	53	48	50
Cho2017	56	60	**63**	53	56	54	51	54
Lee2019_MI	**68**	68	61	**64**	**64**	**58**	**63**	**79**
Ofner2017(I)	50	50	50	50	50	50	50	50
PhysionetMI(I,E)	58	57	57	57	60	54	53	61
Schirrmeister2017	59	58	55	57	54	55	54	62
Weibo2014	56	57	59	55	59	53	51	55
Zhou2016	63	64	60	60	57	56	57	**79**

(c) All - Accuracy sc.

Test dataset / Pretraining dataset	AlexMI	BNCI2014001	BNCI2015004	Ofner2017(I)	PhysionetMI(I)	Schirrmeister2017	Weibo2014	Zhou2016
AlexMI	38	28	20	14	22	31	16	34
BNCI2014001	41	**36**	**21**	**15**	23	39	18	46
BNCI2014004	38	29	20	14	21	36	18	48
BNCI2015001	40	34	20	**15**	22	36	19	45
BNCI2015004	34	27	20	14	22	30	16	34
Cho2017	35	27	20	14	22	28	16	36
Lee2019_MI	37	33	20	14	22	34	19	52
Ofner2017(I)	33	24	20	14	12	25	14	33
PhysionetMI(I,E)	**44**	35	**21**	**15**	**25**	41	**20**	46
Schirrmeister2017	41	34	**21**	**15**	23	**45**	18	49
Weibo2014	42	33	**21**	**15**	23	35	17	43
Zhou2016	40	33	20	**15**	23	37	18	**60**

Table 3. Compatibility tables when using 2 calibration examples per class. Boldface values indicate the best score in each column.

(a) *f-rh* - AUC score

Test dataset / Pretraining dataset	AlexMI	BNCI2014001	BNCI2015001	BNCI2015004	PhysionetMI(I)	Schirrmeister2017	Weibo2014	Zhou2016
AlexMI	57	57	52	51	53	67	51	55
BNCI2014001	62	**72**	61	50	58	82	56	79
BNCI2014004	64	59	60	**52**	54	76	58	73
BNCI2015001	67	68	**69**	51	60	82	**67**	83
BNCI2015004	50	55	52	49	52	62	51	53
Cho2017	54	54	52	51	55	59	50	56
Lee2019_MI	64	64	62	50	60	74	65	82
Ofner2017(I)	50	50	50	50	50	50	50	50
PhysionetMI(I,E)	**68**	69	63	50	**62**	84	63	77
Schirrmeister2017	66	64	66	49	58	**89**	63	80
Weibo2014	65	64	61	51	59	79	56	76
Zhou2016	64	64	66	50	60	78	65	**89**

(b) *lh-rh* - AUC score

Test dataset / Pretraining dataset	BNCI2014001	BNCI2014004	Cho2017	Lee2019_MI	PhysionetMI(I)	Schirrmeister2017	Weibo2014	Zhou2016
AlexMI	53	56	58	52	56	56	50	52
BNCI2014001	69	62	61	59	62	55	55	69
BNCI2014004	62	**79**	60	62	59	60	57	76
BNCI2015001	62	63	59	58	56	54	57	62
BNCI2015004	53	58	57	52	55	55	49	52
Cho2017	57	63	**66**	55	59	54	51	55
Lee2019_MI	**72**	72	63	**68**	**67**	**61**	**65**	83
Ofner2017(I)	50	50	50	50	50	50	50	50
PhysionetMI(I,E)	61	60	59	60	63	55	55	65
Schirrmeister2017	62	61	57	59	57	57	55	67
Weibo2014	58	60	60	57	61	55	52	56
Zhou2016	65	67	62	63	60	59	59	**84**

(c) All - Accuracy sc.

Test dataset / Pretraining dataset	AlexMI	BNCI2014001	BNCI2015004	Ofner2017(I)	PhysionetMI(I)	Schirrmeister2017	Weibo2014	Zhou2016
AlexMI	39	29	21	15	24	34	17	35
BNCI2014001	43	**41**	21	15	26	44	20	54
BNCI2014004	41	32	21	14	23	41	20	54
BNCI2015001	43	37	20	**16**	25	41	21	50
BNCI2015004	32	28	20	14	24	31	16	35
Cho2017	33	28	20	14	23	30	16	38
Lee2019_MI	39	37	21	15	24	38	22	60
Ofner2017(I)	33	24	20	15	12	25	14	33
PhysionetMI(I,E)	**49**	39	**22**	15	**29**	46	**23**	52
Schirrmeister2017	44	38	21	15	26	**52**	21	55
Weibo2014	43	35	21	15	26	40	19	46
Zhou2016	42	36	21	**16**	26	42	21	**66**

[5] Color tables: https://huggingface.co/PierreGtch/EEGNetv4/blob/main/results/tables_colour_full.pdf.

Table 4. Compatibility tables when using 4 calibration examples per class. Boldface values indicate the best score in each column.

(a) *f-rh* - AUC score

Test dataset / Pretraining dataset	AlexMI	BNCI2014001	BNCI2015001	BNCI2015004	PhysionetMI(I)	Schirrmeister2017	Weibo2014	Zhou2016
AlexMI	56	60	54	51	54	72	51	56
BNCI2014001	66	**77**	64	51	61	87	61	84
BNCI2014004	67	62	62	**53**	57	80	61	77
BNCI2015001	70	71	**73**	**53**	62	86	**73**	85
BNCI2015004	51	57	53	49	53	67	51	55
Cho2017	51	55	53	50	57	62	51	60
Lee2019_MI	68	68	65	50	63	79	70	86
Ofner2017(I)	50	50	50	50	50	50	50	50
PhysionetMI(I,E)	68	73	67	**53**	**66**	88	68	81
Schirrmeister2017	**71**	70	68	49	61	**92**	68	84
Weibo2014	69	68	63	52	61	83	59	78
Zhou2016	68	67	69	51	61	82	69	**92**

(b) *lh-rh* - AUC score

Test dataset / Pretraining dataset	BNCI2014001	BNCI2014004	Cho2017	Lee2019_MI	PhysionetMI(I)	Schirrmeister2017	Weibo2014	Zhou2016
AlexMI	55	59	59	53	58	58	50	52
BNCI2014001	73	66	63	61	65	57	57	76
BNCI2014004	65	**82**	61	65	60	62	62	81
BNCI2015001	65	66	61	60	59	56	60	65
BNCI2015004	53	60	58	53	57	58	48	53
Cho2017	60	66	**69**	57	62	57	51	58
Lee2019_MI	**74**	76	64	**71**	**70**	**65**	**70**	87
Ofner2017(I)	50	50	50	50	50	50	50	50
PhysionetMI(I,E)	64	63	60	62	67	57	57	70
Schirrmeister2017	65	64	59	62	60	59	59	73
Weibo2014	62	63	62	58	65	58	53	57
Zhou2016	69	70	63	66	63	62	63	**89**

(c) All - Accuracy sc.

Test dataset / Pretraining dataset	AlexMI	BNCI2014001	BNCI2015004	Ofner2017(I)	PhysionetMI(I)	Schirrmeister2017	Weibo2014	Zhou2016
AlexMI	38	31	21	15	27	37	18	36
BNCI2014001	45	**47**	22	16	30	49	23	59
BNCI2014004	42	35	21	15	25	45	22	61
BNCI2015001	46	40	21	**17**	28	45	24	55
BNCI2015004	32	29	21	15	26	34	18	36
Cho2017	33	30	20	15	25	32	17	40
Lee2019_MI	44	41	21	16	27	44	25	66
Ofner2017(I)	33	24	20	15	12	25	14	33
PhysionetMI(I,E)	**49**	43	**23**	16	**34**	51	**26**	58
Schirrmeister2017	48	42	22	16	28	**57**	25	60
Weibo2014	45	38	22	16	29	45	23	50
Zhou2016	45	40	22	16	28	45	25	**72**

Table 5. Compatibility tables when using 8 calibration examples per class. Boldface values indicate the best score in each column.

(a) *f-rh* - AUC score

Test dataset / Pretraining dataset	AlexMI	BNCI2014001	BNCI2015001	BNCI2015004	PhysionetMI(I)	Schirrmeister2017	Weibo2014	Zhou2016
AlexMI	60	62	56	51	56	77	52	58
BNCI2014001	70	**82**	68	52	64	90	67	87
BNCI2014004	70	66	65	**54**	60	84	66	81
BNCI2015001	70	74	**76**	53	64	89	**77**	87
BNCI2015004	50	61	55	50	54	72	51	57
Cho2017	52	58	55	50	59	66	51	62
Lee2019_MI	71	71	68	51	66	84	74	88
Ofner2017(I)	50	50	50	50	50	50	50	50
PhysionetMI(I,E)	**73**	78	70	53	**69**	90	72	85
Schirrmeister2017	72	75	71	50	64	**94**	73	88
Weibo2014	71	73	65	**54**	64	86	65	81
Zhou2016	68	71	71	52	64	86	73	**94**

(b) *lh-rh* - AUC score

Test dataset / Pretraining dataset	BNCI2014001	BNCI2014004	Cho2017	Lee2019_MI	PhysionetMI(I)	Schirrmeister2017	Weibo2014	Zhou2016
AlexMI	57	62	61	55	61	60	50	54
BNCI2014001	**78**	70	64	64	68	61	59	80
BNCI2014004	68	**85**	62	67	63	65	65	84
BNCI2015001	68	70	63	63	62	59	61	72
BNCI2015004	56	62	60	53	60	61	48	55
Cho2017	63	69	**71**	58	67	59	52	62
Lee2019_MI	77	79	66	**74**	**73**	**68**	**73**	90
Ofner2017(I)	50	50	50	50	50	50	50	50
PhysionetMI(I,E)	68	67	62	65	70	60	60	74
Schirrmeister2017	69	68	62	66	64	64	62	78
Weibo2014	65	66	64	60	68	61	54	61
Zhou2016	72	74	65	69	66	66	68	**91**

(c) All - Accuracy sc.

Test dataset / Pretraining dataset	AlexMI	BNCI2014001	BNCI2015004	Ofner2017(I)	PhysionetMI(I)	Schirrmeister2017	Weibo2014	Zhou2016
AlexMI	39	33	22	15	30	41	20	38
BNCI2014001	47	**52**	**24**	**17**	34	54	28	63
BNCI2014004	46	37	23	15	28	49	26	64
BNCI2015001	48	43	23	**17**	31	49	27	59
BNCI2015004	33	31	22	15	29	38	19	38
Cho2017	35	32	20	15	28	34	18	43
Lee2019_MI	47	43	21	**17**	30	49	28	70
Ofner2017(I)	33	24	20	16	12	25	14	33
PhysionetMI(I,E)	**51**	47	**24**	16	**38**	56	**30**	62
Schirrmeister2017	50	46	22	16	31	**62**	28	66
Weibo2014	45	41	22	**17**	33	49	26	53
Zhou2016	47	43	23	**17**	31	50	28	**77**

Table 6. Compatibility tables when using 16 calibration examples per class. Boldface values indicate the best score in each column.

(a) *f-rh* - AUC score

Pretraining dataset \ Test dataset	AlexMI	BNCI2014001	BNCI2015001	BNCI2015004	PhysionetMI(I)	Schirrmeister2017	Weibo2014	Zhou2016
AlexMI	63	66	57	51	60	81	54	60
BNCI2014001	73	**85**	71	53	67	92	72	89
BNCI2014004	72	70	67	55	63	86	71	85
BNCI2015001	70	77	**79**	53	67	90	**80**	89
BNCI2015004	52	65	57	52	56	76	51	60
Cho2017	56	61	57	49	61	70	51	65
Lee2019_MI	74	75	71	51	70	88	78	90
Ofner2017(I)	50	50	50	50	50	50	50	50
PhysionetMI(I,E)	**78**	82	73	**56**	**71**	92	77	88
Schirrmeister2017	74	80	75	51	67	**96**	77	91
Weibo2014	71	78	69	54	67	89	72	83
Zhou2016	71	75	74	53	67	88	78	**95**

(b) *lh-rh* - AUC score

Pretraining dataset \ Test dataset	BNCI2014001	BNCI2014004	Cho2017	Lee2019_MI	PhysionetMI(I)	Schirrmeister2017	Weibo2014	Zhou2016
AlexMI	61	64	62	56	65	64	51	56
BNCI2014001	**81**	75	66	69	72	65	64	83
BNCI2014004	71	**87**	64	70	66	68	69	86
BNCI2015001	72	73	64	66	66	63	64	78
BNCI2015004	58	65	62	55	63	64	50	57
Cho2017	66	72	**74**	60	70	62	52	65
Lee2019_MI	79	82	68	**77**	**75**	**72**	**77**	91
Ofner2017(I)	50	50	55	50	50	50	50	50
PhysionetMI(I,E)	72	70	65	68	74	65	64	80
Schirrmeister2017	74	73	64	70	68	69	66	84
Weibo2014	68	69	65	63	71	64	57	66
Zhou2016	75	78	66	72	69	70	70	**93**

(c) All - Accuracy sc.

Pretraining dataset \ Test dataset	AlexMI	BNCI2014001	BNCI2015004	Ofner2017(I)	PhysionetMI(I)	Schirrmeister2017	Weibo2014	Zhou2016
AlexMI	43	37	23	17	34	46	23	41
BNCI2014001	49	**56**	**25**	**18**	38	58	32	68
BNCI2014004	45	41	23	15	31	53	29	68
BNCI2015001	48	47	23	**18**	34	53	30	63
BNCI2015004	34	34	23	16	32	43	22	41
Cho2017	36	34	21	16	31	37	20	46
Lee2019_MI	48	47	23	17	33	53	32	74
Ofner2017(I)	33	24	20	17	12	25	14	33
PhysionetMI(I,E)	**56**	51	**25**	17	**43**	60	**36**	67
Schirrmeister2017	54	50	23	17	35	**66**	33	69
Weibo2014	46	46	23	**18**	38	54	31	55
Zhou2016	49	46	24	17	34	54	32	**80**

Table 7. Compatibility tables when using 32 calibration examples per class. Boldface values indicate the best score in each column.

(a) *f-rh* - AUC score

Pretraining dataset \ Test dataset	BNCI2014001	BNCI2015001	BNCI2015004	Schirrmeister2017	Weibo2014	Zhou2016
AlexMI	71	60	50	84	57	65
BNCI2014001	**88**	74	54	93	78	91
BNCI2014004	72	70	54	89	75	87
BNCI2015001	80	**82**	56	92	**82**	90
BNCI2015004	69	60	51	80	55	63
Cho2017	64	58	51	74	52	68
Lee2019_MI	79	75	53	91	80	92
Ofner2017(I)	50	50	50	50	50	50
PhysionetMI(I,E)	86	77	**58**	94	**82**	91
Schirrmeister2017	83	77	52	**97**	81	92
Weibo2014	82	72	54	91	77	85
Zhou2016	79	76	54	90	80	**96**

(b) *lh-rh* - AUC score

Pretraining dataset \ Test dataset	BNCI2014001	BNCI2014004	Cho2017	Lee2019_MI	Schirrmeister2017	Weibo2014	Zhou2016
AlexMI	64	67	64	59	66	52	60
BNCI2014001	**85**	79	68	72	70	71	86
BNCI2014004	73	**89**	65	73	71	72	89
BNCI2015001	75	76	67	69	67	68	82
BNCI2015004	62	68	64	58	67	51	60
Cho2017	69	73	**76**	62	64	54	67
Lee2019_MI	82	84	70	**79**	**75**	**79**	**93**
Ofner2017(I)	50	50	58	50	50	50	50
PhysionetMI(I,E)	76	75	67	72	70	69	84
Schirrmeister2017	78	77	66	73	74	70	88
Weibo2014	72	72	66	67	68	61	71
Zhou2016	77	81	68	74	72	73	**93**

(c) All - Accuracy sc.

Pretraining dataset \ Test dataset	BNCI2014001	BNCI2015004	Ofner2017(I)	Schirrmeister2017	Weibo2014	Zhou2016
AlexMI	41	24	18	50	26	46
BNCI2014001	**59**	**26**	**19**	62	38	72
BNCI2014004	44	24	16	56	33	72
BNCI2015001	50	25	18	57	35	66
BNCI2015004	38	23	17	47	25	45
Cho2017	37	22	17	41	21	49
Lee2019_MI	51	23	17	58	37	77
Ofner2017(I)	24	20	18	25	14	33
PhysionetMI(I,E)	56	**26**	17	64	**41**	72
Schirrmeister2017	54	24	17	**70**	38	73
Weibo2014	50	24	**19**	58	34	59
Zhou2016	50	25	18	58	36	**82**

Table 8. Compatibility tables when using 64 calibration examples per class. Boldface values indicate the best score in each column.

(a) *f-rh* - AUC score

Pretraining dataset \ Test dataset	BNCI2015001	Schirrmeister2017	Weibo2014
AlexMI	64	86	61
BNCI2014001	78	95	81
BNCI2014004	73	91	79
BNCI2015001	**84**	93	84
BNCI2015004	64	84	58
Cho2017	61	78	54
Lee2019_MI	79	93	82
Ofner2017(I)	50	50	50
PhysionetMI(I,E)	81	95	**85**
Schirrmeister2017	80	**97**	84
Weibo2014	76	92	81
Zhou2016	78	92	83

(b) *lh-rh* - AUC score

Pretraining dataset \ Test dataset	BNCI2014004	Cho2017	Schirrmeister2017	Zhou2016
AlexMI	77	66	69	56
BNCI2014001	89	69	73	74
BNCI2014004	**94**	66	74	73
BNCI2015001	86	68	71	68
BNCI2015004	78	65	70	54
Cho2017	80	**78**	67	55
Lee2019_MI	91	71	77	**79**
Ofner2017(I)	50	60	50	50
PhysionetMI(I,E)	85	68	75	72
Schirrmeister2017	88	68	**78**	74
Weibo2014	83	67	72	65
Zhou2016	89	69	75	75

(c) All - Accuracy sc.

Pretraining dataset \ Test dataset	Schirrmeister2017	Zhou2016
AlexMI	54	30
BNCI2014001	65	43
BNCI2014004	60	36
BNCI2015001	61	39
BNCI2015004	51	29
Cho2017	44	23
Lee2019_MI	62	41
Ofner2017(I)	25	14
PhysionetMI(I,E)	69	**46**
Schirrmeister2017	**73**	42
Weibo2014	62	39
Zhou2016	62	40

A.3 Experimental Details of the Example Application

We attempted to reproduce the results that Xie and colleagues [19] presented in their Sect. 4.1. (entitled *Classification accuracy of the DL models when fine-tuning on the whole training set*), in particular their Table 2, of their article. Because the corresponding source code was not published, we had to re-create the experimental settings according to what was reported in the article. Unfortunately, we faced obstacles in this process. We will describe them in this section.

The first difficulty was to establish which fine-tuning scheme had been used in the experiment of Sect. 4.1. In Sect. 2.3, four different fine-tuning schemes were presented but it was not clear, from the text, which one was used to obtain the results in Table 2. Later in the article, the four fine-tuning schemes are compared (only with Schirrmeister2017 as donor) in Table 4 and it seems that the results of the fourth scheme are relatively similar to those presented in column "PT_by_HGD" of Table 2, despite not being perfectly equal. Therefore, we made the assumption that the whole Table 2 was obtained using fine-tuning scheme 4 and also used this scheme in our replication.

Then, it is mentioned that the same training strategy as Schirrmeister et al. [37] was used. However, the article follows up by explaining a training strategy different from the one presented by Schirrmeister and colleagues. Furthermore, the strategy of Xie and colleagues reads as *"In the first stage, only training sets were used for model training. When the loss on the training set does not decrease for some epochs, we stop training and record the lowest loss on the training set. Then, training and validation sets were used to train the model and stop training when the loss on the validation set dropped to the same value as the lowest loss at the first training stage."*. This suggests that the early-stopping mechanism of their *first stage* may not take into account the validation loss. We assumed this was a simple inaccuracy in the textual description and chose to implement the training strategy initially described by Schirrmeister and colleagues. Additionally, the number of epochs without improvement to wait before the end of the *first stage* was not provided. We chose to utilize the same value for early stopping as previously mentioned in the text but in another context, i.e., 100 epochs.

Concerning the cross-validation procedure, it is mentioned that *"Each configuration was evaluated twenty times using different random seeds"*. However, it was not clear whether the different folds over a given test subject were all based on the same pre-trained model or if a new pre-training was done for each fold. We choose the first option as it is significantly faster to compute.

The construction of the train/validation/test data splits was also relatively obscure. Because of the absence of source code, the exact data split is unknown. For pre-training, it is mentioned in their Sect. 3.4.1. that the data of all the subjects was *"divided into 90% training and 10% validation sets"*. We assumed the examples from all subjects were first shuffled, leading to having all subjects present in both sets. Nevertheless, it would be highly unlikely that we reached the exact same split as the original authors. For fine-tuning, it is mentioned in Sect. 4.1. that the *"train-test splition is the same as in the BCI Competition IV and the original paper* [37]*"*. These train/test splits have been annotated in the MOABB library, so we used the library's annotations to obtain the train/test splits. Then, it is stated that the training data is split into *"80% training set and 20% validation set"*. For each subject, we split the training data 20 times, each with a different random seed and in a stratified way, to create 20 folds. Again, it would be highly unlikely that we reached the exact same splits as the original authors. For sanity check, we reproduced the Table 1 of the original work compiling the amount of data in the training, validation and testing sets of each dataset. This leads to our Table 9. We can observe that the numbers in the two tables do not match but we suspect that the main difference can be explained by a confusion in the author's table. Indeed, their line *"Our dataset"* is relatively similar, except regarding N_Subjects, to the Schirrmeister2017 line in our Table 9. The other disagreements are much smaller and could be explained by a difference in the counting methods. Regardless, we conducted our experiments despite the potential disagreement between the two tables.

Table 9. Number of examples in the training, validation and testing sets of the fine-tuning phase in our reproduction of the work of Xie et al. (2023), Sect. 4.1. The eventual "$\cdot \pm \cdot$" indicate the average and standard deviation in case the number of examples is not constant across subjects within a dataset.

Dataset	N_Subjects	N_train	N_valid	N_test
BNCI2014001 (2a)	9	230	58	288
BNCI2014004 (2b)	9	320 ± 11	82 ± 3	315 ± 13
Schirrmeister2017 (HGD)	14	644 ± 121	161 ± 30	160

Finally, some choices seemed rather unconventional to us. First, the band-pass frequency filtering is done after the epoching steps which can cause edge artefacts. Second, the signal is passed at 250 Hz to the neural networks. While Deep ConvNet and Shallow ConvNet were indeed developed for signals at this frequency [37], EEGNet was developed for signals at 128 Hz [23]. It would typically be recommended to adapt the hyperparameters of EEGNet to use it on such signals. Third, an electrode-wise exponential moving standardisation (EMS) step is also applied after epoching using an initialisation on the first 1000 samples. At 250 Hz, this means that the EMS is initialized on an interval of 4 s and only "moves" over the last 0.5 seconds of each epoch. Nevertheless, we implemented these preprocessing steps the way they were described in the original article.

The rest of the experimental settings strictly follow what was described in the original article by Xie and colleagues [19]. The source code of our attempt to reproduce these results, along with the list of libraries we used with their versions, can be found on github[6].

References

1. Luck, S.J.: An Introduction to the Event-Related Potential Technique, 2nd edn. MIT Press, Cambridge (2014)
2. Höhne, J., Krenzlin, K., Dähne, S., Tangermann, M.: Natural stimuli improve auditory BCIs with respect to ergonomics and performance. J. Neural Eng. **9**(4), 045003 (2012)
3. Van Der Waal, M., Severens, M., Geuze, J., Desain, P.: Introducing the tactile speller: an ERP-based brain-computer interface for communication. J. Neural Eng. **9**(4), 045002 (2012)
4. Clerc, M., Bougrain, L., Lotte, F.: Brain-Computer Interfaces 2. Wiley-ISTE (2016)
5. Müller, K.-R., Tangermann, M., Dornhege, G., Krauledat, M., Curio, G., Blankertz, B.: Machine learning for real-time single-trial EEG-analysis: from brain-computer interfacing to mental state monitoring. J. Neurosci. Methods **167**(1), 82–90 (2008)
6. Meinel, A., Castaño-Candamil, S., Reis, J., Tangermann, M.: Pre-trial EEG-based single-trial motor performance prediction to enhance neuroergonomics for a hand force task. Front. Hum. Neurosci. **10**, 170 (2016)
7. Kolkhorst, H., Tangermann, M., Burgard, W.: Decoding perceived hazardousness from user's brain states to shape human-robot interaction. In: Proceedings of the Companion of the 2017 ACM/IEEE International Conference on Human-Robot Interaction, Vienna, Austria, pp. 349–350. ACM (2017)
8. Mane, R., Chouhan, T., Guan, C.: BCI for stroke rehabilitation: motor and beyond. J. Neural Eng. **17**(4), 041001 (2020)
9. Musso, M., et al.: Aphasia recovery by language training using a brain–computer interface: a proof-of-concept study. Brain Commun. **4**(1), fcac008 (2022)
10. Van Erp, J., Lotte, F., Tangermann, M.: Brain-computer interfaces: beyond medical applications. Computer **45**(4), 26–34 (2012)

[6] Code of example application: https://github.com/PierreGtch/CrossDataset_Xie2023.

11. Tangermann, M., et al.: Playing pinball with non-invasive BCI. In: Advances in Neural Information Processing Systems, vol. 21. Curran Associates, Inc. (2008)
12. Goodfellow, I., Bengio, Y., Courville, A.: Deep Learning. MIT Press, Cambridge (2016)
13. Jayaram, V., Alamgir, M., Altun, Y., Schölkopf, B., Grosse-Wentrup, M.: Transfer learning in brain-computer interfaces. IEEE Comput. Intell. Mag. **11**(1), 20–31 (2016)
14. Zhu, Y., Li, Y., Lu, J., Li, P.: EEGNet with ensemble learning to improve the cross-session classification of SSVEP based BCI from ear-EEG. IEEE Access **9**, 15295–15303 (2021)
15. Samek, W., Meinecke, F.C., Müller, K.-R.: Transferring subspaces between subjects in brain-computer interfacing. IEEE Trans. Biomed. Eng. **60**(8), 2289–2298 (2013)
16. Jeon, E., Ko, W., Yoon, J.S., Suk, H.-I.: Mutual information-driven subject-invariant and class-relevant deep representation learning in BCI. IEEE Trans. Neural Netw. Learn. Syst. **34**, 1–11 (2021)
17. Kobler, R., Hirayama, J.-I., Zhao, Q., Kawanabe, M.: SPD domain-specific batch normalization to crack interpretable unsupervised domain adaptation in EEG. In: Advances in Neural Information Processing Systems, vol. 35, pp. 6219–6235 (2022)
18. Wei, X., et al.: 2021 BEETL competition: advancing transfer learning for subject independence and heterogenous EEG data sets. In: Proceedings of the NeurIPS 2021 Competitions and Demonstrations Track, pp. 205–219. PMLR (2022)
19. Xie, Y., et al.: Cross-dataset transfer learning for motor imagery signal classification via multi-task learning and pre-training. J. Neural Eng. **20**(5), 056037 (2023)
20. Aristimunha, B., de Camargo, R.Y., Pinaya, W.H.L., Chevallier, S., Gramfort, A., Rommel, C.: Evaluating the structure of cognitive tasks with transfer learning (2023)
21. Deng, J., Dong, W., Socher, R., Li, L.J., Li, K., Fei-Fei, L.: ImageNet: a large-scale hierarchical image database. In: 2009 IEEE Conference on Computer Vision and Pattern Recognition, pp. 248–255 (2009)
22. Aristimunha, B., et al.: Mother of all BCI benchmarks. Zenodo (2023)
23. Lawhern, V.J., Solon, A.J., Waytowich, N.R., Gordon, S.M., Hung, C.P., Lance, B.J.: EEGNet: a compact convolutional network for EEG-based brain-computer interfaces. J. Neural Eng. **15**(5), 056013 (2018)
24. Xu, F., et al.: A transfer learning framework based on motor imagery rehabilitation for stroke. Sci. Rep. **11**(1), 19783 (2021)
25. Raza, H., Chowdhury, A., Bhattacharyya, S., Samothrakis, S.: Single-trial EEG classification with EEGNet and neural structured learning for improving BCI performance. In: 2020 International Joint Conference on Neural Networks (IJCNN), pp. 1–8 (2020)
26. Schneider, T., Wang, X., Hersche, M., Cavigelli, L., Benini, L.: Q-EEGNet: an energy-efficient 8-bit quantized parallel EEGNet implementation for edge motor-imagery brain-machine interfaces. In: 2020 IEEE International Conference on Smart Computing (SMARTCOMP), pp. 284–289 (2020)
27. Riyad, M., Khalil, M., Adib, A.: Incep-EEGNet: a ConvNet for motor imagery decoding. In: El Moataz, A., Mammass, D., Mansouri, A., Nouboud, F. (eds.) ICISP 2020. LNCS, vol. 12119, pp. 103–111. Springer, Cham (2020). https://doi.org/10.1007/978-3-030-51935-3_11
28. Deng, X., Zhang, B., Yu, N., Liu, K., Sun, K.: Advanced TSGL-EEGNet for motor imagery EEG-based brain-computer interfaces. IEEE Access **9**, 25118–25130 (2021)

29. Barachant, A.: Commande robuste d'un effecteur par une interface cerveau machine EEG asynchrone. Ph.D. dissertation, Université de Grenoble (2012)
30. Tangermann, M., et al.: Review of the BCI competition IV. Front. Neurosci. **6**, 55 (2012)
31. Leeb, R., Lee, F., Keinrath, C., Scherer, R., Bischof, H., Pfurtscheller, G.: Brain-computer communication: motivation, aim, and impact of exploring a virtual apartment. IEEE Trans. Neural Syst. Rehabil. Eng. **15**(4), 473–482 (2007)
32. Faller, J., Vidaurre, C., Solis-Escalante, T., Neuper, C., Scherer, R.: Autocalibration and recurrent adaptation: towards a plug and play online ERD-BCI. IEEE Trans. Neural Syst. Rehabil. Eng. **20**(3), 313–319 (2012)
33. Scherer, R., et al.: Individually adapted imagery improves brain-computer interface performance in end-users with disability. PLoS ONE **10**(5), e0123727 (2015)
34. Cho, H., Ahn, M., Ahn, S., Kwon, M., Jun, S.C.: EEG datasets for motor imagery brain–computer interface. GigaScience **6**(7) (2017)
35. Ofner, P., Schwarz, A., Pereira, J., Müller-Putz, G.R.: Upper limb movements can be decoded from the time-domain of low-frequency EEG. PLoS ONE **12**(8), e0182578 (2017)
36. Goldberger, A.L., et al.: PhysioBank, PhysioToolkit, and PhysioNet: components of a new research resource for complex physiologic signals. Circulation **101**(23), e215–e220 (2000)
37. Schirrmeister, R.T., et al.: Deep learning with convolutional neural networks for EEG decoding and visualization. Hum. Brain Mapp. **38**(11), 5391–5420 (2017)
38. Yi, W., et al.: Evaluation of EEG oscillatory patterns and cognitive process during simple and compound limb motor imagery. PLoS ONE **9**(12), e114853 (2014)
39. Zhou, B., Wu, X., Lv, Z., Zhang, L., Guo, X.: A fully automated trial selection method for optimization of motor imagery based brain-computer interface. PLoS ONE **11**(9), e0162657 (2016)
40. Guetschel, P., Papadopoulo, T., Tangermann, M.: Embedding neurophysiological signals. In: 2022 IEEE International Conference on Metrology for eXtended Reality, Artificial Intelligence, and Neural Engineering (MetroXRAINE), Rome, pp. 169–174. IEEE (2022)
41. Kumar, A., Raghunathan, A., Jones, R., Ma, T., Liang, P.: Fine-tuning can distort pretrained features and underperform out-of-distribution. In: ICLR. arXiv (2022)
42. Provost, F., Fawcett, T., Kohavi, R.: The case against accuracy estimation for comparing induction algorithms. In: ICML, vol. 98, pp. 445–453 (1998)
43. Conover, W.J.: Practical Nonparametric Statistics. Wiley, Hoboken (1999)
44. Benjamini, Y., Hochberg, Y.: Controlling the false discovery rate: a practical and powerful approach to multiple testing. J. Roy. Stat. Soc.: Ser. B (Methodol.) **57**(1), 289–300 (1995)
45. Sajda, P., Gerson, A., Müller, K.-R., Blankertz, B., Parra, L.: A data analysis competition to evaluate machine learning algorithms for use in brain-computer interfaces. IEEE Trans. Neural Syst. Rehabil. Eng. **11**(2), 184–185 (2003)
46. Blankertz, B., et al.: The BCI competition 2003: progress and perspectives in detection and discrimination of EEG single trials. IEEE Trans. Biomed. Eng. **51**(6), 1044–1051 (2004)
47. Blankertz, B., et al.: The BCI competition III: validating alternative approaches to actual BCI problems. IEEE Trans. Neural Syst. Rehabil. Eng. **14**(2), 153–159 (2006)
48. Jayaram, V., Barachant, A.: MOABB: trustworthy algorithm benchmarking for BCIs. J. Neural Eng. **15**(6), 066011 (2018)

49. Bauer, R., Fels, M., Vukelić, M., Ziemann, U., Gharabaghi, A.: Bridging the gap between motor imagery and motor execution with a brain-robot interface. Neuroimage **108**, 319–327 (2015)
50. Miller, K.J., Schalk, G., Fetz, E.E., den Nijs, M., Ojemann, J.G., Rao, R.P.N.: Cortical activity during motor execution, motor imagery, and imagery-based online feedback. Proc. Natl. Acad. Sci. **107**(9), 4430–4435 (2010)
51. Batula, A.M., Mark, J.A., Kim, Y.E., Ayaz, H.: Comparison of brain activation during motor imagery and motor movement using fNIRS. Comput. Intell. Neurosci. **2017**, 1–12 (2017)
52. Wriessnegger, S.C., Kurzmann, J., Neuper, C.: Spatio-temporal differences in brain oxygenation between movement execution and imagery: a multichannel near-infrared spectroscopy study. Int. J. Psychophysiol. **67**(1), 54–63 (2008)
53. Guetschel, P., Moreau, T., Tangermann, M.: S-JEPA: towards seamless cross-dataset transfer through dynamic spatial attention (2024)
54. Hübner, D., Verhoeven, T., Müller, K.-R., Kindermans, P.-J., Tangermann, M.: Unsupervised learning for brain-computer interfaces based on event-related potentials: review and online comparison [research frontier]. IEEE Comput. Intell. Mag. **13**(2), 66–77 (2018)
55. Martínez-Cagigal, V., Thielen, J., Santamaría-Vázquez, E., Pérez-Velasco, S., Desain, P., Hornero, R.: Brain-computer interfaces based on code-modulated visual evoked potentials (c-VEP): a literature review. J. Neural Eng. **18**(6), 061002 (2021)
56. Sosulski, J., Tangermann, M.: Introducing block-Toeplitz covariance matrices to remaster linear discriminant analysis for event-related potential brain-computer interfaces. J. Neural Eng. **19**(6), 066001 (2022)
57. Sosulski, J., Tangermann, M.: UMM: Unsupervised Mean-difference Maximization (2023)

Assessing the Optimality of Decentralized Inspection and Maintenance Policies for Stochastically Degrading Engineering Systems

Prateek Bhustali(✉) and Charalampos P. Andriotis

Faculty of Architecture and the Built Environment, TU Delft, Delft, The Netherlands
{P.Bhustali,C.Andriotis}@tudelft.nl

Abstract. Long-term inspection and maintenance (I&M) planning, a multi-stage stochastic optimization problem, can be efficiently formulated as a partially observable Markov decision process (POMDP). However, within this context, single-agent approaches do not scale well for large multi-component systems since the joint state, action and observation spaces grow exponentially with the number of components. To alleviate this curse of dimensionality, cooperative decentralized approaches, known as decentralized POMDPs, are often adopted and solved using multi-agent deep reinforcement learning (MADRL) algorithms. This paper examines the centralization vs. decentralization performance of MADRL formulations in I&M planning of multi-component systems. Towards this, we set up a comprehensive computational experimental program focused on k-out-of-n system configurations, a common and broadly applicable archetype of deteriorating engineering systems, to highlight the manifestations of MADRL strengths and pathologies when optimizing global returns under varying decentralization relaxations.

Keywords: Inspection and maintenance planning · Decentralized partially observable Markov decision processes · Multi-agent deep reinforcement learning · Actor-critic methods · Stochastic deterioration

1 Introduction

Inspection and maintenance (I&M) planning of deteriorating engineering systems, such as bridges, roads, aircraft, etc., is an optimization problem of seeking a policy that minimizes the expected life-cycle cost over a given time horizon. The problem is particularly challenging for engineering systems with multiple heterogeneous components that exhibit distinct system-level and component-level behaviours because the space of possible policies is intractably large. To make the problem tractable, risk-based and condition-based approaches use heuristics to confine the policy space over which the objective is minimized [12,44]. Although these methods provide fast and explainable policies, it is well understood that they can be far from optimal [4,32].

F. A. Oliehoek et al. (Eds.): BNAIC/Benelearn 2023, CCIS 2187, pp. 236–254, 2025.
https://doi.org/10.1007/978-3-031-74650-5_13

Alternatively, since I&M is a problem of decision-making under uncertainty, several works leverage the partially observable Markov decision process (POMDP) framework to model the environment and state uncertainties inherent to real-world systems [7,8,24,26,29,32]. This enables us to leverage single-agent deep reinforcement learning (SADRL) algorithms, which unlike heuristics, access the entire policy space. They also circumvent many complexity limitations of traditional Bellman backup operator-based POMDP solvers [37,38] when applied to I&M planning problems [6,33].

Although, in theory, neural networks can tackle arbitrarily high-dimensional spaces, SADRL approaches do not scale well under practical computational constraints because the joint space of states, observations and action spaces grow *exponentially* with the number of agents. A natural way to address this is to decentralize the problem by assigning an agent to each component or subsystem, thus articulating the problem as a cooperative multi-agent task. This relaxation is an extension of the single-agent POMDP to multi-agent systems and is formally known as a decentralized POMDP (Dec-POMDP) [3,30,31]. Likewise, we can move from SADRL to multi-agent deep reinforcement learning (MADRL) to solve the Dec-POMDP.

On the one hand, decentralization in reinforcement learning is key to addressing scalability. On the other hand, it can introduce certain side effects, such as environment non-stationarity, equilibrium selection, multi-agent credit assignment, and other issues, which encumber the learning task and may hinder convergence to optimal policies [11,14,27]. These can become potentially predominant in I&M settings due to strong global reward signals, risk costs, and other dependencies common in the mathematical description of deteriorating engineering systems. It, therefore, remains to be understood how the various multi-agent learning pathologies manifest in various I&M planning settings.

In this work, we focus on understanding the optimality characteristics of the three major MADRL paradigms: centralized training with centralized execution (CTCE), centralized training with decentralized execution (CTDE) and decentralized training with decentralized execution (DTDE) in the context of I&M planning. Specifically, we study this through the lens of a 5-component k-out-of-n system, a common and broadly applicable archetype of deteriorating engineering systems, modelled as a (Dec-)POMDP. This allows us to conduct extensive numerical experiments with several MADRL architectures. Finally, we obtain empirical insights on the performance of decentralized algorithms, which can ultimately impede the convergence of MADRL algorithms to global optima.

2 Related Work

Some recent works in the maintenance planning context have leveraged the Dec-POMDP framework to tackle the component multiplicity challenge. Andriotis & Papakonstantinou exploit the independence of agent actions and factorize the policy network output agent-wise, effectively converting the Dec-POMDP into a multi-agent POMDP (MPOMDP) [4,5] (similar to [18]). Although action factorization curbs the exponential growth of the policy network output to linear in the number of agents, the policy input space can still grow exponentially, unless dependencies are properly broken down into likewise factorized representations [4,5,28].

CTDE and DTDE are two practical paradigms for solving Dec-POMDPs, which try to address this challenge [2,17,31,42]. Various CTDE approaches such as COMA [13], QMIX [36], FACMAC [35], VDN [39] have been proposed that can address the credit assignment problem. Leroy et al. extensively compare the performance of various CTDE approaches in the maintenance planning context for k-out-of-n systems with varying n and demonstrate empirically the limitations of current CTDE algorithms in a large system with more than $n = 50$ components [23].

An extensive empirical comparison of the CTDE and DTDE paradigms in cooperative settings has been carried out on standard MARDL environments by Papoudakis et al. to benchmark the efficacy of MADRL algorithms in practice [34]. Lyu et al. provide a theoretical and empirical study on the effectiveness of centralized and decentralized critics and show that both critics have the same policy gradient in expectation. However, the variance in centralized critics is at least as much as their decentralized counterparts. They empirically demonstrate the performance of the CTDE and DTDE paradigms in several environments to highlight shortcomings of training under centralized critics [25]. Guillaume et al. were among the first to compare all MADRL paradigms to solve Dec-POMDPs [9]. They empirically compare CTCE, CTDE and DTDE paradigms on benchmark problems and use RNN-based policy networks, among others, to encode the action-observation history.

In this work, we also compare all MADRL paradigms in the context of I&M planning, emphasizing on k-out-of-n deteriorating systems. However, unlike [9], we encode action-observation histories using beliefs over component states. We do this for three reasons: transition and observation models are often available in this context; belief-based policies are more explainable than RNN-based agents that learn to encode action-observation histories, which is particularly important in risk-sensitive settings; and learning stability is improved as training directly on the belief space is more robust to environment noise. The goal is to understand the strengths and shortcomings of MADRL approaches, specifically when solving real-world I&M planning problems.

3 Background

3.1 Dec-POMDPs

We decentralize the I&M planning problem for a multi-component system by assigning an agent to each component and requiring the agents to cooperatively minimize the inspection and maintenance cost over the system's lifetime. The objective can be extended to include risk thresholds, minimum component health states, budget constraints, etc. [5]. This decentralized cooperative multi-agent setting is formally called a Dec-POMDP [30,31], defined by the tuple $\langle \mathcal{M}, S, \mathbf{A}, T, C, \mathbf{O}, \Omega, t_H, \gamma \rangle$, where $\mathcal{M} := \{1, \ldots, M\}$ is the set of agents, S is the state space, $\mathbf{A} = \times A_m$ is the joint action space, $T : S \times \mathbf{A} \times S \rightarrow [0,1]$ is the transition model, $C : S \times \mathbf{A} \rightarrow \mathbb{R}$ is the system cost model, $\mathbf{O} = \times O_m$ is the joint observation space, $\Omega : \mathbf{O} \times S \times \mathbf{A} \rightarrow [0,1]$ is the observation model, t_H is the time horizon, and $\gamma \in [0,1)$ is the discount factor.

The solution to the Dec-POMDP is an *optimal joint policy*, $\boldsymbol{\pi}^*$, that minimizes the expected sum of discounted costs:

$$\boldsymbol{\pi}^* = \arg\min_{\boldsymbol{\pi}} \mathbb{E}_{\mathbf{a}\sim\boldsymbol{\pi}} \left[\sum_{t=0}^{t_H-1} \gamma^t c_t \middle| \boldsymbol{\pi} \right] \tag{1}$$

where $c_t \in C(s_t, \mathbf{a}_t)$ is the cost following the joint action $\mathbf{a}_t \in \mathbf{A}$ prescribed by the joint policy $\boldsymbol{\pi} = \langle \pi_1, \ldots, \pi_M \rangle$ in state s_t. The policy $\boldsymbol{\pi}$ can be stochastic, mapping the agent's action-observation history to a probability distribution over actions, or deterministic, mapping the agent's observation history to agents' actions. It is known that every Dec-POMDP has at least one optimal deterministic joint policy [31].

In several I&M planning scenarios, the system components deteriorate independently, enabling a factorization of the state space, $S = \times S_m$, transition model, $T_m : S_m \times A_m \times S_m \rightarrow [0,1]$ and observation model, $\Omega_m : S_m \times A_m \times O_m \rightarrow [0,1]$ making it a Dec-POMDP with transition and observation independence [15,21]. In scenarios where components are correlated or dependent, they can be transformed into independent representations through proper reconstruction of the underlying dynamic Bayesian network [28].

The deterioration models are often available or learnable offline, which enables us to maintain beliefs over the states of each agent [4,19,45]. When an inspection action is taken, we use the observation o_m to update the belief over a component's state s'_m using the Bayes' rule:

$$b_{m,t+1}(s'_m) = \frac{\Omega_m(o_m|s'_m, a_m) \cdot \sum_{s_m \in S_m} T_m(s'_m|s_m, a_m) b_{m,t}(s_m)}{\sum_{s'_m \in S_m} \Omega_m(o_m|s'_m, a_m) \sum_{s_m \in S_m} T_m(s'_m|s_m, a_m) b_{m,t}(s_m)} \tag{2}$$

An agent's policy, typically tied to a specific component, maps component beliefs to actions $\pi_m : B_m \rightarrow A_m$.

3.2 Baseline Performance

We establish baseline performance using the classical time-periodic inspections with condition-based maintenance (TPI-CBM) approach as in [5,16,24]. In this strategy, we inspect components at fixed time intervals (Δt_{insp}) and, at the inspection step, take maintenance actions based on observations ($\boldsymbol{o}_{\text{insp}}$), denoted by a sub-policy $\hat{\pi}(\boldsymbol{o}_{\text{insp}})$.

$$\boldsymbol{\pi}^*_{TC}(\Delta t^*_{\text{insp}}, \hat{\pi}^*(\boldsymbol{o}_{\text{insp}})) = \arg\min_{\Delta t_{\text{insp}}, \hat{\pi}(\boldsymbol{o}_{\text{insp}})} \mathbb{E}_{\mathbf{a}\sim\boldsymbol{\pi}_{TC}} \left[\sum_{t=0}^{t_H-1} \gamma^t c_t | \boldsymbol{\pi}_{TC} \right] \tag{3}$$

Intuitively, we formulate the inspection and maintenance planning problem as a combinatorial optimization problem by evaluating the objective defined in

Table 1. Single- and multi-agent DRL architectures studied in this work.

Paradigm	*Mathematical Framework*	*Algorithm*	*Observation*	*Action*	*Critic*	*Actor*
CTCE	POMDP	**JAC** (SADRL)	Joint	Joint	Centralized	Shared
	MPOMDP	**DCMAC**		Factored		Shared
		DDMAC		Factored		Separate
CTDE	Dec-POMDP	**IACC**	Independent	Independent	Centralized	Separate
		IACC-PS		Independent		Shared
DTDE		**IAC**	Independent	Independent	Decentralized	Separate
		IAC-PS		Independent		Shared

Eq.(3) for each policy $\boldsymbol{\pi}_{TC}(\Delta t_{\text{insp}}, \hat{\pi}(\boldsymbol{o}_{\text{insp}}))$ using Monte Carlo rollouts. Additionally, failed components are immediately repaired, enabling the strategy to retrogress to simple corrective maintenance when necessary.

3.3 Multi-agent Deep Reinforcement Learning (MADRL)

In this work, we study the 7 variants of MADRL as listed in Table 1. In all of them, we employ an off-policy actor-critic approach as in ACER [41] for sample efficiency. Following standard nomenclature [17], we categorize these algorithms based on information available during training and execution, as explained below and summarized in Table 1.

Centralized Training with Centralized Execution (CTCE). This paradigm essentially converts the Dec-POMDP either into a single-agent POMDP to directly learn the mapping between the joint belief space and joint action space or a multi-agent POMDP (MPOMDP) to learn the mapping between the joint belief space and the agent-wise factored action space. Although the single-agent POMDP approaches are not scalable, they theoretically encompass global optima in their solution space. MPOMDP solutions relax the requirement for joint action spaces and can be seen as a semi-CTCE paradigm that can approximate well the POMDP solution space under mild conditions. Specifically, we consider three actor-critic algorithmic approaches:

- **Joint actor-critic (JAC)**, where the actor learns the joint stochastic policy $\boldsymbol{\pi}(\mathbf{a}|\mathbf{b};\theta)$, mapping the joint beliefs to joint actions, and the critic learns the value function $V^{\boldsymbol{\pi}}(\mathbf{b};\phi)$ under that policy.
- **Deep centralized multi-agent actor-critic (DCMAC)**, where we exploit the factorizable nature of the joint action space and learn a policy for each agent that maps the joint belief to agents' actions, $\boldsymbol{\pi} = \langle \pi(a_m|\mathbf{b};\theta)\rangle_{m=1}^{M}$, and a centralized critic $V^{\boldsymbol{\pi}}(\mathbf{b};\phi)$ guides each agent as in [4,18].
- **Deep decentralized multi-agent actor-critic (DDMAC)**: Like DCMAC, we exploit the factorizable action space but employ independent networks for each agent mapping the joint belief to component action, $\boldsymbol{\pi} = \langle \pi(a_m|\mathbf{b};\theta_m)\rangle_{m=1}^{M}$, and a centralized critic $V^{\boldsymbol{\pi}}(\mathbf{b};\phi)$ guides each agent as

introduced in [5]. This approach aims to model policy distributions independently, thus alleviating potential training complexities stemming from parameter sharing in the centralized paradigm.

Centralized Training with Decentralized Execution (CTDE). This paradigm assumes that the agents may have access to centralized information signals, such as joint observations, joint actions and critic gradients, only during training but act independently based on local observations during execution/inference. We consider two information accessibility scenarios:

- **Independent actor centralized critic (IACC)**, where each agent only has access to its own component's beliefs and learns the local stochastic policy $\pi_m(a_m|b_m;\theta_m)$ guided by a centralized critic $V^{\pi}(\mathbf{b};\phi)$.
- **IACC with parameter sharing (IACC-PS)**: A special case of IACC where agents share the same policy network $\pi(a_m|b_m, m;\theta)$ but the beliefs are indexed (using one-hot encoding) to enable the network to learn distinct policies.

Decentralized Training with Decentralized Execution (DTDE). Agents only have access to local information during training and execution and never have access to centralized information as in the previous cases. We consider two cases:

- **Independent actor-critic (IAC)**, where each agent learns a stochastic policy mapping its belief to actions $\pi_m(a_m|b_m;\theta_m)$ and is guided by a decentralized critic $V^{\pi_m}(b_m;\phi_m)$.
- **IAC with parameter sharing (IAC-PS)**, where agents share both policy networks $\pi(a_m|b_m, m;\theta)$ and critic networks $V^{\pi}(b_m, m;\phi)$ but the beliefs are indexed (using one-hot encoding) to enable distinct outputs.

Generally, the parameter-sharing approach can be extended to agents with heterogeneous action space cardinalities [40]. Several works have empirically demonstrated the benefits of parameter sharing in environments with homogeneous agents (in terms of observations and actions) [13,18,43]. However, Christianos et al. demonstrate empirically that these benefits are environment-specific, and such parameter sharing can become detrimental in certain environments [10]. Therefore, we study both variants in this work.

Decentralization presents several challenges due to the presence of other agents that impede convergence to optimal policies. From the perspective of a single agent, the presence of other agents affects [2,14,27]:

- Transitions: The environment is perceived as non-stationary by one agent due to the actions of other agents;
- Rewards: Reward received due to joint actions must be disentangled to identify an individual agent's contribution (known as multi-agent credit assignment problem), and exploratory actions by agents obfuscate the reward signal (also known as alter-exploration issue);

- Agent policy: Action selection must be coordinated when multiple optimal joint policies exist (referred to as equilibria selection). Agents can converge to a sub-optimal equilibrium because miscoordination due to unilateral deviation from an optimal equilibrium has lower gains/higher penalties than unilateral deviation from the sub-optimal equilibria. In such cases, a sub-optimal equilibrium is said to *shadow* the optimal equilibrium.

4 Experimental Setup

4.1 Environment: k-out-of-n System

This work studies the optimality characteristics of MADRL approaches, focusing on a k-out-of-n system with heterogeneous components. The k-out-of-n:G (G: good) is a common archetype of deteriorating systems in which the system is functional when at least k out of its n components are working and, therefore, $n \geq k$. The system has two notable special cases, namely $k = n$, a series system, and $k = 1$, representing a parallel component configuration. Examples of such systems include road networks, transmitters in communication networks, human kidneys, etc. [20,22].

We consider a system with $n = 5$ components and assign an agent to each component, thus $M = n$. The state space of each component (S_m) describes its range of health states, $S_m := \{s^1 = \text{no-damage}, s^2 = \text{minor-damage}, s^3 = \text{major-damage}, s^4 = \text{failure}\}$ and similarly the component-wise actions are given by $A_m := \{a^1 = \text{do-nothing}, a^2 = \text{repair}, a^3 = \text{inspect}\}$. Each component m has a unique and stationary deterioration model T^d_m, the natural deterioration of the environment (e.g. ageing due to corrosion, fatigue or other stressors):

$$\overset{T_1^d}{\begin{bmatrix} 0.82 & 0.13 & 0.05 & 0 \\ 0 & 0.87 & 0.09 & 0.04 \\ 0 & 0 & 0.91 & 0.09 \\ 0 & 0 & 0 & 1 \end{bmatrix}} \overset{T_2^d}{\begin{bmatrix} 0.72 & 0.19 & 0.09 & 0 \\ 0 & 0.78 & 0.18 & 0.04 \\ 0 & 0 & 0.85 & 0.15 \\ 0 & 0 & 0 & 1 \end{bmatrix}} \overset{T_3^d}{\begin{bmatrix} 0.79 & 0.17 & 0.04 & 0 \\ 0 & 0.85 & 0.09 & 0.06 \\ 0 & 0 & 0.91 & 0.09 \\ 0 & 0 & 0 & 1 \end{bmatrix}}$$

$$\overset{T_4^d}{\begin{bmatrix} 0.8 & 0.12 & 0.08 & 0 \\ 0 & 0.83 & 0.12 & 0.05 \\ 0 & 0 & 0.89 & 0.11 \\ 0 & 0 & 0 & 1 \end{bmatrix}} \overset{T_5^d}{\begin{bmatrix} 0.88 & 0.12 & 0 & 0 \\ 0 & 0.9 & 0.1 & 0 \\ 0 & 0 & 0.93 & 0.07 \\ 0 & 0 & 0 & 1 \end{bmatrix}}$$

The above synthetic transition models capture the main characteristics of a deterioration model, namely, they are upper-triangular (component state cannot be improved without repair) and unit-mass at the terminal state (failure is an absorbing state).

The *repair* action restores the component back to state s^1, but this action only succeeds with a probability r_m and the transition model corresponding to this action is given by:

$$T_m^r(s_m'|s_m, repair) := \begin{bmatrix} 1 & 0 & 0 & 0 \\ r_m & 1-r_m & 0 & 0 \\ r_m & 0 & 1-r_m & 0 \\ r_m & 0 & 0 & 1-r_m \end{bmatrix} \tag{4}$$

where r_m is the repair accuracy of agent m, reflecting the uncertainty in the duration the action requires to be completed, or other. We use the following value of r_m for each of the m components $1, 0.9, 0.95, 0.85, 0.8$, respectively. The chance of unsuccessful repair actions aims to capture the inevitable human error during maintenance activities in practice.

We summarize the transition model for a component as follows:

$$T_m := \begin{cases} T_m^d, & \text{if } a = \text{ do-nothing or } a = \text{ inspect} \\ T_m^r \times T_m^d, & \text{if } a = \text{ repair} \end{cases} \tag{5}$$

The cost model is divided into component-level costs (repair and inspection costs) and system-level costs. For each component m, the repair costs c_m^{repair} are 30, 90, 80, 250, 350, respectively, and inspections costs $c_m^{inspect}$ are 20, 40, 25, 50, 100, respectively. System failure leads to a penalty $c^{failure}$ equal to 3 times the sum of component repair costs. The cost model can be summarized as follows:

$$C(s,a) = \mathbb{1}_{failure}(s) \cdot c^{failure} + \sum_{m=1}^{M} \mathbb{1}_{a^2}(a_m) \cdot c_m^{repair} + \mathbb{1}_{a^3}(a_m) \cdot c_m^{inspect} \tag{6}$$

where $\mathbb{1}_y(x)$ denotes the indicator function, taking a value of 1 if x=y, and 0 otherwise. This penalty necessitates the agents to cooperatively coordinate maintenance actions to ensure global system functionality.

Each component has a unique observation model Ω_m through which the respective agent obtains imperfect observations of its true state when the inspection action is chosen and is given as follows:

$$\Omega_m := \begin{bmatrix} p_m & 1-p_m & 0 & 0 \\ \frac{(1-p_m)}{2} & p_m & \frac{(1-p_m)}{2} & 0 \\ 0 & 1-p_m & p_m & 0 \\ 0 & 0 & 0 & 1 \end{bmatrix} \tag{7}$$

where p_m describes the observation accuracy of component m for the inspection action and takes values of 0.8, 0.85, 0.9, 0.95, and 0.8 for the five agents. Component failure, however, is assumed to be self-announcing, i.e. information about failed components is noise and cost-free. The objective is to minimize the operation cycle cost of the system over $t_H = 50$ with $\gamma = 0.99$.

4.2 MADRL Algorithms and Baselines

For brevity, we only describe the algorithm for JAC in detail in Appendix 1. The same off-policy features are used for all seven multi-agent approaches. All MADRL algorithms hyperparameters are tuned on the 4-out-of-5 setting, and the

Table 2. Comparison of the best performance observed for each algorithm (with ± indicating the 95% confidence interval when evaluating the optimization objective (1) with 10,000 MC rollouts. Bold indicates best in the respective k-out-of-n setting.

		1-out-of-5	2-out-of-5	3-out-of-5	4-out-of-5	5-out-of-5
Baseline	TPI-CBM	1485.74 (±8.43)	1498.8 (±8.62)	1654.19 (±14.11)	3998.41 (±43.51)	19728.42 (±95.45)
CTCE	JAC	365.51 (±10.90)	**735.96 (±13.59)**	1686.41 (±18.56)	**3413.96 (±33.88)**	**12595.17 (±67.70)**
	DCMAC	363.64 (±10.96)	**735.56 (±14.08)**	1789.00 (±21.25)	**3396.92 (±32.64)**	**12509.88 (±66.73)**
	DDMAC	364.10 (±10.67)	**732.62 (±13.49)**	1858.60 (±24.16)	**3384.11 (±32.95)**	12764.02 (±67.13)
CTDE	IACC	**298.01 (±7.96)**	820.21 (±13.80)	**1600.01 (±15.00)**	3460.20 (±35.57)	12685.70 (±66.53)
	IACC-PS	**285.64 (±7.99)**	833.55 (±10.28)	**1578.24 (±14.88)**	**3421.71 (±35.39)**	**12543.43 (±69.51)**
DTDE	IAC	563.99 (±21.91)	1422.94 (±18.13)	**1603.05 (±14.76)**	**3421.37 (±32.43)**	13291.65 (±73.41)
	IAC-PS	**296.57 (±8.42)**	850.90 (±16.11)	1646.18 (±14.46)	3395.78 (±34.13)	13370.26 (±76.00)

best-performing ones are reported in Table 4 (see appendix). We use these tuned hyperparameters and train ten instances of each agent with random seeds on all k-out-of-n settings. To pick the best policy, we evaluate the agent periodically every 4,000 training episodes using 10,000 Monte Carlo rollouts. A large number of rollouts is needed due to the high variance of expected discounted cost Eq. (1), as also highlighted in [23].

For the TPI-CBM heuristic, the policy space has $t_H \times (|S_m|-2) = 50\times 3 = 150$ policies, assuming policy uniformity over components. We subtract 2 since the initial and final states' actions are fixed, i.e., do-nothing and repair, respectively. However, if we were to allow different component-wise policies, the search would grow to $150^5 = 7.5 \times 10^{10}$, rendering the combinatorial optimization of Eq. (3) intractable since evaluating the objective requires a large number of Monte Carlo evaluations. Therefore, we optimize the heuristic, assuming the same policy for all components and find an optimum over the smaller search space of 150 policies.

All code and experimental data are publicly available: https://github.com/omniscientoctopus/optimality-of-decentralization

5 Results and Discussion

We summarize the performance of the MADRL algorithms in all k-out-of-n settings using box plots and the test performance of agents during training in Fig. 1. Additionally, we report the best performance observed for each algorithm in Table 2. For a more detailed comparison, we report mean performance with 95% confidence intervals over ten random seeds in Table 3 in the appendix. To enable a concise performance comparison of the paradigms, we aggregate the results across settings using mean, interquartile mean (IQM) and median in Fig. 2 as demonstrated by Agarwal et al. in [1]. Before aggregating the performance, we normalize the results with the respective baselines in each setting.

CTCE: Figure 1 shows that JAC, DCMAC, and DDMAC are all able to consistently outperform the heuristic in most settings, and the equivalence of their individual aggregate performance is shown in Fig. 2, where the confidence intervals have a significant overlap. However, in the 3-out-of-5 setting, while their best instance remains competitive, we observe discrepancies in their performance, as reported in Table 2. Sub-optimalities in the CTCE paradigm have been previously reported by Bono et al. and have been attributed to the difficult exploration

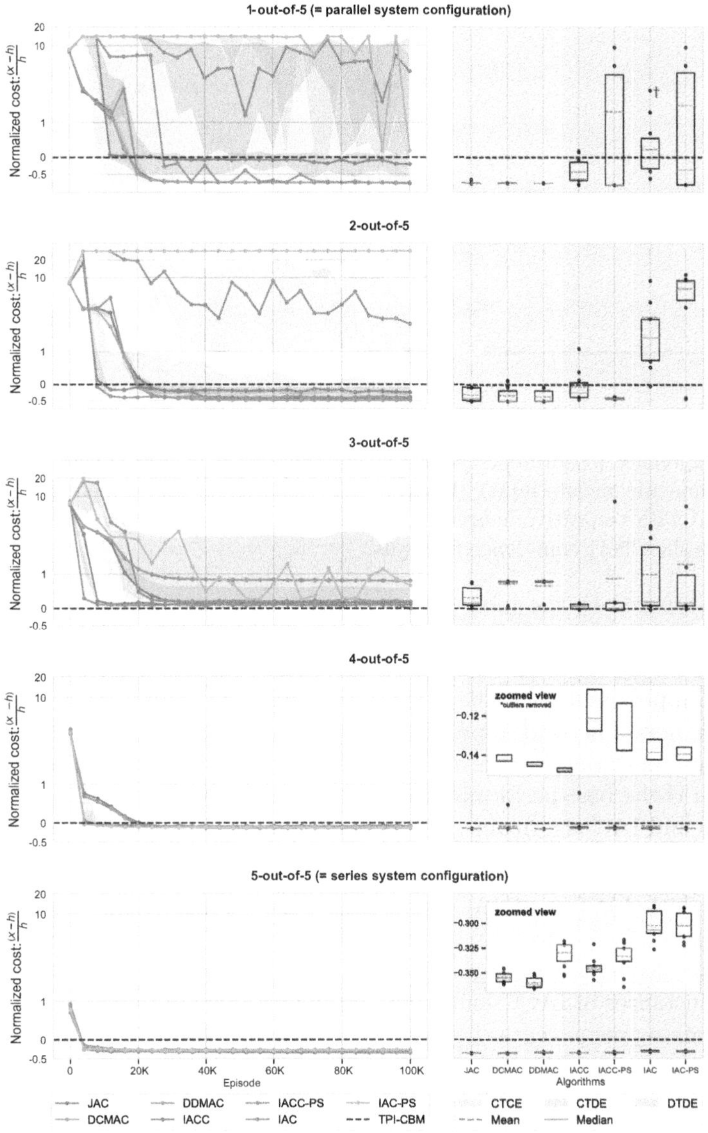

Fig. 1. Performance of CTCE, CTDE and DTDE algorithms in different k-out-of-n settings, normalized w.r.t. the heursitic (h) (lower is better). **Left**: Performance of the algorithms evaluated every 4,000 episodes during training, using 10,000 rollouts. The curve for each algorithm is aggregated over ten training instances. The bold line and the shaded region indicate the median and interquartile range respectively. **Right**: Each box plot summarizes the performance of the best policies across ten training instances, where the box represents the interquartile range and circles denote the outliers.

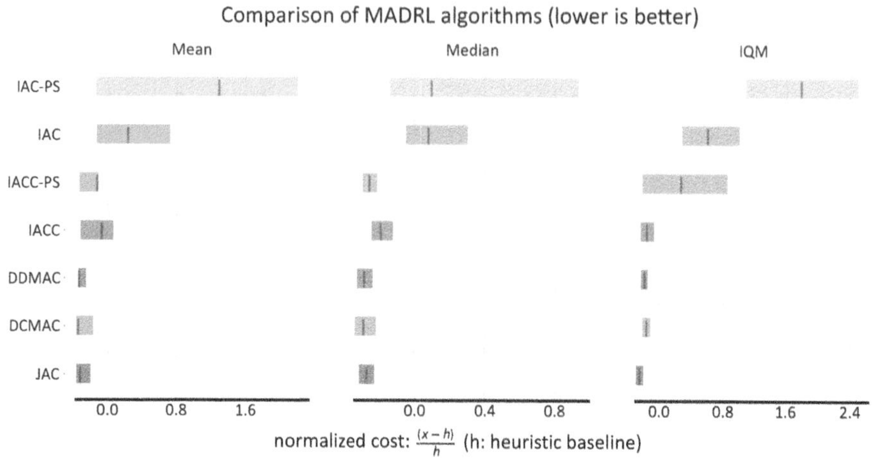

Fig. 2. Aggregate performance over the different k-out-of-n settings: mean, median and interquartile mean (IQM) (lower is better). Results for individual settings are normalized with respective heuristic baselines. Vertical lines indicate point estimates, and bands show 95% confidence intervals.

problem imposed by the joint state and action spaces [9]. We concur with this observation, especially because, unlike [9], we encode action-observation histories using beliefs and thus eliminating any additional complexities arising due to alternate approximations. The observed discrepancy cannot be merely an artifact of low neural network representational capacity as long as the same network architecture performs well in other settings. Another observation underpinning this claim is the best-performing training instance (random seed) of the IACC, IACC-PS and IAC algorithms, reported in Table 2, that are able to surpass the performance of CTCE algorithms and prove the existence of better policies.

CTDE: Both IACC and IACC-PS exhibit performance equivalent to CTCE algorithms in the 5-out-of-5 setting, but begin to exhibit variability as we move towards the 1-out-of-5 setting as shown in Fig. 1. However, surprisingly, the best training instances of IACC and IACC-PS algorithms outperform JAC, the best CTCE training instance, in the 3-out-of-5 setting by about 7%. We examine this closely by comparing the histogram of returns from 10,00 rollouts for the IACC-PS and JAC policies in Fig. 5 and contrast it with the corrective repair heuristic policy. We clearly observe how the environment under JAC policy is slightly more likely to witness at least one system failure. Additionally, we also plot individual rollouts under these polices in Figs. 3 and 4, respectively. In most time steps, the IACC-PS policy chooses corrective repair actions, however, it is able to marginally outperform the corrective repair heuristic by avoiding costly repair actions closer to the end of the life-cycle, such as for component 4 after $t = 40$. In contrast, the JAC agent chooses to monitor component 3 via inspections, and chooses a combination of predictive and corrective repair actions to keep

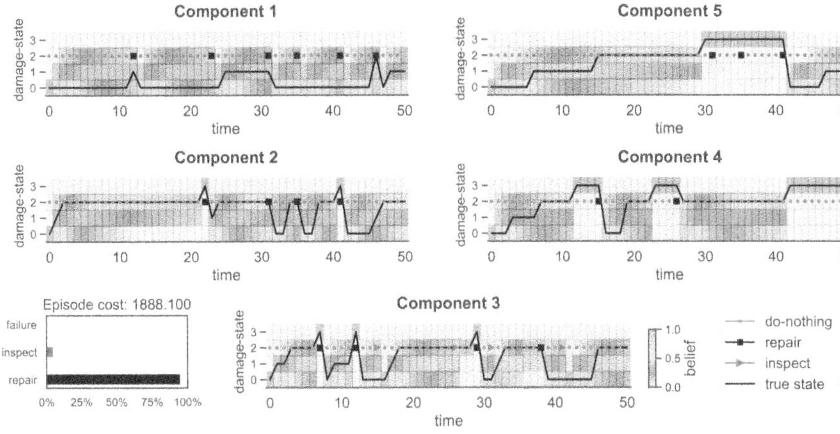

Fig. 3. Sample rollout of the best JAC policy in the 3-out-of-5 setting. The JAC agent chooses to monitor component 3 via inspections, and uses a combination of predictive and corrective repair actions to keep the system functional.

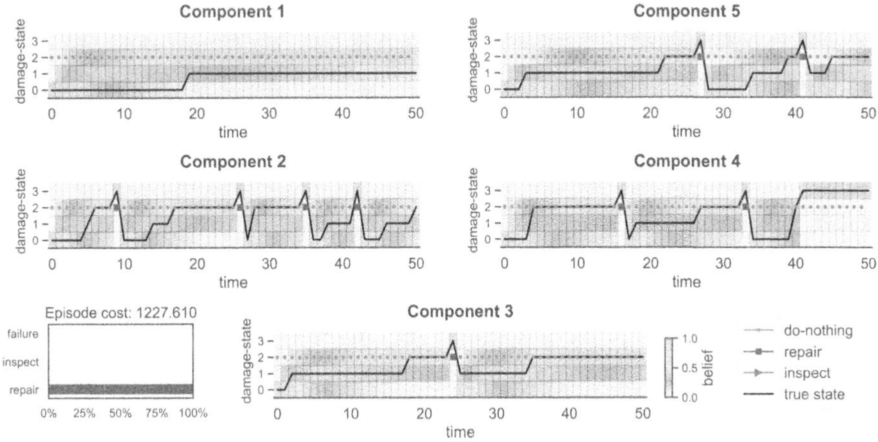

Fig. 4. Sample rollout of the best IACC-PS policy in the 3-out-of-5 setting. In most time steps, the agents choose simple corrective repair actions, however, they are able to marginally outperform the corrective replace heuristic policy by avoiding costly repair actions closer to the end of the life-cycle. We observe this for component 4 after $t = 40$, where the agent chooses do-nothing despite component failure.

the system functional. A possible explanation is that this component combines aggressive deterioration and low inspection to repair cost ratio.

DTDE: In terms of aggregate performance, fully decentralized algorithms are outperformed by both CTCE and CTDE algorithms, as shown in Fig. 2. Similar to CTDE algorithms, DTDE algorithms exhibit increasing variability in performance as we move from the 5-out-of-5 setting to the 1-out-of-5 setting, i.e. towards environments requiring more coordination among agents, as shown in Fig. 1. However, the performance of DTDE algorithms is more adversely

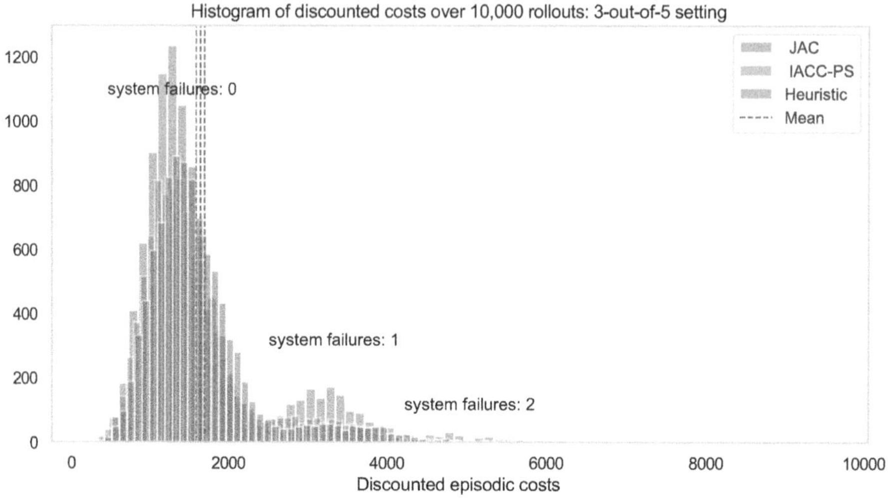

Fig. 5. Histograms of the discounted episodic costs of the best performing training instances (as highlighted in Table 2) in the 3-out-of-5 setting compared against a corrective repair heuristic policy over 10,000 environment rollouts. The modes in the histograms correspond to episodes in which system failures occur. Note that the IACC-PS policy closely resembles the corrective repair policy, but is marginally better as explained in Fig. 4.

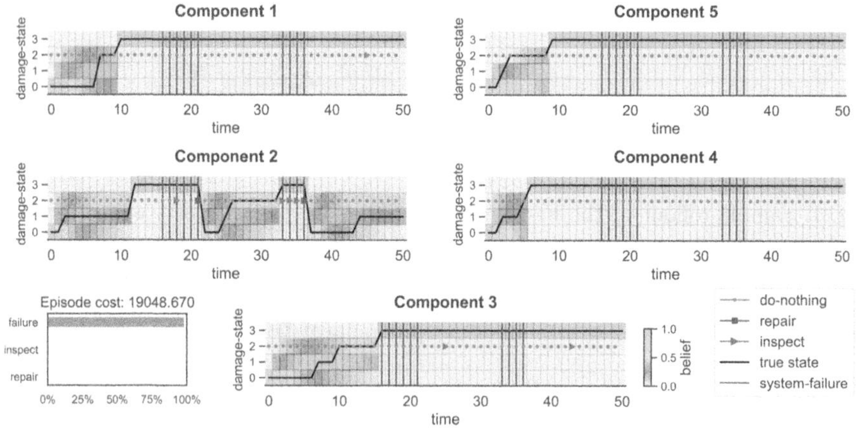

Fig. 6. Sample rollout of an outlier IAC policy in the 1-out-of-5 setting (indicated with † in Fig. 1), where the agents succumb to multi-agent learning pathologies, resulting in a poor policy. Agents 1,3,4,5 choose do-nothing actions even during system failure, and only agent 2 takes necessary repair actions. (Color figure online)

impacted as the need for cooperation in the environment increases. We illustrate this using a sample rollout of an outlier policy in the 1-out-of-5 setting (indicated with † in Fig. 1) in Fig. 6. Although the best performing instance is able to outperform the heuristic, this training instance succumbs to multi-agent learning pathologies and results in a poor policy. The performance of the parameter-sharing variants show similar variability, but can sometimes stumble into good policies, as reported in Table 2 for the 1-out-of-5, 4-out-of-5 and 5-out-of-5 settings.

Overall, as we move from the 5-out-of-5 setting to the 1-out-of-5 setting, environments demand more coordination among agents. In Fig. 2, we observe a clear trend: CTCE algorithms are unaffected by coordination requirements and thus show little variability in aggregate performance. In contrast, DTDE algorithms show large variability highlighting their susceptibility to multi-agent learning pathologies. CTDE algorithms are able to mitigate these and foster coordination among agents, thus performing better than their DTDE counterparts. Lastly, in Fig. 2, we also observe that the performance of the parameter sharing variants is comparable to their independent counterparts, in addition to being significantly more computationally efficient to train.

6 Conclusions

Multi-agent deep reinforcement learning provides a scalable approach to optimal inspection and maintenance (I&M) planning for multi-component systems. In this work, we study the three major multi-agent learning paradigms, i.e., centralized training with centralized execution (CTCE), centralized training with decentralized execution (CTDE) and decentralized training with decentralized execution (DTDE), through the lens of a k-out-of-5 system to investigate their efficacy and limitations in I&M planning. Our key conclusions are listed below:

- While CTCE methods are shown to be superior overall, they also remain susceptible to sub-optimal policies due to exploration challenges induced by the joint state/action spaces. More importantly, the large joint spaces hinder scalability of these algorithms in real-world I&M problems.
- CTDE and DTDE approaches, although more scalable, face challenges stemming from decentralization, such as the emergence of non-stationary environments, multi-agent credit assignment issues, shadowed equilibria, etc. Vanilla CTDE approaches are observed to mitigate these pathologies and consistently outperform their decentralized counterparts. However, due to the large variability in performance, DTDE algorithms are sometimes still able to converge to competitive policies.
- The overall performance of parameter-sharing variants in both CTDE and DTDE paradigms is comparable to their independent counterparts, despite heterogeneity in system components in terms of costs, deterioration characteristics, and action effects. Additionally, parameter-sharing variants are significantly more computationally efficient to train.

– Finally, with increasing number of redundant components in the system, more cooperation among agents is needed to maximally exploit these redundancies. As such, environments with redundant system components can serve as a good benchmark to test agent cooperation in the context of I&M planning.

We aim to continue this line of work and study more rigorously the influence of component connectivity configurations in deteriorating engineering systems, such as series-parallel systems, and homogeneity/heterogeneity of system components on policy learning.

Acknowledgements. This material is based upon work supported by the TU Delft AI Labs program. The authors gratefully acknowledge this support.

A Appendix

Table 3. Mean performance of the algorithms aggregated over ten training instances (random seeds) with ± indicating the 95% confidence interval. Bold indicates best in the respective k-out-of-n setting.

		1-out-of-5	2-out-of-5	3-out-of-5	4-out-of-5	5-out-of-5
Baseline	TPI-CBM	1485.74	1498.8	**1654.19**	3998.41	14780.43
CTCE	JAC	**372.46 (±2.51)**	**1070.24 (±178.81)**	**2487.57 (±285.79)**	**3488.80 (±11.30)**	**12698.22 (±50.20)**
	DCMAC	**377.01 (±5.83)**	**1146.16 (±162.51)**	**2774.12 (±256.45)**	**3451.70 (±9.68)**	**12642.19 (±56.38)**
	DDMAC	**379.71 (±21.31)**	**1194.30 (±188.91)**	2965.18 (±152.77)	**3517.82 (±12.38)**	**13097.86 (±160.00)**
CTDE	IACC	13467.32 (±940.42)	13844.57 (±988.96)	14329.28 (±850.25)	9952.01 (±723.77)	20830.69 (±277.56)
	IACC-PS	13311.32 (±1326.17)	13320.42 (±1316.56)	11802.21 (±2468.70)	7449.54 (±1025.22)	17457.71 (±2312.53)
DTDE	IAC	4797.06 (±3042.81)	4892.51 (±2266.34)	**3917.98 (±1273.71)**	4319.42 (±49.72)	13528.65 (±278.93)
	IAC-PS	5442.69 (±3246.56)	7326.18 (±2951.19)	**4051.89 (±2519.96)**	**3632.35 (±86.58)**	13505.44 (±131.70)

Table 4. Tuned hyperparameters of the algorithms used to train agents on various k-out-of-n settings

Paradigm		CTCE			CTDE		DTDE	
Algorithm		JAC	DCMAC	DDMAC	IACC	IACC-PS	IAC	IAC-PS
Episodes (E)		100,000						
Timesteps		$E \times t_H = 100,000 \times 50 = 5M$						
Architecture	Actor	[21, 64, 64, 243]	[21, 32, 32, 15]	[21, 16, 16, 3] x 5	[5, 16, 16, 3] x 5	[10, 32, 32, 3]	[5, 16, 16, 3] x 5	[10, 32, 32, 3]
	# parameters	21,363	2,255	3,375	2,095	1,507	2,095	1,507
	Critic	[21, 64, 64, 1]	[21, 64, 64, 1]	[21, 64, 64, 1]	[21, 64, 64, 1]	[21, 64, 64, 1]	[5, 16, 16, 1] x 5	[10, 64, 64, 1]
	# parameters	5,633	5,633	5,633	5,633	5,633	1,925	4,929
	Total # parameters	26,996	7,888	9,008	7,728	7,140	4,020	6,436
learning	batch size	64 (timesteps)						
Actor	optimizer	Adam						
	initial lr	0.0001	0.0001	0.0001	0.0005	0.0005	0.0001	0.0005
	decay factor	0.1						
	decay episodes	20,000	20,000	20,000	10,000	10,000	25,000	25,000
	decay type	linear						
Critic	initial_lr	0.005	0.005	0.001	0.005	0.001	0.001	0.001
	decay factor	0.1						
	decay episodes	20,000	20,000	20,000	10,000	25,000	25,000	25,000
	decay type	linear						
ϵ-greedy strategy	ϵ-start	1						
	ϵ-end	0.005	0.005	0.005	0.001	0.005	0.001	0.001
	decay episodes	20,000	20,000	20,000	10,000	10,000	25,000	25,000
	decay type	linear						
Replay Buffer	timesteps	500,000	500,000	500,000	10,000	10,000	10,000	10,000

As described in the main text, we use the 4-out-of-5 setting for hyperparameter optimization and report the tuned hyperparameters in Table 4. We note that decentralized agents often exhibit instabilities when using large replay buffers, thus, their replay buffers are much smaller than their centralized counterparts. This is because random samples from a large replay buffer can correspond to policies significantly different from the current policy, forcing agents to modify their recently learned policy drastically.

Algorithm 1: Joint Actor Critic (JAC)

Initialize: Actor $\boldsymbol{\pi}(\mathbf{a}|\mathbf{b};\theta)$, Critic $V^{\pi}(\mathbf{b};\phi)$, Experience Replay buffer $\mathcal{D}$, exploration scheduler ε, learning rates α_a^0, α_c^0, learning rate schedulers ζ_a, ζ_c, optimizers η_a, η_c, batch size $\mathtt{B}$, Episodes E, global time step $t' = 0$, exploration probability ϵ_0.

for $e = 1$ *to* E **do**
    $\mathbf{b}_0 = \text{env}()$ `// get initial belief`
    for $t = 0$ *to* $t_H - 1$ **do**
        if `explorationstrategy`$(\epsilon'_t) = \textit{random}$ **then**
            $\mathbf{a}_t \sim \mathcal{U}(\mathbf{A})$, $\mathbf{A}$ is the joint action space
        else
            Sample action: $(\mathbf{a}_t, \mathbf{p}_t) = \boldsymbol{\pi}(\mathbf{b}_t;\theta)$
        Environment step: $(\mathbf{b}_{t+1}, c_t, \mathtt{d}_t) = \text{env}(\mathbf{a}_t)$ `//` $\mathtt{d}_t := \mathbb{1}_{t_H-1}(t)$
        Store experience: $(\mathbf{b}_t, \mathbf{a}_t, p_t, \mathbf{b}_{t+1}, r_t, \mathtt{d}_t) \cup \mathcal{D}$
        if $t' > 10 \times B$ **then**
            Sample batch from buffer: $\mathcal{B} = \{(\mathbf{b}_t, \mathbf{a}_t, p_t, \mathbf{b}_{t+1}, c_t, \mathtt{d}_t)\}_{i=1}^{\mathtt{B}} \sim \mathcal{D}$
            $\boldsymbol{\pi}(\mathbf{a}|\mathbf{b};\theta^{t+1})$, $V^{\pi}(\mathbf{b};\phi^{t+1}) =$ `Train()`
        $\mathbf{b}_t \longleftarrow \mathbf{b}_{t+1}$
    $\epsilon_{t'+1} \longleftarrow \varepsilon(\epsilon'_t)$ `// update exploration parameter`
    $\alpha_a^{t'+1} \longleftarrow \zeta_a(\alpha_a^{t'})$ `// update actor learning rate`
    $\alpha_c^{t'+1} \longleftarrow \zeta_c(\alpha_c^{t'})$ `// update critic learning rate`
    $t' \longleftarrow t' + 1$

`Train():`
    For each sample i in batch,
    $\mathtt{future} = \mathtt{sg}(V^{\pi}(\mathbf{b}'_i;\phi)) \cdot \mathtt{d}_i$ `// stop gradients: sg(·)`
    Advantage: $\mathtt{A}_i = c_i + \gamma \cdot \mathtt{future} - V^{\pi}(\mathbf{b}_i;\phi)$ `// TD error`
    $\rho_i = \log \boldsymbol{\pi}(\mathbf{a}_i|\mathbf{b}_i;\theta)$
    Importance sampling weights: $w_i = \frac{\mathtt{sg}(\boldsymbol{\pi}(\mathbf{a}_i|\mathbf{b}_i;\theta))}{p_i}$
    Clipping weights: $w_i \longleftarrow \min(w_i, \bar{w})$
    Actor gradients: $\mathrm{g}_\theta = \frac{1}{\mathtt{B}} \sum_{i=1}^{\mathtt{B}} w_i \cdot (\nabla_\theta \rho_i \cdot \mathtt{A}_i)$
    Critic gradients: $\mathrm{g}_\phi = \frac{1}{\mathtt{B}} \sum_{i=1}^{\mathtt{B}} w_i \cdot \nabla_\phi \mathtt{A}_i$
    $\theta' \longleftarrow \eta_a(\mathrm{g}_\theta, \theta, \alpha_a)$
    $\phi' \longleftarrow \eta_c(\mathrm{g}_\phi, \phi, \alpha_c)$
    return $\boldsymbol{\pi}(\mathbf{a}|\mathbf{b};\theta')$, $V^{\pi}(\mathbf{b};\phi')$

For training, we employ a variant of the actor-critic with experience replay (ACER) algorithm for learning [41] as introduced for I&M in [4,5] and outlined above. To minimize the variance caused by the importance sampling weights, we clip the values w_i by setting $\bar{w} = 2$.

References

1. Agarwal, R., Schwarzer, M., Castro, P.S., Courville, A.C., Bellemare, M.: Deep reinforcement learning at the edge of the statistical precipice. In: Advances in Neural Information Processing Systems, vol. 34, pp. 29304–29320. Curran Associates, Inc. (2021). https://proceedings.neurips.cc/paper/2021/hash/f514cec81cb148559cf475e7426eed5e-Abstract.html
2. Albrecht, S.V., Christianos, F., Schäfer, L.: Multi-Agent Reinforcement Learning: Foundations and Modern Approaches. MIT Press, Cambridge (2023)
3. Amato, C., Chowdhary, G., Geramifard, A., Ure, N.K., Kochenderfer, M.J.: Decentralized control of partially observable Markov decision processes. In: 52nd IEEE Conference on Decision and Control. pp. 2398–2405. IEEE, Firenze (2013). http://ieeexplore.ieee.org/document/6760239/
4. Andriotis, C.P., Papakonstantinou, K.G.: Managing engineering systems with large state and action spaces through deep reinforcement learning. Reliab. Eng. Syst. Saf. **191**(March), 106483 (2019). https://doi.org/10.1016/j.ress.2019.04.036
5. Andriotis, C.P., Papakonstantinou, K.G.: Deep reinforcement learning driven inspection and maintenance planning under incomplete information and constraints. Reliab. Eng. Syst. Saf. **212**(March), 107551 (2021). https://doi.org/10.1016/j.ress.2021.107551
6. Andriotis, C.P., Papakonstantinou, K.G., Chatzi, E.N.: Value of structural health information in partially observable stochastic environments. Struct. Saf. **93**, 102072 (2021). https://doi.org/10.1016/J.STRUSAFE.2020.102072
7. Arcieri, G., Hoelzl, C., Schwery, O., Straub, D., Papakonstantinou, K.G., Chatzi, E.: Bridging POMDPs and Bayesian decision making for robust maintenance planning under model uncertainty: an application to railway systems. Reliab. Eng. Syst. Saf. **239**, 109496 (2023). https://www.sciencedirect.com/science/article/pii/S0951832023004106
8. Bismut, E., Straub, D.: Optimal adaptive inspection and maintenance planning for deteriorating structural systems. Reliab. Eng. Syst. Saf. **215**, 107891 (2021). https://www.sciencedirect.com/science/article/pii/S0951832021004063
9. Bono, G., Dibangoye, J.S., Matignon, L., Pereyron, F., Simonin, O.: Cooperative multi-agent policy gradient. In: Berlingerio, M., Bonchi, F., Gärtner, T., Hurley, N., Ifrim, G. (eds.) ECML PKDD 2018. LNCS (LNAI), vol. 11051, pp. 459–476. Springer, Cham (2019). https://doi.org/10.1007/978-3-030-10925-7_28
10. Christianos, F., Papoudakis, G., Rahman, A., Albrecht, S.V.: Scaling multi-agent reinforcement learning with selective parameter sharing (2021). http://arxiv.org/abs/2102.07475, arXiv:2102.07475 [cs]
11. Claus, C., Boutilier, C.: The dynamics of reinforcement learning in cooperative multiagent systems. In: Proceedings of the Fifteenth National/Tenth Conference on Artificial Intelligence/innovative Applications of Artificial Intelligence, pp. 746–752. AAAI 1998/IAAI 1998, American Association for Artificial Intelligence, USA (1998)

12. Deodatis, G., Fujimoto, Y., Ito, S., Spencer, J., Itagaki, H.: Non-periodic inspection by Bayesian method I. Probab. Eng. Mech. **7**(4), 191–204 (1992). https://www.sciencedirect.com/science/article/pii/026689209290023B
13. Foerster, J., Farquhar, G., Afouras, T., Nardelli, N., Whiteson, S.: Counterfactual multi-agent policy gradients (2017). http://arxiv.org/abs/1705.08926, arXiv:1705.08926 [cs]
14. Fulda, N., Ventura, D.: Predicting and preventing coordination problems in cooperative Q-learning systems. In: Proceedings of the 20th International Joint Conference on Artifical Intelligence, pp. 780–785. IJCAI 2007, Morgan Kaufmann Publishers Inc., San Francisco, CA, USA (2007)
15. Goldman, C.V., Zilberstein, S.: Decentralized control of cooperative systems: categorization and complexity analysis. J. Artif. Intell. Res. **22**, 143–174 (2004). https://doi.org/10.1613/jair.1427
16. Grall, A., Bérenguer, C., Dieulle, L.: A condition-based maintenance policy for stochastically deteriorating systems. Reliab. Eng. Syst. Saf. **76**(2), 167–180 (2002). https://doi.org/10.1016/S0951-8320(01)00148-X
17. Gronauer, S., Diepold, K.: Multi-agent deep reinforcement learning: a survey. Artif. Intell. Rev. **55**(2), 895–943 (2022). https://doi.org/10.1007/s10462-021-09996-w
18. Gupta, J.K., Egorov, M., Kochenderfer, M.: Cooperative multi-agent control using deep reinforcement learning. In: Sukthankar, G., Rodriguez-Aguilar, J.A. (eds.) AAMAS 2017. LNCS (LNAI), vol. 10642, pp. 66–83. Springer, Cham (2017). https://doi.org/10.1007/978-3-319-71682-4_5
19. Kaelbling, L.P., Littman, M.L., Cassandra, A.R.: Planning and acting in partially observable stochastic domains. Artif. Intell. **101**(1–2), 99–134 (1998). https://doi.org/10.1016/S0004-3702(98)00023-X
20. Kapur, K.C., Pecht, M.: Reliability Engineering, 1st edn. Wiley, Hoboken (2014)
21. Kochenderfer, M.J., Wheeler, T.A., Wray, K.H.: Algorithms for Decision Making. MIT Press, Cambridge (2022)
22. Kuo, W., Zuo, M.: Optimal Reliability Modeling: Principles and Applications. Wiley, Hoboken (2003). https://catalogimages.wiley.com/images/db/pdf/047139761X.07.pdf
23. Leroy, P., Morato, P.G., Pisane, J., Kolios, A., Ernst, D.: IMP-MARL: a suite of environments for large-scale infrastructure management planning via MARL (2023), http://arxiv.org/abs/2306.11551, arXiv:2306.11551 [cs, eess] version: 1
24. Luque, J., Straub, D.: Risk-based optimal inspection strategies for structural systems using dynamic Bayesian networks. Struct. Saf. **76**, 68–80(June 2017) (2019). https://doi.org/10.1016/j.strusafe.2018.08.002
25. Lyu, X., Baisero, A., Xiao, Y., Daley, B., Amato, C.: On centralized critics in multi-agent reinforcement learning. J. Artif. Intell. Res. **77**, 295–354 (2023). https://www.jair.org/index.php/jair/article/view/14386
26. Madanat, S., Ben-Akiva, M.: Optimal inspection and repair policies for infrastructure facilities. Transp. Sci. **28**(1), 55–62 (1994). https://doi.org/10.1287/trsc.28.1.55,https://pubsonline.informs.org/doi/10.1287/trsc.28.1.55
27. Matignon, L., Laurent, G.J., Le Fort-Piat, N.: Independent reinforcement learners in cooperative Markov games: a survey regarding coordination problems. Knowl. Eng. Rev. **27**(1), 1–31 (2012). https://www.cambridge.org/core/product/identifier/S0269888912000057/type/journal_article
28. Morato, P.G., Andriotis, C.P., Papakonstantinou, K.G., Rigo, P.: Inference and dynamic decision-making for deteriorating systems with probabilistic dependencies through Bayesian networks and deep reinforcement learning. Reliab. Eng.

Syst. Saf. **235**, 109144 (2023). https://www.sciencedirect.com/science/article/pii/S0951832023000595
29. Morato, P.G., Papakonstantinou, K.G., Andriotis, C.P., Nielsen, J.S., Rigo, P.: Optimal inspection and maintenance planning for deteriorating structural components through dynamic Bayesian networks and Markov decision processes. Struct. Saf. **94**(August 2021), 102140 (2022). https://doi.org/10.1016/j.strusafe.2021.102140
30. Oliehoek, F.A., Amato, C.: A Concise Introduction to Decentralized POMDPs. SpringerBriefs in Intelligent Systems, Springer, Cham (2016)
31. Oliehoek, F.A., Spaan, M.T.J., Vlassis, N.: Optimal and approximate Q-value functions for decentralized POMDPs. J. Artif. Intell. Res. **32**, 289–353 (2008). https://doi.org/10.1613/jair.2447
32. Papakonstantinou, K.G., Shinozuka, M.: Planning structural inspection and maintenance policies via dynamic programming and Markov processes. Part II: POMDP implementation. Reliab. Engi. Syst. Saf. **130**, 214–224 (2014). https://doi.org/10.1016/j.ress.2014.04.006
33. Papakonstantinou, K.G., Andriotis, C.P., Shinozuka, M.: POMDP and MOMDP solutions for structural life-cycle cost minimization under partial and mixed observability. Struct. Infrastruct. Eng. **14**(7), 869–882 (2018). https://doi.org/10.1080/15732479.2018.1439973
34. Papoudakis, G., Christianos, F., Schäfer, L., Albrecht, S.V.: Benchmarking multi-agent deep reinforcement learning algorithms in cooperative tasks (2021). http://arxiv.org/abs/2006.07869, arXiv:2006.07869 [cs, stat]
35. Peng, B., et al.: FACMAC: factored multi-agent centralised policy gradients (2021). http://arxiv.org/abs/2003.06709, arXiv:2003.06709 [cs, stat]
36. Rashid, T., Samvelyan, M., de Witt, C.S., Farquhar, G., Foerster, J., Whiteson, S.: QMIX: monotonic value function factorisation for deep multi-agent reinforcement learning (2018). http://arxiv.org/abs/1803.11485, arXiv:1803.11485 [cs, stat]
37. Shani, G., Pineau, J., Kaplow, R.: A survey of point-based POMDP solvers. Auton. Agent. Multi-Agent Syst. **27**, 1–51 (2013). https://doi.org/10.1007/s10458-012-9200-2
38. Spaan, M.T.J., Vlassis, N.: Perseus: randomized point-based value iteration for POMDPs. J. Artif. Intell. Res. **24**, 195–220 (2005)
39. Sunehag, P., et al.: Value-decomposition networks for cooperative multi-agent learning (2017). http://arxiv.org/abs/1706.05296
40. Terry, J.K., Grammel, N., Son, S., Black, B.: Parameter sharing for heterogeneous agents in multi-agent reinforcement learning (2022). http://arxiv.org/abs/2005.13625
41. Wang, Z., et al.: Sample efficient actor-critic with experience replay (2017). http://arxiv.org/abs/1611.01224
42. Wong, A., Bäck, T., Kononova, A.V., Plaat, A.: Deep multiagent reinforcement learning: challenges and directions (2022). http://arxiv.org/abs/2106.15691, arXiv:2106.15691 [cs]
43. Yu, C., et al.: The surprising effectiveness of PPO in cooperative, multi-agent games (2022). http://arxiv.org/abs/2103.01955, arXiv:2103.01955 [cs]
44. Zhu, B., Frangopol, D.M.: Risk-based approach for optimum maintenance of bridges under traffic and earthquake loads. J. Struct. Eng. **139**(3), 422–434 (2013). https://doi.org/10.1061/(ASCE)ST.1943-541X.0000671
45. Åström, K.J.: Optimal control of Markov processes with incomplete state information. J. Math. Anal. Appl. **10**(1), 174–205 (1965). https://doi.org/10.1016/0022-247X(65)90154-X

Human Recognition of Emotions Expressed by Human-Like Avatars on 2D Screens

Erik van Haeringen(✉), Marco Otte, and Charlotte Gerritsen

Vrije Universiteit, De Boelelaan 1111, 1081HV Amsterdam, The Netherlands
e.s.van.haeringen@vu.nl

Abstract. Understanding emotions of others is important for effective interactions among people. Therefore, it is likely similarly important in applications where people interact with or via virtual humans. However, while some studies have examined the recognisability of expressions by virtual avatars, it is currently unclear how generalisable the findings are across technologies and designs. To empirically examine how well people (N = 100) recognise dynamic facial expressions for a set of 12 proposed avatars, the expressions are tested at high (75%) and low intensity (25%) in the context of 2D computer screens. Also, the effects of the self-reported age, gender, mood and ability to recognise emotions by the annotator are examined. Then, these findings are compared to emotion recognition literature for avatars and real people with a similar context. Finally automated recognition models are applied to test automated emotion detection, as well as to establish what facial action units may contribute to the found patterns in recognisability of the proposed avatars. We conclude that on average the emotional expressions of the proposed avatars are recognisable and confusion patterns resemble those of real people, where specific emotion pairs are more difficult to distinguish. Negative effects are found for male avatar gender and the age of the participant, while no effect is found for the self-reported mood or ability to recognise emotion. Moreover, no difference is found in the mean recognition-rate between human and avatar-based studies, yet the variation among avatar recognition studies is substantial.

Keywords: Emotion recognition · Avatars · Virtual human · Facial expression · Facial action coding

1 Introduction

With evolving technology digital avatars have become increasingly human-like over the past decades, where emotionally expressive avatars have found their way into society, for example in education, gaming and customer service [8,34,40,50,54]. Many of the current applications are powered by artificial intelligence, highlighting the relevance of studying human-avatar interactions as a path

F. A. Oliehoek et al. (Eds.): BNAIC/Benelearn 2023, CCIS 2187, pp. 255–273, 2025.
https://doi.org/10.1007/978-3-031-74650-5_14

for delivering new AI capabilities to broad audiences [11,70]. Moreover, with predictions that in the future human-to-human communication may shift in part towards digital avatars representing people in virtual online spaces, it is becoming increasingly important to understand how human-avatar interactions may affect social interactions among people [19,21]. Understanding the emotions of others is important for effective interactions [35]. Therefore, it stands to reason that this may also apply to interactions with human-like avatars. While a number of studies have examined emotion recognition of avatars (see related work), it is currently unclear how generalisable the results are. This is because the avatars examined in different studies vary significantly in design, appearance and context.

In the present study we empirically test the ability of people to recognise dynamic emotional expressions shown on computer monitors. First, this is done by showing participants short video clips via an online survey. The context of regular computer screens, as opposed to virtual or mixed reality, was chosen to allow for a direct comparison to emotion recognition studies with human stimuli. Moreover, even though emotional communication via avatars in immersive and extended reality has received significant attention in recent years [1,28,64], the current use of virtual reality by consumers is still relatively low compared to the use of two-dimensional screens [4]. To match, we designed avatars with state-of-the-art software that can run on consumer-level computers in online social applications. Then to examine the generalisability of the obtained results, these are compared to results of other studies with a similar context for recognition of expressions of both avatars and real people. In addition, the effects of the age, gender, mood, and emotion recognition ability reported by the participants on recognition accuracy are explored.

Since in future work the proposed avatars will be used to study emotion contagion in group settings mediated by human-like avatars [32], a secondary objective of this study is to understand the recognisability of this particular set of avatars. For this we also applied two automated techniques. Besides human recognition, we use a novel method by testing the ability of several facial emotion recognition (FER) models to automatically detect the emotional content of the proposed virtual expressions. To gain further insights in the proposed expression animations, we also analysed facial action unit activation of the expressions with a machine learning model. This creates profiles indicating which virtual muscle groups are activated per expression, allowing objective comparison between expressions, and may answer why certain pairs are more often confused.

The remainder of this paper is structured as follows. In section two, related literature on emotion recognition in virtual and real human faces is discussed. Section three describes the proposed avatar expressions and how these were implemented in a survey, followed by a description of the participant sample and the analysis method for human and automated recognition. Section four shows the results for human recognition of the virtual expressions, followed by a comparison to literature and an examination of the effects of several participant characteristics on the recognition rate. Finally, the results for the automated facial emotion recognition and facial action unit analysis of the virtual expressions are discussed. In section five the results and limitations are discussed and recommendations are made for future work.

2 Related Work

An avatar in a broad sense is a representation that marks a person's entity, and can therefore be used for both highly realistic virtual human characters as for a much simpler representations, like a coloured pawn in a game [2]. In this work we focus on avatars designed to approximate real people. This is further narrowed down to avatars with dynamic expressions of emotion. Even though emotions can be recognised from still images of avatars [20] and more abstract depictions like emoji's [12], the focus on dynamic expressions of emotion is chosen because they have been shown to be more recognisable [66], and result in stronger mimicry [59].

Studies that examine emotion recognition of avatars or virtual humans vary in their aims. Some examine expression recognisability to validate their avatar designs. An example of this is Amini et al. [3], who designed a tool for users without 3D-modelling skills to produce static and dynamic expressive avatars. Other works compare recognition accuracy between avatars and human stimuli, such as Fernández-Sotos et al. [24], against the Penn Emotion Recognition Test (ER-40), or Gutiérrez-Maldonado et al. [31], against the PERT96 dataset. Studies have also examined the effects of various animation features on the recognition rate. Suma et al. examine the effect of expression intensity, both for facial and vocal expressions [63]. Durupinar and Kim also examine emotion recognition at different intensity levels in adults and children [18]. In addition, they also vary the appearance of the avatar to study the effects of skin-colour and gender appearance of the avatars. Saquinaula et al. [60] test whether graphical realism affects empathy for avatars. They find participants tend to empathise more and are better able to recognise expressions of avatars that are less realistic.

A more applied use can be found in studies that employ avatar expressions to compare atypical medical and psychological groups to a typical population. Marcos-Pablos et al. [47], Muros et al. [53] and Torregrossa et al. [65] use avatar expressions in establishing the difference in between healthy adults and people with schizophrenia. Monferrer et al. use dynamic virtual expression to study the effects of depression on emotion recognition [52], whereas Chevalier et al. compare emotion recognition by people with autism among avatars, embodied agents, and real people [13]. Another application is in education. Daher et al. designed an emotionally expressive avatar powered by a chatbot to train emotion recognition and empathy, aiming to solve issues with data imbalance and biases present in other applications that use material of real people [16]. All in all, the use of avatars or virtual humans in emotion research appears to be growing. However, to our knowledge there is currently no systematic literature review that offers a comprehensive overview and summarises the challenges in the field.

Next, to relate the recognition of avatar expressions to human expressions, we collected literature on the human recognition of human facial expressions with a similar context as the present work. The large majority of studies has used photographs to test the ability of people to recognise the emotional expressions of others [33,71]. However, since the present study focusses on dynamics expressions of avatars, a more direct comparison lays in studies that show human emotional expressions in videos. Moreover, because the expressions of the avatars are designed using typical characteristics for a certain emotional expression, for comparability only stimuli sets of posed human expressions, rather than spontaneous, are considered [39].

3 Methods

3.1 Emotional Avatars

The avatars are designed with Reallusion Character Creator and IClone[1] and recorded using the game engine Unity[2]. A set of twelve avatars was composed, six with a male appearance and six with a female appearance (Fig. 1). To optimise comparability with literature, a set of six basic emotions is used, believed by some to be universal emotions [15,36]. These include anger, disgust, enjoyment, fear, sadness and surprise. The expressions are based on the descriptions of the facial action coding system [22]. For each of the 12 avatars, 6 emotion expressions were recorded with high intensity (75% intensity), and 6 with a low intensity setting (25% intensity), yielding 144 recordings in total. Each expression starts with a neutral expression. After one second of neutral expression, the expression of the avatar transitions to the emotion expression, where the transition takes one second and the full emotion is then maintained for four seconds before the video fades to black and starts over. The intensities and durations were chosen empirically to maximize realism of the expressions, while clearly distinguishing between the two intensities. The videos of the emotional expression can be found in the supplementary materials.

3.2 Survey

To measure how well people can recognise the emotional expressions of the avatars, the expressions were shown as short videos to the participants in an online survey designed using the Qualtrics platform[3]. The participants made a forced choice for one of the six emotion labels by clicking a button below the video. Neutral or unclear answering options were not offered to not underestimate the detection of subtle emotional expressions. Since the present study is a pilot for further research on emotion contagion in virtual groups, this was chosen to learn whether subtle emotional expressions of avatars can be recognised and therefore have the potential to infect. The 144 expressions videos were shown in a random order to each participant to mitigate any learning effects. Additionally,

[1] https://www.reallusion.com.
[2] https://www.unity.com.
[3] https://www.qualtrics.com.

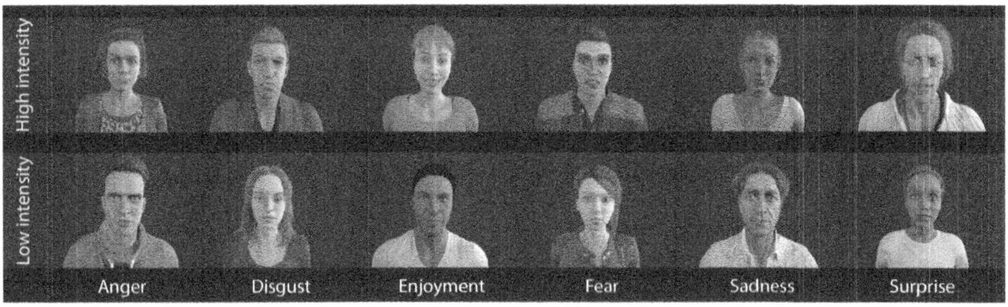

Fig. 1. Emotional expressions at high and low intensity demonstrated by the twelve proposed avatars. Please note that the expressions are dynamic, where the figure shows the final intensity after transition from a neutral starting state.

at the start of the experiment the participants reported their age (numerical), gender (male/female/other), mood (five-point Likert scale from very negative to very positive) and ability to recognise the emotion of others (five-point Likert scale from far below average to far above average). To prevent effects of the smaller display size, the survey was available for users on computers and tablets, but not on phones.

3.3 Participants

The online platform Prolific[4] was used to recruit participants. Two pre-screening filters were applied. People could not enter the experiment if they had labelled themselves with autism spectrum disorder (whether diagnosed or suspected). This was chosen as on average autism spectrum disorder is known to negatively affect emotion recognition [42]. Further, only people residential in the western half of Europe were included. Cultural differences are known to affect how people express emotions and interpret expressions [23]. Thus, because the present study serves as a pilot for future experiments taking place in the Netherlands, the geographical limitation was set to approximate the cultural composition in the population of future work, while still allowing for a sufficient pool of people on the Prolific platform that could choose to participate. At the start of the survey people were presented with an information letter and informed consent. In total 100 participants completed the survey, for which they received a financial compensation. One participant was excluded afterwards, because they completed the survey unrealistically fast. An additional participant was recruited as a replacement.

3.4 Analysis of Human Recognition

Emotion recognition is analysed as the recognition rate per emotional expression. We use confusion matrices to visualise both the recognition rate and patterns in

[4] https://www.prolific.com/academic-researchers.

mislabelling. To compare the present findings to literature, studies were collected with Google Scholar. A study is included if it examines emotion recognition of posed dynamic expressions of emotion, for either virtual humans or real people. The expressions need to be clear, meaning at high intensity and without parts of the face being obscured. Further, only studies are included that either present an appropriate confusion matrix or have published the raw data, as this allows us to construct combined confusion matrices for literature. As some literature examines more emotions than the six basic emotions in the present study, to make a fair comparison the accuracies are recalculated with only these emotions. In total, eight studies are examined that measure emotion recognition of avatars, and eight studies that examine human expressions (Table 1). All analyses are performed using RStudio[5]. The data and scripts used in the analysis can be found in the supplementary materials.

Table 1. Overview of the literature included in the comparison.

Study	Design	Condition used	N
Avatar dynamic facial expressions			
Amini et al. [3]	Haptek	Video high intensity	82
Durupinar and Kim [18]	Adobe Mixamo	Adults	208
Fernández-Sotos et al. [24]	Adobe Fuse CC	DVF	204
Garcia et al. [27]	Adobe Fuse CC	High intensity	204
Gutiérrez-Maldonado et al. [31]	3ds Max	VR	98
Muros et al. [53]	Adobe Fuse CC	Control	56
Saquinaula et al. [60]	Unreal MetaHumans	Meta human	30
Vicente-Querol et al. [67]	Adobe Fuse CC	High intensity	23
Human dynamic facial expressions			
Calvo et al. [7]	KDEF + FantaMorph	Dynamic	96
Fujimura and Umemura [26]	Own recordings of actors	Dynamic	39
Geraets et al. [28]	BLERT	Video task	100
Krumhuber et al. [38]	9 datasets of dynamic posed expressions	Posed	70
Martinez et al. [48]	Own recordings of actors	Face only	32
Richoz et al. [57]	Gold	Dynamic	444
Rodger et al. [58]	Gold	Dynamic hearing	45
Wingenbach et al. [68]	ADFES	High intensity	92

3.5 Analysis of Automated Recognition

We collected several facial emotion recognition (FER) models to test how recognisable avatar expressions are for automated methods. Specifically, we selected the highest-scoring model for the Affectnet [51], RAF-DB [43] and FER2013 [30] datasets as found on Paperswithcode[6] that met the selection criteria. To be selected, the model also needed to have its code published at the time that

[5] https://posit.co.
[6] https://paperswithcode.com/task/facial-expression-recognition.

we performed the analysis, provide clear documentation and pretrained checkpoints. This resulted in the selection of the models RMN [55] and POSTER++ [46]. The FER model of the LibreFace toolkit [10] was also included despite it obtaining lower scores on several datasets than the state of the art, because it offers as an accessible open-source toolkit that runs in real time on both GPU and CPU. Similar to the human annotations, the results were analysed using confusion matrices over all the predictions made between 4 and 6 s, when the emotional expression is at top strength for the particular clip. Neutral expressions were taken from the period between 1 and 2 s of each clip. For all models default settings were used as much as possible. For POSTER++ no default model is specified, thus the pretrained model that performed best on our data was chosen.

Second, to objectively describe the facial animations of the proposed avatars, ME-GraphAU [44] and LibreFace [10] were used to detect facial muscle movements as so-called action units. ME-GraphAU was chosen as it has highest scores for the BP4D and DISFA datasets of the models that had published their code at the moment of our analysis on Paperswithcode[7]. Specifically, we used the OpenGraphAU version of the model trained on a combination of six datasets. Action unit measurement by LibreFace was also included for its accessibility and real-time capabilities, while reporting reasonable performances across datasets for action unit detection. This way future work may easily use the same methodology to compare new avatar designs to ours. For both models the provided pretrained models were used. To gain insights in what aspects may have contributed or challenged the detection of the designed expressions, we focus on the action units that literature finds are associated with specific emotional expressions (Table 2).

4 Results

4.1 Emotion Recognition of the Proposed Avatars

Recognition of the emotional expressions by the proposed avatars depends on the type of emotion that is displayed and the intensity of the expression (Fig. 2). For all emotions, more intense expressions are recognised better than weaker expressions. However, this effect is stronger for anger, disgust, fear and sadness, while for enjoyment and surprise the accuracy decreased with only one percent for the subtle expressions. Further, there are several significant patterns in the confusion of emotions. Anger-disgust and fear-surprise form pairs that are often mixed up. In case of fear-surprise the confusion is not balanced, where fear is more often mislabelled as surprise than vice versa. Also notable is that while sadness has a high recognition rate at high intensity, at low intensity it is more often labelled as surprise. Further, while there are specific emotions that were recognised less well for particular avatars, there are no individual avatars of which the expressions were universally recognised less accurately (See supplementary materials).

[7] https://paperswithcode.com/task/facial-action-unit-detection.

Table 2. Association between action units and emotion categories in literature.

Emotion	Action units		
	Matsumoto et al. [49]	Cordaro et al. [14]	Keltner et al. [37]
Anger	4 + 5 or 7 + 22 + 23 + 24	4, 7	4 + 5 + 17 + 23 + 24
Disgust	9 or 10, 25 or 26	4, 6, 7, 9, 10, 25, 26 or 27	7 + 9 + 19 + 25 + 26
Enjoyment	6 + 12	6, 7, 12, 16, 25, 26 or 27	6 + 7 + 12 + 25 + 26
Fear	1 + 2 + 4 + 5 + 20, 25 or 26	1, 2, 5, 7, 25, 26 or 27	1 + 2 + 4 + 5 + 7 + 20 + 25
Sadness	1 + 15, 4, 17	4, (43), (54)	1 + 4 + 6 + 15 + 17
Surprise	1 + 2 + 5 + 25 or 26	1, 2, 5, 25, 26 or 27	1 + 2 + 5 + 25 + 26

This overview is based on Table 1 of Barrett et al. [5]. The '+' indicates action units appear simultaneously, while a ',' indicates action units are statistically likely, but do not necessary occur at the same time

4.2 Comparison to Literature

To place these findings in context, a comparison is drawn with literature. The present results are not significantly different from literature (Fig. 3). Moreover, it can be observed that the expressions of anger, disgust enjoyment and sadness of the proposed avatars are well recognisable compared to both avatar and human literature, while the accuracy is on the lower side for surprise and fear. Overall, no significant differences are found between avatars and human emotion recognition in the examined literature, except for fear, that is recognised significantly less from human faces. However, the variation among studies that examine recognition of avatars is larger than those examining human expressions. This suggests that there are larger differences among avatar designs than there are among dataset of posed human expressions. Our expectation was that this may be the result of technological advances over recent years in the graphical realism of the avatars. Yet, the variation in recognition rate for avatars does not relate to the year of publication (Fig. 4).

When looking at the patterns in confusion (Fig. 2), on average the strongest confusion in both avatar and human literature occurs in the same two pairs as found in the present study, namely anger-disgust and fear-surprise. Also notable is the confusion of sadness in avatar literature with disgust and fear, while this pattern is less clear with human faces or for the present findings.

4.3 Effects of Gender, Age, Mood and Recognition Ability

Both the gender of the avatar and participant are found to affect emotion recognition for particular emotions (Fig. 5). The male gender appearance of the avatar negatively affects recognition accuracy for fear and surprise compared to female appearance, while for the other emotions no significant difference is found. Additionally, participants who identified as male on average had significantly lower

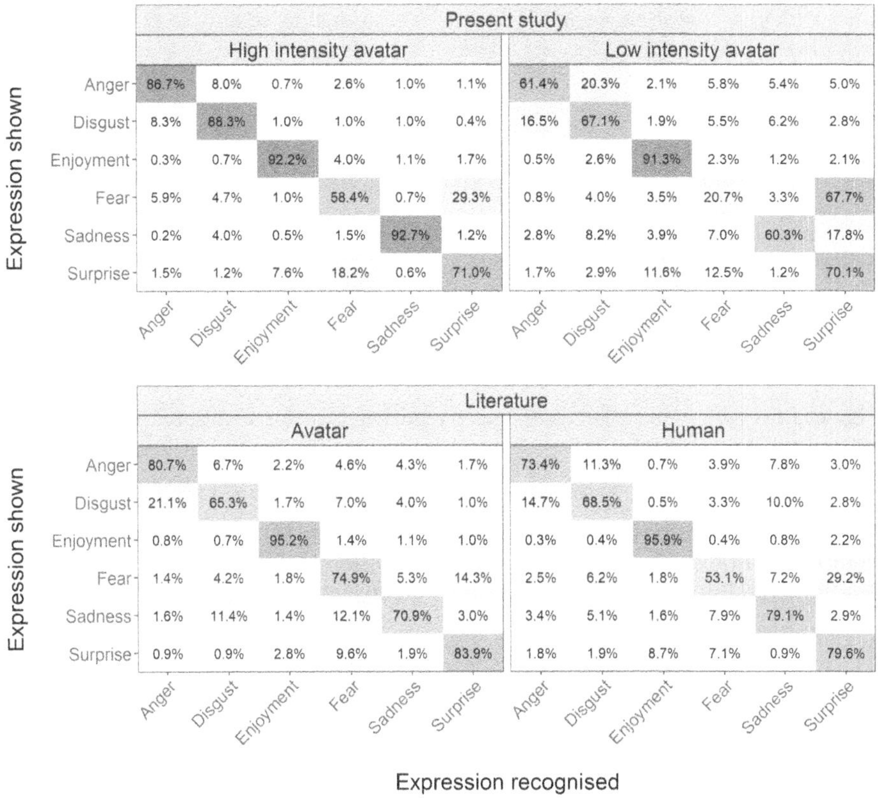

Fig. 2. Confusion matrices of the shown expressions and the recognised emotions for the present study (top) and literature (bottom).

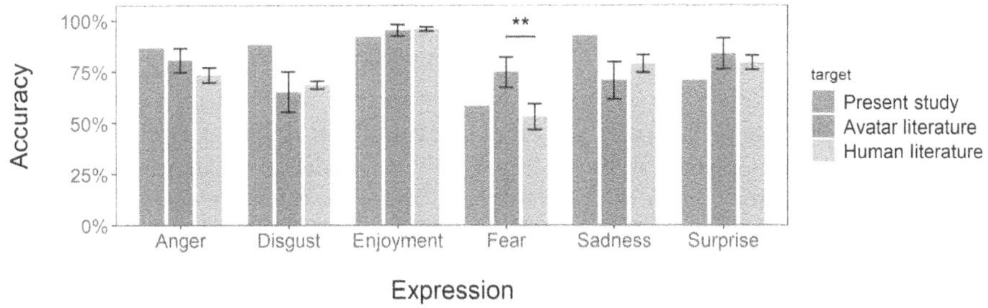

Fig. 3. Emotion recognition accuracy compared to literature (mean ± SE). The ** symbol indicates a significant difference between groups ($p \leq 0.01$) according to the Wilcoxon test. Other differences among groups are not significant ($p > 0.05$).

recognition scores than those who identified as female for expressions of surprise shown by avatars with a female appearance, and expressions of sadness regardless of avatar appearance. Overall, most studies examining the recogni-

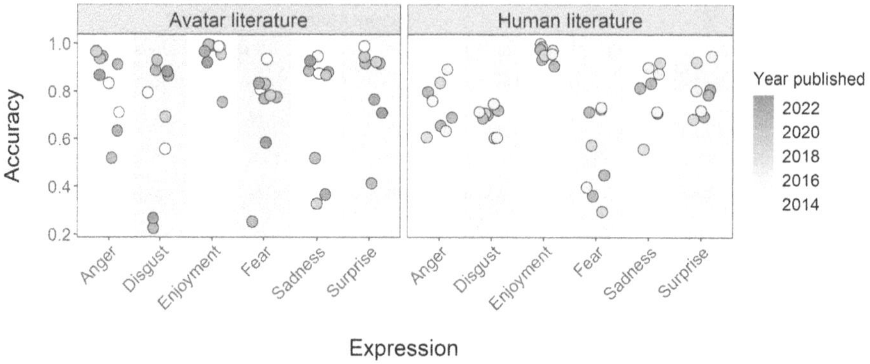

Fig. 4. Effect of publication year on recognition rate for emotional expressions by avatars and human faces

tion of human expressions find women perform better on emotion recognition than men, though there are also studies that find no gender differences [25,56]. Studies examining the effect of stimulus gender are mixed [56].

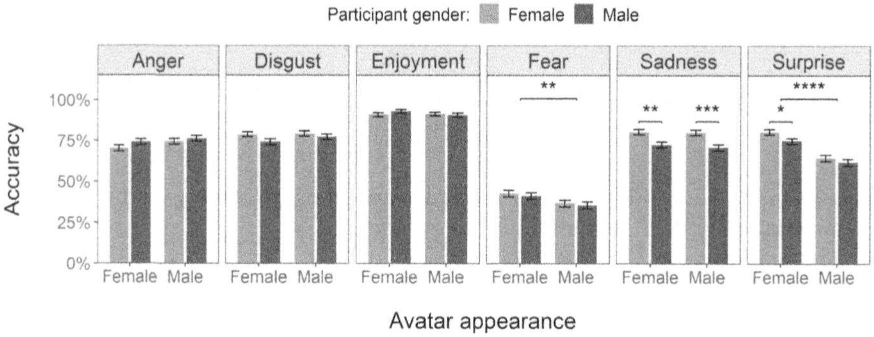

Fig. 5. Emotion recognition rates per combination of self-reported annotator gender and avatar gender appearance (mean ± SE, F = female, M = male). The ‘other’ category for annotator gender is not shown due to the low sample size. The symbols * ($p \leq 0.05$), ** ($p \leq 0.01$), *** ($p \leq 0.001$) and **** ($p \leq 0.0001$) indicate significant differences according to the Wilcoxon test, while unmarked pairs are not significant ($p > 0.5$).

The age of the participants in the present study negatively relates to emotion recognition for anger, enjoyment and surprise, while no correlation was found for sadness, disgust and fear (Fig. 6). This partly matches a recent meta-analysis of Gonçalves et al., who find a negative effect of age on recognition of all examined emotions except for disgust [29]. Contrary to literature [45,61], no effects are found of the self-reported mood of the participant on recognition accuracy (see

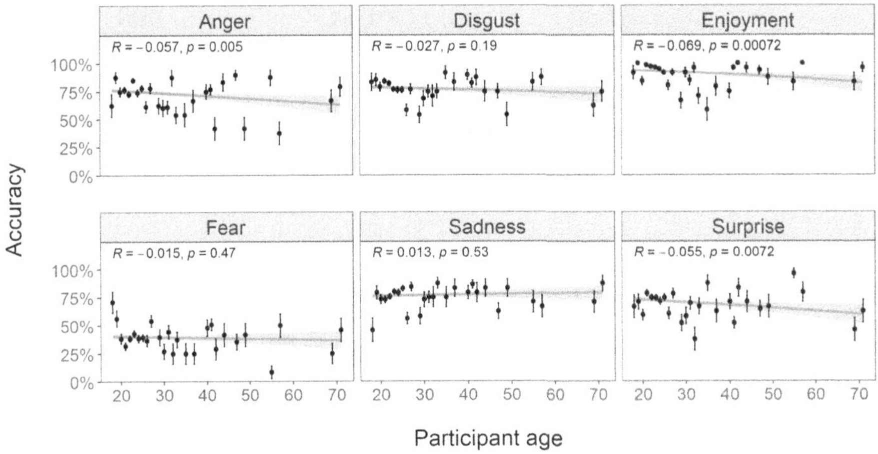

Fig. 6. Pearson correlation of emotion recognition against age of the participants. The points and error bars indicate the mean ± SE.

supplementary materials). Also, no significant effects were found for the self-reported ability to recognise emotions. This on the other hand is in line with literature that finds self-perceived emotional intelligence is not a reliable predictor for accurate emotion recognition [25]. Important to reflect is that while participant gender was nearly balanced in our data, age, mood and emotion recognition ability were not, possibly obscuring effects of these factors.

4.4 Automated Recognition

The performance of the examined FER models varies substantially with the intensity of the avatar expressions, with close-to-human performance on strong emotions and low performance on subtle emotions (Fig. 7). LibreFace [10] yields the highest accuracy for the high intensity expressions with 71%, approaching the 82% accuracy of the human participants. In fact, it performs on par or better than the participants on all emotions, except for disgust that is often mislabelled as anger. POSTER++ [46] and RMN [55] give slightly lower accuracies for the high intensity expressions, with 67% and 59% respectively. None of the models performs well on recognising low-intensity expressions, with the highest accuracy for RMN with 25%, compared to 62% for human participants. Moreover, the low-intensity expressions are also not always recognised as having a lack of emotion (neutral), what may be expected if expressions are too subtle. LibreFace and RMN mislabel a significant part of the subtle expressions as anger, whereas POSTER++ assigns fear to many subtle expressions.

An explanation for the sub-human performance on the present task could lay in the challenge to develop FER models that generalise well. We speculate that using avatar faces as input instead human faces brings a similar challenge for these models as "in the wild" source material does. Affectnet [51] for example is

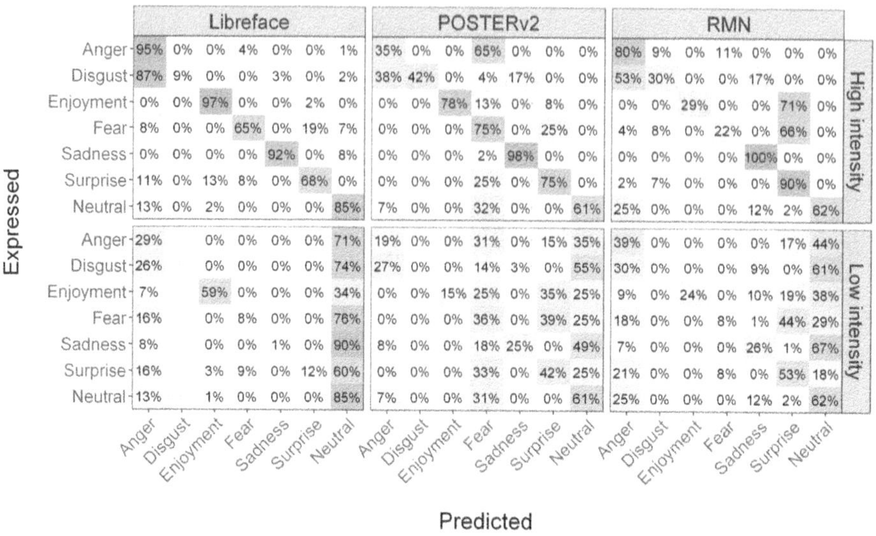

Fig. 7. Confusion matrices of the proposed avatar expressions and the predictions of three FER models.

composed from social media videos with the diverse lighting conditions, camera angles and recording qualities, resulting in consistently lower performance than other datasets. This matches our finding that of the three pretrained models provided for POSTER++, the model trained on Affectnet performed noticeably better than those trained on RAF-DB [43] or CAER-S [41]. Still, the examined FER models are more capable in recognising avatar expressions than expected, based on a recent study where recognition rates did not surpass 30% [17].

As shown in Fig. 8, the virtual muscle groups activated in the proposed expressions include many of the actions units commonly associated with the examined emotions (the coloured bars). Showing the action unit intensity relative to the neutral state was chosen because the annotated videos with the avatar expressions always started with a neutral expression, which then transitioned into an emotional expression. Since this pattern was also communicated at the start of the survey, the meaning of the expression was likely interpreted by participants relative to the neutral state.

The action unit profiles may also give insights in why some emotions may have been more difficult to recognise. While not all associated action units need to be activated at the same time to convey emotional meaning [5], the lower intensity of certain actions units can explain some of the confusion patterns we found in human and computer recognition. The detected profiles of fear and surprise, the pair most often confused, are strikingly similar. These emotions share five associated action units, while there are three action units only associated with fear (4, 7 and 20). The intensities of these action units are not much higher for expressions of fear than of surprise, especially for low-intensity

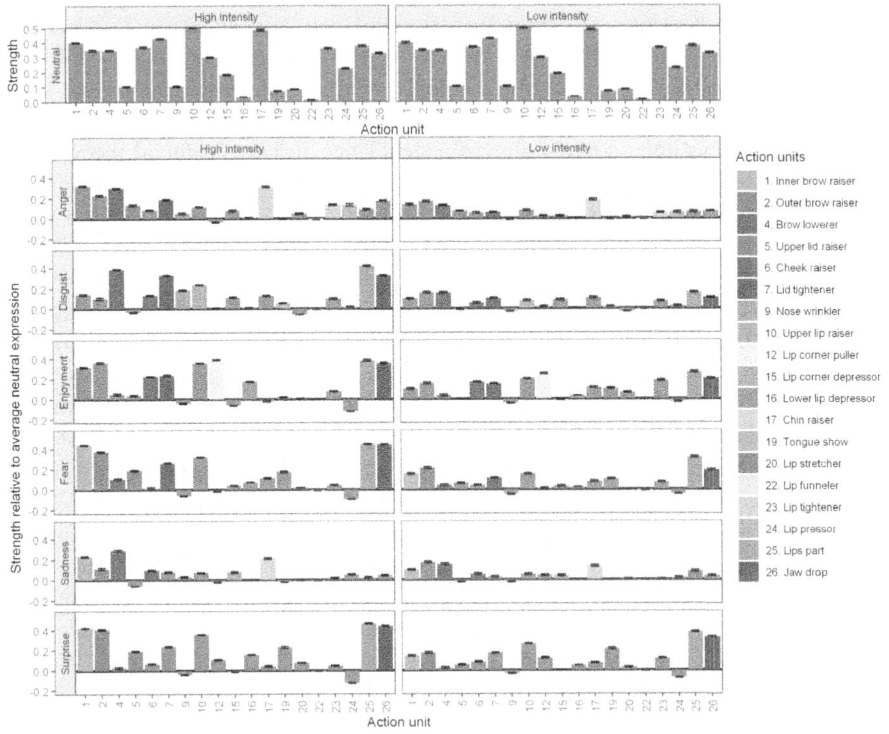

Fig. 8. Action unit strength as detected with ME-GraphAU [44]. On top the absolute strength of neutral expressions. Below the action unit strength relative to the mean neutral expression for each emotional expression. The action units associated with each emotion are coloured (see Sect. 3.5). Only action units associated with at least one emotion are shown.

expressions. Another pair that is often confused for low-intensity expressions is anger and disgust, while confusion at high intensity is lower. This matches the difference in the action unit profiles. For high-intensity expressions there are clear differences in action unit intensity for 9, 25 and 26, that are only associated with disgust, and 17, that is only associated with anger. For the low-intensity expressions these differences are smaller or absent, which may explain the higher confusion rate.

5 Discussion

The aim of this pilot study was to examine the recognisability of emotions expressed dynamically by a set of human-like avatars, and to determine the generalisability of the findings by examining literature with a similar context. The results indicate that the recognition rate of the proposed avatars for most expressions is high compared to other studies of emotion recognition in avatar and human faces. Exceptions are the expressions of fear and surprise. Particularly when the expression intensity is low and the avatar has a male appearance, fear is often confused with surprise for the proposed avatars. This could signal an issue with the design of the male avatars. The lower recognition of fear and surprise, but not other emotions, could point to a deficiency in certain facial movements that are shared between fear and surprise. We found that the overall action unit profiles of fear and surprise are remarkably similar, where the action units only associated with fear are detect with similar intensity for either emotion type. However, comparing action unit activation between avatars with male and female appearance, we found no pattern that could explain why the accuracy is lower for the male appearance (see supplementary materials). It should also be noted that the difference in accuracy between the avatar genders is not large compared to the differences among emotions. Moreover, the found recognition rates for fear and surprise do not fall outside the range of accuracies reported in literature for human faces. Therefore, the result may also be an accurate reflection that fear and surprise are difficult for people to distinguish [9].

In fact, the collected literature shows that the average recognition accuracy of avatars is in on par, or, in case of fear, better than for human faces. However, the variation among avatar studies is large, hinting at an influence of the particular avatar designs. Computer graphics have considerably improved over the years, yet, contrary to our expectation, the year of publication does not clearly relate to the recognition rate of the avatars. We therefore speculate that the large variation is the result of animation choices. In other words, which muscles are moved to what extend to create the expressions. Future studies may consider using automated tools to objectively measure recognisability across designs. Combining empirical evaluation with automated facial action unit detection gave insights in what animation characteristics may be responsible for conveying the emotional meaning, and what might be improved to increase recognisability. We suggest this method could be applied across avatar designs, as well as in comparison with human datasets, to develop deeper knowledge about which (combinations) in facial movements are essential for emotions to be recognisable and whether these combinations differ between human and avatar faces.

A limitation of the comparison in the present work is that these designs were not examined in the same context. Other aspects than the design may also explain the larger variation in accuracies in avatar studies compared to human studies, such as the number of answer options, the intensity of the displayed emotions, the population from which participants were recruited and the way the avatars are shown to the user. Future work could therefore attempt to study avatars from a wide range of available technologies for the same animation sequences, methodology and population. However, since avatar designs are often not shared or shared in compiled form (videos or photos), making adjustments or standardising expression animations and intensities across most designs is not possible. A reason not many avatars are shared in editable form could come forth out of licence restrictions of the technology used to design the avatars. Therefore, an alternative way forward may be for future work to introduce a standardised protocol to examine the recognisability of emotional expressions, that researchers can use for benchmark testing their designs. However, it should be noted that strict animation descriptions result in a form of posed expressions, which is also a limitation for the present findings. Posed expressions only represent a fragment of the ways emotions are expressed in daily life, while people are known to differ strongly in their representations of what and emotion should look like [6]. Future work may therefore wish to use motion capturing or action unit detection in naturalistic settings to compile a collection of spontaneous emotional expressions with a high similarity to human expressions [69]. This would allow a more realistic comparison between avatar expression and everyday emotional expressions of people, for example as done by Sollfrank et al. for static images [62].

Together, we conclude that avatars have the potential to be similarly or more recognisable than human faces for emotional expressions, while offering repeatability and configurability at less investment than for collecting human stimuli. Yet results from one avatar design cannot simply be generalised without further study. This may also have implication for other work reliant on emotion recognition, such as studies examining the emotional influence of avatars on participants, or the emotional exchange between people mediated by avatars.

Supplementary materials

The materials can be found at https://osf.io/x3ukm/

Acknowledgements. This work is part of the research programme Innovational Research Incentives Scheme Vidi SSH 2017 with project number 016.Vidi.185.178, which is financed by the Dutch Research Council (NWO).

Disclosure of Interests. The authors have no competing interests to declare that are relevant to the content of this article.

References

1. del Aguila, J., González-Gualda, L.M., Játiva, M.A., Fernández-Sotos, P., Fernández-Caballero, A., García, A.S.: How interpersonal distance between avatar and human influences facial affect recognition in immersive virtual reality. Front. Psychol. **12**, 2925 (2021)
2. Ahn, S.J.G., Fox, J., Bailenson, J.: Avatars. In: Bainbridge, W. (ed.) Leadership in Science and Technology: A Reference Handbook, pp. 695–702. Sage, Thousand Oaks, CA (2012)
3. Amini, R., Lisetti, C., Ruiz, G.: HapFACS 3.0: FACS-based facial expression generator for 3D speaking virtual characters. IEEE Tran. Affect. Comput. **6**(4), 348–360 (2015)
4. ARtillery Intelligence: VR Usage & Consumer Attitudes, Wave VII - ARtillery Intelligence (2023). https://artilleryiq.com/reports/vr-usage-consumer-attitudes-wave-vii/

5. Barrett, L.F., Adolphs, R., Marsella, S., Martinez, A.M., Pollak, S.D.: Emotional expressions reconsidered: challenges to inferring emotion from human facial movements. Psychol. Sci. Public Interest **20**(1), 1–68 (2019)
6. Binetti, N., Roubtsova, N., Carlisi, C., Cosker, D., Viding, E., Mareschal, I.: Genetic algorithms reveal profound individual differences in emotion recognition. Proc. Nat. Acad. Sci. United States Am. **119**(45), e2201380119 (2022)
7. Calvo, M.G., Avero, P., Fernández-Martín, A., Recio, G.: Recognition thresholds for static and dynamic emotional faces. Emotion **16**(8), 1186–1200 (2016)
8. Cao, Q., Yu, H., Charisse, P., Qiao, S., Stevens, B.: Is high-fidelity important for human-like virtual avatars in human computer interactions? Int. J. Netw. Dyn. Intell. 15–23 (2023)
9. Chamberland, J., Roy-Charland, A., Perron, M., Dickinson, J.: Distinction between fear and surprise: an interpretation-independent test of the perceptual-attentional limitation hypothesis. Soc. Neurosci. **12**(6), 751–768 (2017)
10. Chang, D., Yin, Y., Li, Z., Tran, M., Soleymani, M.: LibreFace: an open-source toolkit for deep facial expression analysis. Preprint (2023)
11. Chattopadhyay, D., Ma, T., Sharifi, H., Martyn-Nemeth, P.: Computer-controlled virtual humans in patient-facing systems: systematic review and meta-analysis. J. Med. Internet Res. **22**(7), e18839 (2020)
12. Cherbonnier, A., Michinov, N.: The recognition of emotions conveyed by emoticons and emojis: a systematic literature review. Technol. Mind, Behav. **3**(2: Summer 2022) (2022)
13. Chevalier, P., Martin, J.C., Isableu, B., Bazile, C., Tapus, A.: Impact of sensory preferences of individuals with autism on the recognition of emotions expressed by two robots, an avatar, and a human. Auton. Robots **41**(3), 613–635 (2017)
14. Cordaro, D.T., Sun, R., Keltner, D., Kamble, S., Huddar, N., McNeil, G.: Universals and cultural variations in 22 emotional expressions across five cultures. Emotion **18**(1), 75–93 (2018)
15. Crivelli, C., Fridlund, A.J.: Inside-out: from basic emotions theory to the behavioral ecology view. J. Nonverbal Behav. **43**(2), 161–194 (2019)
16. Daher, K., Bardelli, Z., Casas, J., Mugellini, E., Khaled, O.A., Lalanne, D.: Embodied conversational agent for emotional recognition training. In: ACHI 2020 : The Thirteenth International Conference on Advances in Computer-Human Interactions, pp. 384–390. IARIA, Valencia, Spain (2020)
17. de Araújo Luz Junior, J., Formico Rodrigues, M.A.: Comparative analysis of facial expression recognition systems for evaluating emotional states in virtual humans. In: ACM International Conference Proceeding Series, pp. 38–47 (2023)
18. Durupinar, F., Kim, J.: Facial emotion recognition of virtual humans with different genders, races, and ages. In: Proceedings - SAP 2022: ACM Symposium on Applied Perception, vol. 22 (2022)
19. Dwivedi, Y.K., et al.: Metaverse beyond the hype: multidisciplinary perspectives on emerging challenges, opportunities, and agenda for research, practice and policy. Int. J. Inf. Manage. **66**, 102542 (2022)
20. Dyck, M., Winbeck, M., Leiberg, S., Chen, Y., Gur, R.C., Mathiak, K.: Recognition profile of emotions in natural and virtual faces. PLoS ONE **3**(11), 1–8 (2008)
21. Ekdahl, D., Osler, L.: Expressive avatars: vitality in virtual worlds. Philos. Technol. **36**(2), 1–28 (2023)
22. Ekman, P., Friesen, W.V.: Facial action coding system. Environ. Psychol. Nonverbal Behav. (1978)
23. Elfenbein, H.A., Ambady, N.: On the universality and cultural specificity of emotion recognition: a meta-analysis. Psychol. Bull. **128**(2), 203–235 (2002)

24. Fernández-Sotos, P., García, A.S., Vicente-Querol, M.A., Lahera, G., Rodriguez-Jimenez, R., Fernández-Caballero, A.: Validation of dynamic virtual faces for facial affect recognition. PLOS ONE **16**(1), e0246001 (2021)
25. Fischer, A.H., Kret, M.E., Broekens, J.: Gender differences in emotion perception and self-reported emotional intelligence: a test of the emotion sensitivity hypothesis. PLOS ONE **13**(1), e0190712 (2018)
26. Fujimura, T., Umemura, H.: Development and validation of a facial expression database based on the dimensional and categorical model of emotions. Cogn. Emotion **32**(8), 1663–1670 (2018)
27. García, A.S., Fernández-Sotos, P., Vicente-Querol, M.A., Lahera, G., Rodriguez-Jimenez, R., Fernández-Caballero, A.: Design of reliable virtual human facial expressions and validation by healthy people. Integr. Comput.-Aided Eng. **27**(3), 287–299 (2020)
28. Geraets, C.N., et al.: Virtual reality facial emotion recognition in social environments: an eye-tracking study. Internet Interventions **25**, 100432 (2021)
29. Gonçalves, A.R., Fernandes, C., Pasion, R., Ferreira-Santos, F., Barbosa, F., Marques-Teixeira, J.: Effects of age on the identification of emotions in facial expressions: a metaanalysis. PeerJ **2018**(7) (2018)
30. Goodfellow, I.J., et al.: Challenges in representation learning: a report on three machine learning contests. In: Lee, M., Hirose, A., Hou, Z.-G., Kil, R.M. (eds.) ICONIP 2013. LNCS, vol. 8228, pp. 117–124. Springer, Heidelberg (2013). https://doi.org/10.1007/978-3-642-42051-1_16
31. Gutiérrez-Maldonado, J., Rus-Calafell, M., González-Conde, J.: Creation of a new set of dynamic virtual reality faces for the assessment and training of facial emotion recognition ability. Virtual Reality **18**(1), 61–71 (2014)
32. van Haeringen, E.S., Veltmeijer, E.A., Gerritsen, C.: Empirical validation of an agent-based model of emotion contagion. IEEE Trans. Affect. Comput. (2023)
33. Hayes, G.S., et al.: Task characteristics influence facial emotion recognition age-effects: a meta-analytic review. Psychol. Aging **35**(2), 295–315 (2020)
34. Hofer, M., Hüsser, A., Prabhu, S.: The effect of an avatar's emotional expressions on players' fear reactions: the mediating role of embodiment. Comput. Hum. Behav. **75**, 883–890 (2017)
35. Israelashvili, J., Fischer, A.: Recognition of emotion from verbal and nonverbal expressions and its relation to effective communication: a preliminary evidence of a positive link. J. Intell. **11**(1) (2023)
36. Jack, R.E., Garrod, O.G., Yu, H., Caldara, R., Schyns, P.G.: Facial expressions of emotion are not culturally universal. Proc. Nat. Acad. Sci. United States Am. **109**(19), 7241–7244 (2012)
37. Keltner, D., Sauter, D., Tracy, J., Cowen, A.: Emotional expression: advances in basic emotion theory. J. Nonverbal Behav. **43**(2), 133–160 (2019)
38. Krumhuber, E.G., Küster, D., Namba, S., Shah, D., Calvo, M.G.: Emotion recognition from posed and spontaneous dynamic expressions: human observers versus machine analysis. Emotion **21**(2), 447–451 (2021)
39. Krumhuber, E.G., Küster, D., Namba, S., Skora, L.: Human and machine validation of 14 databases of dynamic facial expressions. Behav. Res. Methods **53**(2), 686–701 (2021)
40. Kyrlitsias, C., Michael-Grigoriou, D.: Social interaction with agents and avatars in immersive virtual environments: a survey. Front. Virtual Reality **2**, 786665 (2022)
41. Lee, J., Kim, S., Kim, S., Park, J., Sohn, K.: Context-aware emotion recognition networks. In" Proceedings of the IEEE International Conference on Computer Vision, vol. 2019-Octob, pp. 10142–10151 (2019)

42. Leung, F.Y.N., et al.: Emotion recognition across visual and auditory modalities in autism spectrum disorder: a systematic review and meta-analysis. Develop. Rev. **63**, 101000 (2022)
43. Li, S., Deng, W.: Reliable crowdsourcing and deep locality-preserving learning for unconstrained facial expression recognition. IEEE Trans. Image Process. **28**(1), 356–370 (2019)
44. Luo, C., Song, S., Xie, W., Shen, L., Gunes, H.: Learning multi-dimensional edge feature-based au relation graph for facial action unit recognition. In: Proceedings of the Thirty-First International Joint Conference on Artificial Intelligence, IJCAI-22, pp. 1239–1246 (2022)
45. Manierka, M.S., Rezaei, R., Palacios, S., Haigh, S.M., Hutsler, J.J.: In the mood to be social: Affective state influences facial emotion recognition in healthy adults. Emotion (Washington, D.C.) **21**(7), 1576–1581 (2021)
46. Mao, J., Xu, R., Yin, X., Chang, Y., Nie, B., Huang, A.: POSTER++: a simpler and stronger facial expression recognition network. Preprint (2023)
47. Marcos-Pablos, S., González-Pablos, E., Martín-Lorenzo, C., Flores, L.A., Gómez-García-Bermejo, J., Zalama, E.: Virtual avatar for emotion recognition in patients with schizophrenia: a pilot study. Front. Human Neurosci. **10**, 12 (2016)
48. Martinez, L., Falvello, V.B., Aviezer, H., Todorov, A.: Contributions of facial expressions and body language to the rapid perception of dynamic emotions. Cogn. Emoti. **30**(5), 939–952 (2016)
49. Matsumoto, D., Willingham, B.: Spontaneous facial expressions of emotion of congenitally and noncongenitally blind individuals. J. Pers. Soc. Psychol. **96**(1), 1–10 (2009)
50. Miao, F., Kozlenkova, I.V., Wang, H., Xie, T., Palmatier, R.W.: An emerging theory of avatar marketing. J. Market. **86**(1), 67–90 (2022)
51. Mollahosseini, A., Hasani, B., Mahoor, M.H.: AffectNet: a database for facial expression, valence, and arousal computing in the wild. IEEE Trans. Affect. Comput. **10**(01), 18–31 (2019)
52. Monferrer, M., et al.: Facial emotion recognition in patients with depression compared to healthy controls when using human avatars. Sci. Rep. **13**(1), 1–10 (2023)
53. Muros, N.I., et al.: Facial affect recognition by patients with schizophrenia using human avatars. J. Clin. Med. **10**(9), 1904 (2021)
54. O'Rourke, S.R., Branford, K.R., Brooks, T.L., Ives, L.T., Nagendran, A., Compton, S.N.: The emotional and behavioral impact of delivering bad news to virtual versus real standardized patients: a pilot study. Teach. Learn. Med. **32**(2), 139–149 (2019)
55. Pham, L., Vu, T.H., Tran, T.A.: Facial expression recognition using residual masking network. In: Proceedings - International Conference on Pattern Recognition, pp. 4513–4519 (2020)
56. Rafiee, Y., Schacht, A.: Sex differences in emotion recognition: investigating the moderating effects of stimulus features. Cogn. Emot. (2023)
57. Richoz, A.R., Lao, J., Pascalis, O., Caldara, R.: Tracking the recognition of static and dynamic facial expressions of emotion across the life span. J. Vis. **18**(9), 5–5 (2018)
58. Rodger, H., et al.: The recognition of facial expressions of emotion in deaf and hearing individuals. Heliyon **7**(5) (2021)
59. Rymarczyk, K., Zurawski, Ł., Jankowiak-Siuda, K., Szatkowska, I.: Emotional empathy and facial mimicry for static and dynamic facial expressions of fear and disgust. Front. Psychol. **7**(NOV), 1853 (2016)

60. Saquinaula, A., Juarez, A., Geigel, J., Bailey, R., Alm, C.O.: Emotional empathy and facial mimicry of avatar faces. In: Proceedings - 2022 IEEE Conference on Virtual Reality and 3D User Interfaces Abstracts and Workshops, VRW 2022, pp. 770–771 (2022)
61. Schmid, P.C., Schmid Mast, M.: Mood effects on emotion recognition. Motiv. Emot. **34**(3), 288–292 (2010)
62. Sollfrank, T., et al.: The effects of dynamic and static emotional facial expressions of humans and their avatars on the EEG: an ERP and ERD/ERS study. Front. Neurosci. **15**, 651044 (2021)
63. Suma, T., Sonia, B., Agyemang Baffour, K., Oyekoya, O.: The effects of avatar voice and facial expression intensity on emotional recognition and user perception. In: Proceedings - SIGGRAPH Asia 2023: Technical Communications, SA Technical Communications 2023 (2023)
64. Sun, Y., Won, A.S.: Despite appearances: comparing emotion recognition in abstract and humanoid avatars using nonverbal behavior in social virtual reality. Front. Virtual Reality **2**, 694453 (2021)
65. Torregrossa, L.J., et al.: Decoupling of spontaneous facial mimicry from emotion recognition in schizophrenia. Psychiatry Res. **275**, 169–176 (2019)
66. Trautmann, S.A., Fehr, T., Herrmann, M.: Emotions in motion: dynamic compared to static facial expressions of disgust and happiness reveal more widespread emotion-specific activations. Brain Res. **1284**, 100–115 (2009)
67. Vicente-Querol, M.Á., García, A.S., Fernández-Sotos, P., Rodriguez-Jimenez, R., Fernández-Caballero, A.: Development and validation of basic virtual human facial emotion expressions. In: Ferrández Vicente, J.M., Álvarez-Sánchez, J.R., de la Paz López, F., Toledo Moreo, J., Adeli, H. (eds.) IWINAC 2019. LNCS, vol. 11486, pp. 222–231. Springer, Cham (2019). https://doi.org/10.1007/978-3-030-19591-5_23
68. Wingenbach, T.S., Ashwin, C., Brosnan, M.: Validation of the Amsterdam dynamic facial expression set - bath intensity variations (ADFES-BIV): a set of videos expressing low, intermediate, and high intensity emotions. PLOS ONE **11**(1), e0147112 (2016)
69. Zane, E., Yang, Z., Pozzan, L., Guha, T., Narayanan, S., Grossman, R.B.: Motion-capture patterns of voluntarily mimicked dynamic facial expressions in children and adolescents with and without ASD. J. Autism Dev. Disorders **49**(3), 1062–1079 (2019)
70. Zhang, J., Chen, Q., Lu, J., Wang, X., Liu, L., Feng, Y.: Emotional expression by artificial intelligence chatbots to improve customer satisfaction: underlying mechanism and boundary conditions. Tourism Manage. **100**, 104835 (2024)
71. Zupan, B., Eskritt, M.: Facial and vocal emotion recognition in adolescence: a systematic review. adolescent research review (2023)

Author Index

F. A. Oliehoek et al. (Eds.): BNAIC/Benelearn 2023, CCIS 2187, pp. 275–276, 2025.
https://doi.org/10.1007/978-3-031-74650-5

SPRINGER NATURE

GPSR Compliance

The European Union's (EU) General Product Safety Regulation (GPSR) is a set of rules that requires consumer products to be safe and our obligations to ensure this.

If you have any concerns about our products, you can contact us on ProductSafety@springernature.com

In case Publisher is established outside the EU, the EU authorized representative is:

Springer Nature Customer Service Center GmbH
Europaplatz 3
69115 Heidelberg, Germany

The manufacturer's authorised representative in the EU is Springer Nature Customer Service Centre GmbH, Europaplatz 3, 69115 Heidelberg, Germany. If you have any concerns regarding our products, please contact ProductSafety@springernature.com

Printed and bound by CPI Group (UK) Ltd, Croydon, CR0 4YY
28/09/2026
02224076-0009